# REFRAMING INTERNATIONAL DEVELOPMENT

# REFRAMING INTERNATIONAL DEVELOPMENT

## *Globalism, Postmodernity, and Difference*

**Nelson W. Keith**

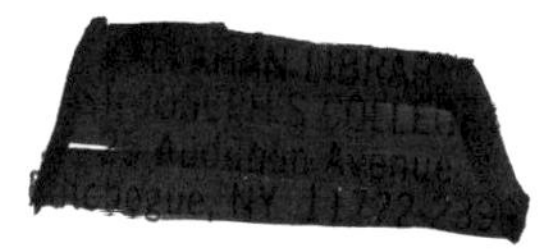

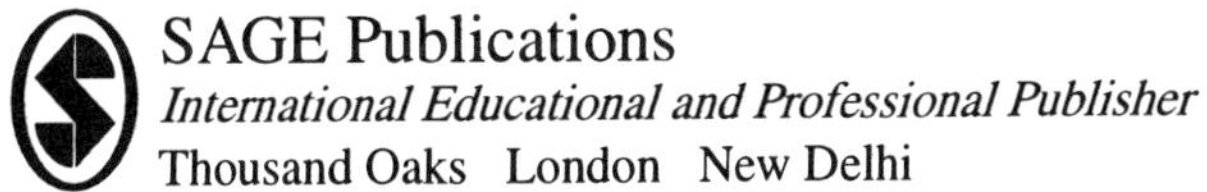

SAGE Publications
*International Educational and Professional Publisher*
Thousand Oaks London New Delhi

For information:

SAGE Publications, Inc.
2455 Teller Road
Thousand Oaks, California 91320
E-mail: order@sagepub.com

SAGE Publications Ltd.
6 Bonhill Street
London EC2A 4PU
United Kingdom

SAGE Publications India Pvt. Ltd.
M-32 Market
Greater Kailash I
New Delhi 110 048 India

Printed in the United States of America

*Library of Congress Cataloging-in-Publication Data*

Keith, Nelson W.
Reframing international development: globalism, postmodernity, and difference / by Nelson W. Keith.
p. cm.
Includes bibliographical references (p. ) and index.
ISBN 0-8039-7061-7 (cloth: acid-free paper). — ISBN 0-8039-7062-5 (pbk.: acid-free paper)
1. Postmodernism—Social aspects. 2. Economic development—Social aspects. 3. International economic relations. 4. Enlightenment. I. Title.
HM73.K42 1997
337—dc21 97-4764

This book is printed on acid-free paper.

97 98 99 00 01 02 03 10 9 8 7 6 5 4 3 2 1

*Acquiring Editor:* Peter Labella
*Editorial Assistant:* Corinne Pierce
*Production Editor:* Sherrise M. Purdum
*Production Assistant:* Karen Wiley
*Typesetter/Designer:* Danielle Dillahunt
*Indexer:* Teri Greenberg
*Cover Designer:* Candice Harman
*Print Buyer:* Anna Chin

# CONTENTS

## PART II



## PART III

---

## PART IV

# Preface and Acknowledgments

In a truly profound sense, this book draws its major impetus from a growing annoyance with the main approaches taken to contemporary globalization, particularly global interdependence. The truth is that mainstream theory and practice on the subject appears to view the admitted changes as variations on the old theme of superordination versus subordination. Nothing of the qualitative changes evident in the dynamics of nonmodern cultures, in wide-ranging feminist counteroffensives against modernist patterns of thought and action, in the depletion of strategic resources, in the degradation of the environment, in the relative sterility of Enlightenment thought—nothing, or precious little, of the combined effect of these truly novel definers of our present global reality appears to be dislodging a pervasive myopia to the extent that it should be disturbed. If the reaction does not take some form of "anti-Doomsday-ism," championed by an invincible science, it becomes entangled with a hackneyed Eastern philosophical aphorism: *This, too, shall pass!*

The urgency to disturb and then dislodge is coerced by the need to ensure that the oncoming globalized, interdependent world receives the kind of thoughtful and perceptive conceptualization that avoids our headlong march down the wrong fork in the road. The evidence now strongly suggests that our slavish and sometimes cavalier adoption of certain key features of the Enlightenment—a preponderantly Cartesian orientation, for instance—has taken us along one such fork. The evidence is now directing, with like assuredness, that we construct a framework of global relations with an attentive eye to the new definers and symptoms of the present global reality, some of which are mentioned above. Together, these loom as the unintended, but clearly implicit, consequences of our obedience to Descartes, to his unwavering commandment that there is but one permanent way to arriving at knowledge and truth. The related processes required nothing short of the marginalization and sometimes outright eradication of nonmodern practices and habits of mind.

The new undertaking suggested by the current crisis in international relations is that these marginalized phenomena, many of which exist in the Third World (or in Third World-like contexts, such as inner-city areas of large metropolitan cities!) and bear the label of "backwardness," be brought in from the cold. Once deplored, backwardness signals its contemporary relevance in present permutations of politics, economics, and social arrangements in modern, metropolitan contexts. Their role is no longer ad hoc and peripheral.

Although the evidence for qualitative adjustment to our view of global reality is overwhelming, the penchant for clinging to old formulas is highly visible. The reality of global interdependence cannot but be accepted—such is the nature of the beast—yet the approaches to its definition are inordinately misguided. The awkward admixture of inattentiveness, apathy, insouciance, confusion, masterly inactivity, suspect conceptualization, and the like does communicate an urgency to which my efforts in writing this book are obedient. As a reviewer of the manuscript observes, the voice in this book is a non-Western voice to the West that says, "Welcome to global reality. Perhaps now we can share the challenge of common survival without the presumption that you know best." This is a perceptive precis of the work. My hope is that the message and its supportive arguments will attract the attention of those of the world community who, like myself, see the plight of humankind hanging in a balance. The hope is also that those who have not so far given serious thought to the matter will find in this work suitable food for thought and action. In truth, Big Brother has never known best and the time to forge a new world order, one sensitive to more representative voices, is never more opportune.

In the course of producing this work, I have incurred many debts, the acknowledgment of which time and space do not permit. But I would be remiss if I did not register my profound gratitude to those whose contributions have been truly singular. My first offer of thanks is to my wife, Novella. Members of two-professor families know only too well the trials and tribulations involved in the constant competition for a stock of time that is never sufficient for individual agendas, less so when scholarly interests and other professional exigencies diverge. Novella would always find it agreeable to avoid the impasse. She would always appear at those critical junctures when the colors of the flag of distress begin to take shape. The book has benefited, as a whole, from her illuminating criticism and recommendations, especially in matters of content and style. Her editorial assistance was also quite instructive, as were her timely translations from French and Italian. Finally, I must also register my appreciation for her encouraging me to scale with greater enthusiasm those confining walls within which our disciplines would often like to hold us prisoners. I took a leap from law and sociology and, without abandoning them, found the view beyond quite sparkling and exhilarating!

Two of my former students, now young professors of inestimable promise, read large portions of the manuscript and made many helpful comments and insightful suggestions. Michael Rosano and Bruce Pietrykowski, both of the University of Michigan at Dearborn and earlier undergraduates at Rutgers, New Brunswick, are the two young, vibrant minds that came to my rescue. Both assisted in putting me straight on pivotal issues in political theory and political economy, respectively. No, I was not allowed to take too many liberties that one is so often tempted to do in a work of which polemics are inseparably a part. At the same time, they were not above bolstering the polemics at critical junctures. On an aside, these two young minds have really presented me with a two-course meal. They have enticed from me that special sense of pride that a father experiences at the coming of age of his sons. The sensations of humility and satisfaction evoked are quite unspeakable.

A fair measure of thanks falls also to the lot of my distinguished colleague at West Chester, Paul Stoller. Paul took valuable time out from his own extremely busy research and writing schedule to read, with great care, significant portions of the manuscript. Sections directed at culture are the better for his critical and searching comments. My last debt, in this vein, is owed to Professor Michael Allen of Bryn Mawr. Mike's fingerprints are all over the book, from its early life as a prospectus to the final arrival of this moment. I have come to depend on and respect his intellectual acuity, erudition, and sharp, but fair, critiques. If the work does not reflect these qualities, together with other scholarly perspicacities for which I am deeply indebted, lay not this sin to their charge.

Debts of another sort must also be acknowledged. The first is to Peter Labella, my editor at Sage. Peter could detect when the pressures of time were taking their toll. With admirable and welcome disengagement, he would beat those strategic retreats from which my ragged mind and the progress of the work drew much sustenance. Finally, research for this book received material support from a variety of sources. I wish to thank the College of Arts and Sciences at West Chester University for a number of research grants and reduced workloads, without which this book would never have been completed at this time. My hope is that the final product is worthy of this highly appreciated support.

## *Chapter One*

# THE NATURE AND ORBIT OF CHANGE

## *A Statement of Central Themes*

*We have scorched the snake, not killed it:*
*She'll close and be herself, whilst our poor malice*
*Remain in danger of her former tooth*
William Shakespeare.[1]

*Civilization progresses from agriculture to paradox.*
E. M. Cioran (1993)

In one of his famous tragedies, *Macbeth*, Shakespeare has three witches put into the head of Macbeth, the trusted general and eventual assassin of Duncan, King of Scotland, the idea that the treachery would go unpunished. His destruction would only come about, the witches confide, after Birnam Wood came to Dunsinane. How can a forest walk to a castle? Furthermore, Macbeth's death could not come at the hands of anyone born of a woman. So because the script did not legislate pugnacious encounters with dragons, lions, or pythons, but with men, Macbeth had really nothing to fear but fear itself.

As the tragedy proceeds, Macbeth discovers that forests can indeed move toward castles, as the avenging armies from England, camouflaged with the vegetation from Birnam Wood, marched toward Dunsinane. Later, in his duel with Macduff, a loyal nobleman and friend of the slain King, Macbeth is rudely awakened by another revelation—Macduff was "from his mother's womb untimely ripped." Delivered through a caesarean section, the eventual conqueror of Macbeth was technically "not born of a woman."[2]

I have revisited the Shakespearean canon to focus attention on a comparable irony that is no less befuddling to those for whom metropolitan hegemony is a state akin to a Divine Right. Dependence and its real implications for a currently emerging global interdependence form the subject matter of this irony. In certain quarters of the Third World and among like-minded metropolitan scholars, dependence stands unmitigatedly for nothing short of the systematic exploitation of the Third World by the metropolitan world. The Macbeths in the tragedy are the duplicitous twins, colonialism and imperialism, whose instructions encompassed the candor of a William Pitt and Ludwell Denny: The first would have Britain exercise every power over the colonies "short of taking their money out of their pockets" (Knaplund, 1927, p. 91), and the latter declared in the 1960s, with some braggadocio, that "[Americans] shall not make Britain's mistake. Too wise to govern the world, we shall merely own it" (cited in Levinson, 1971, p. 91).

The irony extracts its vitality from the "balance-of-power" picture of international economics and politics. The view is based mainly on the military superiority of the metropolitan world, coupled with its concomitant economic and political might. It mirrors a certain "arrogance of power" that abounds in the history of most nations engaged in the venture of domination. The role of the dominated is embodied in a famous couplet from Alfred Lord Tennyson's *The Charge of the Light Brigade*: "Their's not to reason why/their's but to do or die!"

But that perception is being altered by a hidden dimension to dependence now manifesting itself most visibly in the metropolitan world. The consequence is a shift from one-dimensional dependence to two "dependences" (Dependence I and II, discussed in Chapter 2). Dependence I is analogous to *dependencia.* Briefly, this is the economic exploitation of the Third World by the metropolitan countries mainly through the unequal exchange occurring in trading relations. Dependence II, on the other hand, reflects the arrival of forces inherent in the modern project but that are only now maturing. Modern man was cast in the image of the supreme controller of Nature and the absolute architect of humanity's march from necessity to freedom. The inherent weaknesses in the design are now appearing in full force. He is not able to lead the Other(s) to freedom; now, he suffers with the Other(s) a certain cunning of modernity.

The forces at work—which combined, I have labeled *globalism*—do appear to be forging a global interdependence fashioned from the interplay between these "dependences." Globalism is a normative agenda that extracts from the Enlightenment and certain aspects of modernity the broad principles geared to eliminate at once the cunning of modernity and flatten the dichotomies originating in this source. It is my contention that this interplay is aided by a much wider and enveloping crisis. The shift is not occurring along the developmental continuum suggested by modernization theory—the point is hardly that dependent societies are now forced to see the wisdom of an interdependence implied by Ricardian comparative advantage. Likewise, I am not referring to those conventional definitions embodied in the three ideological postures jostling for our political souls—those employing the balance-of-power framework from conservative, liberal, and radical perspectives.

The interdependence analyzed in this book diverges from these frameworks in fundamental respects. Let me provide three representative examples. First, the entire mix of causal factors is more heterogeneous and numerous than the narrow economic, political, and political-economic or political-psychological variables we often confront in conventional analyses. To be added to the old mix—sometimes as new inflections on old relations—are race, ethnicity, gender, culture, and Nature, to mention the more significant. In fact, this expanded causal base is partly the result of the diminishing (but still very active) role of political economy as the dominant ontological force. Just as Adam Smith employed this new paradigm, via his celebrated *The Wealth of Nations,* to marginalize the outmoded, static, zero-sum formulations of mercantilism, so the time has arrived for a new ontology to take its place. This new ontology is the product of a global compression that is altering the multiple formative dimensions of time and space, as well as enacting qualitative changes in capitalist relations. The power of production and distribution forces to determine contemporary social definitions, meanings, and a host of social relations appears to be lessened. Accordingly, as activity shifts away from production to consumption in the emerging paradigm, new types of social relations are coming into view. Rita Felski (1995, p. 61) points aptly to the nature of some of the dynamics at play:

> The view of modernity as driven by the logic of productive forces gives way to a recognition that consumer demand is not simply a passive reflection of economic interests, but is shaped by a variety of relatively independent cultural and ideological factors. . . . This is the result of the loosening of the constraints imposed in the process of production. (p. 61)

The increased reflexivity and human agency coextensive with the growing encroachment of the sensual is another distinct feature of what appears to be an emerging social formation. For although political economy privileges the values of freedom and security of private consumption as well as material progress, its emerging substitute is distinctly partial to "personal autonomy and identity, as opposed to centralized control" (Offe, 1987a, p. 73)—a drift toward the pole of compassion, away from the preserves of individualism. This new behavioral inflection explains the rashes of humanism now appearing with greater frequency throughout the world: comfortable middle-class people forsaking the lucre to follow the "ideal of the citizen-pilgrim" (Falk, 1992, p. 16); members of social movements in the Third World (India, Kenya, Nigeria, for example) putting the fate of the environment ahead of important economic considerations; the conscious courtship of "convivial poverty": "The belief that the answer to imposed forms of material poverty has been found in [a] people's own ethical and cultural approach to poverty" (Rahnema, 1992, p. 171).

The resultant theory and practice are refigured because the heterogeneous mix of variables allows noneconomic factors, such as culture, to play a more centrally defining role. In other words, what functioned as dependent variables in the political economy paradigm are now emerging as independent variables (Eder, 1993). There are also indications that the inclusion of these formerly excluded variables often throws standard interpretations off line.[3]

The second example involves dependence itself. Notions of metropolitan dependence did not exist, in any real sense, during the heyday of dependencia, which was thought to be the self-inflicted backwardness of Third World societies unwilling to heed the messages of socioeconomic redemption delivered by the disciples of modernization theory. Today, it is tantamount to received truth that those recipes have aided, in no small way, the underdevelopment of the Third World (Chapter 2). Then, Third World advocates would ritualistically frame their discourse and polemics within the underdevelopment orbit, intimating at the same time, somewhat contradictorily, that such was the path to the salvation of the bloc. Strategies fluctuated between exercising some control over the underdeveloped country's economic surplus (democratic socialism) and attempting to negotiate the best conditions for dependence (Quijano, 1971).

But the "development-by-growth" model is a double-edged sword, carving out a complementary form of dependence in advanced societies (Dependence II). This largely obscured form of dependence is situated within a paradox: the master plan of modernist science delivers on its promise of material plenty but does so with the classic flair of a Jekyll and Hyde. The Jekyll-esque stance is sustained by the growing realization, now evident in environmental decay, pollution, nuclearism, and industrially induced diseases, that something is amiss. The evidence assumes a certain poignancy, in that these sources of growing discomfiture arise from the very processes that promote material plenty and prosperity. For quite some time, this camouflage deflected probity, thanks to the effective use of a smug ideology of *independence,* such as that displayed by our Mr. Ludwell Denny! This is the Hydean counterpoint.

The symbiosis between these two expressions of dependence (Dependence I and II) is exposed in contemporary analyses of "risk" and the structure and rationale of social movements. At issue are quality-of-life questions that are increasingly viewed in opposition to modernity's largesse of affluence and material plenty. In the words of one observer, "There seems to be an inverse relationship between GDP and the quality of life: the more GDP grows, the more the quality of life deteriorates" (Mies & Shiva, 1993, p. 61). It should be added that the crises of the modern individual, the "unencumbered Man," are closely bound up with this cluster of processes.

My last example draws on the causal factor I consider most significant in this very complex process of change. Indeed, it explains the reasons for placing greater stress on the ideational as distinct from the material factors involved in interdependence. Suffice it to say here that the Enlightenment crises show themselves to be little short of a thought revolution. Confronting sustained challenges are its pivotal principles and concepts: reason, logic, a unitary conception of reality, and the "unencumbered" Self are all caught in the midst of the fray. Subsequent analysis will indicate that in the case of many traditionally material variables (depletion of strategic resources, ecology, population, and so on) ideational factors have permeated and are exerting formative influence on their relations. The analysis will be conducted in the expansive context of Nature as Other.

In the end, interdependence comes to represent the interplay of economic, political, and heretofore dismissed noneconomic variables. It also yields theoretical explanations and emancipatory agendas that are transnational, transcultural, and transracial and that seem increasingly to be more cosmopolitan than narrowly self-interested and parochial. The taken-for-granted superiority, the fixity of metropolitan hegemony, are being set upon by a new train of forces, some of which are generated by globalism, whereas others are unleashed from the restraints previously imposed by the dominance of "rational" (namely Western-centric) economic development. Generally, these are phenomena that one comes to associate with cultural and socioeconomic "backwardness"—nonrational modes of thought and action ascribed to Africa and other outposts existing on the leeward side of Western civilization. The label of backwardness would later, as we shall see, be pinned to women and Nature.

A major consequence of the new twist to interdependence is the flattening of old dichotomies erected by both modernization theory and Marxism-

Leninism. Indeed, a very clear and persuasive deduction to be drawn from this analysis is that current relations should not be viewed in the old terms of self-centered independence (a common metropolitan stance) and a lingering, self-conscious dependence (a posture common to the dependent world). The required agenda, rather, is to attack collectively this "poisoned gift of an unresolved tension between universalism and particularism" (Laclau, 1991, p. 57), by constructing a theory and practice situated outside of the main defining principles of modernity. The "poisoned gift" exists in the literal sense of poisoned food and environment but also in a poisoned culture of relations in which the Self-Other dialectics are situated.

## ❖ About Scope and Method

Let me now attempt to erect some boundaries commanded by a topic whose immensity does, in a strange way, excite and invite, instead of discourage, discourse. The bulk of humanity lives its life and has its being in successive installments of incrementalism in the economic, political, and ideological spheres of life; hardly are there the opportunities to visualize the outlines and begin to perceive a new dawn. Few are those flashpoints in human history where, as Wordsworth waxed rapturously about the French Revolution, people could exclaim "bliss was it in that Dawn to be alive/but to be young was very Heaven" (cited in Toulmin, 1992, p. 175). The indications are that a dawn of this sort is upon us, complete with its unpredictabilities, its ironies, its mixed blessings.

I am not the tender nineteen-year-old Wordsworth then was, but this oncoming age of paradox stirs deep feelings of a personal nature. For much that represents the new thinking in which interdependence is embodied does appear as a vindication of those long neutralized, though largely unsilenced, voices. Mine is a Third World voice of a particular timbre, which long registered the virtues of "border crossings" before the concept became justifiably fashionable. It is a voice that along with other voices—"Other(s)" as will be used throughout the book in the context of alterity—has inveighed against seemingly eternal inequities, systematized with the construction of the Big Ditch (the space created between the modern and nonmodern) by Descartes and his men. The air is astir with expectancy. One confesses readily to a quickening of the spirit, even though the irrepressible enthusiasm and anticipation it entices have the enormous weight of history aligned against them. The opportunity to close that ditch, at least to some degree, has arrived. The task is not to go back to Aristotle with Alasdair MacIntyre or to bask in the supreme cosmopolitanism of a Montesquieu, suitably outfitted with the argumentative skills of a Socrates. This is Thomas Pangle's antidote. In truth, we must close that ditch or we die!

At the same time, I am only too aware that such zeal must be tempered by at least two sobering injunctions: The one appeals to my professional terms of reference, and the second cautions about manifold historical slips between cup and lip. In the first place, I must avoid any surrender to those diversions that could compromise my responsibilities as a scholar. I cannot pretend that this will be an easy task. The temptation in the present context is profound, as one is cast adrift in a sea of unformed and imprecise analytic methods and concepts. Here the subjective and the narrowly experiential must be kept in check. As for the role of history, some of its unerring lessons are cautionary, abounding at times in the most cruel of ironies. The liberals, genuinely taken in by the putative civilizing potentialities of the Enlightenment, were confident that the Age of Reason had truly arrived. And how did that light fail? Let me count the ways. . . . The French Revolution followed by the Terror; the First World War; the Second World War; the Holocaust. . . . And the disappointments—Bosnia, the Persian Gulf War, and the carnage in Rwanda—keep falling into that petty pace from day to day. It has been so again! The tormented poet must be so informed.

The outlines of the interdependence that appear to be taking shape are conceptually of the scale in which historical disappointments abound. Yet one must redress the proper balance between measured optimism and necessary skepticism; dare to hope. The world is untidy, yet it manages by its sometimes precious little offerings to keep hope and effort alive.

Let me, then, continue to speak of the book's scope and method, remaining quite sensitive to these injunctions but no less exhilarated by what appears on the horizon. If these are excesses, then, in this age of articulated rights and truth claims, I claim the moment's surcease, as the spirit gives me utterance!

First, this book is synthetic in nature, without being a synthesis. A synthesis, properly speaking, is the product of reasonably well-defined opposing arguments shaped into a new, discernible entity. The truth is that the bulk of the analysis in this book is quite comfortable with discussing structures and institutions breaking apart, as is the case with the Enlightenment crisis and the changing nature of global economic practice. It is on a less sure footing when attempts are made to discuss replacements—a situation having less to do, one hopes, with glaring ineptitudes of the author than with the nascent and evolving character of a global order caught in the uncertainties and ambiguities of becoming. As John Gerard Ruggie (1993) expresses the dilemma in the case of international relations, most contemporary efforts exist as "pretheoretical task[s]" directed at the "search for a vocabulary and for the dimensions of a research agenda" (p. 144). Indeed, the lack is found in anthropology (Marcus, 1992); in sociology (Bauman, 1992); in economics (Thurow, 1984); in political theory (Held, 1991). The list is truly extensive.

Analysis is hampered, for the most part, by formulations and concepts losing their traditional meaning and influence as the old paradigm crumbles and by expectancy and frustration as replacement concepts and the appropriate tools of analysis prove at best rudimentary. Inchoateness is rife and has led to a rash of "problematizing," or to the practice of sketchily aligning ideas and insights to congenial explanatory frameworks. In context, we *know* that the nation-state, international banking, social class, and an extensive list of concepts and institutions are changing. But we do *not* yet know what their replacements or reconfigured forms will be, although a number of these are farther along the path of comprehension than others.

This book could be described justifiably as a partial portrait of emerging social structures and an attempt to relate their tendencies to an international order in the process of change. Nonetheless, for all its partial nature, the work identifies and analyzes major organizing principles moving toward what can been termed "a shared general direction." This approach finds menace in the traditional practice of placing societies along a developmental continuum—a coerced general direction. Instead, it conceptualizes each society as moving largely along its own path of development but being subject, to some degree, to "a shared general direction" that is defined by diversity. The perspective encompasses the concept of *difference*, which is a main building block of this work.

The task of mapping a shared general direction excludes certain analyses that might be generally expected. The book cannot present an integrated structural analysis of the newly emerging global system. Consequently, it will not, for instance, discuss the role of the state or the nature of international relations or global economics, except in the general context of explanation. Such analyses are really posterior to the main thrusts of this work, whose primary purpose lies in sketching the broad outlines of that system. The task requires, rather, a review of critiques, offered not as reenactments of old exchanges won, lost, or unsettled but as the crucial materials from which the new paradigm is created. Formerly, these materials existed primarily as critique; now the tack is to discover through that critique a discourse of possibilities, creating a whole that will be much more than the sum of its parts.

There is a perspectival unease that I would like to dispatch. The first strain relates to the book's trek into deep history, and the other speaks to the limited role of economics in the analysis, as a whole. A good many readers might be perplexed by my long retreat to the land of the Enlightenment and the trek into even earlier times. I have visited Simonides, the Greek poet, and Cicero! These excursions are necessary to uncover crucial explanatory linkages: the truth is that although we might be separated by the distance of centuries, debates today, whether they address the continued existence or the abandonment of the Enlightenment, do have their loci of support or points of departure in this body of thought. It is difficult to dispute Charles Taylor's (1989) point that the Enlightenment makes us what we are. Even though we might currently be going over a historical watershed, "We still reach for the old vocabularies" (p. 393) provided by the Enlightenment. (A number of contemporary Realist theorists in international relations might dispute the statement; if that is so, their advocates must go even farther back to establish their line of descent—Thucydides and the Peloponnesian War!!) The Enlightenment's monstrous embrace of our contemporary reality explains why its principles have been seen, rightly or wrongly, as "a code word for everything we ought to distrust" (Phillips, 1993, pp. 55-56).

Parenthetically, this work shares a measure of that distrust, without, however, fully deserting the tradition. Although its unitary definition of reality and its slavish attachment to a constraining form of logocentrism call for a strong attack, its credentials for providing spheres of emancipation for the varieties of human beings living on earth remain impressive. In a world now defined increasingly by the criteria of difference, Enlightenment principles are not obsolete. Rather, concepts such as universal humanity, free labor, government by consent, and others need to be appropriately recast. Enlightenment principles devolve from a unitary system in which all expressions that fall outside of its purview are defined as deficits. And yet these principles do support a politics of recognition from which a politics of difference and like political forms congenial to the Other(s) can be suitably grounded (more in Chapter 10).

The method used in this book is resolutive-compositive. Roughly speaking, it breaks down phenomena into their constitutive parts as a way of demonstrating how they were initially constructed. Such a methodological approach allows us to grasp the strengths and weaknesses inherent especially in the Enlightenment tradition. The book combines analyses from the history of ideas, the history of philosophy, and the social sciences, with an uncharacteristic emphasis on culture as a direct agent of change.

As the book was originally conceived, a fair measure of Marxism-dependency theory served as animating factors. But the perspective gradually changed. Marxism is a creature of the Enlightenment; Richard Falk (1992, pp. 24-25) is quite right in locating it within modernity, and Frazer and Lacey (1993) support the thesis by stipulating that, like social democracy, it is essentially a modern theory. It is also true, however, that Marxism contributes to the construction of the new paradigm. Redefinitions of the Subject, now situated in "communicative praxis," are still located, nonetheless, within historical forms of domination that Marxism remains unparalleled in explaining. Indeed, I agree with Luke Martell (1992, p. 153) that Marxist methods rather than its ends have been the system's setbacks, yet care must be taken in evaluating relationships between ends and means. Marxist internationalism is quite congenial in principle, but it is limited vis-à-vis globalism, as it is linked in telling ways to modernity in a fashion that denies difference.

What is at stake in the crisis, as a whole, are not matters centrally related to production and distribution, as such. The major problems are fundamental to issues from which production and distribution draw their theory, practice, and ethics. Accordingly, philosophical issues take precedence, because the prime causal factors appear to be ontological, epistemological, and linguistic in nature. I have consciously, with much theoretical and historical justification, shoved economics from the center of the stage. It has for much too long been sustained by a fetishism that is partly the legacy of neo-Smithian and Marxist economics. It cannot be overstressed that the economic moment under interdependence is not muted but, rather, shows signs of a significant qualitative transformation. But these changes are not self-induced, however much we are being advised that human beings' thought, perspectives, and action adhere to an economistic imperative. In other words, biology is bound to economics.

I address briefly the narrow economic issue here, partly as a response to the structure of the book. Crucial for situating interdependence, I propose, are themes whose transformative power emerges from foundational principles of the Enlightenment that are presently in deep crisis. For another reason, the book must address the narrow economic moment so as to situate it within the emerging scheme of things. Therefore, I draw attention to the manner in which its traditional foundations, erected on the "economistic fallacy," are subject to transformation by other forces excluded from its definition and the singular worldview it attempts to foist on all and sundry.

Accordingly, one treats the economic moment in relation to its "denaturalization." The concept, as Fred Block (1990, p. 27) defines it in terms of the "economistic fallacy," stipulates that pursuit of economic gain is natural to human beings and that other cultures not displaying it are primitive and backward. Ludwig Von Mises (1960) in whose economics such a fallacy originates, states pointedly that "the spheres of rational action and economic action are . . . coincident. All rational action is economic. All economic action is rational" (pp. 112-113). Perhaps the most daring claim is that made by Jack Hirshleifer (1977): "As economics 'imperialistically' employs its tools of analysis over a wide range of social issues, it will *become* sociology and anthropology and political science" (pp. 3-4). This unimpeachable truth flows from such stipulations as that all aspects of life are ultimately governed by scarcity; that self-interest is ultimately the driving force behind all expressions of life; and that competition is the widespread law of "natural-economy interactions." Current rational-choice theories are heavily infected by this line of reasoning (Becker, 1976).

The fact is that "rational" economic orthodoxy is itself coming under the sway of elements of the Other(s)—a development somewhat perplexing, for the reasons indicated above. In addition, these tendencies to the "de-naturalization" of economics feed noticeably into the structure of globalism, which is explicated more fully in the next chapter. From the state of contemporary economic thought and action, the economic is *not* rational in the Cartesian-Kantian sense in which the term is used. It uses added components of Other-inflected phenomena. And in so doing, it demonstrates the manner in which the other ideational forces, those defined in relation to a crisis-ridden Enlightenment, are anterior in their new definitional role and paramount in their effects.

The analysis that the preceding propositions requires falls outside the immediate format of this book. Indeed, it would take perhaps another book for that purpose, even though the sketches they provide are wholly consistent with the principal rationale of the work. There are complementary strains to be found in such phenomena as resource depletion, ecology, and so on, which will be addressed from the perspective of Nature as Other, making more explicit the deep-seated character of Dependence II. These issues appear in the next chapter. Of the others, I have isolated two phenomena for their demonstrated complicity and highly probable continued involvement in the overall process of the "de-naturalization" of the economic: advanced technology and deindustrialization. I will use a broad brush to administer a number of suggestive strokes from which, perhaps, more in-depth research may originate. The dominant discourse hardly ever contemplates issues in the present light. Birnam Wood can never come to Dunsinane! What I present, by extending the Shakespearean metaphor, is a number of leaves shed by trees making their way to Dunsinane, with globalism as their Duncan.

*Technology Unbound.* Since the late 1970s, there have been very clear signs that advanced technology is implicated in the creation of the global economy and the concomitant weakening of the nation-state (Held, 1991; Falk, 1992).[4]

Often what is not fully grasped is its inherent capacity to act autonomously, away from the dictates of capitalist domination. The history of technology shows clearly that it has been equally the servant of the dominant mode of production, because it is capable of changing allegiance (Westrum, 1991, p. 26; Winner, 1980) or, at least, withdrawing from involvement and enabling alternative "spaces" to be created (see Sclove, 1995, pp. 69-71, concerning democratic communities of work established in Holland, Belgium, and Switzerland).[5]

Advanced technology today appears to be involved in the process of disengagement from capitalist domination, if not a substantial articulation with alternative socioeconomic principles. Now, there is justifiable dispute as to whether the "alternative" technologies claimed as departing from narrow, instrumentalist definitions are really as claimed. Old technologies are often merely relocated to new sites (Mexico, for example) and then become alternative merely by the structural and cultural constraints imposed by these new sites. On the other hand, there are those instances in which technology is appropriated differently. One is the *Swadhyaya* movement originating in the states of Gujarat and Maharashtra as well as in the city of Bombay. It has a membership of several hundred thousands, with Vedic cosmologies being quite instrumental in orienting sophisticated technologies to social needs. Claude Alvares (1991, p. 16) speaks of a "survival technology," where profits are subordinated to such imperatives as the necessary balance to be struck between population and environment. Cuba provides another example. It has replaced the instrumental technology provided by the former Soviet Union with sustainable development. Such examples tend to belie the old truism that "industrial advance at every stage [in dependent economies] depends greatly on the acquisition of knowledge from a more industrialized country" (Hagen, 1975, p. 156).

*The Other Side of Deindustrialization.* Deindustrialization is defined mainly from the perspective of Macbeth, the metropolitan world. Bluestone and Harrison (1982) define the concept as "a widespread systematic disinvestment in [a] nation's productive capacity" (p. 6). Of course, the definition has sparse relevance to the Third World, except as an adjunct of some kind. But there is a dimension to this admittedly very complex concept that shows the possibilities of (a) contributing to the "denaturalization" of the economic dimension and (b) leveling out the First World-Third World dichotomy. In fact, deindustrialization makes commodity production more accessible to an increasing range of interests, within the First World and the Third World, because huge financial outlays are no longer a requirement for these operations (Froebel, Heinrichs, & Kreye, 1980; Sanderson, 1985).

*Informalization vs. Friedman.* As Portes, Castells, and Benton (1989) illustrate, the concept takes under its umbrella a variety of features—legal and illegal activities, social as well as economic aspects, modern as well as nonmodern and traditional aspects, nonmarkets dynamics, and so on. Again, in the best traditions of Macbeth, the phenomenon is defined from the perspective of the metropolitan world, not as a "B," by which its difference is acknowledged but as a "not-A," in which case it is seen as representing deficiencies of "A," the metropolitan world, particularly its market orientation (see Sethuraman, 1981, 1985). But informalization has forced itself into positive reckoning by quantitatively and qualitatively influencing metropolitan economic and social practices: in 1985, the informal economy accounted for some 15% to 20% of all economic activity in the United States (Denton, 1985; Greenfield, 1995; Wiegand, 1992); by the year 2000, it is estimated that barter—a widely despised practice by the metropolitan world, which banishes it to the Third World and confidently isolates it as the bane of Third World backwardness—will account for about 50% of all world trade (Neimark, 1990). There is growing evidence, too, that a number of these "backward" practices get settled in the metropole via immigration: some examples are particularistic forms of business practices, "banking" activities (Goozner, 1987; Keith, 1995a).

Informalization displays a social and cultural dimension as well. Some of the salutary results usually attributed to informalization in the Third World are now appearing in England, Italy, and Spain. The flexible work hours it promotes stall the encroachment of the "McDonaldization" syndrome, by allowing people to simultaneously engage in productive work and retain strong family and social ties (Capecchi, 1989; Mingione, 1994; Piore & Sabel, 1984; Roberts, 1994; Smith, 1994).

## ❖ A Statement of Themes

Finally, we come to the issue of selection. Why are some topics selected and others excluded? The choices are made for their capacity to illuminate and help to structure the framework this book is attempting to sketch. There will be omissions, to be sure. My hope is that strictures on this account will center more on the absence of proper ballasting for conclusions perhaps too hastily drawn than on major defects in the conceptual framework.

In fact, the reader should be put immediately on notice. If the arrival of a new global order inheres in breakdowns, modifications, or changes in its defining ideational and material aspects, why do key processes get short shrift or become subsumed under others? Under the ideational, one should expect to observe the explicit contributions of philosophy, literature/aesthetics, political theory, and perhaps, architecture. Yes, architecture! The case for its active involvement in the ethical and communitarian definitions of the contemporary world has been insightfully made by Karsten Harries (1996) in his *The Ethical Function of Architecture*. At bottom, architecture is woven more intimately into the cross- and interpenetrating disciplinarity induced by postmodernism. One injunction is to provide people with the type of built environment reflecting the way they look and feel, with a clear rejection of the priority usually given to the technical, the practical, the efficient (Hutcheon, 1987-87; Seabrook, 1991). *Multiple vernaculars* is a term commonly associated with this new approach. One could make a strong case for religion, whose "postmodern" impact has been persuasively recorded (Cox, 1984; Falk, 1992; Toulmin, 1983)[6] and for advanced technology, about which not nearly enough will be provided. Instead, we must rest content with their subsumption under headings such as "citizen-pilgrim," and "convivial poverty," in the case of religion along with pointed references to its role in social movements from which, ideally, appropriate extrapolations can be made. Technology, in its turn, will depend mostly on like extrapolations to be drawn from its impact on the global industrial process, on its influence in heightening agency and reflexivity, enabling the erosion of dominant metropolitan ideologies, or forging unity across class, gender, ethnic, and racial lines. Of course, there are other examples.

In the present work, selectivity is determined by a regime of convenience that does not transgress, at least not too much, by the canons of interpretations and analysis, by theoretical bias, and by the scope of the work. In the text, I have subsumed some political theory under philosophy, and literature/aesthetics, some political theory, and linguistics are absorbed within culture. Such analyses make for a predictable density that can potentially obscure. Much effort is made to minimize this possibility. Where density does appear, I would hope that it serves to prepare the soil for useful insights instead of providing a seeding-bed for obfuscation.

Part I (Chapters 2 and 3) provides theoretical and historical specificity for the book's themes. The new slant to interdependence is explained within the framework of globalism. Globalism speaks to a way of life, to the unfulfilled and largely ignored or marginalized aspects of the Enlightenment on which an interdependent world, less hampered by distorting dichotomies, depends.

Its arrival is announced by shifts in structure and in the logic of concepts supplying them with meaning. Under the weight of contemporary capitalist contradictions and the ontological shifts from the central view of a world structured according to political economy, a complementary form of dependence begins to take shape. Dependence of the Third World (the type so vigorously analyzed by the dependencia school) and, now, a dependence of the First World are combining against a force—modernity. Modernity was always seen as an ally of the First World in a strategic and hegemonic regime of independence vis-à-vis the other worlds. The analysis suggests that the incubus was always inherent in modernity. It has now become visible.

In the course of analysis, some attention is devoted to the peculiar origins of this cancerous and totalitarian system of hegemony, one without precedent, despite the imperialisms of Alexander of Macedonia and Julius Caesar. I employ the concept of the *grand narcissism,* without the deep psychoanalytic connotations of the term. The concept is used interchangeably with the label, "idols of the tribe," less as an application of Francis Bacon's methodology than as a vividly descriptive term for the guardians of Western thought. In the course of the analysis, we see what there is about these peculiar hegemonic strains that are inseparable from the creating and maintaining of dichotomies. Central to the analysis is the explanation of the Self and the Other(s), as the contours of the "negated double" are etched.

The main ideational definers and causal factors originate in the crises and transformations taking place within the Enlightenment tradition. These are explored in Part II (Chapters 4-7). These crises and transformations are analyzed under two main headings, rationalism and culture. Under the first heading (Chapter 4), I devote the bulk of the analysis to epistemology, for, arguably, it is here that the key detonators of modernity—including crisis of the Subject, leading to the sustained attack on logocentrism; the recasting of the structure of reason and rationality; the inadequacy of a preferred "consciousness" to grasp the world—are to be isolated and understood. Overall, these analyses enable us to grasp the scope of dependence and the ways in which ideologies and theories are urged in its construction and continuing existence.

There are subtexts here. One that filters throughout the analysis is, by implication, reconstructive. In the first sense, there is the constant reminder to contemporary theorists of an abstractionist, ahistorical bent that the purity and objectivity of their current exercise are flawed. Another fragment of this subtext relates to the Enlightenment and reason. Its foremost advocates (Hume, Kant, Hegel, among others) were in deep struggles with the principles and commands of these forces. The contradictions would surface in prejudices and strongly proestablishment politics in which the venerable Newton himself was implicated. This fragment of the subtext exists as partial redemption of the Enlightenment. For it is the position of this book that the tradition is not dead. It is not possible to situate interdependence without the input of Enlightenment principles, although there is the necessity to purge that input of modernist contagion. Another subtext of note implicates Marxism. The radical undertone to the work owes much to this source. Without being tempted to digress, I can state explicitly that Marxism, despite its limitations, did point the way to *difference*.

Part III (Chapters 8-10) analyzes the new dynamics of culture now released from the constraints of a disintegrating modernity. To provide the required context, I discuss the changing face of culture, emphasizing the specific historical conditions from which each mutation emerges. Within the breakdown of modernity, culture becomes more praxis oriented and begins to inform a more globally inclusive politics. Of central significance is the part played by postmodernism. The attack of this body of formulations on modernity, especially its *logocentric* underpinnings, helps to set the stage for a loosening of those modernist structures in which culture was held captive. Logic is gradually, but perceptibly, supplanted by *rhetoric*. This concept is more complex than the term commonly used in everyday speech, "a battle of words," as I. A. Richards (1936)would say. It is more a source for comprehending the world that eschews the decontextualized, ahistorical laws of Descartes. As developed in Chapter 10, rhetoric challenges "logic" (with its emphasis on quantitative truth) by claiming that knowledge and truth derive from language and the epiphanies of lived experience.

A new mutation of culture informs (and is informed by) an emerging politics of difference. This politics spills over its former metropolitan boundaries to coalesce with like strains in the global community. The use of fresh theorizing is crucial for the theories and practices of this politics—for, in the current state of the theoretical agenda, these exercises are multiple. Freedom has a strange, but predictable, way of giving perhaps an overblown legitimacy and importance to autonomy. Be that as it might, we see culture forming the ballast for many theories of difference—standpoint theory and Afrocentricity, among them.

Two other crucial points also form a part of the analysis. The first is that this politics does not originate only in Other-derived recalcitrance; it also has its roots in democratic traditions. The second point is that this politics is supported, at present, more by elective affinities than by the earthy everyday practice in which strange incongruities abound. In other words, the politics is driven less by pluralism, whose focus is directed more at equality (every interest securing adequate time to plead its case, without any consideration for distributive issues), than by broad questions of justice animated by the epochal need to yield recognition to all, as a function of the current dictates of planetary survival.

Part IV consists of the concluding chapter. Some attention is devoted to the obstacles lying in the path of the agenda I have sketched in this book. There must be no illusions that a politics of difference and the multiple transformations to which they beckon are anything but hugely problematical projects.

## ❖ Notes

1. *Macbeth,* Act 3, Scene 2 (Shakespeare, 1980, p. 870).
2. *Macbeth,* Act 5, Scene 8 (Shakespeare, 1980, p. 881).
3. An excellent example is the debate between Lawrence Kohlberg and Carol Gilligan on male- versus female-oriented morality, in Seyla Benhabib (1992, chap. 5).
4. Old-style national economies and monetary systems give way to greater fluidity and interdependence. Key consequences are (a) the emergence of autonomous "spaces" in which *difference* flourishes (Appadurai, 1990; Keith, 1995a; Vattimo, 1992); (b) the rise of NGOs and other nonstatist organizations in supplanting old hierarchical practices and promoting more direct, egalitarian participation of former marginals in such global issues as the environment, narcotics, and sustainable development (Alger, 1990; Farrington & Bebbington, 1993b; Edwards & Hulme, 1992; Fisher, 1993; Meyer, 1995; Paul & Israel, 1991).
5. Technological complicity with the Other(s) is increasingly visible in "cultural invention" (Lee, 1994, p. 33); "indigenous media" (Ginsburg, 1994); applied technology (Mitchell, 1980); and in the rapidly expanding areas of "ecological engineering" and "ecotechnology" (Mitsch, 1991; Mitsch & Jorgensen, 1989). With a large pool of technical personnel, India (third after the United States and Soviet Union) is advanced in appropriate technology. Technologists such as the well-known C. V. Seshadri are working on new approaches (*Shakti*) to solve the riddle created by the law of entropy (Giri, 1995, pp. 207-213).
6. This is a general theme, shared by thinkers such as Paul Feyerabend. Religion, as the "dwarf, ugly and wizened, and kept out of sight" (Peukert, 1984, p. 10), is emerging forcefully. Richard Falk (1992) implies a religious revival of some kind, as "secularism itself has 'killed' God by denying the relevance of spiritual perspectives in the conduct of public affairs" (p. 24). Harvey Cox (1984) places the task of a worldwide religious regeneration in the postmodern possibilities of liberation theology. Religion-oriented social movements are prominent in Third World development: At the 1992 Earth Summit in Rio, 200 scientists, including 27 Nobel laureates, expressed concern to the assembled Heads of States about the rise in irrational ideologies often challenging scientific and industrial progress. The complaint was spurred by the rise of religion in the environmental movement.

# PART I

# *Chapter Two*

# GLOBALISM AND DEPENDENCE IN THE NEW WORLD ORDER

*My point is that there is a general autonomy and "logic" to the globalization process, which operates in relative independence of strictly societal and other conventionally studied sociocultural processes.*
Roland Robertson (1992, p. 60)

*The past, more or less imaginary, or more or less rationalized, after the event, acts upon the future with a violence only equaled by the present itself.*
Paul Valery (1958, p. 12)

In this chapter, I provide an alternative construction to the concepts of dependence and interdependence, locating them within the larger context of globalism, a parent concept to be defined. In the end, it is the peculiar characteristics assigned to dependence and globalism that give to interdependence its equally peculiar status, one that challenges other current approaches to this phenomenon. Interdependence, on this view, results from a paradigm shift away from modernity that secures its terms of reference from the phenomenon of *difference*.

*Difference*, as used in this work, shares many similarities with a concept used by Anne Phillips (1993) to depict certain kinds of political exclusion experienced by particular social groups and interests, largely because of characteristic differences they possess. Examples include race, ethnicity, and gender, which have not been appropriately accommodated within certain renditions of democratic practice. Phillips uses a comparison of two such renditions originating in classical Greek democracy, first, to depict current commonplace interpretations of democratic practice (mainly in Europe and the United States) and, then, to draw attention to their unfinished business vis-à-vis the excluded mentioned above. The first "story," as she calls it, is the tale of liberal democracy, which, for its advocates, has weathered the storm, despite bouts with fascism and authoritarianism, and is now the model of choice by reason of its proven capacities. The second story begins with a disclaimer of the first, pointing to persistent and "extensive prohibitions that have kept so many people out of the political community" (Phillips, 1993, p. 2); it thus negates the claims of any regime as the model of choice based on performance. This void has instigated the search for a politics, still anchored to democracy, which satisfies the urgent requirement to "recognize and legitimate group difference while resisting fragmentation into discrete and local identities, and the kind of solidarity that becomes possible if we give up on the presumption of an undifferentiated humanity" (p. 2).

The need for such a politics is given greater urgency by the collapse and continuing erosion of models of redress on which the excluded often pinned their hopes. The first model is radical democracy in Europe, of socialist and social-democratic derivations, which collapsed with the fall of the Berlin Wall. The second is radical democracy, American style, which is seriously eroded. The frustration comes with the inability to excite the quality of political participation required to fulfill democratic expectations. Implied here is the role played by political apathy.

Like Phillips's, my concept of difference also focuses on the failure of democracy to, as yet, account equitably for the difference of various constituencies, animate but also inanimate. However, although I share the general antipathy she harbors against the use of difference as crippling forms of exclusion, my framework is more inclusive. The current globalizing processes of the world succeed in accomplishing two results that foster inclusivity. First, they generalize. Thus, there is a generality to the structure and application of the excluded (hereafter, the Other[s]). Gender issues share remarkable similarities in Europe, the United States, and elsewhere in the world. Second, they facilitate the formation of coalition, by allowing a more ready view of the processes of cause and effect. Women can now relate much more easily to the processes that at one and the same time bestow an identical status of inferiority on Nature. Women's difference, like that of Nature, originates in Matter.

Matter is not a basis from which truth and knowledge can ever be expected to spring forth! Identical interrelationships exist as well between that duo and indigenous peoples, Third World cultures, homophobia, and so on. A political corollary here is that objectives, if not strategies, of emancipation, will have much in common. The homogenizing of causation to which the Other(s) are exposed under modernity tends to have that effect. And this consequence appears less a function of a general commonality than it is spurred on by shared perspectives with huge normative implications for humankind's continued existence.

Modernity makes no secret of its principal mission. It is bent on making alike the "unlike," with the model peculiarly modern. In the process, it deploys its key ontological and epistemological definers to marginalize, make neutral, or even destroy the *differentia specifica* of the Other(s). These are themselves a largely contrasting set of definers claimed by the Other(s) as consisting in their valuable contribution to humanity. Their exclusion impoverishes, whereas for the modern tradition (including Marxism in some instances), their existence looms as an obstacle in the march from the realm of necessity to freedom. The exclusionary nature of the democratic agendas discussed by Anne Phillips is situated here. Her emancipatory politics, although agreeable in the spirit of a democracy yet to be actualized, should not lose sight of the much wider and diverse terrain to which it applies in principle.

Interdependence then emerges, unlike other approaches addressed later, as processes suggestive of the leveling of modernist dichotomies. This is partly the result of difference being integrated into a more inclusive interpretation of the workings of the present global community. The global connectedness by which it is marked is less defined by old binary forms of power definitions (power over) than by new types of confluences and coalitions (power to). The claims for emancipation by women and ethnicity and race and Nature are largely identical and have strong tendencies to converge in the desired politics that Professor Phillips, among others, has insightfully volunteered (more in Chapter 10). This network of claims also appears to converge in another way, further threatening old-divide explanations like First World and Third World. Often all expressions of the Other(s) can be found existing within modern settings, not as adjunct or obtruded oddities but as dynamic, serviceable forms. As a result, the modern and the nonmodern, the formal and the informal, coexist in profound structural unity. Does this phenomenon not undermine the conceptual exclusivity and operational inevitability of the "modern"? Do these developments not, at least, confound the notion of modernity's inevitable erosion of nonmodern and nonrational cultural forms?

Globalism, partly on the foregoing account, involves much more than an expanded scope for international and transnational activities. It is a transformative process. It possesses a corrosive quality that is intolerant of the hierarchies and dichotomies that are inherent in modernity. At its barest, globalism is a value system fed by an ethics drawn from global diversity. In turn, this diversity is the result of the now widely recognized limits of a view of reality as a privileged interpretation from the perspective of the Subject—a "Philosophy of Consciousness."[1] Reality is intersubjective and socially constructed in its ideational aspects (how people arrive at social meaning) and material aspects (how economic systems and technological applications are devised and implemented), hence the stress on diversity that lies at the core of a *globalismic* view of the emerging world order. In turn, the Subject and the apodictic reason he commands under Kant is being replaced by "the logic of scientific language," namely, the replacement of "Kant's transcendental logic of objective experience" (Apel, 1980, p. 78). "The subject does not belong to the world: rather it is a limit of the world" (Wittgenstein, cited in Apel, 1980, p. 10).

Even though globalism extracts much of its validity from the spirit of the Enlightenment and likewise from the modernist agenda—it does appropriate, often without much contestation, key aspects from democracy, justice, freedom, and much that science and technology provide in unlocking the secrets of Nature—this perspective can be viewed as the antithesis to the parent system from which these positive forms of human emancipation derive. But as I introduced in the previous chapter, the antithesis encompasses far more than one would expect from a dialectical process confined mainly to the stuff of modernity. Much of the paradigmatic shift originates in the social and existential counterpoints that come with the ontologies radiating from the conceptual statement, "it is different," as against "it is not."

Indisputably, a major flaw of the Enlightenment—pronouncedly, its Cartesian rendering—is its limited and mechanistic view of human life and of much, like Nature, by which that life is defined and sustained. Here, a particular segment of the human race is privileged—ostensibly by developing the emancipatory powers of the machine within us—to dictate to the rest a singular interpretation of reality that they (the Other[s]) are coerced or inveigled to accept on pain of their civilizational demise. History has shown this "privilege" to be enjoyed by several conquering nations laying claim to some form of Divine Preference, which, at once, sanctions the path all humankind must follow and turns a blind eye to concomitant tyranny and plunder. As Voltaire remarked, spells and incantations are known to kill great flocks of sheep, but not without the use of a little arsenic.

For the moment, let it suffice to state, as the globalismic counterpoint, that human beings do not function like a machine, nor should their application of reason involve merely making "unlikes alike" (Benhabib, 1986, p. 164). As modernity diminishes in importance, as the arsenic that is instrumental rationality correspondingly dissipates, old derivative dichotomies (i.e., First World-Third World, Self-Other) come under attack. Such assaults are the combined results of the unfulfilled promises of modernity and the denial of alternative and complementary perspectives. *Other*-driven theoretical forms (postmodern theory, neocritical theory [Agger, 1993; Ray, 1993], standpoint theory, for instance) and their praxiological expressions (the politics of *affinity* or *location*, for example) are part of the newly emerging framework in which these attacks are expressed.

Thus globalism is really situated in a new ontology and epistemology. These orbits of interpretation must perforce implicate economics, but not as the fountainhead giving fixity to human behaviors and values (Chapter 1). Globalism takes serious issue with this line of reasoning. It does so from a broadened conceptual and methodological base. First, the economic aspect, and one that is so imperialistically defined, is not the only ingredient of which reality is constructed. The economic aspect, as it is integrated into capitalism, has a distinct historical specificity. Human beings and their societies tend to be reduced to the economic dimension. This formula requires that human beings function as just another resource required by the economy (Rahnema, 1992, p. 169). Second, theoretical modes of deriving knowledge and placing it within satisfactory frames of meaning and action can hardly be unitary. The evidence that reality is intersubjective and constructionist, with language playing a pivotal interpretive role, becomes progressively more persuasive. In such a context, reality is negotiated, as in the case of the negotiated self (more in Chapters 9 and 10).

On account of these and other departures from orthodoxy, globalism, in the end, undermines the illusion that dependence can reside one-sidedly and in a narrow way only in the Third World (Dependence I) and reveals a much more complex (and different) phenomenon in which First World independence makes little sense. The absurdity is worse if the analyses of related crises originate in, or substantially from, narrow economic calculations, except as a point of very substantial departure. The antidote for any of the well-known social pathologies generated by the crisis of the modern self (narcissism, proteanism, and so on) is not providing people with more leisure time under current economic regimes. The solution to pollution and poverty could do well without modernity's version of a technological fix.

I have termed the dynamics of these negations "Dependence II." The role of economics is certainly implicated, but it impinges on other psychic, psychological, ontological and other philosophical dimensions that, although integral to human emancipation, have been marginalized in modernity's passion for creating all the world's peoples into a single image. In this view, interdependence emerges as the interplay between two "dependences," both engaged in a complex process of emancipation from the excesses of modernity.

For these reasons, the approach that best explains interdependence is hardly one that resides in the interplay between the independence of the metropolitan world and the dependence of the Other(s). This represents a crucial flaw in the major interpretations of interdependence, despite, as I will show later, their patently dissimilar and sometimes hostile interideological exchanges. By situating interdependence in a globalismic context, we avoid such analytic imprecision and enhance our understanding of what currently exists as international relations in a state of flux.

## ❖ The Parameters of Globalism

Let me begin by distinguishing globalism from a battery of concepts to which it is related. First, globalization. This concept has two inflections: It suggests that "political, economic, and social activity is becoming worldwide in scope"; and it connotes "an intensification of levels of interaction and interconnectedness among the states and societies which make up international society" (Held, 1991, p. 206). I am partial to the second inflection, although it is far too general and descriptive, because it admits comfortably under its umbrella all sorts of competing theories of global relations.

Transnationalism and internationalism need to be distinguished from globalism, to which they are superficially related. First, transnationalism connotes, generally, a specific organization of international capitalism. In its narrow contours, the term describes a particular phase in the preparation of the world for entrenched capitalist hegemony. To that end, it escalates the process of synchronization and generalizes patterns of standardization allowing for the globally integrated nature of capitalist production and distribution (Gill & Law, 1988, pp. 146-156). Transnationalism is superficially supportive of a central aspect of globalism—difference—inasmuch as the success of economic transactions often depends on a "respect" for the culture of the Other. What is thinly disguised repeatedly are the metropolitan biases inherent in this view: The stress on "intercultural communication," which addresses the surface aspects of the culture of the Other, really serves the purpose of making the rest of the world accessible to metropolitan domination. In turn, internationalism carries a slightly more liberal connotation. It is usually couched in a naïveté that at times becomes indistinguishable from deception, as the principle of cooperation among nations, for the pursuit of their common good.

The arrival of globalism has long been foreshadowed as an outgrowth of, or reaction to, the negative features of modernity, to wit, the Enlightenment's claim to leadership of the whole of humankind. In Condorcet's words, the Enlightenment was involved in a truly global process, one reflecting liberty, truth, happiness, virtue. It would be unlike his world of separated and incompatible people; rather, people would become well and truly "inseparable, as soon as enlightenment has reached a certain level simultaneously among a large number of nations and has penetrated the whole mass of a great people, whose language is universally known and whose commercial relations embrace the whole globe" (cited in Schapiro, 1963, p. 187). Condorcet speaks of the Enlightenment in equalitarian tones that suggest a marked preference for universalistic values such as social participation by all (including all peoples and women) as opposed to the politics of difference (Schapiro, 1963, pp. 190-193 in the case of women). Sharing some of the cosmopolitanism of Condorcet's liberalism, globalism exists as a normative component of the spirit of the Enlightenment, with the "tradition"—I make a distinction between *tradition* and *project* in the next chapter—providing supportive ballast. Of course, the problem is that the Enlightenment lends itself to a variety of interpretations, a point that Alasdair MacIntyre addresses and to which I return in the next chapter.

But globalism surfaces also as a watchdog, as a potential political agenda, a stance it assumed when the principles of the Enlightenment took concrete form. The impetus for that political agenda was preempted when Cartesian epistemology laid down the irrevocable edict that human beings and the life they lead are reducible to the working principles of the machine. A similar duty attaches to Locke's *tabula rasa,* by which the cultural and historical slates of the Other(s) and non-Western peoples would be wiped clean (because that was the extent of human nature) and replaced by enlightened reason. (Here one of the watchdog functions resides in monitoring the interpretation and application of *reason.*) More in subsequent chapters. Parenthetically, these are key interpretations of the Enlightenment tradition, which do not accommodate the key concepts and assumptions of globalism. Or if they do, there is divergence in terms of the choices of theory and practices selected.

The watchdog function is reinforced further by another troublesome factor associated: This machine, which had Hume in awe, will brook no opposition as to the interpretation of reality it represents and, moreover, it expresses the clear "desire to wipe out whatever came earlier" (de Man, 1969, cited in Gergen, 1991, p. 32). Threatened with extinction are those foundations on which the substantial majority of human beings make sense of life—worldviews and systems of knowledge that have defined their worlds for centuries. That threat was to finally turn inward, as the situation of metropolitan women, including the wife of modern man, testifies.

What explains the relatively sudden active streak to globalism? The answer, I think, lies in the shifting balance of power within and among geopolitical spheres, which is, in turn, exacerbated by maturing contradictions. But above everything else—and those contradictions are directly related to it—is the largely effective attack on the explanatory framework within which these competing expressions of power resonate. I will attempt to make the point with a brief reference to the collapse of a major obfuscatory mechanism employed to maintain hegemony over the Other(s).

First, the point has been made repeatedly that although most hegemonic powers throughout history gained their legitimacy for conquest from some version of divine dispensation, the narcissism of the capitalist experience is different. This Grand Narcissism, as I have labeled it, followed suit but gradually resorted to other means to entrench domination. Science figured prominently in creating subtle means, and the increasing democratization introduced by the Enlightenment made it very difficult to sustain the barbarism and the crudities of earlier times, despite the Conquistadores! The main core of this position is discussed in another context (Chapter 4), so I will merely provide the crux of that argument, together with support from other sources.

Under capitalism, there was a conscious policy to rule without force or overt violence. Arnold Toynbee (1976) makes the point that Western civilization now "no longer felt an obligation or an impulse to impose a majority's creed and rite by force" (p. 536). But this statement is a half-truth that shines luminously vis-à-vis the earlier forms of subjugation. In its own terms, science, on which Toynbee's reflection is based, is not free from a "soft," but nonetheless effective, form of force. This force is often obscured by a rationality through which objective determinations can be made about the differing values of comparative cultures and races. Newtonianism, which simultaneously determined the dependence of non-Western nations as well as the inferiority of women, serves up two good examples. Both acquired their disability via a common form of explication—the Mind-Matter discourse discussed in Chapter 6.

Edward Sampson (1993) refers to this force as "soft force" and its technique as that of a "silent killer." The agendas are embodied in "forms of domination that center primarily around the construction of the other: forms that deny life by controlling its definition of reality" (p. 4). These forms are indeed silent in their approach but have not the theme that has historically set them apart from predecessors: the continued institutionalization of attributes, and the like, of the Other(s), as the way to represent them as the vigorously "negated double" (Mudimbe, 1994, p. xii). In other words, this form of narcissism sustains its vitality by maintaining the gulf between itself and the Other(s) through a superficially attractive, yet functionally unachievable, agenda. Likewise, it creates a bond with the Other(s) as host(s) in a set of parasitic relations.

## ❖ Narcissism and the Negated Double

The *negated double* is a most revealing concept, because it alludes at once to organic relations between the two—the Self and the Other(s)—which are contradictory in nature. Grasping the manner in which these relations are structured under capitalist modernity allows us to appreciate how the normative aspects of globalism came into play. As I will illustrate, the liberatory contradictions result from the exercise of a soft force that lost its ability to rule by reification and distracting ideologies.

Operating as a total system that incorporates modern and peripheral capitalism, the capitalist mode of production is compelled to execute two main functions: to accumulate and to legitimate. Both functions are expected to occur in a dynamically competitive system where many key participants (Third World peoples, women, indigenous peoples, homosexuals, and so on) participate and share in the process of accumulation. That system is exclusive, as modernization theory makes clear. And much is done via ideology, symbolism, and the like, to separate the participating entities—the Other(s)—from their indigenous endowments and other social and cultural features that form the basis of their worldviews. In concrete terms, accumulation is anything but consistent with the theoretical principles underpinning it; well-known critiques on the negative consequences of uneven development, on class-dominated distribution, on racism, on sexism, on homophobia, for example, are commonplace and need not delay us here.

The entrenchment of the negated double occurs here mainly through a spurious mirror image. It is spurious for the identical reasons expressed in the contradictions of democracy mentioned above. Other(s) will never, via the actual practice of capital accumulation, achieve parity or fairness in distribution. Generally speaking, this asymmetry has little to do with subjective deficiencies, and the like. There is a systemic mutual exclusivity about the two sets of interests, as Marx demonstrates. Capitalist accumulation is erected on these structural disparities. At the same time, the complementarity of the two (i.e., the Self and its negated double) is partly achieved by (a) the process of its integration (economics, politics, and ideology) and (b) a definition of success imposed by that process of integration. In the first case, the economic and related formulas of the Other(s), the negated double, are largely rejected and become central to systemic definitions, primarily by denial. They are the ingredients of the negative limb of several dichotomies of modernization theories. In the second case, the negated double now draws its formulas of success from the demonstration effects of the single, the "Self"—the positive limb of those dichotomies, as well as from systemic strategies of legitimation (ideologies, including hegemony a la Gramsci and other ruses that allow domination to appear as part of the natural order of things—*habitus,* as Pierre Bourdieu labels some of those processes. Just the same, denied, marginalized, or even destroyed in the construction of each negative limb of these dichotomies are the treasured unique elements of the Other(s)—race, culture, gender, and so on.

The Other(s) is made the conscience of the Self through a process occurring from early capitalism (under colonialism, for example) up to the present. On the one hand, there is vulgar exploitation of native peoples, often accompanied by acts of unspeakable genocide. The records are replete with such barbarous acts as the contamination of the Australian aborigine's flour with arsenic or the dispassionate killing of Kaingang Indians in Brazil by mixing strychnine in their drinking water. But there was, at the same time, the coveted image of the "Noble Savage." He was the personification of primeval Nature, the exemplar of a coexistence with Nature that Modern Man would increasingly crave. Other(s) were victimized by the absence of *the* proper interaction with reason but possessed qualities (emotions, intuition, and so on) without which Modern Man would destroy himself. Maria Mies (Mies & Shiva, 1993) presents the matter rather intriguingly:

> The "savages" . . . must be constructed symbolically as *complementary* "other" to rational Modern Man. And they have to be fixed into a kind of state of nature, as representing . . . the "Golden Age"; this is where they are meant to remain so that modern rational, civilized Man maintains his nature base without which he could not survive. (p. 151)

Fanon (1967) also expresses this dialectic in *Black Skins, White Masks:*

> Man is human only to the extent to which he tries to impose his existence on another man in order to be recognized by him. As long as he has not yet been

> effectively recognized by the other, that other will remain the theme of his actions. (pp. 216-217)[2]

From this account and analysis, we sense a profound connectivity unhampered by physical distances separating peoples. Progressively, it shores up the related contradictions that modernity is incapable of resolving satisfactorily. The Other(s) recognize, first, that parity at the distributive levels is festooned more by words than deeds and, then, that the emperor indeed has no clothes. This realization occurs with force under conditions of Dependence II, to be discussed more fully below. The present activist strains of globalism are situated here.

To the extent that a unitary interpretation of reality is specious, the Other(s) are constrained to take issue violently with its abuses and suspect theories. History also props up the posture of watchfulness provided by the example of "ontological totalitarianism" that eventuated in the Holocaust. Universal reductionism of which the Self is made is vividly displayed here (Bauman, 1989). The Other(s), on the other hand, are also integrally involved with the Self in the process of their joint emancipation. This explains the strong identification with such modernist "inventions" as popular democracy, even though the definitions of the "why," "who," and "how" are matters of profound contestation. The relationship between Self and Other(s), between "A" and "not-A," act(s) as an umbilical cord between these two, as structurally their futures are indivisible, as Hegel, Fanon, and others have stressed repeatedly.

Consequently, globalism is both an outgrowth of and a reaction to modernity. It is defined, partly, by the principles that appear, paradoxically, to work against the modernist agenda—substituting a multiple interpretation of reality, as I mentioned above. Globalism, for instance, supports the concept of difference, with its distinct capabilities of rescuing alterity from the sameness to which it has been condemned "by means of the philosopher's stone of the knowing ego" (Critchley, 1992, p. 6)—to borrow Levinasian terminology. This helps to define the twin tasks of its political agenda: (a) to bring the Other(s) back into a globalismic (as distinct from a modernist) epistemological framework and (b) to assist in laying the groundwork for an ethics appropriate to the "umbilicalism" that characterizes Self-Other(s) relations.

The main links between difference and interdependence exist as bridges between metropolitan (modern) and nonmodern and so-called backward practices and habits of mind. Concretely, the reference is to the impact of those theoretical and praxiological forms to which I referred earlier. Postmodern theory or standpoint theory and a politics of recognition or affinity are partly the complements or negations of the scope of modernity; in this context, we observe much expanded definitions of rationality and market economics, for example, which permit a more inclusive definitional space, one that now integrates the perspectives of women, indigenous peoples, Nature, among like expressions of the Other(s). In the case of an expanded rationality, a globalismic version dispenses with the Cartesian view that there is *a* single and permanent way to get to the truth. In this endeavor, it is heavily supported by postmodernism, with its unsparing, if at times, excessive attack on the Enlightenment. To the extent that this corrective is situated in deeply embedded, but yet-to-be-realized, principles of human emancipation, globalism is engaged in a decoupling of the true spirit of the Enlightenment—its humanistic aspect—from the constraints of modernity.

Yet globalism could not exist without the history of worldwide domination that forms its underside. We can infer this result from Roland Robertson's (1992) claim "that it has not been until quite recently that considerable numbers of people living on various parts of the planet have spoken and acted in direct reference to the 'organization' of the entire heliocentric world" (p. 54). The organizational thrust of which he speaks is directed against an interpretation of the Enlightenment as modernity—which, its flaws notwithstanding, still must adhere to its intrinsic system of critique. In a sense, globalism represents the chickens coming home to roost.

Those principles that animate and sustain legitimate dissent are not disguised or camouflaged by the specter of domination. If we look at the broad definition of the spent structure of modernity (i.e., "hegemonic internationalism") we are able to abstract the basis of legitimate dissent. Hegemonic internationalism, as Fred Halliday (1988) defines it, "destroys . . . old societies and political systems and [imprints] cultural, linguistic, economic and military systems upon [the populations in question]," acting out of an underlying imperialistic belief "that white nations had a right and duty to rule the colonized" (p. 193). Expressed and implied in its fundamental organizing principles, whether as philosophies, political, ethical, or economic theories are patterns of thought and action oriented to justice, fairness, equality—all of which provide contestative points of contact with the major principles of this system. Broadly speaking, it is permitted to lead a revolution to change such a system; this change-oriented action may assume less extreme forms such as criticism, debate on political and moral values, and so on (Plamenatz, 1960). The history of European decolonization, complete with its rash of nation-states since the 1960s (Ghana, Kenya, Nigeria, and so on), testifies to the sometimes happy consequences of many of these forms of dissent. These points support my earlier metaphor of modernity as the emperor without clothes.

When I referred earlier to globalism as a value system hemmed in by an ethics of diversity, these are some of the very principles I had in mind. In the normative form, the Enlightenment manifested these principles of checks and balances, together with a kind of secular custodialism achieved when the *philosophes* marginalized God and usurped his function as the Keeper of his flock. In its civic form, the Enlightenment tradition reinforces the above function through the rights and duties endemic in the right to rule Fred Halliday mentioned above. But rights and privileges carry responsibilities; it is the critical exploration of the hegemon's rights and privileges as well as his duties and responsibilities that supplies globalism with its fulcrum. The well-known apologist for hegemonic internationalism—Rudyard Kipling—concedes that much in the double-edged duty he exacts of British imperialism.

> Take up the White Man's burden
> — The savage wars of peace
> Full fill the mouth of famine
> And bid the sickness cease.
> The ports ye shall not enter,
> The roads ye shall not tread,
> Go make them with your living,
> And mark them with your dead.
> (Kipling's "The White Man's Burden,"
> cited in Snyder, 1962, pp. 87-88)

As Ali Mazrui (1990) interprets these lines, Kipling was making a "virtue of the unintended consequences of imperialism" (p. 21).

Historically speaking, globalism could, perhaps, have gathered substance only through the combination of the forces that created modernity. That combination, at once, seeks to integrate peoples of the world through enlightened philosophical formulations stressing truth, morality, knowledge; through the constant upgrading of technique (mainly through appropriate technology); through economic and political regimes sensitive to the ends of freedom. But globalism moves beyond modernity, especially in its insistence on democratic principles from which diversity partly draws its legitimacy. It does so, to use Jim George's (1995, p. 211) felicitous phrase used in another context, by making the case that terms like " 'democracy,' 'emancipation,' and 'power' might have other valid meanings than those laid down by correspondence rule logic."

Globalism and modernity surfaced from a common mix, as I have stressed above. But they are conceptually and often analytically distinct, while mutually reinforcing. R. R. Palmer, the translator of Georges LeFebvre's *The Coming of the French Revolution*, casts much light on the concept. Palmer draws attention to some of the major contributions of the French Revolution, itself an important weather vane for modernity and globalism: "From it have come the . . . accentuated division of the earth among national sovereignties, the recognition of national self-determination as a desirable principle and at the same time the hope that peace might reign over nations equally free." And yet "paradoxes" abound:

> The revolution liberated the individual, and consolidated the modern state. It confirmed the rule of law, and it launched a tradition of violence. It denounced war as a stratagem of governments, not of peoples, and made war more terrible and more "total" by putting whole nations behind the armies. It cleared the way for the triumph of capitalism, and inspired socialism to subvert it. It based society on the institution of private property, but also on the human rights of the average man. It declared all peoples to be alike, and at the same time . . . persuaded many peoples that their interests were opposed to the "West," and that their peculiar national character forbade assimilation into a uniform world civilization. (LeFebvre, 1973, pp. v-vi)[3]

Concretely, it might be stated that globalism extracts its definition and agenda from the unfilled dimensions of the above paradoxes. It constitutes the normative dimension of the Enlightenment in the fullest and most rational expressions of the tradition. Globalism is *not* the normative dimension of modernity, defined as an Enlightenment variant driven by instrumental rationality. Instrumental rationality is to modernity as substantive rationality is to a truly inclusive Enlightenment, one that accentuates the central place of difference. The heterogeneous framework of globalism is captured nicely by Martin Albrow (Albrow & King, 1990):

> I take [globalism] to refer to those values which take the region of 5 billion people as the object of concern, the whole earth as the physical environment, everyone living as world citizens, consumers and producers, with a common interest in collective action to solve global problems. (p. 8)

## ❖ From Dependence I to Globalism

My use of *dependence* is far more expansive that its association with *dependencia* á la Frank, Baran, or Cardoso and departs from that tradition. In the latter's theoretical framework, the dependent character of the "underdeveloped" areas of the globe (e.g., the Third World) results from centuries-old domination by a Europeanization of the world (see Amin, 1974; Blaut, 1993; Frank, 1968). It has become somewhat of a reflex action to brandish Teotonio Dos Santos's (1970) definition of dependence as "a situation in which the economy of certain countries is conditioned by the development and expansion of another economy to which the former is subjected" (p. 231). This results from a very special set of relations between the dominant, metropolitan, societies and the dependent world, influenced by the three interpenetrating forces of colonialism, imperialism, and exploitation. This I have termed Dependence I.[4]

This original definition of dependence has its theoretical roots in Marxism-Leninism, which then shaded into dependency theory commingled sometimes with various neo-Marxist theories. In their totality, though the theories and practices were diverse, the objective was to release the underdeveloped world from the economic exploitation of the metropolitan world. Strategies of emancipation run the gamut from socialist revolution (Marxism-Leninism), to dependent development under capitalist aeges (Cardoso & Faletto, 1979), to negotiated dependence (Quijano, 1971). In any event, the analyses were fundamentally economic in nature, and the bulk of these strategies had far fewer quarrels with the environmentally, psychically, and humanistically corrosive features of capitalism. Like Oliver Twist, they wanted more. In other words, there appeared to be substantial support for the "development-by-growth" model represented mainly by modernization theory (see Hoselitz, 1960; McClelland, 1961; Rostow, 1962).

Traditional conceptions of dependence, which are aligned mainly to the discourses on underdevelopment, now assume a different shape under globalism. These changes are axial in nature, because our age is undergoing a qualitative shift from political economy, as I stated in the opening chapter. Does it, then, mean that the old conceptions of Dependence I, of metropolitan domination of the Third World, are now outmoded? Yes and no. Indeed, this ambiguous response speaks eloquently to key relations caught in the transition of the axial shift mentioned above. Yes, the analytic flood in which globalism is deluged does indicate that, in a new sense, the traditional notion of "core" exploiting "periphery" needs to be modified. Global processes set in motion, whether as specific agendas, as unintended consequences, or as blatant or misguided theories and practices, are recasting the entire mix of formative social relations into a new phase. In concrete terms, factors such as the combined interplay of advanced technology and its negative effects on environment and of the narrow, yet totalizing, application of reason are extending the scope and meaning of dependence. Although many of these analytic concepts derive from, and are still relevant to, modernity, they are moving away from largely political economic definitions to others in which postmodernism figures prominently.

Such shifts are a historical commonplace. Let me digress a bit to provide substantiation. Jurgen Habermas (1986, pp. 3-4, Vol. 1) indicates correctly that the current, if now beleaguered, reign of political economy resulted when, during the 18th century, it displaced rational natural law as the key organizing principle. The qualitative shift was brought about mainly by Hegel, whose genius rests, in part, in making of history not merely a neutral space for the fulfillment of philosophical ideas; despite his conservatism, he was etching the site for dynamic processes of change. The next step in the progression was Marx, whose quarrels with Hegelianism are well-known and need not delay us here (Avineri, 1971; Ferry & Renault, 1992). It should suffice to indicate that a history whose impetus and process of change was, for Hegel, orchestrated by a force *ab extra,* detached from the originating wellsprings of purposeful action (i.e., reason), was supplanted by a force originating in the social and historical conditions of life—labor—on which the principles of reason depended. Consequently, ontology was historically situated in human-defining and human-sustaining aspects of labor that came to define capitalism. This is the "work model of activity" that looms as the privileged mode for making and shaping human history.

It is the evolution of these shifts that now links, structurally as well as ideationally, the fortunes of dependencia and those of the metropolitan world. The shift toward postmodern measures does not completely eclipse the importance of economic factors. It merely marginalizes an economic definition of reality, one whereby the dynamics of social and spiritual life originate in the characterization of the world as a giant work house (to use Adorno's term; cited in Meszaros, 1989, p. 93). These shifts, often ontological as well as epistemological, now introduce other defining variables—collectively enshrined mainly in the Other(s)—into a new ambit of social conceptualization and interpretation. It is this evolving process in transformation, in which heretofore ignored or marginalized phenomena (culture, for instance) become active, that highlights the hidden dimensions of dependence.

The picture is no longer one of an all-round dominant economic hegemon, exercising total mastery over Nature, directing like socioeconomic development of the backward, outlying reaches of the rest of the world. It is rather of the emergence of a cognate form of dependence of the so-called developed, modern, world created by the limitations and contradictions built into the overarching development agenda as a whole. Both subworlds are victimized by a dependence coming into full flowering from what I contend is a misapplication of Enlightenment tradition, or, more properly, the result of the modernist moment within that hugely encompassing tradition.

This emergent form of metropolitan dependence was always obscured by a widely agreeable, but narrow, form of economic determinism. From Marx (the socialist) to Ludwig von Mises (the libertarian) to Milton Friedman (the conservative), the economic is given a pride of place almost to the total exclusion of the other defining agents of social life. Largely on account of the crippling economic myopia of capitalism, we have lost sight of the role of the noneconomic. Marshall Sahlins (1976) and Pierre Clastres (1974) have documented how significant cultures erected congenial and anthropologically satisfying patterns of life on noneconomic assumptions and practices. Others, such as Amartya Sen (1977) and Alan Sica (1988, in a critique of Weber), point to the unwarranted use of the economic and the rational in attempting to "naturalize" the economy. Naturalization requires the disvaluing of all other social forms, with wants, hopes, and the environment beholden to the market (Esteva, 1992, p. 18).

In truth, the naturalization process is epochal. The picture of an economic definition of reality was to coalesce with the new social system created by capitalism. Naturalization was required to "justify processes through which 'private vices' could become 'public virtues' in the marketplace" (Benhabib, 1986, p. 6). Much that accompanies the rise of capitalist economics via Weber's (1958) analysis (*The Protestant Ethic and the Spirit of Capitalism*) suggests this cleansing process; avarice, for example, became respectable and a driving force for capital accumulation—capitalism's coveted prize. A contemporary truth is that, whether in the form of an alternative economics (sustainable development), politics (postmodern), or other spheres of social analysis, a theory and practice of difference is bent on either limiting or eliminating the corrosive effects of these suspect "public virtues."

At the present stage, globalism is making of dependence a schizoid phenomenon. As eagerly as Third World countries must guard against and ferret out exploitation of all kinds, they must consciously cooperate with the main architects of those conditions from which the region recoils. Indeed, the agenda becomes imperative as much for the exigencies of Third World emancipation as for the pressures urged on by the new, yet derivative, dependence of those architects, the metropolitan world. Reciprocally, the metropolitan world is challenged to follow a less dominating, more collaborative approach in its relations with the other areas of the world, notably the traditionally underdeveloped areas. This is so because there is a conflation of cause and effect: Third World dependence is traceable mainly to the metropolitan world, but contemporary metropolitan social pathologies, many of which reside comfortably in the "developing" world, are of the same piece as underdevelopment.

Take the case of the Four Tigers (Taiwan, Singapore, Hong Kong, and Korea), persistently hailed as the model for the rest of the "developing" world. In truth, economic success has come at a huge price: poisoned water, contaminated soil, and a sea reeling under the destructive impact of chemicals such as mercury compounds. In Taiwan, some 20% of the land is polluted by industrial waste, and some 30% of the rice crops invariably contain dangerous levels of cadmium and mercury (McClintock, 1994, p. 301). (In this case, counteracting strategies involve collaborative efforts with worldwide branches of the environmental movement [Cammack, Pool, & Tordoff, 1993].)

The future of both spheres is now visibly intertwined, as traditional social, political, and economic forms (exemplified by social class, the nation-state, and a growth-driven approach to social development, respectively) either vanish or adjust to the new rhythms. Especially with the economic and political boon provided by Pax Americana, we could pretend that international relations functioned maximally when each nation could blindly pursue its own "peculiar" interests, quite oblivious of its neighbor. Nations were taken to be bouncing off each other, in the manner of billiard balls, without any real inkling of interdependence, in the sense in which I have defined it. There was nothing of the "ecological" that is now a prominent and persuasive view of the physical world as a finite system; there was little appreciation of the limits to the resources on which such an anarchic rendition of the world depends. (This topic will be addressed in Chapter 3.) Such a perspective was greatly influenced by a Hobbesian psychology abounding in narrow, self-interested practices, supposedly dictated by the laws of human survival and anchored to the idea that we inhabit a chaos-ridden, anarchic reality. Such a state of affairs dictates, in part, that a Social Darwinist approach be pursued. Likewise evident is the science-has-defeated-nature posture—a technological utopianism that, though diminishing, remains a popular feature of metropolitan ideology.

Under this regime, the realm of activity is prescribed, for better or worse, by the interplay of democracy and capitalist material plenty. This has allowed an uncomfortable inattentiveness to finitude, defined in the present context as the limits to, and the integrated nature of, the physical environment. Anarchic self-interest thrives maximally in an environment with enough cushion to mitigate the excesses of its claims. Where material plenty flourishes, an epidemic of rights appears that strengthens an individualism of a *possessive* or *asocial* type (MacPherson, 1962; Mulhall & Swift, 1992, pp. 13-18). Abundance at the *intra*society level fosters a divorce of civic freedom from civic responsibility. Two sets of forces that exist in a natural dialectical harmony are attempting to lead independent existences.

This position is, in a related fashion, quite insensitive to the current pornography of global power. Nation-states may be sovereign, theoretically, but, in truth, some states are more equal than others. Sovereignty meant precious little when the U.S. government wanted the president of Panama. Sovereignty in the hands of the weak is no less problematical than sovereignty exercised by the strong. The former has so easily, under the guise of self-determination, inflicted the most heinous deprivations on its subjects—such is the case of Mobutu Sese Seko of Zaire. In the latter situation, it exculpates greed, wanton exercise of unequal power in the name of insupportable exercises of rational choice, and much that sacrifices principle to expediency.

Suggesting that these issues are not profoundly complex would be unspeakably naive. After all, the Somalis were generally pleased to see the U.S. forces board the last military plane from Mogodishu, though they were exposed to the death-guaranteeing policies and practices of their leaders. Students of ideology (Gramsci and Bourdieu) have done well to alert us to the working of hegemony and habitus—the "collective unconscious," as Bourdieu has shown, does much to keep a status quo intact. But in any event, the key issue of human connectivity looms large and ponderously. One detects a persistence and expansion of the separation between freedom and responsibility mentioned earlier in the intrasociety context, which has spilled over into the international sphere. The reality that appears to be inching itself on the stage is cosmopolitan in conception: It is forcing humankind to grapple with a sociological-philosophical point—that we, as human beings, derive our self-understandings and conceptions of the good from broadly communitarian sensibilities. It shares the spirit of Levinasian ethics of "an inherent interhuman responsibility" aligned to "a respect for social difference and particularity" (George, 1995, p. 211).

Today, the obscuring clouds are dramatically lifting and the contours of an increasingly forced fellowship are taking shape—"forced" not so much because it is unnatural but because of the transformative character of the forces at work. This emerging world order can be readily explained as the quickening of the survival impulses triggered by a common humanity coming to recognize its profound connectedness and the perils it now faces.

Of course, survival impulses are deeply involved in the new agendas of change. More specifically, though, their agendas are encoded in the master plan of modernity that imprints on them their shape, their rhythms, and the processes involved in the dynamics of change. This finitude, in its dual meaning, is structurally linked to major thrusts of modernity overtaken by their contradictions and the changes within the global environment. Finitude, as the exposure of the physical limits of the environment (ecological decay, depletion of resources), will undermine (is undermining, as we shall see later) the penchant for fabricating spurious rights and distorted individualisms, based on an outmoded growth-oriented formula of socioeconomic development. Finitude, as an ontological concept that places human beings within a fixed existential scheme of things, is forcing Modern Man to come to grips with mortality and confront the narcissism induced by science and technology, as reflected in the pursuit of everlasting life (organ transplantation, gene splitting, and the like). Modern social theorizing is quite uncomfortable with this aspect of reality: Even the redoubtable Jurgen Habermas, with his penchant for grand theorizing, could find very little room for it in his "universal pragmatics" (Habermas, 1972). These lacunae, which are widely viewed as deeply crippling, are now taken by many to have a counterpoint in various elements of difference. For one, much inheres in the contrasting worldviews defined by either a *logic-driven* or a *rhetoric-driven* interpretation of reality (more later, especially in Chapters 7 and 10).

In both cases, the issues related to finitude result from foundational principles of modernity in a state of deep crisis. In both cases, the trajectories along which solutions are likely to appear bring into reckoning a fresh awareness of human connectivity. There is much to suggest that this awareness moves well beyond the connectivity we may experience as an instinctive and intellectual reflex action. Environmental pollution, resource depletion, the revolt of the Other(s) against logocentric exclusivism—all these and more give a certain prophetic poignancy to W. H. Auden's immortal line: If we do not love each other, we die!

## ❖ The Contemporary Relevance of Dependence I

What is the value of explaining Dependence I in a world where the emphasis has shifted away from its narrow purview? The question is quite legitimate for two major reasons. First, there are those who contend that the conditions giving rise to Third World dependence no longer exist. Alice H. Amsden (1979) and Nigel Harris (1986) use the case of the Four Tigers (Taiwan, Singapore, Korea, Hong Kong) to question the legitimacy of dependence as a whole; indeed, they suggest that radical dependency theories, in particular (the Frankian School), are outmoded, citing the performance of the Four Tigers as irrefutable proof. Strong state interventionism (*etatisme*) and invocations of Weberian conceptualizations of the role of an "entrepreneurial spirit" are among the factors cited (Amsden, 1979; Harris, 1986). Besides, for all of their suggestiveness, dependency theorists were always better at explaining than at offering solutions: There was much "whitewashing," blaming exploitation mainly on the metropolitan elite (Sherman, 1987, p. 230).

Second, this mode of analysis is increasingly at odds, partially if not totally, with the current interplay of forces served up by globalization. Indeed, the range and the scope of critique here are much more comprehensive, as analysis moves beyond narrow economic issues. Take Marxism, for instance. That framework—a point admitted by Marxist and non-Marxist alike (Aronowitz, 1992; Boggs, 1986; Inglehart, 1990)—has assumed a "post-Marxist" and "postdependency" posture. Global relations are now considerably less conditioned by factors on which the Marxist and the dependency theorist relied as bases for strategies and solutions. Let me cite the work of Alain Touraine, Aronowitz, and others as representative examples. For Touraine (1969, 1977), there is a movement from industrial to postindustrial programmed society, one defined largely by the capital/labor dialectic, to a society in which technocracy dominates. Historical change is no longer spearheaded by the working class but by new social movements. And their agenda is hardly to seek more from industrial exploitation but, rather, to halt its expansionist and "progressive" thrust. The act of constraint is necessary to realign human life with the sense of identity and community.

Stanley Aronowitz (1992, p. 61), who maintains sympathetic ties with the Marxist tradition, points to the fact that unionism in many Third World countries, South Africa and Brazil, for example, is heavily imbued with "cultural affinities." Unions are, therefore, "a cultural as well as an economic form." Culture is praxis; no longer is it an epiphenomenon. A similar position is taken on what might be called "political affinities." Some Marxist-Leninist parties of the Third World—some in the circum-Caribbean region, for example—now find it vital to graft liberal democratic principles (rights to property, rights to competitive electoral politics, freedom of worship, and so on) onto new Marxist theoretical reconstructions (see Munroe, 1990, pp. 16-21). It might be noted as well that nationalism and anti-Americanism have also tended gradually to supplant Marxist-Leninist orthodoxy (Rosenau, 1992, p. 153). Much of the tension and avoidance inhere in the distinctions I have earlier drawn between globalism and socialism and in the diminishing importance of the political economy paradigm.

From the perspective of the dependency school, one observes changes of heart. Frank, the putative father of radical dependency theory, now envisions social change in the context of social movements like the Christian Base Communities in Brazil and Chile. In turn, Bjorn Hettne (1978) states, compromisingly, "that there can be no fixed and final definition of development, only suggestions of what development should imply in particular contexts" (p. 7). A like inflection is induced from liberation theology. Here the concept of "integral development," borrowed from Pope Paul VI, is applied at three levels: The first level refers to centrality of aspirations of the poor; the next level focuses on the significance of freedom, the ability of people to control their own lives; and the third deals with liberation, that is the communion with God and other human beings (Manzo, 1991, p. 23). As John Farrington and Anthony Bebbington (1993) put it,

> There is now a greater willingness to recognize the potentially virtuous (sic) contributions of the private sector to development, the limitations of the state as a vehicle of progressive social change, and the need for serious consideration of economic efficiency in the delivery of development services. (p. 2)

Increasing reliance is now being placed on NGOs as constituents of the "third sector." The stress on revolution as the sine qua non to agreeable social change has diminished. The increasing role of noneconomic and nonmodern variables in these solutions should also be noted, suggesting at least two qualitatively new developments: first, a dismantling of traditional cause-and-effect discourses; second, a flattening of old dichotomies. Let me hasten to add that the changes affect competing theories of society equally, given that capitalism and socialism share an exclusivist Enlightenment bias from which globalism is revolting. Neither of these two modes of production is conceptually comfortable with globalism's agenda of diversity.

Indeed, the central purpose of a focus on the etiology of dependence rests perhaps less on its contemporary theoretical insights (especially those related to recipes of change) than on its ongoing significance as an explanatory framework. The substantial weight of the evidence surely supports the view that the underdeveloped world, as we know it, is the product of a peculiar association with a Europeanized model of global development. On the whole, the main body of modernization theory—perhaps the most consistent opposition to the Marxist-dependency tandem—operates less as disagreements with broadly accepted accounts of the origins of dependence. Andre Gunder Frank's famous broadside still possesses the power to dissuade the opposition (Frank, 1968).[5] Objections occur more generally as quarrels with dependencia's recipes for change. Thus, Peter Berger (1986, pp. 119, 126) does not find Walt W. Rostow's famous "stages of growth" analysis "ethnocentric"; rather, he finds it "optimistic." He also volunteers that the colonial powers, by leaving behind railroads, ports, and bureaucracy, have really provided invaluable assets for development in the postcolonial period. This curious statement and many others like it are often induced by the bulk of dependency theorists who had little patience with any agenda of change that failed to contemplate full-blown revolution.

Although much theoretical change is to be expected as the conditions of life and the stuff of human affairs are transformed, the global explanatory force of dependence has not lost its savor. History usually records qualitative breaks in its continuity by measures of equally qualitative specificity. In truth, we may be approaching a new historical conjuncture, but elements of the Hegelian period continue to have their impact, despite the growing disenchantment with progress, with reason, on which its dialectic depends.

We can still recognize the influence of Hegelianism on dependence and its supportive theories. Despite the internal shifts within the "work model of activity" (Benhabib, 1986, p. xi), we are still caught within its embrace. Although fundamental changes in global social processes are indisputably on us, we must avoid excessive declamation, especially if it is induced by the collapse of the Berlin Wall and the demise of the Soviet Union. Those who would remain riveted to the view that Dependence I is old hat are really proverbial ostriches.[6]

## ❖ Dependence II: The Incubus Deserts the Shadows

Dependence II, as I define it, expresses itself less as material scarcity than as psychic and psychological fears and deprivations. There is less dichotomization in international relations here than one would suspect. It is not that the metropolitan world is reeling from the deleterious effects of modernity, expressed as the result of the surfeit of overproduction and material plenty, while the rest of the world wallows in Dependence I. Postscarcity anarchism, to borrow Murray Bookchin's term, and economic scarcity are definitely at large, but they are not necessarily the preserve of one subworld or the other. Traditional dichotomies appear to be flattening, as a result of hybridity and other forces introduced by globalism: the simultaneous existence of particularism and universalism in both developed and underdeveloped societies—an undermining of the modern/backward dichotomy (Keith, 1995b; Robertson, 1992); the spread of reflexivity within the global environment (Giddens, 1990; Lash & Urry, 1994); the operating of that environment as largely independent, but interrelated, "scapes" in an economy that is cultural in nature and less dominated by cultural giantism ("the United States is no longer the puppeteer of a world system of images, but is only one node of a complex transnational construction of imaginary landscapes"; Appadurai, 1990, p. 7). Consistent with this view is that of Jean Baudrillard who notes that although contemporary capitalism can economically and politically reproduce itself in a postindustrial world, it has lost the capacity to do so symbolically. Superfluously, it is the symbolic world that provides us with meaning: We are *homo pictor,* the symbol-producing animal, afloat in a new economics of signs and space (Lash & Urry, 1994).

Much of this translates into a politics of culture, especially the "instanciation" induced by global communications systems. In this context, Scott Lash and John Urry (1994, p. 36) do not overstate the case in suggesting that even though the media thrive on "spectacularization," preferring forms ("signs") to substance, they, nonetheless, promote a "reflexivity" from which even the traditionally oppressed (Third World peoples, for example) are not excluded. By reflexivity is meant one's capacity to exercise more control over his or her life by making choices influenced less by traditional agencies of power, decisions better served by, say, a more widespread access to information.[7]

The presence of Dependence II announces itself in a variety of new forms. We observe, especially in the advanced industrial societies, the shift away from political economy and a concomitant stress on distribution to a growing preoccupation with quality of life. These latter issues, as Ronald Inglehart's (1990) research indicates, emphasize aesthetic, intellectual, as well as belonging and esteem, values. William Julius Wilson (1991) appears to detect traces of this phenomenon among the underclass in large metropolitan cities—the development seems to be the result of a shift from production-oriented definitions to those related to consumption, which at once foster a measure of reflexivity and patterns of emancipation. Emancipation becomes linked to such phenomena as the alleged control the poor exert over style and the "design process" that ultimately interpenetrate and reinforce a politics of the body with its new and growing stress on esteem and aesthetics (see Lash & Urry, 1994, chap. 3, and Poster, 1990, for a sketch of the dynamics of this new shift). In addition, there is the tendency to immerse these values into broadly communitarian contexts, extending to, and incorporating, like interests in the global environment.

It is fashionable as well to speak of a new phase in industrial development in which Dependence II is quite visible: risk. If traditional modernity is defined mainly in terms of the inexorable production of goods and services as an end in itself, a risk-driven modernity revolves around the deleterious consequences of this growth-driven approach to development. These processes are akin to "a culture of death as the basis of capital accumulation" (Shiva, 1989, p. 13) that at once makes the concerns of the metropolitan member and those of Third World populations joined. Risk is prompted by such disastrous industrial by-products as radioactivity and chemical pollution (Beck, 1992). Indeed many of these concerns are spurred on as much by direct metropolitan-centered trepidations, as they are the focus of critical attention initiated by the Other(s).

Overall, two different sets of motivations are evident. The first is sparked by the growing realization that the world is a village. Behold! There is Chernobyl, which dramatizes that nuclear pollution is no respecter of national borders. The second motivation is more cognitive and intellectual and inheres in Enlightenment principles: The custodialism, referred to earlier in the context of globalism, culls a portion of its impetus from a tradition of immanent critique endemic in the Enlightenment. Some of these points were raised earlier with respect to hegemonic internationalism.

Although the history and experience of Dependence I make it difficult to speak of effective immanent critique—such is the distorting effect of the instrumental rationality undergirding that experience—it must be remembered that fidelity to truth and its handmaiden, critique, is among the first commandments of the Enlightenment. The maxim is frequently expressed and implied in a historical chain linking Kant to Popper. Charles Taylor (1989, chap. 22) locates the ethic in an Enlightenment-inspired norm of "moral exceptionalism," and Reinhart Koselleck (1988, pp. 10-11) alludes to the fact that there is a self-policing dimension to the Enlightenment—a "court of last resort"—to which all participants are answerable. For his part, Gianni Vattimo (1992, p. 17) captures this persistent element in the contention that the Enlightenment is not merely "a stage" of or "a prelude to emancipation"; it is the very essence of this condition.

Metropolitan concerns are, then, not wholly affectations animated by greed. After all, an Enlightenment-driven revolution, in displacing God, must assume the custodial role so central to his Divine Plan. God was eclipsed for the very reason that he had not provided the assurance that his methods and strategies would result in any significant improvement. One is reminded of a famous comment on Turgot's insouciance toward Divine Providence: For this philosophe, God was "a sort of honorary President of the development of civilization who might disappear without affecting the proceedings" (Bury, 1932, p. 207).

Current developments in the Third World also make the connection between Dependence I and Dependence II quite evident. New forms of industrialization—deindustrialization, to be precise—suggest the arrival of a more equitable process by which commodities for the world market are produced (Chapter 1).

But these changes are surfacing from a background in which the forces of dependence are still active. The central question is whether the main organizing principles to which the system as a whole is anchored have been qualitatively dislodged. A conclusion is that however crucial asymmetrical changes might be to the logic of the system as a whole, that fact should not per se be the basis for suggesting a qualitative dislodgment of that system. Worse so, if the asymmetries are viewed in isolation, even though they could foreshadow systemic shifts of huge proportions. We must attempt to problematize largely from the inherently contradictory nature of those key principles that define reality.

If we look closely at the examples of shifts mentioned above, this point is borne out. Take postmaterialism. The main contention here is that middle-class affluence in the advanced industrial societies has really extended the principles of Engel's Law to include nonmaterial needs and aspirations. As the industrial middle class becomes more affluent, the shift in commodity choices is away from basic necessities (food, shelter, and so on) to luxuries. With this shift comes a new inflection to political choices and activity, as the affluent, in terms of their own narrow interests, now pursue issues of empowerment, esteem, and self-actualization (Inglehart, 1990, p. 6). World poverty has taken on postmaterialist interests. The affluent in the metropolitan world do fear for the stability of their world and see global inequality and poverty as a major source of global instability and a primary threat to world peace (Snow, 1992). This fact is dramatized by the environmental and demographic aspects of such inequality: The metropolitan world is naturally drawn into a politics of reciprocity and mutuality, as the prospects of ozone layer problems and the flight of "eco-refugees" and "climatic asylum seekers" become increasingly real (Lash & Urry, 1994, p. 33). Mutuality is pressured by survivalism. A world defined as interactive spheres or circles, touching at strategic points but remaining defined and propelled by peculiar self-interest, is a concept that cannot be seriously defended.

So the affluent (and, for that matter, the metropolite of declining fortunes) are not detached from dependence, if it is taken, as it should be, as dynamic, overarching clusters of processes. Often they are fighting the distribution problems of others—the poor at home and abroad; women's issues that have taken on an international scope because of the interpenetration of causal factors between the "core" and the "periphery"; environmental battles, again of an international scope because of the interpenetrative nature of causal factors.

Indeed, it is quite easy to make similar major intrasystemic connections in the cases of the dynamics of risk, postindustrialism, or any other. Let us take risk. The "reflexive modernization" by which it is defined originates, as Ulrich

Beck theorizes, from industrial overproduction. This development involves not only what the Third World regards as a grossly disproportionate use by the metropolitan world of the earth's resources—some 80% of which is to be found in the former sphere—but the resultant productive activity that despoils the Third World, largely through the export of deadly chemicals and the depletion of resources of successive generations. The politics of risk relates in no uncertain terms to questions of waste disposal, the composition of exported chemicals (herbicides and pesticides), and so on. Strategies clearly illustrate the intrasystemic connections. Worldwide, environmental advocates stress the implementation of the so-called right-to-know principle, which would alert Third World buyers to the chemical content of foreign imports. Often these imports are banned from the metropolitan markets. The right-to-know principle has not been fully implemented in the Third World but receives vigorous support from foreign environmentalists. It is well to note also, as Beck (1992, pp. 27-28) reminds us, that the structure that would most impede the broad consensual politics involved here (i.e., the nation-state) is rendered ineffectual. Environmental concerns are constructing new and effective global standards that states are finding more difficult to avoid. These standards are prominently reflected in strict environmental laws (Birnie, 1992) and in the conditionality requirements attached to the involvements of international organizations like the World Bank (Hurrell, 1993).

Dependence is, then, a crucial factor in policy formation and implementation. It exerts a direct bearing on initiatives important to the preservation of resources acquiring the status of a "global good." The above example also shows the obsolete nature of the archaic ways in which dependence has been interpreted up to the present. Although the origins of human motives remain difficult to determine, there is less "do-goodism" here than survivalism and, in some cases, expressions of the custodial function mentioned earlier.

New social movements, in which the advocates of postmaterialist politics and the politics of postindustrialism, or that of risk or sustainable development, find their most effective voices, are also said to betray a postdependence ("postmodern") quality. I will have occasion to return to some of those issues from time to time, but for the moment, it is enough to state that the validity claims of Other(s) quite heavily affect the theories and practices of these movements. In their role as postcapitalist replacements for social class, these movements betray an inherent globalismic character: the substitution of modernist characteristics (self-interest and statism, for example) with conscience, morality, compassion, and global connectivity. Connectivity, as Ulrich Beck (1992) states persuasively in his *Risk Society,* is strengthened because the contemporary world is now called on to share the "bads." In the previous pattern of capital accumulation, production and distribution beckoned to the sharing of "goods" that led to hierarchies and social division (i.e., class, ethnicity). In contemporary "risk society," the distribution of the hazards of technology is indifferent to these social and cultural divisions and counsels solidarity in the search for solutions.

Finally, the expression of dependence with which we are most commonly familiar in the literature—the pillage of the Third World, to borrow Pierre Jalee's graphic term—is now occurring in the metropolitan world. As I have touched on in Chapter 1, one of the most significant results of the extended period of world economic stagnation (1970s to 1980s) was the highlighting of conditions of dependence within metropolitan societies. The phenomenon is commonly referred to as "peripheralization of the core." In large cities where the phenomenon is most visible, practices that are generally associated with the dependence of the Third World (barter and many other nonmarket-driven practices, for example) are taking root. Consequently, we now find in the literature references to "our Third World," as indicative of such conditions existing in the United States (Midgley, 1994, p. 3).

It is quite evident from the above account that dependence has taken on added meanings and dimensions. If we employ a type of periodization, we can confidently suggest that the phenomenon betrays distinct features at specific periods. During the 1950s to the early 1970s, the nature of the First World-Third World dichotomy was revealed. The thrust of the analyses was largely economic. In vogue was the famous "gap approach," subscribed to by dependency theorists such as Raul Prebisch and like-minded sympathizers: As Claude Alvares (1991) put it, "you subtract the ideal or polar features typical of Southern nations [i.e., the Third World] from those of the Northern nations [i.e., the metropole] and the remainder is your development programme" (p. 11). Dependency theorists and those interested in the fate of Third World economies subscribed to the common wisdom peddled by the industrialized world that science's conquest over Nature was complete and that technology could forever wrest growth from its resources. Even the feminist movement, which had perhaps its first real impact in its association with the Marxism/dependency tandem, staged its first battle within economic parameters: the debate over the exploitation of labor within the household (Himmelweit & Mohun, 1977; Molyneux, 1979). Several currents from that stream flow into the expansive river of dependence when the focus becomes directed at issues like the environment (Shiva, 1989). This is a typical example of a narrow contextual meaning being overtaken by the always implied, but now maturing, consequences of the complex, overarching world socioeconomic system. Another example is the connection between Third World poverty and the environment. As Barry Commoner (1972) has shown, we cannot now speak of world poverty without acknowledging the negative impact of the metropolitan world on the environment from which that poverty substantially springs. The deforestation of the Amazon region, the increasing use of pesticides, and the erosion of the topsoil in Third World regions can often be directly traced to the supply of goods for metropolitan appetites. Similar causal relationships exist in the cases of energy consumption and malnutrition (see the ample and well-documented literature from the Worldwatch Institute).

The disclosures of the Club of Rome's famous *Limits of Growth* (Meadows, Meadows, Randers & Bhrens, 1972), usher in the next period. For the first time, a very detailed study was directed at the corrosive ecological effects of the "development by growth" model. In short, population growth, pollution, the production of food, and the generation of energy were collectively analyzed in relation to the earth's capacities to sustain the model. Although its methodology has been severely criticized, many of the strictures do support a concern for the environment (more in Chapter 3).

This shift brought with it a broadened and more analytically diverse set of actors. Most of them (i.e., resource depletion, pollution) surfaced as claims of another Other—Nature—that germinated as a result of the inherent propensity to create dichotomies, animate or inanimate (Chapters 3 and 6). Modernity has, largely through its Cartesian conditioning, defined Nature as inert, passive material without any inner principle of action. It exists, presumably, to be exploited, penetrated, and brought to its knees, as both a function of the mastery science decrees for Modern Man and the preoccupation of that science, under the tutelage of Bacon, with improving the material conditions of life. Now a repressed Nature emerges as another disgruntled Other to join an expanding group of Other(s) marching to the rhythms of difference.

These diverse currents flow into, and are fed by, alternative definitions and strategies calling into play more inclusive kinds of theories and practices. Not only do we witness the increasing number of new phenomena gathering under the umbrella of globalism, but there is more. For example, standard modernist (i.e., capitalist) theories and measures seem misplaced in the new environment. Market economics and rational choice theories are not well placed or, at best, function clumsily. Market economics must now make its peace with informalization (see Chapter 1) and the "economics" of sustainable development (see Chapter 3), both of which stress "communitarian equity" (to coin a phrase) over naked capitalist profitability and individualism and a people-oriented science over one driven by positivistic definitions.

## ❖ Interdependence and a Summary of the Argument

The concept of interdependence I am pursuing differs markedly from the alternatives reviewed in the literature. Such should be the burden of the chapter up to this point. First, interdependence is generally associated, rather narrowly, with international economics and international politics. The difficulty is that these two variables, almost by definition, present a picture of the world in terms of superordinacy and subordinacy. If one were left to draw conclusions based on these two variables alone, the master-servant model of international development would continue to reign supreme. But there are other variables working, at times unobtrusively, to undercut such a static model of power. We should remember the Berlin Wall and the collapse of the Soviet empire in the late 1980s. It is only well after the collapse that one gets a true picture—any picture, in many cases—of the corrosive role non-economic forces (ethnicity, religion, praxes of resistance) have played. We should also remember that the more extensive slate of variables results from the declining importance of political economy as the central organizing principle of international relations.

The truth is that as far as the metropolitan sphere is concerned, if economics and politics are not diminished in their roles in world affairs, they are either facing stiff challenges or being jostled for equal time and attention by other variables anchored to anthropology, sociology, and culture. I will have occasion to discuss more fully the fact that key agents of change that were spawned by economics and politics—social class, for instance—are being eclipsed or rendered secondary by culture-oriented or culture-inspired definers, with new social movements as their carriers.

Second, this notion of interdependence is heavily freighted with a paternalistic, Big Brother connotation. Often the stress is placed largely on appeals to principles of humanity—the Brandt Report is marred by this affliction. The metropolitan world is seen as sharing its mastery of Nature in the name of a compassion that should now assume more humane dimensions. The so-called sovereignty-at-bay model (Vernon, 1971) is a case in point. Briefly, the model is centered on the acceleration of interdependent, mutually beneficial economic growth resulting from transfers of capital and technology from the rich, industrialized countries to the poorer countries. The tide of economic growth is expected to lift all boats, as the saying goes, but it is the metropolitan world that initiates and sustains the chore of lifting through a glorified form of charity.

The other models of interdependence have defects of their own, in addition to the excessive stress placed on economics and politics. The neo-Realists' view of independence puts the choice—the rational choice—into the hands of the metropolitan world (Waltz, 1979). This model has been traced back to Thucydides and the Peloponnesian War, through to Hobbes. On this view, justice, honesty, morality, and the like must be subordinated to the anarchy essential to global politics. "Morality has no place in foreign policy" is a kindred sentiment attributed to one of America's celebrated foreign policy experts, himself an adherent of the Realist school: George Kennan.[8] In sum, it is the metropolitan world that rationally and strategically initiates the changes, however qualitatively different they may be. By inference, the Other(s) remains in its traditionally supine position.

Third, there exists the so-called radical position. Here, the underlying thesis, whether it is expressed in Marxist-Leninist or in a dependency theoretic term, is that interdependence is at best a formalistically descriptive term that poorly obscures inherently exploitative relations—the metropolitan world's pillage of the nonmetropolitan world. Interdependence, then, is nothing short of metropolitan parasitism. Underdevelopment theses mine much of their critical ammunition from this quarry (see earlier references to Dependence I).

Of course, there is even a more outright denial of interdependence. It is the version that forms the basis of the contemporary debate between liberals and conservatives. As Robert B. Reich, himself a prominent spokesman for the liberals, says it, the "we" versus "them" characterization of world affairs is hale and well. Liberals differ in that charity and conciliation toward "them" should be sedulously pursued; for the conservatives, "the only pertinent issue is how much we should concede to "them" (Reich, 1988, p. 49). At best, we can speak only of a mechanical, descriptive—as against a structural, analytic—interdependence.

In the end, none of these widely argued positions quite conveys what is actually taking place. As the analysis throughout this book attempts to support, metropolitan dependence (and the nonmetropolitan world's sympathetic reaction toward it) is the result of the peculiar mold in which the developmental agendas of the two subworlds are cast. In truth, metropolitan-led development succeeded in blighting and distorting not only the nonmetropolitan world but the First World as well. Much that defines this dependence—Dependence II—appears as the direct consequence of a short-term, albeit economically impressive, approach to development. We are now coming face to face with the long-term, negative consequences of modernity as Dependence II. They surface both as the antithesis of a narrow, economistically defined reality, with imperative economic growth as its rationale and the studied exclusion of key noneconomic and nonmodern variables situated at the core of an inherently diverse reality. The excluded are largely the Other(s).

It is not difficult to locate the source of tension within dependence writ large: It is to be extracted from a process that might be called "social and humanistic denudation." This is the price modernity exacts for a state of individual autonomy, and it amounts to a Faustian compact. Membership to modernity demands the renunciation of "particularisms" that would allow us to function in society in the perfectly rational and morally approved way—"externally and instrumentally" (Bauman, 1993, p. 83). These are qualities that Descartes and Kant would have Modern Man display as proof of his final escape from necessity into the realm of freedom.

But the quest to achieve this level of supreme individual detachment has proved inimical to our nature and the recipe for chronic and destructive homelessness, to use Peter Berger's term. Modern Man is morally and emotionally disembodied. The "particularisms" he so despises in himself and the Other(s)—emotions, deep religious sensibilities, attachment to tradition, the "lack" of those rationalities famously analyzed by Max Weber—really exist as the refuge against the psychic and psychological pathologies endemic in the modernist project. Much of this ground has been covered as narcissism (Lasch, 1979), proteanism (Lifton, 1971), homelessness (Berger, Berger, & Kellner, 1974), remissiveness (Carroll, 1977; Lipovetsky, 1992), and irrationalism (Barrett, 1959).[9] It is enough to say here that many of these social pathologies were anticipated by Nietzsche, Kierkegaard, and Alexis de Tocqueville. Where Nietzsche speaks of moderns lapsing into "pitiable comfort," de Tocqueville alludes to a "soft despotism" exerted by democracy (Taylor, 1991, p. 4). At the same time, given the thesis of this book, I must note that these philosophers and social commentators—including Weber, who left us in the cage!—often did not look far enough to see the strains of emancipation unsuccessfully occluded by modernity.

Dependence writ large is, therefore, a far more complex phenomenon than meets the eye. Today, the concept is not well served by those who would cling tenaciously to narrow economistic and teleological analyses of Marxism. For one, there is far more autonomy to the role of causal factors than that agenda admits; for another, a number of these causal factors venture outside of the narrowly economic (as I have stressed above and more fully in subsequent chapters); for yet another, Alain Touraine is quite correct in suggesting that although Marx was exemplary in exposing the intricacies of capitalism as a system, his analysis of the actors and their political activity within it left a lot to be desired. This last revelation helps to clear the way for progressive movements by actors across Descartes's Big Ditch, a construction in which, as we have seen, Marx himself was implicated.

Dependence II is closely related to the formulations of Thierry Verhelst (1990) on the subject. It is not simply that the metropolitan world has become a source of harm rather than help; the problem is that the metropole has become culturally underdeveloped because it, too, has become a victim of the idea of progress and the model of development that it imposed on itself and transmitted to the Third World. The cultures of the Third World, as he continues, offer a way for the metropolitan world to resolve its own cultural crisis. As Bauman (1993) put it in a precis of Emmanuel Levinas, the Other(s) does not merely serve the purpose of replenishing "the life juices" of the Self; it will be "the gatekeeper of [the Self's] moral life" (p. 85). Because the structure of the Other(s) emerges as laminated, bringing together a motley array of causal factors, the call for a breakup of the monolithic modernist paradigm and its replacement by one that is epistemologically diverse is expressed by many voices, from within the metropolitan world and without. So much for neat dichotomies and polar opposites existing on either side of the North-South geographical divide! The feminist and environmental movements are making a mockery of this increasingly beleaguered position.

The analysis of interdependence actually requires the investigation of two apparently antithetical, yet profoundly compatible and interpenetrating, sets of processes—Dependence I and II. Let me now proceed with an analysis of the Enlightenment tradition from which many of the paradoxes outlined in this chapter are to be traced.

## ❖ Notes

1. The philosophy of consciousness or subject-centered reason makes the white, middle-class male the measure of reality (see Apel, 1980, chap. 3; Benhabib, 1986; Habermas, 1987; Lacoue-Labarthe, 1989; Rorty, 1979; Schrag, 1989a, chap. 7).

2. A tension is expressed in Hegel's (1969) master and slave dilemma (see Frazer & Lacey, 1993).

3. Orlando Patterson (1991) detects a similar strain in the U.S. Constitution: "We the politically free body of men, always, it would seem, tragically the *them* who do not belong" (p. 405). The historicity of the "we" is denied by the power of the state.

4. Dependence I describes the exploitation of the Third World by the First World but is served by a variety of theories. Among the most prominent are *the development of underdevelopment, dependent development, world systems theory, modes of production theory,* and *Marxism* (for excellent analyses, see Bjorn Hettne, 1990; Cristobal Kay, 1989; Larrain, 1989).

5. Frank's critique remains a *tour de force.* He saved his most effective barbs for Rostow's *Stages of Economic Growth* (Cockcroft, Frank, & Johnson, 1972).

6. UNICEF shows, for instance, that in 1988, some one-half million children died directly from debt-related adjustment policies tied to metropolitan derivation. Third World women are still disadvantaged, despite changes in global accumulation. See Ward (1990) for an excellent collection of articles on the point as well as Giri (1995); for an example in the United States, see Axinn and Stern (1988).

7. Reflexivity as people oriented results from a breakdown of systems such as positivism (which attaches meaning to a unified, rational Subject—the white male) and structuralism (which situates social agents as effects of social structures). Reflexivity owes much to the new theorizing of Foucault on the subject of power, which he sees as being accessible to the dominant and the dominated alike (Giddens, 1990, pp. 36-45; Poster, 1990, pp. 131-134).

8. In his latest book, Kennan (1996) has modified his stance. Noted also is a softening of the neorealist anarchic position in the newly evolving concept of "relative" gains versus the old "absolute" gains favored by the old school members like Morgenthau, Waltz, and Tucker. Greater reciprocity within the world community is implied here (see Grieco, 1990, for a discussion of the concept).

9. In order, these are the disciplinary analysis for the problems related to the fall of the modern Subject. Proteanism and narcissism are *psychological;* remissiveness tends to be narrowly *Freudian;* irrationalism is *philosophical;* and *homelessness* is sociological.

# *Chapter Three*

# INTERDEPENDENCE AND ITS INTERFACE WITH NATURE'S REVOLT

*In permitting man, Nature has committed much more than a mistake in her calculations: a crime against herself.*
E. M. Cioran (1993, p. 78)

*We [can] expect essentially an eternal abundance of energy, the only requirements being that the sun keep shining and modest technological progress continue for a few years.*
Herman Kahn et al. (1976, p. 89)

The analysis of the revolt of Nature draws from the ideational as well as the material aspects to which the phenomenon is reducible. The main thrust of the chapter is more ideational than material, because the former exposes the faulty bases from which material, economic practices proceed. A general contention of this book is that an economics-led approach to the crisis and the consequential search for solutions are stillborn. Modern economics lies at the heart of the problem. Although the logic of Nature's revolt is coextensive with the Enlightenment crisis (the core of Parts II and III), its effects are quite visible in related economic practices; for these phenomena provide Dependence II with the contradictions that would gradually mature against the systems within which these practices operate. The interplay is expressed aptly by Vandana Shiva's (1989) depiction of global economics as "a culture of death as the basis of capital accumulation" (p. 13). The main purpose of the present analysis, given these explicit guidelines, is to align Nature's revolt and *difference* to Dependence II. The analysis illustrates sharply the manner in which the logic of modernity affects not only the fortunes of the Third World and the nonmodern world generally but also the metropolitan world, despite Descartes's bestowing on Modern Man the title of *maitres et possesseurs de la nature*.

This aspect of the analysis brings into sharp relief the full force of Nature as Other; the remaining portions of the discourse appear in Chapter 7. In that chapter, I discuss the symbiotic association between Nature and women as Other(s) as part of the very complex phenomenon of dependence.

The problematic place of Nature in the grand scheme of things is proverbial. From the rich and highly nuanced historical accounts now in existence, it is clear that Nature's stock has run the gamut from a force to be revered to one that has to be conquered. In his well-received book, *Nature, Technology, and Society*, Victor Ferkiss (1993) takes us on a quick, instructive journey of Nature's fortunes from the time of the Mesopotamian civilizations, through the Greeks, the Romans, the Middle Ages, to Descartes. Over that considerable period of time, Nature's lot has moved from a feared and fearsome force to a crucial element in the general scheme of things, to mere matter to be controlled by and in the service of human beings. Although notable voices relegated Nature to a servile role throughout these earlier times—Aristotle among the Greeks, and Cicero among the Romans, for example—the Greeks and the Romans venerated Nature. In nonmodern cultures, such as India, the fates of men and animals were intertwined. The Hindus, for example, see all species to be woven into a single, unending web of *Karma* and reincarnation.

The evidence is quite persuasive that the shift to Nature as slave came with the advent of Christianity (Ferkiss, 1993; White, 1968; Young, J., 1990). The posture, as Robin Attfield (1994) relays it, lies "in the Judeo-Christian belief that man, being made in God's image, is set apart from nature, and that the entire physical creation was brought into being for human benefit and rule" (p. 21). Indeed, Ferkiss (1993, pp. 16-17) identifies Augustine (A.D. 354-430) as the player of no small part in the transformation. Augustine's embrace of Manicheism and later, Christianity comes through, in the view of some researchers, as a rejection of matter, a disdain for the physical works of God. Nature as a villain was the result of a combination of classical philosophy, this anathema to Nature—and the concomitant dualism between the world of spirit and the world of the flesh, between Mind and Matter—and Jehovah's injunction in the Book of Genesis that we should be fruitful and multiply and in the process subdue the earth. Playing a dynamic role in the drama is science, which makes "our fundamental relationship with [Nature] come down to war and property" (Serres, 1995, p. 32).

At the same time, the anti-Nature sentiments and formulations were not without their pronounced counterpoints, naturalistic as well as religious. In mid- to late-16th-century France, there is strong evidence of Nature's inclusive role in what might be termed *the natural contract,* to borrow Michel Serres's term. Luc Ferry (1995, pp. ix-xvi) recounts, with all seriousness, the austere legal proceedings conducted between weevils and the owners of vineyards whose harvests had been savaged by the little "creepers." In noteworthy legal proceedings, advocates would often win the day on behalf of their little clients, engulfed in the solemn notion that animals possessed the same rights as human beings. Contemporary sentiments would find it ludicrous to have a bishop assail leeches for noncompliance with a court order. But such was the case of the recalcitrant leeches of the lake of Berne in the Switzerland of 1451. The bishop of Lausanne cursed them with a fury inspired by God: "In the name of God almighty, of the heavens, of the Divine and Holy Church, I curse you, wherever you go, and you will be damned, you and your descendants, for the rest of your days on earth" (cited in Ferry, 1995, p. xii). Such proceedings continued well into the 18th century. Nature was taken, like human beings, to possess the power of self-generation, which "called attention to her prodigious creativity" (Mies & Shiva, 1993, p. 206). Although these expressions of coexistence and coevolution between man and Nature were obviously diminishing in number and importance, Francis Bacon and Isaac Newton were well on their way to preparing the ground for Nature to be exploited "for the relief of man's estate" (Francis Bacon), treating it as "a limitless provider without needs of its own" (Plumwood, 1993, p. 21).

Pro-Nature religious sentiments were hardly subdued and managed to maintain a presence even within Christianity for quite an appreciable period. First, there were the female-centered religions revolving around the myth of the ancient goddess who ruled before the arrival of Christianity and other patriarchal religions (Carmody, 1992; Spretnak, 1981). A second example is enshrined in St. Francis of Assisi and his reverence for all the multitudinous forms of life. It is speculated that he was a member of the Celtic monastic tradition, for which Nature held an exalted place. Of St. Francis, it is remarked that he "tried to substitute the idea of equality of all creatures, including man, for the idea of man's limitless rule of creation" (White, 1968, cited in Ferkiss, 1993, p. 21). Another pro-Nature tendency existed in Calvinism. For Calvin (1509-1564) spoke of man "as the steward of all his possessions and the earth as a leasehold which people may not plunder of its goods" (Attfield, 1994, p. 16).

In the end, it was that very Christianity that would justify the initiative of science to pry open Nature's secrets in order to dominate it. In his own words, Bacon envisioned "the enlargening of the Human Empire, to the effecting of all things possible" (Bacon, 1974, cited in Attfield, 1994, p. 30). After his fulsome support for empirical science, which had its first major institutionalization in the Royal Society (1662), science went full-bloodedly in pursuit of Nature for the relief of man's estate: Bacon would have it bound to man's service and enslaved (Hooykaas, 1972; Passmore, 1974; White, 1968). In short, the ensuing disembodiment of Nature, which proceeded with dispatch after Descartes, succeeded in "strip[ping] nature of the intentional and mindlike qualities which make an ethical response to it possible" (Plumwood, 1993, p. 5).

From quite diverse positions, "relief" has evoked charges of rape, pillage, and exploitation. To some degree or other, we have all been disappointed or frustrated by a technological Prometheus gone wild. But there has been a shift. Nature, partly in concert with a number of Other(s)—indigenous peoples, Third World cultures, metropolitan women—is now reasserting its claims to difference. The concerted effort results from certain commonalities, especially those whose epistemologies go deeply against the "technology-as-growth" model; in short, the notion is that people function like a machine and that the sum and substance of their humanity amounts to nothing more than needs to be met in the marketplace in the context of perpetual scarcity. For, as I elaborate in Part II, these complex definitions informed by "machinist" thinking were to extend from Nature to the Other(s), because of a common, vital, quality they share: a supposed composition from, and definition by, inert Matter—the *fons et origo* of deleterious sensuality and irrationality—the virus, which via its infection of history and culture, exists as a constant source of error in our quest for certainty.

Difference, with which claims of Nature are coextensive, appears to avoid, generally, the temptation to reverse the traditional binary oppositions—woman to replace man, traditional to eclipse modern, and so on. As I discuss mainly in the context of the Self-Other interchange in Parts II and III, there is still a strong sentiment to refashion human rehabilitation in the general spirit of globalism. Nature's revolt eventuates mainly as negative consequences—for Nature and humankind—when Nature's intrinsic structure and its need to be rehabilitated are dismissed by the pejorative term *inanimate*. In truth, Nature consists of multiple ecosystems. It is not a material substrate to be treated as an "externality" by economics, namely, a factor for which there is no maintenance-cost index built into the process of production. Conventional economics, as Nicholas Georgescu-Roegen (1971) observes,

> neither induces any qualitative change nor is affected by the qualitative change of the environment into which it is anchored. It is an isolated, self-contained and ahistorical process—a circular flow between production and consumption with no outlets and no inlets. (p. 2)

In stark opposition, an agreeable economic framework would be sensitive to the complex interconnectedness of ecosystems, to their need to provide the source from which Nature's "prodigious creativity" derives. That creativity and the need for its constant rejuvenation must be recognized, facilitated, and promoted by all those operating within Nature's purview. "Evolutionary adjustment" is sine qua non to ecosystems that adjust to new and excessive patterns of resource use over considerable periods of time. Accordingly, ecosystems must be protected from rapid change (Capra, 1996; Redclift, 1987, p. 18); they are "communit[ies] where parts fit together in symbiosis" (Rolston, 1988, p. 311). These facts make startlingly anachronistic any notion related to the conquest of Nature.

To explain Nature as an externality is to demonstrate how this creativity is stymied, both as a function of the basic inertness to which it is reduced and as the larger project of control that is deemed consistent with "the relief of man's estate." The revolt surfaces as strains on Nature's carrying capacity (population, for example) and dysfunctions, such as diseases, which are the consequences of ecosystems prevented from rehabilitating themselves. Simultaneously, these phenomena highlight the gross limitations of modern science and the absence of human deep-rootedness within the dynamic and intricate processes of Nature. In other words, man, contrary to Cartesianism, is "not apart from nature" but is, indeed, "a part of nature" (O'Briant, 1974).

The first segment of the chapter addresses the main economically inflected features against which Nature has directed its assault. These phenomena, presented as thumbnail sketches, are resource depletion, environmental pollution and ecology, and population growth. All three spring directly from the logic of the technology-as-growth model in which Nature is reduced to a mere factor of production to satisfy the artificial scarcities endemic in modern economics. These sketches are presented against the backdrop of a number of reasonable expectations. First, it is hard to imagine many people, especially those to whom this book is directed, who are not familiar in some way with the crises presently addressed. The sketches merely strive for a suitable impressionistic rendering from which the analysis will be initiated. Second, there is an expectation that my selective use of statistics will satisfy the trite but true maxim that *more isn't necessarily better.* In a sense, statistics are merely adornments for the substantial points discussed in this chapter.

The second segment of the chapter identifies some of the ways in which the Other-inflected aspects of Nature reinforce the dynamics of Dependence II. In the process, I indicate some of the main arguments generated from the various perspectives into which the crises have ramified. The final segment addresses the patterns and traces of collaboration that are surfacing through such corrective approaches as sustainability and global norms.

## ❖ A Thumbnail Sketch: Depleted Resources

For our purposes, resource depletion is divided into two main branches. The first relates to the dramatic decimation of wildlife, both flora and fauna; the second, to the equally dramatic reduction of strategic industrial resources that feed the seemingly insatiable appetites of metropolitan industrialization. Included in the second category is water. As reported in the late 1980s, underground water supplies were falling in Africa, China, India, and North America as demand outstripped the capacity of aquifers to replenish themselves. In the United States, 50 pesticides contaminated the groundwater of 32 states, and 2,500 toxic waste dumps required attention (Brown, Flavin, & Wolf, 1988). Wetlands and marshes, which act to preserve shorelines and purify water, are being lost at the rate of 450,000 acres annually (Carpenter, 1990).

The unconscionable destruction of flora and fauna has passed into a proverb. In the Third World, where perhaps the bulk of such destruction is occurring, there are some 90% or so of all the 100 million species of plants and animals existing in the world. But the process of extinction proceeds; it is estimated that by the year 2015, one quarter of all known species will have disappeared. Along with this disappearance will go the capacity to develop new kinds of medicines, for the forests continue to remain the main sources of new discoveries in the drug industry.[1] But this is not all. There is the aesthetics issue. The systematic depletion of wildlife and fauna robs humanity of an indispensable heritage. Old-growth forests, some with ancient trees dating back several hundreds of years, "have acquired a mystique that stimulates and rouses passions [not] only among conservationists" *but among most people who have a sense of connectivity to the vast complexity of the universe* [italics added] (Renner, 1991, p. 36). The Chipko leader, Sunderlal Bahuguna, declared, out of a profound reverence for the forests, that a total prohibition be enforced against the felling of trees, "irrespective of whether they were meant for satisfying local needs or noncommercial needs" (Tewari, 1995, p. 153).

The destruction of forests is an allied form of depletion that dramatizes the integrated nature of the crises. Acid rain—to cite one causal factor—has "killed" thousands of lakes and rivers in North America and Europe. In Siberia, it has ruined more than 1,500 square miles of timber; that is about half the size of Rhode Island (Feshbach & Friendly, 1992). It is in the nature of the case that this mode of depletion brings with it many subsidiary depletions. Forests are cleared for the lumber they provide. The operations are indiscriminate and injudicious: Each day, at this writing, there are 116 square miles less of these forests. Much of the activity occurs in Amazonia, which supplies half of the earth's oxygen. Deforestation accelerates desertification and soil erosion. Each day, 70 square miles of new desert and 57 million tons of valuable top soil are lost to erosion. In the case of indigenous populations, deforestation eliminates fuel, sources of food, medicines, and other income-generating uses (Dwyer, 1990). It is estimated that some 200 million indigenous peoples depend on forests for their livelihood. Indeed, as Holmes Rolston III (1988, chap. 1) enumerates, 14 types of value are associated with the natural environment: life support, economic, scientific, aesthetic, genetic diversity, historical, cultural symbolization, character building, diversity-unity, spontaneity, stability, dialectical, life, and religious. If one, then, chooses to focus merely on the *economic* dimension of these depletions and losses, such myopia is quite tragic. The tragedy is prominently portrayed by one of America's leading economists, the Nobel laureate Robert Solow. In a flush of rational choice headiness, he volunteers that as long as natural resources can be substituted, their loss or exhaustion should be taken as "just an event, not a catastrophe" (cited in Mies & Shiva, 1993, p. 208). This detachment is coextensive with an indifference to Nature that sees no distinction between real and plastic trees. The point is made unequivocally by Martin Krieger (1973) who says that because society (i.e., culture), not Nature, determines what appeals to us, the latter is truly disposable. This represents an undialectical view of reality, a mechanistic one in which relations between society and Nature are largely fixed and strive for shifting patterns of equilibrium. The issue here, as Laurence Tribe (1974) observes, is that such a position could perhaps be justified, if human interests were the only interests to be regarded. He speaks, instead of the inherent rights of trees, forests, and the like. Of course, human interests—their aesthetic expressions, for example—cannot be separated from the endowments of Nature of which trees are a major constituent (Rolston, 1988).

The depletion of strategic resources (extractive and nonextractive) is another vexed issue. The list of extractive resources generally revolves around some nineteen items (see Meadows, Meadows, Randers, & Behrens, 1974, pp. 372-373), but the stress is usually placed on oil, coal, and natural gas. The significance of these three resources is bound up with practical as well as symbolic implications. Central to these implications is the continuing subjugation of Nature; the coevolutionary relationship between humankind and Nature diverged when fossil fuels and their related technologies "freed" us from a codependent relationship with nature (Norgaard, 1995, p. 488). It is impossible to avoid Nature as the key aspects of modern civilization depend on increasing exploitation to meet the needs of an energy-driven civilization. Fully 85% of the energy consumed in this regime is wasted. Such enormous expenditure of energy is locked into impermanent and frivolous products required by our consumption ethic (Leiss, 1990, p. 94). Zygmunt Bauman (1993) summarizes the dilemma quite well:

> "Economic growth" represents the insatiable hunger of industry for new and larger profits—but profits (that is, the surplus of money at the end of the productive cycle) are but claims on new sources of energy to be burned in the next cycle. (p. 214)

New products are really deteriorated materials.

Often the issues involved here are multiple, but questions of equity and sustainability are prominent. Two of the oft-recurring questions in this context are (a) whether strategic resources that have so demonstrably improved human life are fairly distributed and (b) because many of these resources are nonrenewable, should better approaches to resource husbandry not be adopted to ensure sufficient levels for succeeding generations? The issues germane to the major questions ramify into subsidiary forms, as one would expect. But the heavy political freight evident in their slightest contemplation doubtless originates in questions of distribution. A graphic statistic that invariably excites these questions resides in energy use: Between 1950 and 1990, energy usage increased sevenfold, with the bulk of the increase accounted for by fossil fuels, namely, nonrenewable resources. In context, 20% of the world's population, those living in the industrialized societies, consume some 80% of the world's energy! The United States, with less than 6% of the world's population, consumes 40% of the world's natural resources!

This last graphic captures much of the tension that resides within the areas of problem solving and causation. It also takes us to the heart of a political climate in which privilege comes face-to-face with the unconscionable inequity, one in which proffered principles of justification (rationalism, science, competition, individualism, and so on) bounce jarringly against the realities of the law of entropy. I will have a bit more to say on the topic in the final segment.

## ❖ A Thumbnail Sketch: Ecological Degradation

For the purposes of this book, ecological degradation encompasses the ecology (pollution, soil erosion, global warming, acid rain). Individually and in the collective, these have generated a huge, largely negative, literature against the technology-as-growth model (Capra & Pauli, 1995; Chiras, 1992; Sachs, 1992; Stone, 1992). The pattern of Nature's revolt depicted here radiates principally from its impetuous exclusion as the crux of the complex ecosystems on which the needs of man are really dependent. This imprecise and vindictive definition of Nature, namely, that it is inert, there to be exploited—stifles its regenerative capacities, with the result that this lack of creativity presents problems for human beings; wastelands eliminated translate into less shoreline and more polluted water for plant and animal life, as we saw above.

What this negative set of results is gradually revealing is a perceptible shift from the notion of Man, the Conqueror, to Man, the proverbial Sorcerer's Apprentice—one who is only just beginning to grasp the enormity of an injudicious agenda of tinkering. We are witnesses to a development for which our instrumental rationality has not prepared us: As Holmes Rolston III (1988) puts it, "technology does not release us from natural dependencies; it only shifts their location and character" (p. 37).

It is perhaps not inaccurate to suggest that the main impetus for the continuing intense focus on environmental degradation owes much to Zhores Medvedev's expose of the nuclear destruction in his *Nuclear Disaster in the Urals*. In short, Soviet nuclear technology had, in 1957 or 1958, wreaked havoc on the Soviet environment. It happened that an area in the Urals, between the cities of Sverdlovsk and Chelyabinsk, was irretrievably contaminated by nuclear radiation. The region in question, about the size of Rhode Island, had not been spared relative to its life forms. Birds, fishes, soil animals, field plants, and of course, people have all been adversely affected by this nuclear disaster. In the particular case of birds, there has been the issue of contamination beyond the Soviet borders. Many of the species found in the contaminated region make their yearly pilgrimages to the Mediterranean, Central Asia, Georgia, North Africa, and Iran. What is absolutely frightening is the prognosis that the area will remain contaminated for hundreds of years!

The awareness that technology was not playing to the script soon brought similar incidents, albeit of lesser magnitude, to world attention. Thus, the United Nations Conference on the Human Environment convened in Stockholm in 1972. The impetus came mainly from Sweden, which was then experiencing acid rain, degradation of the environment evidenced, in part, by high levels of pesticides and heavy metal deposits in fish and birds. Disclosures about America's own bouts with environmental degradation surfaced: the death of Lake Erie under the heavy bombardment of toxic chemical effluents. Later, in the 1970s, Japan had acquired an unflattering status: the octopus that eats its own legs! By the late 1970s, all the major pollution-caused diseases appeared in Japan. By the beginning of 1979, the government "extended official recognition as pollution victims to over 73,000 people, and hundreds had died directly from these diseases" (McKean, 1981, p. 20).

Although the hazards of degradation are now an open book, the evidence of technology has multiplied, largely the result of the legitimacy provided by the Stockholm conference of 1972. Take the Third World. In the case of Brazil, a star newly industrializing country (NIC), some 10 million kilograms of raw sewage is pumped daily into the three contiguous rivers in the Rio area, of which 99% is untreated. One of these rivers, the Thiele, has an oxygen content of zero after taking on its burden. In a 14-city area washed by (perhaps *flushed* is more appropriate) these rivers, the infant mortality directly attributable to the condition of the water was 200 per 1,000 births (Faber, 1992, pp. 5-6). Brazil's southern neighbor, Argentina, faces a similar plight. Rivers such as the Matanza and the Reconquista, tributaries of the Plate River, bear no oxygen, because of the heavy degradation inflicted by chemical toxins and other hazardous industrial waste (Long, 1993, p. 199).

There is much to be said of the complacency that remoteness can generate. People usually fail to attach the appropriate significance to occurrences in other people's backyards. As much as Bhopal shocked many in the metropolitan world, there was a degree of comfort that Nature had released its venom elsewhere. But that has changed, and the United States is no exception. At Union Carbide's plant in Institute, West Virginia—a close replica of its Bhopal plant—there have been 190 leaks of highly toxic substances, such as phosgene gas, during the early 1980s. Cancer rates in the surrounding Kanawha Valley are twice those of areas outside of the immediate vicinity of the plant (Barry, 1986). In this climate of deflated confidence in technology, it hardly bodes well for its image to use cloaking devices to avoid responsibility. Thus, A. H. Robins and Johns-Manville, manufacturers of the IUD (a birth control device used by women) and asbestos, respectively, filed for Chapter 11 protection in anticipation of future lawsuits (Weir, 1988, p. 52).

**TABLE 3.1** Leading Causes of Death in the United States, 1900 and 1990: Selected Statistics

| 1900 | | 1990 | |
|---|---|---|---|
| Cause | Percentage of All Deaths | Cause | Percentage of All Deaths |
| Cancer (9) | 4 | Cancer (2) | 24 |
| Pneumonia (1) | 12 | Heart disease (1) | 34 |
| Diarrhea (3) | 8 | Stroke (7) | 7 |

SOURCE: National Center for Health Statistics, "Advance Report of Final Mortality Statistics," 1990, *Monthly Vital Statistics*, Report 41, No. 7.

NOTE: Numbers in parentheses indicate the rank order of each causal factor for each decade.

Other troubling disclosures revolve around the safety of chemicals. During the late 1980s, only 289 of the 700 chemicals used in the production of pesticides had been sufficiently tested to determine their side effects (Commoner, 1990, p. 50). Up to the time of Bhopal, only 70 of some 40,000 pesticides on the open market had been checked by the Environmental Protection Agency (EPA), as required by Congress (Asinoff, 1985). The combined effects of ecological degradation and pollution have been directly linked to the growing incidence of cancer. Comparative statistics are instructive (see Table 3.1).

The experience of Europe kept pace with the rest of the industrialized world. In 1986, after Bhopal, there was Chernobyl; then occurred what is commonly referred to as "ChernoBasel" toward the end of that year. It consisted of a fire at a chemical warehouse owned by Sandoz, Inc., the transnational corporation. Massive tonnages of toxic substances, including 66,000 pounds of pesticides, were dumped into the Rhine (Weir, 1988, pp. 6-7). During the late 1980s, up to 10% of all deaths in Hungary were attributed directly to pollution.

More specific examples of the shift into a Dependence II posture will be provided. But a cardinal factor in the process was a final agreeable meeting between modern science and Other-derived cosmologies. The coalescence assumed the shape of theories of ecosystems thought, where science has supplied the rational proof of what the Gaia cosmology, the earth-bound ethnophilosophies of Native American peoples, the Australian aborigines (with their emphasis on "dream time"), among others, have been claiming often in the face of metropolitan derision.[2] It is that the earth and all that dwell on it—animate or inanimate—are part of a single, interconnected system. The irony of this fortuitous happenstance is stated aptly by Wolfgang Sachs (1992):

> The environmental movement seems to be the first antimodernist movement attempting to justify its claims with the enemy's own means. It resorts not only to the arts . . . , to organicism . . . , to the glory of nature . . . , or to a transcendental creed . . . , although all these themes are present, but it bases its challenge on ecosystems theory, which integrates physics, chemistry and biology. (p. 30)

Chernobyl and many other lesser mishaps have reinforced the notion that pollution is, at bottom, no respecter of nation-states or their borders but that the earth is truly an integrated system—an ecosystem. It is not "a fortuitous juxtaposition of plants [and animal life]," as the noted botanist Henry Gleason remarked (cited in Rolston, 1988, p. 160); an ecosystem is a set of overlapping systems and subsystems and not a mere collection of isolated organisms. Contemporary thinking associated with the parent science of ecology challenges much of the prevailing zero-sum thought that inform international relations and economics, for instance. Viewing the various interactions within the world as essentially symbiotic—a perspective that must infiltrate the many theories and practices engaged in by the peoples of the world—is definitive.[3] Increasingly, options must be formulated in recognition of this stubborn fact, although, as we shall see, modern science still persists in attempting to put a square peg into a round hole in the form of "ecological modernisation" (Hajer, 1996).

This spectacular nuclear disaster has initially drawn attention to the dangers of nuclear technology. But that is not all. It helped, as well, to put into proper perspective pollution of other kinds—chemical pollution, perhaps above the others. The burgeoning interest in these and other kinds of pollution owes much to the pioneering activities of Rachel Carson (1962) and Barry Commoner (1972). Carson's book, *Silent Spring,* drew attention to the fact that all animal life is directly and deleteriously affected by the presence of pesticides, herbicides, and the new synthetic hydrocarbons now integral to metropolitan industrial production. Barry Commoner, for his part, showed in *The Closing Circle* that the major causes in the dramatic increase in postwar environmental degradation are changes in the technology of production. Natural products (soap, cotton, wood, and so on) have been replaced by synthetic products (i.e., detergents, synthetic fibers, plastics); natural fertilizers have been supplanted by chemical fertilizers; natural forms of pest control have, in turn, been replaced by synthetic pesticides. Today, the stubborn fact is that every single day, 1.5 million tons of hazardous waste is discharged into the air, the sea, and the land.

There has always been—and continues to be—the crucial question of causation. Not unnaturally, metropolitan fingers point first in the direction of the Third World (and the Second World, when it existed). The breakdown of the ozone layer, the erosion of valuable, life-sustaining topsoil, and the pollution of water resources have been attributed, to an unconscionable degree, to Third World nonrationality or irrationality. Much has been placed at the doors of Third World elites whose mode of maintaining their wealth and lifestyle is viewed to be contributory. Some United Nations Conference on Environmental Development (UNCED) documents have suggested that the rapid growth of toxic chemicals is due to the population explosion (Mies & Shiva, 1993, p. 58). Such a blatant misrepresentation is strongly indicative of the power of the status quo and the degree of control it exerts. For with the project of economic reconstruction (sustainable development) and environmental control (UNCED is subject to much pressure from the metropolitan economies) yielding to the stewardship of these larger economies, pointing the accusing finger is a relatively simple matter. The value of challenging modernity in its own scientific terms, as Wolfgang Sachs indicates above, proved to be a double-edged sword. In one sense, the challenge is liberating and impresses on the consciousness of the modern scientist dimensions of his discipline whose relevance vis-à-vis Nature has been ignored or underconceptualized. But in another sense, the modernist perspective is provided with a stay of execution. As Bronislaw Szerszynski (1996) states insightfully, all currents critical of modern technology are trapped in its problematic, for "they continue to ask the question 'how can we know what to do?' in terms laid down by modernist thought, however much they might give what appear to be very unmodernist answers to that question" (p. 106).

The truth, as Barry Commoner, among others, including the Green movement, has shown, is that the main culprit is really the type of technology that now unifies the interests of the metropolitan world and the Third World against a truly monstrous incubus. The passion of blaming the victim, whether for his lack of "environmental consciousness" or for any of the other reasons mentioned in the preceding paragraph, is greatly misplaced. To revert to the earlier analyses in the previous chapter, Dependence I—traditional *dependencia*—is now making common cause with Dependence II, as both sets of economies are umbilically linked to a common system now the subject of profound concern. In Barry Commoner's words (1972), "the phalanx of powerful economic, political, and social forces is driving the ecology crisis" (p. 300). "The same systems of production that have generated [America's] enormous wealth," he says, "are also responsible for the present excessive levels of environmental pollution" (Commoner, 1990, p. 46). The evidence is compelling that the ozone layer has much more to fear from exhaust emissions from automobiles of the industrialized societies and to the exports they dispatch abroad than from slash-and-burn practices in the Amazon. Exercising a measure of control over the politics of information deployment can be strategic,but is hardly enough to deflect metropolitan culpability: Each American contributes five times more to air pollution than the average Brazilian (Easterbrook, 1989). In turn, soil erosion is more directly attributable to the export-driven practices encouraged by metropolitan tastes—the clearing of scarce agricultural land by the Thai farmer to produce manioc for the animal feed industry in West Germany or the clearing of fragile Amazonian environment and the overgrazing of Botswana's plains to produce beef for the metropolitan market, are good examples (French, 1994; Young, 1990).

The symbiosis is direct. The neorealist position on the anarchic nature of the world is belied here in the areas of trade and commodity exchange. Vegetables produced by the Third World fertilized by hazardous chemicals banned in the metropolitan countries find their way back to the dining tables of metropolitan families. The rivers that flow into Jakarta Bay in Indonesia carry the combined pollution and degradation (from raw sewage, from acidic effluent from the rubber industry, from palm oil production, from fertilizers leached into the underground waters) that feed directly into the seafoods that ultimately make their way to metropolitan dining tables. The banned herbicides and pesticides that are unconscionably sold to the Mexican vegetable farmers or the Chilean grape producers find their way into the international marketplace. As if to wreak vengeance on the parties operating on either side of the economic divide as well as to instill a sense of urgency and the realization of a forced fellowship between First World and Third World, Nature likewise afflicts the grape, shrimp, or banana producer. Thus, unions in Ecuador and other Latin American countries found it necessary to institute court proceedings against Shell, Standard Fruit, and Dow Chemical, among others, because of the sterility to workers on banana plantations brought about by the pesticide DBCP. Reports indicate that there are several thousands so afflicted in Ecuador, Honduras, and Costa Rica (Martinez-Alier, 1995, p. 514). This is the nature of the "Russian roulette" that science has inflicted, one that is commonly termed "the circle of poison"; it is leading the metropolitan consumer and the Third World producer to become genuine partners in a real drama of survival. It is a consequence of this crisis in which one observes vividly the interdependence of First World, Third World, and Nature.

And what does this drama say about the much vaunted sophisticated quality of life provided by this economic regime? When the dust finally settles, one is forced to look skeptically at the impressive "bottom line" figures that often quell dissent. Negatively adjusted growth statistics often appear as the result of Nature appearing as an externality touched on earlier. Take the example of Malaysia. Its rate of economic growth between 1971 and 1980 was an impressive 7.1% annually. When the price of environmental degradation is factored in, that figure falls to 4.0% (Stone, 1992, p. 30). On another note, one can well understand a seeming irony prevalent in metropolitan societies; it is, as I stated in the previous chapter, a growing disenchantment with the "quality" of life, even in the face of impressive GDP statistics. The increasing technologization of our lifeworld deepens the perception that "our own interventions and appropriations" are "potentially problematic, even threatening" (Beck-Gernsheim, 1996, p. 148).

## ❖ A Thumbnail Sketch: Population

Population growth has always been positively and negatively associated with socioeconomic development. The demographic histories of the United States and Australia, for instance, typify the positive correlation between ample natural resources and copious supplies of suitable labor. On the other hand, "overpopulation" is opposing the concept for the situation in which population either outstrips, or threatens to outstrip, the growth potential of existing resources. There is much controversy concerning when this state of affairs is reached—giving rise to many theories often clustering around the ideas of Thomas Malthus or the technological utopianism, in which the ideas of Marx can be included. In rather crude terms, the first approach assesses the effect of population on the carrying systems of the environment. The neo-Malthusian approach employed by Dennis Meadows et al. (1974) projected a figure of 3 billion, based on the capacities of the environment's carrying systems; Robert Katz (1973), on the other hand, thought that 100 billion is more realistic, as we can depend on the creativity of scientists, engineers, and geniuses to make it an achievable probability. The numerical disparity in evidence is far more than a quantitative one. It is a distinction that derives from the position taken as to whether the notion that the bucket will, in time, overflow if water is constantly being added or not. With the aid of scientists and geniuses, the bucket will be getting bigger and the supply of water should not abate (Percival, 1989; Simon, 1983). The approach conforms with Robert Solow's thesis that "the ancient concern about the depletion of natural resources no longer rests on any firm theoretical basis" (cited in Mies & Shiva, 1993, p. 208).

The issue of population growth draws its most compelling arguments for population control from the stubborn reality of finitude. Unchecked population growth is a fundamental threat to life on the planet. At the beginning of the 19th century, it required over a century for the world's population to double. In 1900, there were 1.7 billion people; this figure increased to 5.3 billion in 1990 and by 2025 there will be some 8.5 billion (Wallimann, 1994, p. 44). Other projections suggest that the figure will mount to 10 to 14 billion during the 21st century, with the bulk of the growth centered in the Third World. As U.N. sources reveal, the countries of the South will, by the year 2000, add some 900 million people to their populations, and those of the North will remain fairly stable. Most of the growth—71%—will nestle in Third World cities, whose present infrastructures are already falling into irredeemable disrepair under the pressures of comparatively smaller numbers. Take the cities of Central America. Their population increased from 2.8 million to 13.7 million between 1950 and 1990. By 2025, the figure is projected to reach some 30 million (Farah, 1993).

When we take a retrospective of population studies, we note a progression. If population issues were not entangled in religion—it still does, recall the recent Population Conference in Cairo and the role of the Vatican[4]—it is nestled in the private sphere. The size of a family was a matter for the couples involved to decide. The next stage came clearly in view with the UN World Population Conference held in Bucharest in 1974. There the responsibility for demographic stability was placed in the lap of each nation. Currently, we are at a new stage, the global stage, in which the often autonomous, private, and subjective decisions touching the population issue are now centrally public and global concerns.

The movement to the present has a parallel in demographic transition theory by Frank Norestein.[5] Briefly, Norestein, using demographic patterns in Europe, identified three phases by which to make sense of population dynamics. During the first stage, birth and death rates are usually high, leading to slow population growth. These patterns are usually found in preindustrial societies. The second stage occurs when the benefits of industrialism are felt. Better health and nutrition, immunizations, and so on lead to birth rates remaining high, death rates declining, and population growth increases. The third stage occurs when economic and social gains reduce the desire to have large families. This stage is represented by the contemporary industrialized societies.

But democratic transition theory is modeled on the notion of progress, with its slavish dependence on technology that assists in entrenching the notion that the bucket will always find the space to hold the additional water. Accordingly, we detect the presence of modernization theory a la Rostow here. Like the "stages-of-growth" thesis, democratic transition theory has encountered insurmountable obstacles: Although a relative handful of societies has reached the third stage—the Western capitalist nations and the People's

Republic of China—the majority appear to be irredeemably trapped at the second stage. As Brown and Jacobson (1986) relate the conundrum,

> [Democratic transition theorists] did not say what happens when developing countries get trapped in the second stage, unable to achieve the economic and social gains that are relied upon to reduce birth rates. Nor does the theory explain what happens when second-stage population rates of 3% per year—which means a twentyfold increase per century—continue indefinitely and begin to overwhelm local life-support systems. (p. 6)

Polarization or dichotomization seems to be the force driving these population dynamics.

Is the population issue generally accepted in globalismic terms? First, let me sketch the gravamen of that position. Its main theses derive from contemporary ecological principles in which social, cultural, and ecological patterns must be kept in some semblance of equilibrium. Accordingly, it would see the crucial importance of matching population densities to the carrying capacities of the various ecosystems on which these populations depend. For these reasons, it can be said to be quasi-Malthusian, as it does not place its faith and future into the hands of modern technology. (I have used the term *quasi-Malthusian* because Reverend Malthus was little concerned with depleted resources or with the environment's carrying capacity. His main predilection had to do with the growth of the population in relation to the ability to produce food.) At the same time, technology is not banished—how could it be? The task is really to make it *appropriate*, given the ecologically defined parameters within which it should be compelled to function. Nevertheless, the compulsion at work seeks to strike the required medium between—to use Maarten Hajer's apt phrasing—the urge to protect "nature as it is" and "nature as it was"; the one often comes with "barbed wire into the prairie," and the other leads to "bizarre engineering exercises" (Hajer, 1996, p. 265).

The wholesale application of the type of modern technology supported by Robert Katz and Herman Kahn as well as the various splinter constituencies spawned by his ideas runs counter to the ecology-driven approach favored by globalism. More about Kahn later. Overall, the growth-propelled logic that informs modern capitalism has yet to provide patterns of equalitarian distribution to enable poor people to bring demographic levels and socioeconomic well-being into respectable balance. Modern capitalism appears to be incapable of extricating itself from its inherent tendency to propagate uneven development; within this tendency, dichotomies (rich and poor, modern and backward, and so on) flourish. Furthermore, the ability of the Third World to "catch up"—an argument used recklessly by modernization theorists—is impossible. Above all other reasons, it is quite improbable that the required levels of strategic resources and energy use could be maintained. Let us take the case of energy. To maintain current levels of socioeconomic development in the United States, Europe, and Japan requires some 75% of *all* energy production. It is not difficult to imagine the increased level of pollution and the deepened environmental degradation that would result, even were we to think of this project as being feasible. It is estimated that even at current levels if the world's energy supply were shared equally, Americans would have to subsist on just one fifth of present per capita usage. Finally, is it in the nature of this "development-by-growth" model to have standards remain stagnant? No. (See Mies & Shiva, 1993, pp. 54-68, and Trainer, 1989, for convincing critiques of the propositions.) Indeed, the nonmodern world would be mindless to endorse the catch-up initiative, based on the current record and performance of modern technology. How has the revolt of Nature and the allied effect of the Other(s) been affecting the world population problem? The response resides in a combination of distrust and gradualism. But the results are enough to inspire hope, as the long-excluded input of the Other(s) is figuring increasingly in searches for solutions.

First, the distrust factor. The metropolitan world, with its seemingly fanatical devotion to the question of population growth, wins the suspicion of the Other(s). Non-Western societies have been at the receiving end of much metropolitan chicanery. This distrust was vigorously displayed at the UN World Population Conference held at Bucharest in 1974. The majority of African leaders opposed any attempts to implement policies to reduce population growth in their respective countries. In fact, many suspected that "racist motivations" were at the heart of the initiative (Burdett, Fornos, Kinkade, & Meyer, 1988). A second factor is tradition. Large families are marks of distinction in many non-Western societies, often the consequence of strong traditions inflected at once by patriarchy and the anthropological urge to perpetuate one's being. Of course, the pattern has been enforced by metropolitan religious contagion (Catholicism) where birth control is discouraged.

Overall, it is safe to suggest that although inroads are gradually made on the population issue, it has not assumed the proportions of a revolution. The urgency of the problem renders anything less than appreciable progress something in the nature of a qualified failure. At the same time, it would be a little disingenuous to think of population policymakers as the proverbial conscientious bull in a china shop.

The truth is that those who express deep concern for the rate at which the world's population increases are not alarmist. In basic terms, there is much to the old adage that if one keeps pouring water in a tub, one day it will spill over. The evidence is that the natural support systems of the earth are finding it difficult to cope with burgeoning population growth. Indeed, the argument for population control is buttressed by two main principles of ecosystems theory: First, natural resources are finite, as ecosystems have a limited carrying capacity, and second, if a balance is not maintained within the systems, it will lead to dysfunctions, as everything is related to everything else (Commoner, 1972, p. 33). When one gets beyond the instrumentally inflected politics that has sullied the record of much metropolitan effort—using Third World population as mere research subjects, for example—and a counteracting initiative, which would often fall just short of glorifying population excesses in its effort to protect the interests of the subjects, the prospects of deleterious overpopulation are formidable.

It is evident that the message is finding its way across the globe. More encouraging, it has caught the attention of the major industrialized countries. Indeed, if it is yet to reap rich rewards, it has begun to produce change in the thinking of Nature and society and in the conceptualization of population problems. In the Third World, one witnesses a variety of approaches geared to population stabilization: Some use tax incentives for keeping family sizes to a minimum (Korea, China, India); several other Third World countries (many African countries among them) employ disincentives, such as denial of maternal benefits; still others (India and Bangladesh, for example) offer incentives to encourage sterilization and the use of contraceptives; other countries (Nigeria, for example) contemplate using the tax system to reduce or stabilize population growth and curb rural/urban migration—all these are examples of steps taken in the right direction.[6] These are encouraging developments, but it remains the case that far more effective efforts are desperately required.

Let me move from the state of the population crisis to the wider debates involving the other manifestations of Nature's revolt. We will notice that a positive reevaluation of Nature is gaining acceptance perceptibly but not without predictable resistance.

## ❖ The Nuanced Oppositional Voices

It would be mistaken to leave the impression that the forces that appear to be most resistant to the demands being made by the revolt of Nature—those clustering around ecological modernization, for example—reside mainly in the metropolitan world. Nonmodern practices and habits of mind have been clearly inimical to Nature, despite an aura of romanticism surrounding them.

One can readily identify any number of spheres in which nonmodern practices are quite hostile to Nature's best interests. Much has been correctly reported on the agreeable complementarity between indigenous agriculture and Nature. One thinks immediately of the farming practices of the Australian aborigines, where the wisdom of their slash-and-burn agricultural techniques has now received the cachet of modern scientific approval (Young, J., 1990). And yet, we should not lose sight of the horror of the countless exotic animals killed yearly in Southeast Asia to provide aphrodisiac for men's sexual pleasures; of the high levels of illegality (30% or so) in the global wildlife trade ($5 billion to $8 billion annually) in which significant numbers of Third World people are deeply implicated (French, 1994); of the fact that many of these destructive policies (in Brazil and Thailand, for example) result from faulty government policies (Farber, 1991). We should not allow exoticism that often accompanies current thinking on nonmodern cultures to obscure the view to a host of practices in need of immediate correction.

## ❖ Nuanced Opposition: The "Kahn-esque" Posture

A review of the general rational and scientific positions against the broad "limits-to-growth" perspective makes useful contact with the ideas of Herman Kahn, whether the concern is with depleted resources, pollution, or any of the other key issues making up that genre. The late Kahn, a physicist by training, took a robust attitude in his defense of science as the solver of all problems. I will draw from his well-known, if controversial, book, *The Next 200 Years: A Scenario for America and the World,* as a convenient point of reference.

Kahn and his collaborators scoff at the idea of depletion and pollution. Science has the answer. Just sunlight and a modest rate of technological advance will do, as we see in the epigraph at the head of this chapter. Their book is quite useful as, in its critique, it presents the prominent position against which it inveighs. The book, which was published in 1976, surfaced as an antidote to *The Limits to Growth,* which appeared in 1973. Its arguments support the technology-for-growth thesis for which its authors express an unbounded enthusiasm. In fact, it was this very enthusiastic Kahn who recommended that Amazonia be created into a huge lake for generating hydroelectric power.

In their analysis, Kahn and his collaborators divide the contestants into two main categories, whose positions on key issues such as technology and capital, management and decision making, resources, growth, innovation, industrial development, income gaps and poverty, and quality of life are contrasting. The two opposing positions, which are taken to be extreme, are the "neo-Malthusian" and the technology-and-growth postures. The first is an adaptation from the Reverend Thomas Malthus's famous thesis: If population grows at a faster rate than the production of food supply, starvation is inevitable. The other position holds that in the next century, material needs can be met so easily in the developed world that its success will provide a model for the rest of the world.

But reality occupies a less extreme position, on the authors' view. The realistic neo-Malthusian position is one of moderation—that of the guarded pessimist. Guarded optimism is its opposite. Both positions take generally similar approaches to many key issues; the differences are largely a matter of degree. Accordingly, both expect serious problems relative to energy supply, food, and other resources; foresee the possibility of cataclysmic or irreversible environmental damage; think that with technological progress, wise policies, competent management, and good luck humankind can combat its problems and survive. Where, then, is the main distinction? In the case of the guarded pessimist, the neo-Malthusian, the prospects are only "barely" encourageable. For the guarded optimist, the technology-and-growth devotee, success is in the offing, even in the face of injudicious policies, poor management, or bad luck. He holds that position mainly on the strength of technology. Technology and capital solve almost all problems, and even though some mishaps are caused by carelessness, none is without a remedy. Most problems result from too little technology and capital, not from an excess. The guarded optimist also volunteers that enough resources exist to fuel ongoing progress in the world and that sophisticated management and decision making resulting from modern communications systems make the notion of serious problems rather outmoded.

This schema ramifies in a variety of directions. But before I trace some of them, it is important to make a point of a significant nature. That such a debate, as that sketched above, did occur was, in a sense, far more important than the points of disagreement between these two branches of the materialist school (Norgaard, 1995). One might note also that in the early to the mid-1970s, it was the habit of speaking as if a discrete disconnectedness existed between the metropolitan and the other quarters of the globe. Let me get back to the derivative positions that are influenced greatly by Herman Kahn's forthrightly expressed ideas. The appeal of these ideas receives considerable support from three added factors. I have called the first "the politics of statistical imprecision." If attempts at measurement prove imprecise (as in the case of the limits-to-growth initiative), their self-induced rejection was sufficient to deflect attention away from the original premise. The central focus shifted away from the measurable exhaustion of natural resources to the inability to measure the levels of their depletion accurately. By a deft sleight of hand, the consequential underreporting of these reserves was accordingly presented as an index of seemingly inexhaustible supplies. Take the example of Julian Simon (1983). After stating that all natural resources, except oil and lumber, have been increasing rather than decreasing in the long run—a conclusion measured by *cost or price,* he adds that

> there is no reason to believe that the supply of energy is finite, or that the price will not continue its long-run decrease. This statement may sound less preposterous if you consider that for a quantity to be finite it must be measurable. (cited in Finsterbusch & McKenna, 1990, p. 326)

The second factor is the "doomsday syndrome." In the late 1960s, it was fashionable to predict the likely decade in which population explosion would bring the operations of the world to a halt (Ehrlich, 1968; Paddock & Paddock, 1967). An otherwise distinguished economist, Stanley Jevons, predicted that British industry would decline with the depletion of coal, only to be confounded by the switch to petroleum. Instead, the world's carrying capacity for human population has vastly exceeded the dire projections of Ehrlich and the supply of oil has not complied with the predictions of the authors of *The Limits to Growth,* as indeed it failed to do in earlier noteworthy instances. The earth has seemingly accommodated, quite comfortably, more people than the projections contemplated; oil reserves have expanded.

The third factor is one that applies equally to metropolitan, Third World, and non-Western contexts. It inheres in religious and secular expressions of the notion of "the Chosen." Richard Falk (1992, p. 39) speaks of the religious bent within Western civilization as one in which progress and its methodologies are sanctified; in evidence as well is a form of Freudianism in which one detects behavior hemmed in by the notion that we find it impossible to imagine our own death. It is as though the dynamic nature of life, complete with its wellsprings of hope, overshadows any significant attempts to cope realistically with basic questions of finitude. I have drawn attention to this strain that is deeply embedded in Enlightenment thought (Chapter 2). In a related context, William Sheehan (1978) alludes to a human "illusion" that "nature's bounty is limitless." In his words,

> when some competent expert says apprehensively, "don't waste" or, "at this rate of consumption the world's supply soon will be exhausted" (p. 48) one's inclination is to dismiss this as unduly pessimistic. We tend to prefer the assurances of

> [those] who say new discoveries, substitution of products, or man's ingenious technology will take care of things amply.

For its part, non-Western fidelity in the benevolence of the supernatural appears as some variant of the Gaia hypothesis (which, incidentally, is being adopted by certain strains of the environmental and other grassroots movements (Lash, Szerszynski, & Wynne, 1996; Miller, 1991). Here the earth is seen as a single, self-regulating organism, with unfathomable powers of recuperation. Hence, there is nothing that science and technology can visit on her that cannot be absorbed or dispelled (Miller, 1991)—a fallacy empirically disproved by ecological degradation and theoretically undermined by scientists like Shiva and Capra.

These are, then, some of the extrinsic ballasting that provides a backdrop for the daring of the guarded optimist of the Kahn-esque sort. Following are a number of derivative theses, circumscribed by a number of singular points in refutation:

- *The growth of know-how is unlimited, given the ingenuity of hand and brain.* Generally, this accurate statement is restricted to an incomplete sphere of operation. Brain and hand do not define the parameters of the social order; they are constrained to work within specific limits. The perspective of man, the knower, is a feature of the philosophy of consciousness—a tenet of the Enlightenment—that is now being vigorously controverted (see Chapter 2).
- *There is a shrinkage of raw material usage.* Between 1960 and 1970, for example, the shrinkage was 0.6%; since 1990, that figure has risen to about 3.0%. In a sense, this projects modern science and technology in a positive light. This might be beneficial in the short run but is seemingly of dubious value if economic practice remains wedded to the growth-at-all-costs approach.
- *The record of science finding substitutes is impressive.* In Robert Solow's words, if substitutes can be found for natural resources, the depletion of natural resources will be just another event, not a catastrophe. Robert Solow's conclusion is particularly troubling. First, it shares the now-problematic "philosophy-of-consciousness" posture. Second, Nature is not a mere material substrate; its various dimensions, as Holmes Rolston indicates above, are vital to a complete sense of human and social requirements. Human, cultural, and environmental dimensions are not related only in an instrumental sense. Third, depletion of nonrenewable resources is making the renewable (rivers and forests, for example) nonrenewable. Fourth, the use of substitutes removes just one element from the cluster that devastates Nature. As long as economic practices are of an energy-dependent kind that pollutes and depletes, substituted

inputs may be of minor significance unless the energy production and its related waste disposal systems are qualitatively changed.

- *Shifts in resource use patterns that accompany developing technologies provide a built-in controlling mechanism.* The tendency is for these shifts to entrench human dependency and relocate it within other areas. If the shift is away from, say, oil to coal, the dependency has not disappeared, and moreover, in this example, there might be increased ecological and environmental problems.
- *Automatic mechanisms of the market will regulate resource use.* The remedy for possible pollution and ecological degradation (Smith & Kushner, 1990) is privatization. In short, reduce the environment (air, land, and water) to private enterprise. With private ownership and the profit motive will come the protection that the capitalist exercises over a valuable investment. Quickly, to summarize Max Dublin's (1992, pp. 213-215) critique, one does not have any evidence that capitalism will do any better than it has done so far. Wryly, he asks this crucial question relative to the prospect of absentee ownership in which such transfers of property rights would largely reside: "Why not clear-cut your tract of timber wood if you do not live in or beside it and do not have to look at it afterward?" (p. 214). The market has not the wherewithal to predict long-term scarcity; the price of oil does not signal that oil will become scarce, "if anything, [it signals] an ever growing supply" (Wallimann, 1994, p. 48).

In all the rejoinders proffered by guarded optimists, the arguments march headlong into obstacles erected by ecosystems thinking and the obsolescent nature of outmoded economics. In turn, both oppositional stances are conditioned by a more pervasive one—the implications of the law of entropy or the second law of thermodynamics.[7] Briefly, the message is that modern production is based on patterns of energy usage that increasingly require more energy to maintain and keep stable the levels of production achieved. Modern production can only be continued alongside dramatically increasing use of energy resources, and as, per the law of entropy, the universe evolves irreversibly toward degradation, not resuscitation, such practices as the voracious consumption of energy and other strategic resources merely expedite the inevitable process of universal degradation. In any event, although entropy is inevitable, if we are to justify our claims to rationality, if we remain faithful to the psychical and anthropological impulses that have so unabatedly impelled us toward the perpetuation of life in all its dimensions, we must be guided by the limits, options, and strategies inherent in this law.

Evidence of a compatible *thinking* and *reconceptualization,* if not a pervasive process of *translation,* exists. In this final segment, a few sketches suggest a number of distinct areas in which encouraging strategies appear, if overburdened at times by a recalcitrant status quo.

## ❖ The Emerging Shape of Global Cooperation

Is the world listening to the defiant voices of Nature? What can we make of these responses? We have already seen, in the case of the population crisis, that the reactions are mixed—a reading that does not, so far, embolden one to speak of a substantial trend in the right direction. But the trend is, however, quite unmistakable.

We can get a reasonable sense of changing global perceptions on the topics discussed in this chapter by taking a look at global public opinion. Certainly it can hardly be denied that the two extreme positions on which the present growth-by-production model is driven still exist. There remains a widespread technological utopianism and the belief that science has the answer; second, there is still among the Third World the notion that the tack ought not to be a change of the paradigm of development. Two major justifications usually accompany this latter view: The first is that nonmodern cultures, as the traditionally exploited, are being excluded from achieving the enviably high standard of living that the metropole has enjoyed; the second relates to metropolitan deception. This reaction was exemplified at the Rio conference of 1992, when the industrial economies suggested that lumber-exporting Third World countries should reduce that activity, mainly to save the environment. The perception of chicanery was fortified, in part, by the fact that the timber industry of the American Northwest—comparatively quite substantial—was not saddled with such a constraint!

Nonetheless, there is evidence of a growing agreement, despite the setbacks in the management of population growth and the saturnalia of suspicion that the metropolitan world does so richly deserve. In 1992, a Gallup poll indicated that a majority of peoples from 20 of the 22 countries surveyed endorsed stronger action to protect the environment, even if it required a decrease in economic growth (Dunlap, Gallup, & Gallup, 1992). In 1986, a CBS/*New York Times* Poll showed that 66% of Americans agreed that protecting the environment was paramount, despite the probability of increased prices. That figure increased to 80% in 1989 (Commoner, 1990, pp. 60-61). This development suggests a dramatic change in attitude from that of the metropolitan consumers of the late 1960s and the 1970s. Consumers are now less likely to feel exonerated from any culpability associated with pollution or environmental degradation—a burden that was usually placed on industry and/or the operation of market forces. Boycotts, conservation, recycling, and like activities, are all indications that sustainability—or, at least, some version of the concept—is taking hold in the metropolitan world. The qualification is hardly spurious. For sustainability (ecological modernization) is conceptualized as being comfortably functional *within* the current capitalist regime. It grates against the more pervasive view that the concept is without a future, unless it is aligned to a qualitatively different framework. I will elaborate on this theme below.

Are comparable changes detectable in the rest of the world? In countries such as Taiwan, where pollution and ecological degradation reach scandalous proportions, local populations often take matters into their own hands. Other examples include that of the Chipko movement of rural people of Northern India who organized to save their forests and the initiative of Penan and other indigenous peoples from Sarawak and Malaysia against the logging interests that were depleting their forests. We are likewise aware of the much heralded "swidden fallow" agricultural strategies used by the Bora Indians of the Peruvian Amazon to reduce ecological and socioeconomic vulnerabilities (Redclift, 1987, p. 154).

At this writing, there is the case of the Ogoni people of the Niger delta in Nigeria. Much attention has justifiably been drawn to the execution of Ken Saro-Wiwa, the human rights activist, who, along with the Ogoni people, defied the expansion of Shell Petroleum operations within Ogoniland. It is true that the question of the receipt of benefits was important; after all, since the discovery of oil in 1958, Shell Petroleum extracted some $30 billion worth of oil and natural gas while the Ogoni people have little to show for it but poor health care and increasing levels of poverty. But there is a parallel and seemingly stronger motivation—it is the state of the environment. It is true that the UNCED designates the coastal rain forests and mangrove swamps of the delta as fragile and in need of protection as one of the most endangered river deltas in the world. But the Ogoni people did not wait on the UN to provide them with a deep sense of care for their environment, the lure of money notwithstanding. They have paid dearly with their lives: Since 1993, some 20 Ogoni towns have been destroyed, with 1,800 people losing their lives, and 50,000 people left homeless. In 1989, another nonmodern culture turned its back on the benefits of modern technology, with revolutionary activity as a last resort. The reference is to the societies of Papua-New Guinea who inhabit the ecologies washed by the Kawerong River. Although Papua-New Guinea's copper mine provided about 40% of that country's national export earnings, the daily discharge of some 130,000 tons of toxic pollutants and the destruction of the ecology were enough to trigger antitechnology responses leading to the closure of operations in 1989. The indigenous peoples of Brazil provide another example. The Brazilian Pastoral Commission on Land indicates that some 1,200 murders of activists, peasant leaders, and union representatives, among others, have their origins in the prevention of deforestation of Amazonia. These are but a few representative examples that now appear with increasing regularity.

Increasingly, these events and transformation in attitudes come to form significant elements in new patterns of thinking. These patterns are often situated within discrete matrices from which the impact of the new elements can be observed. Three prominent examples must suffice. The first resides in the new politics of recognition (see Chapters 2 and 9) whose effects are implicated in the dynamics of new social movements. As the nature of these effects will be scattered throughout the text, I will not addresses them here. The second matrix is provided by new global norms and ethics, and the third encompasses the ethic of sustainability. What is provided below are mainly impressionistic sketches, not exhaustive analyses.

### *New Global Norms and Ethics?*

The rise of new global norms and ethics is situated in a new climate of global reality. If one were asked to identify one of the more influential causal factors, the decline of realist/neorealist paradigm and its concomitant power politics approach would rate rather highly. Especially crucial is the fate of its derivative ethics. Nicholas Georgescu-Roegen (1971) volunteers an observation on neoclassical economics that applies equally to these ethics. He states that this brand of economics is the product of conditions of plenty and could, as such, direct its logic in line with the principles of anarchy and self-sufficiency. Likewise, systems of ethics, which have a parallel and derivative existence—those of Hobbes, Kant, and the libertarians about which I will say a bit more in the next chapter—are exposed to identical pressures to conform with present realities. If neoclassical economics has to conform to the increasing pressures of new economic impetuses—ecological economics, for example (Constanza, 1991)—the examples of new global norms and ethics, to be exemplified below, are clearly the result of pressures exerted by Nature in revolt. Doubtless, the new passion for generating these norms and principles of ethics owes much to survivalism. If we take the example of environmental degradation, there is definitely a collective sense that our "global commons"—air, water, the oceans, soils, and so on—are threatened. Of diminishing importance is the "billiard ball" concept of internationalism, of *realpolitik,* to which I referred in Chapter 2.

Examples of new global norms gaining currency are (a) the need to democratize technology to guarantee full disclosure about hazards and (b) universal principles of "the right to know" and "freedom of information" on health and safety issues. Of related activism: the Pesticide Action Network (PAN), formed in May 1982, following an International Organization of Consumers Unions, cohosted by Sahabat Alam (Friends of the Earth) in Penang, Malaysia. In 1985, PAN instituted the "dirty dozen" (i.e., the targeting of 12 hazardous pesticides for global action). At that time, PAN participants were active through hundreds of groups in over 50 countries (Weir, 1988, p. xiii). In 1985, the "No More Bhopals" network was inaugurated in Nairobi, Kenya, in a conference on sustainable development.

Other examples are to be found in the general area of *rights*. Thus, much reformulation now revolves around the notion of human rights being international in scope. A concomitant issue relates to the growing influence of grassroots participation; its impact arrives via the epidemic spread of NGOs in Third World development. In a study conducted on behalf of the Club of Rome (Schneider, 1988), it was discovered that there were 2,087 NGOs involved in development in the metropolitan societies and 67,000 participating in like activities in Latin America, Asia, and Africa. In both situations, these organizations saw themselves as the needed alternatives to the nation-state and the most reliable sources for the alternative theory and practice by which sustainable development is broadly defined (Alger, 1990; Padron, 1987). Emerging from this developing process is the claim for a new global value: grassroots participation, central to which are the emancipatory qualities of "self-reliance" and "the full flowering of individual human potential" (Alger, 1990, p. 156).[8]

A Nature in revolt also spurs the theoretical imagination into exploring the dimensions of an ecological ethic. Many scholars working especially in the area of the "environmental philosophy" (Regan, 1986; Rolston, 1986; Taylor, 1986) place the question at the top of their agenda. Should the endowments of Nature now be seen as "being worthy of respect in [their] own right?" (Plumwood, 1993, p. 166). Presently, an interesting debate rages on the issue, with, decreasingly, a concern as to whether such an ethic exists than its proper epistemological basis. Should it be Kantian, where reason and cognition play a key defining role? Or should the value be anchored to a more extensive conceptualization of rights, a form of ecoliberalism? On the view of Arne Naess (1973, p. 96), originating in deep ecology, is there not a growing irrefutability that the world cannot be analyzed "into separately and independently existing parts?" (see Attfield, 1994, part III; Plumwood, 1993, ch. 7; Taylor, 1986, for nuanced approaches to the issue). From this short list of examples, global norms and values are gradually inching their way to center stage. One is struck by the new brand of theorizing in which they reside and by a de-dichotomizing principle by which they are nearly always guided.

### *The Ethic of Sustainability*

Sustainability is a variously defined concept originating in the crisis of the development-by-growth model. In the literature, the concept ramifies into three main spheres: (a) maintaining intergenerational welfare, productivity, and the resilience of economic systems; (b) maintaining capital stocks; and (c) maintaining the regenerative capacities of the environment (O'Hara, 1995). It is not misleading to suggest that versions one and two are preponderantly dependent on version three, inasmuch as the viability of economic activity is paramount. Accordingly, it is small wonder that it is the regenerative capacities of the environment that subsume much of the contemporary debate. It should also be stressed that the particular charges embedded in the injunction have long been a centerpiece of nonmodern cultures all over the globe. So, whether the admission was grudging or not, the input of the Other(s) was unavoidable.

Dissatisfactions with the unsettling consequences of the development-by-growth model—many of which are expressed in the revolt of Nature—became legitimized by the Brundtland Commission Report, *Our Common Future* (World Commission on Environment and Development, 1987). This report appears both as a corrective to the earlier Brandt Commission Reports, with their top-down management approaches and the call to have economic activity accord with the physical limits of the environment.[9] The Brundtland Report appears to reverse this strategy in a number of recommendations, three of which will be quickly recorded. First, it advocated that small rural producers, primarily women, must be given preference in allocating resources. These producers must also be involved directly in policy formation. Second, the management of resources was also recommended for centralization. Local communities were to be given substantial control over the use of those resources. Third, there should be the evolution of a political system to ensure effective participation in decision making.

Sustainability calls for three main strategies. The first is the conservation of finite resources. We must bear in mind the needs of future generations. Resources must be used more efficiently and alternatives must be sought. The second focuses on reducing waste, and the third addresses the stabilization of world population.

Sustainability has been underpinned by new theoretical efforts. One example is the approach called PAR (participatory action research), which is found in a number of countries in Latin America, Asia, and Africa. The approach has found immense favor as it gives pride of place to self-awareness. As Orlando Fals-Borda (1990) expresses it in the case of Latin America—but a formulation equally applicable in other parts of the Third World,

> [Participatory discourse] postulates an organization and structure of knowledge in such a way that the dominated, underdeveloped societies articulate their own sociopolitical position on the basis of their own values and capacities and act accordingly to achieve their own liberation from the oppressive and exploitative forms of domination imposed by opulent (capitalist) foreign powers and local consular elites and thus create a more satisfactory life for everyone. (p. 81)

PAR stresses the upholding of people's countervailing power, their grassroots empowerment, if you will. The approach to sustainability, as Borda continues, revolves around four interlocking methodological strategies. First, *collective research.* Briefly, the process involves a thorough collection of data via fact-finding trips, public assemblies, committees, and so on. Public assemblies are employed by the people to assess the value of the information gathered. Second, *critical recovery of history.* These processes enable the people to select, through their collective memory, those elements of the past that have been useful to counteract domination. Much use is made of witness accounts of older members of the communities "possessing good analytic memories" as well as "family coffers." Third, *valuing and applying folk culture.* This allows such deeply embedded traditions like storytelling to be resuscitated. In addition, these *rhetorical* forms (more on this topic especially in Chapter 10) feed into a politics in which beliefs, myths, music, drama, and so on, are fundamental. Fourth, *production and diffusion of new knowledge.* In short, this dimension involves a complex process of sifting and evaluating pertinent knowledge that is then disseminated to communities and workers' organizations for implementation. In context, "they may determine the priorities concerning its use and authorise and establish the conditions for its publication and dissemination" (Fals-Borda, 1990, p. 94).

But there remain the vastly complex issues associated with interpretation and execution. Often the species of sustainability contemplated by Third World advocates (ecofeminists, for example) and many branches of the environmental movement within the metropolitan world is of a different stripe. The feisty, anti-imperialist, self-sufficient language used by Orlando Fals Borda above spawns notions that are not identical in conception and execution with the intent of the Brundtland approach (ecological modernization). It is clear that, for Borda, sustainability connotes the birth of a "space" in which dominated societies can extricate themselves from crippling denials (of their culture, economics, and politics) and work more closely in a global environment in which those systems of denial are now proved fallacious, an environment in which common dangers call forth efforts at a new fellowship. A major argument from Borda (for the Third World) and Richard Norgaard (for the First World) is that the environmental crisis *writ large* is not simply a matter of insufficient knowledge and insufficiently well-assigned property rights, and so on. It requires, in large part, a sedulous rejection of the materialist paradigm, where progress reigns disembodiedly, and Nature is a mere point of departure and not one of return.

But this is hardly the agenda of ecological modernization that is embedded in the Brundtland Commission report. In principle, the formal agenda speaks the language of the ecologist (complete with the tools of ecosystems science), concedes the ravages of the earth, and even admits the role of a Promethean technology. But it has, so far, refused to abandon the key principles on which such a Prometheus thrives. As Bronislaw Szerszynski states earlier, this persistence, this legitimacy, obtains in part from the continuing key position occupied by modernity in the manner in which ecological questions are asked. In the end, there is a powerful thrust toward the "rationalization of ecology" (Hajer, 1996, p. 261), one in which a dominant theme is not to discontinue an economics of growth and a technology geared to Nature's submission, as it is to making the related systems more efficient. The agenda is not to reduce the production of automobiles and change from fossil fuels but to produce more fuel efficient and more environmentally friendly units. The tack, as Wolfgang Sachs (1992) notes, was to create "a marriage between the craving for development and concern for the environment" (p. 28). The somber postulates of the law of entropy appear, at least for the moment, to be superseded by the still potent residues of the instrumental notion of progress.

This unyielding, though often modified, view of modernity puts ecological modernization into fierce exchanges with still other renditions of sustainability. Many of them are predominantly Nature-centered, which serve to ensure a prominent spot for Nature on the development agenda. Likewise, they expose the obfuscatory ploys used by the industrial economies to blame the victim for such environmental ravages as the decay of the ozone layer and other environmental pollution. Deep ecology (Macy, 1991; Naess, 1973, 1986) provides examples of the near total indivisibility of Nature and humanity. Extreme branches of movement have even campaigned to maintain wilderness areas free from human usage, canvassing vigorously in the process for population controls in the name of Nature's sovereignty. Ecofeminism (Mies & Shiva, 1993; Shiva, 1989), in its turn, seeks to create a coalition between the oppression of Nature with that of women. At the core of the movement is a strong anticapitalist, antimodernist bent, one that places great stress on self-reliance and working in substantial harmony with Nature. A noteworthy branch of deep ecology—biocentric egalitarianism—is to be cited. Its agenda takes us back to those court battles of 16th-century France, when, as Luc Ferry relates it at the top of this chapter, weevils and leeches had legitimate rights. In short, Nature assumes a major cluster of rights—"the equal right of all right to live and blossom" (Attfield, 1994, p. 205). I will add as a final example a form of socialist sustainability, inaugurated by *Capitalism, Nature, Socialism: A Journal of Socialist Ecology.*[10] Succinctly, its agenda is this:

> to [contribute] to the shift in emphasis from the traditional neo-Marxist tradition of analyzing the Latin American crisis in terms of contradictions between productive forces and relations of production to a broader ecological Marxism that focuses on contradictions between these forces and relations, on the one hand, and the ecological conditions of production, on the other. (Faber, 1992, pp. 4-5)

This is not the place to raise the obvious theoretical issues germane to Marxism's profound modernist orientation, one to which modern technology is central. From the perspective of Nature, this new initiative does well, if it should do so only rhetorically, to keep Nature at center stage.

What we usually find is a kind of diversity in approach that is committed to the principles of sustainability. In short, to take the examples above, there is sustainability a la capitalism, sustainability a la socialism, and other approaches distrustful of the preceding two. In this climate of *chaos* a couple of dust-laden platitudes come to mind. First, too many cooks do tend to spoil the broth, but equally, one can hardly make an omelette without breaking eggs. We are in the presence of "constructive" chaos!

The matrices used to explore the changing approaches toward Nature are quite dynamic. New global norms, an evolving ethic of sustainability, and a contingent global politics are all directly involved in Nature's revolt. If we are not yet able to settle on clearly defined analytic trajectories—a good many of these "positions" being quite inchoate—the glaring diversity serves to make a cardinal point. It is that Nature will not be conceptualized as a mere point of departure; it is a point of theoretical return. In the process, it is taking many casualties, preeminent among them are a number of key foundational principles of modern economics.

In summary, the contents of this chapter lay bare the many dysfunctions that result from utilizing Nature as a mere material substrate. In the general climate of constructive chaos, a number of cogent conclusions are evident. The first is that present and future developmental agendas must adopt a different approach, one in which the role of Nature must accord with the new knowledge we are increasingly acquiring about it; the science of ecosystems contributes hugely here, as do the principles and prospects of environmental philosophy. Second, corrective approaches to the emerging globalism must integrate nonmodern perspectives, as progressively they are proving invaluable in global reassessments of all kinds. Far too often traditional environmental knowledge is devalued and not consulted in the planning process (Alger, 1990; Redclift, 1987). Third, the neoclassical economic system is clearly out of step with the dynamics of a new economic order in which Nature's role is quite different. Indeed, this point serves to underscore the contention that the emerging interdependence underlying the economic and other complex clusters of global processes can no longer be based primarily (or even fundamentally) on an economics-led rehabilitation. New economic habits of mind and practices are indeed in critical demand, but they must draw sustenance from equally new ethical and philosophical principles logically anterior to them. At the same time, the old economics is not fading away but stubbornly situates itself within ecological modernization, as it stresses efficiency. An economic agenda has clearly a key role to play. The cardinal question is whether it will merely function as the proverbial wolf in sheep's clothing or yield to the mounting pressures that announce with increasing frequency and greater assurance its demonstrably anachronistic posture in a world perceptibly moving beyond its concepts, premises, and assumptions.

## ❖ Notes

1. Results are encouraging. NGOs work with drug companies to develop new drugs and preserve forests in Costa Rica and Ecuador (see Meyer, 1995).

2. Much support is provided by the work of the noted anthropologist David Maybury-Lewis (1992). He links the ecological connectedness of the universe now established by quantum physics with the cosmologies of Australian aborigines and native Mexicans (see also Booth & Jacobs, 1990, and Rappaport, 1979, p. 41, regarding the "ritually regulated ecosystem" maintenance of the Tsembaga of Papua).

3. Ecological systems are now seen as the best models for sustainability, especially the "climax ecosystem," which has the capacity of "closing the cycle" (see Constanza, 1991, p. 333—an excellent resource for questions on the general topic; see also Capra, 1996; Farber & Nelson, 1993).

4. The Pope responded critically to the tone of the International Conference on Population and Development held in Cairo, September 1994. He appears to express more concern for moral issues tied to the nuclear family and heterosexuality than for narrow population and economic

growth issues. This conference also highlights the role of women in challenging the Pope and in leading worldwide initiatives to curb population growth. See the Pope's strictures in his *International Conference on Population and Development: Letter to President Clinton and Address to Dr. Nafis Sadik*, Vatican City, March 18/19, 1994.

5. See Notestein, Kirk, and Segal (1963) for an elaboration of his theory. For its application to Third World settings, see McNamara (1982).

6. China's one-child family campaign is noteworthy; since its start in 1979, the birth rate has been halved. Population growth in Kenya dropped from 8.1 children per woman in 1979 to 5.4 in 1993. Attitude to population growth appears to be changing. World Bank surveys show that 50% to 90% of Third World women want to stop childbearing or delay the birth of other children.

7. The rule here is that we must maintain energy flows at a low level (i.e., slow down the entropic process). To do so, we must devise decentralized, small-scale units that use renewable energy.

8. A few First World countries had contributed to the concept for many years (Holland, Belgium, France). In the 1980s, much activity surrounded "the European development education movement" involving such projects as "Twinning cities in Europe and the Third World," creating Third World awareness groups, etc. In 1989, 39 of the 40 largest cities and towns in Holland were directly involved in such initiatives (see Alger, 1990; van Tongeren, 1984).

9. The Brandt Reports were prepared in the spirit of the technology-for-growth model. Equity is the main theme. The Brundtland report stresses sustainability linked to environmentally appropriate technology and ensuring a healthy productive earth for succeeding generations. For problems with this agenda see Hajer (1996), Grove-White (1996), and Beck (1992, chap. 7 re. the role of science).

10. A Marxist ecology is problematical, as Marxism is technology driven. See Rudolf Bahro (1984, 1986), Martinez-Alier (1991, pp. 118-136), and Banton (1996) for the pros and cons of the issue.

# PART II

# *Chapter Four*

# CRISIS AND THE FRAGMENTED SHADOWS OF THE ENLIGHTENMENT

*In the deepest recesses of one's egocentric*
*fortress a voice softly but tirelessly repeats*
*"our walls are made of plastic, our acropolis of papier-mâché."*
Cornelius Castoriadis (see Bauman, 1993, p. 46)

## ❖ The Relief

The upcoming quartet of chapters directly addresses the epistemological crisis of the Enlightenment. Together they are intended to focus mainly on the way a particular regime of knowledge garrisoned the world and how its fissures have been breached by competing perspectives, notably those of the Other(s). To prepare the way for this complex analysis, I provide a relief to project the nature of the major positions presented in this part of the book.

The present exercise erects a basic architectonic framework by which one understands the historical and structural interplay between dependence and the Enlightenment tradition. This will convey, I hope, a better sense of the special features ascribed to interdependence. The largely narrow economic and historical explanations extended to the concept in the previous chapter have been foreshadowed by the larger crisis of modernity's parent structure. The breakdown is of the very system of knowledge from which economics, history, politics, and international relations, among others, extract their theory and practice.

By using the so-called resolutive-compositive method, I show how the main building blocks of that system are set in place. Then, through an analysis of building blocks, mortar, tools, and workmanship, we can better grasp the overall crisis in which the Enlightenment is mired. It is from such breakdown that we are able to observe the suspect quality of the edifice. Overall, the analysis is intended to provide a measure of substantiation for many concepts and issues that were only tentatively raised in the previous chapter. But the quartet of chapters really can be described as a retrospective look at the present, from the vantage point of the past.

It should, likewise, be noted that research materials from, and about, the dependent world are used sparingly. The paucity hardly relates to the availability of data; rather, it is driven by the principal foci of the analysis. The present task is to look mainly through the eyes of those who fabricated what J. M. Blaut (1993) refers to as "the colonizer's model of the world." In the process, we should get no less a vivid sense of the manner in which dependence articulates with the project of the Grand Narcissist, the idols of the tribe. We will, as a reconstructive analysis of the crisis permits, be better able to observe the fault lines of the parent framework. These fault lines provide a better focus on interdependence that results from a different set of structural combinations.

The analysis will be largely thematic. Parts, like reason, rationality, natural law, and heliocentrism, among others, will be used to explain the whole. In the end, it will be epistemological issues that dominate. We will observe how epistemological issues induce the belief in hierarchies, notably those between nations; how a systematic deployment of knowledge would in time broaden the dichotomizing propensity to bring a greater number of Other(s) under some form of dichotomous control—Nature and women; how the fetish for generating dichotomies would turn on itself, as the prince of all dichotomies—the First World-Third World dichotomy—becomes entrapped and begins to implode. The revolt is led by women, gays, and people of color, among others, whose growing political activity finds common cause with the Other(s) against the Cartesian tradition.

Chapter 4 begins by mapping out an outline of the Enlightenment crisis as it appears today. It is largely impressionistic, presented more in a narrative than in an analytic form, to set the stage for subsequent analysis. It foreshadows many of the major issues to be addressed in the other chapters.

Chapter 5 looks more closely at the general features of the Enlightenment, particularly rationalism. It will elucidate a good many concepts impressionistically drawn in the previous chapter. Likewise, it locates rationalism within a dynamic historical context from which abstract rationalist notions extract their impetus and meaning. The final segment of the chapter sketches the logocentrism-emotivism dichotomy forming the central platform for Self-Other interplay.

Newtonian cosmology occupies the bulk of Chapter 6. The analysis enables us to observe how Newton's laws, which establish certain fixed relations among planets within the solar system—relations of superordination and subordination—are applied to the affairs of the social world. Newtonian cosmology also establishes patterns of social behavior away from the dynamics of lived experience toward decontextualized, ahistorical, first principles in which geometry occupies a central place. Discussed in this context as well is the rise of dependence as domination of nonmodern societies (Other[s]) by modern societies (Self).

Chapter 7 provides a summary of key points of analyses in Part II. First, it sketches some examples of the modernist consequences of dispensing with history. Descartes, Voltaire, and other Enlightenment figures had no patience with history. With the rule of the Method, there was no realistic avenue for the worldviews of other cultures to be understood. Second, the chapter looks closely at the specific weaknesses of the Cartesian-driven rationalism and hints as substitutes drawn from a diverse range of critiques, many of which originate in the principles of Otherness.

## ❖ The Current Contortions Within Humanism

Although the newfound symbiosis between Dependence I and II can be satisfactorily explained by factors largely intrinsic to it (see Chapter 1), the fullness of the current perils of the Enlightenment is required to place these factors into their proper perspective. There is a fairly substantial consensus that the Enlightenment, as both a *project* and a *tradition*, is in deep crisis. Indeed, judging by the varied sources of the issues involved and their organic relationship, there can be little doubt that the crisis is systemic.

By project, I mean the modernity–Modern Man interplay. In turn, tradition refers to the paradigm from which the project draws its key definitions and ethical commands. The implication is that tradition is capable of giving rise to other "projects"; but the history of the Enlightenment, so far, is that its application has been monopolized by the above interplay. The combination receives its terms of reference from a basic Cartesian theorem, namely, that reality can be accurately understood and fashioned for the enlightened development of humanity only when there is a Subject (Modern Man), a rational being who stands outside the world of objects and exercises control by knowing them. Complementarily, modernity is the peculiar organizational matrix in which the exercise of control by knowing occurs. We have excellent analyses of this matrix from Marx (economic organization), Weber (rationality), the Frankfurt School, and Habermas (the philosophy of consciousness), among others, and need not dwell on the topic any longer.

Alternative projects, as mentioned above, have not been institutionalized. But there are clearly such models endemic in the Enlightenment tradition. Side by side with the natural philosophy from which sprung a Descartes or a Newton was a profound humanism represented by such figures as Erasmus (1466-1536), Montaigne (1533-1592), and Shakespeare (1564-1616), among others. In Stephen Toulmin's nicely crafted line, they "speak across the centuries in ways we feel upon our pulses" (Toulmin, 1992, p. 23). A similar position is also taken by Hugh Trevor-Roper (1969), who places the greater stress on Erasmus. Condorcet, as we saw in Chapter 2, displayed a fair degree of the humanist touch. The strain is also present in a good many current critiques of modernity.

The capacity to accommodate a variety of existential options is an inherent feature of the Enlightenment tradition. It allows advocates to situate, often with deceptive ease, quite a variety of arguably attractive images of man, all of which can be fiercely defended. This Procrustean quality enables the tradition to be defended as ideally suited, as long as the uncertainties of reality persist and the protection of minority and dissenting voices and positions remain anchored to freedom and democracy (Parker, 1993; Popper, 1992, p. 118). On the other hand, those like Alasdair MacIntyre (1984, 1988; Gergen, 1991) are clearly ill at ease with, among other things, the lack of explicit guidelines for clarity of debates and the resolution of issues for which a variety of "truths" seems to be permitted. This inherent weakness, on these views, leads to confusion in what is really rational and to a lack of specificity on many key moral issues: "The facts of disagreement themselves frequently go unacknowledged, disguised by a rhetoric of consensus" (MacIntyre, 1988, p. 2). Relative to consequent moral dilemmas to result, MacIntyre (1984) makes the point, based on the "conceptual incommensurability of rival arguments," in the following way:

> It is precisely because there is in our society no established way of deciding between these claims that moral argument appears to be necessarily interminable. From our rival conclusions we can argue back to our rival premises; but when we do arrive at our premises, argument ceases and the invocation of one premise against another becomes a matter of pure assertion and counterassertion. (p. 8)

Whether we are faced with mere confusion or a discussion of the rules inimical or congenial to the phenomenon of *difference*, one quickly realizes that we are embroiled in a crisis in which the fate of humanism is at stake.

Shorn of their technical argumentation on justice and rationality, Gergen and MacIntyre are really throwing down a challenge defined and sustained by a sense of community, both interpretations of which are hardly compatible, except in the sense of a revolt against the principles of the Enlightenment. By allowing for a more inclusive definition of what constitutes reality, one that takes cognizance of diverse worldviews, the former is hinting at a humanism in which a particular identity obtains. In Jeffrey Weeks's (1995) words, "Identity [would] become more of a process than a given, offering a choice of beings rather than the truth of ourselves" (p. 31). The self now lives a fragmented existence (Bauman, 1995); it derives meaning from oscillating between "belonging and disorientation" (Vattimo, 1992, p. 10).The process, though speaking in terms of multiples, does not reside in the confusions that abound when a single, unitary definition is pushed into a variety of directions by the huge contradictions aligned to the concept of unitariness. This is the insurmountable problem to which MacIntyre alludes, even though his concern appears less animated by unitariness per se than by the lack of a consistent defining principle that would avoid conceptual confusion and incommensurability. He is definitely in favor of a *telos* that eliminates conflicts about ultimate ends. On the other hand, the humanism implied by Gergen originates from different sites, where the Other(s) extract their legitimacy. The core principle of multinucleated humanism has the conceptual and practical possibilities of accommodating the multiple islets of often zealously guarded particularities—race, gender, ethnicity, class, global egalitarianism—now striving to fit themselves in an agreeable position in the emerging global order. For his part, MacIntyre does speak agreeably of community. The difficulty his agenda faces is that he wishes us to go back to Aristotle or face, for him, the debilitating nihilism of Nietzsche—not the postmodern, those potentially liberating contributions this philosopher makes to the concept of difference. The choice is the "*Ubermensch,* the man who transcends, finds his good nowhere in the social world to date, but only in that in himself which dictates his own new law and his own new table of virtues" (MacIntyre, 1984, p. 257). One of the difficulties with the MacIntyrean agenda is that, according to Brian Barry (1989), the return to Aristotle would be the equivalent of "keeping 'em down on the farm after they've seen Paree" (p. 168). On the other hand, Gergenesque conceptualizations are desperately in pursuit of congenial praxes.

The fortunes of humanism and the Enlightenment, as is well known, are intertwined. The primacy of human dignity, values, and interests—first to surface as an integrated agenda during the Renaissance—is the logical adjunct to Enlightenment principles. Indeed, humanism conflated with timely attempts to define the new Man rising from the thrall of absolutism and disengaging from an undifferentiated world of status (in the sense that Sir Henry Maine uses the term).

Perhaps individualism was this nascent creature's main impetus, but the meaning of the newly emerging humanism, in social, political, and philosophical terms, was ambiguous. Indeed, its ambiguity was equally matched by the pressure to ensure that choices of definition and their actual execution take proper stock of what was at stake for the future of the race. As the Italian ascetic, Pico della Mirandola, poses the dilemma in his *Oration on the Dignity of Man*, "Man is born his own master in all liberty. . . . He can degenerate into a beast or be born anew to become like God" (quoted in Todd, 1971, p. 6). The consequences of this choice appear to be at the heart of the crisis in which the Enlightenment is mired.

The crisis that now threatens modernity originates, largely, in the maturing tensions between two competing approaches to humanism. The first approach, one that is currently under severe attack, may be labeled "rationalistic"; the other, "historicist." It is on the foundation of the first that modernity rests. This emphasis on the rational has a long history whose origins can be discerned during the Renaissance and the Middle Ages. Its reliance on externally derived principles for taking the measure of humanity and in plotting a future from necessity resides in a profound lack of confidence in the human body and its experiences. These frailties, in which a historicist humanism abounds, are rejected. Of course, such frailties were a metaphor for the masses, the populous classes who were "judged to be brutal, dirty, and totally incapable of holding their passions in check so that they could be poured into a civilized mould" (Muchembled, 1988, cited in Bauman, 1993, pp. 23-24).

Should humanism be a subjectively defined set of principles with considerations of self-interest dictating the moral content of human behavior? Generally speaking, the rationalist agrees with the proposition. On the other hand, does humanism inhere in unbreakable and anthropologically imperative bonds with larger forces from which peoples are socially constructed? Is humanism coextensive with the ingredients of social institutions that afford "the necessary context within which we become individuals?" (Bellah, Masden, Sullivan, Swidler, & Tipton, 1992, p. 6). Is it attached, indissolubly, to what Charles Taylor (1989, pp. 4-5) refers to as "inescapable frameworks"? If I understand him correctly, he suggests that there are moral intuitions—powerful and universal—that compel people to act out "a natural susceptibility to feel sympathy for others." This "natural susceptibility" is fortified by a socialization informed by Enlightenment principles that results in a "moral exceptionalism." These are some of the major questions to which the historicist responds in the affirmative.

If comment on the current contortions of humanism has, so far, been largely conceptual, the empirical evidence has become more pronounced. Already, attention has been drawn to the "denaturalizing" of the economy currently undertaken by Fred Block, among others (Chapter 2). Concurrently, a huge offensive has been launched against the long-suspect claims of the ethic of rational self-interest. Many of the research findings in political science, psychology, and economics, among others, announce that notions of the common good are not as diminutive as the rational choice school would have us believe (Frost, 1996; Mansbridge, 1990; Sampson, 1993). This erosion appears to be matched by a recrudescence in communitarianism, offered, in part, to offset the Kantian excesses residing in the notion that right (against the common good and its situation within community) resides within the individual by virtue of his being a moral agent. Indeed, the contemporary philosopher Tom Regan (1991) announces a new declaration based on the eclipse of Descartes: "The malign logic of Descartes's *cogito* is dead. In its place a new declaration is alive: *Ego vivo in civitate, ergo sum* (I live in community, therefore I am)" (p. 3). Reflected in these habits of thought is a rash of new thinking, with such issues as global ethics and international justice forming a crucial part of the mix. Of some prominence is the rise of ecological thought that suggests an ethics rooted in Nature, one that abjures the fact-value dichotomy, inasmuch as the driving force propelling this body of thought is holism and interconnectedness (Chapter 3).

Parenthetically, the ethic of broad moral concern for human beings all over the world is one of the bases of globalism. By itself, it has not been singularly effective. But its limited impact finds responsive allies in the pressures of survivalism and other ethical issues indicated in the previous chapters.

## ❖ The Degrees From Which They Do Ascend

The rationalistic and the historicist approaches are not mutually exclusive. Both are committed in their respective ways to further the ends of individual freedom and justice. But the first approach seeks to do so through principles and methods treating as secondary (and, at times, irrelevant) the empirical content of lived experience. In the case of Hobbes, for example, there is much to suggest that his model of the social contract derives from Euclidean geometry (Forsberg, 1990; Kavka, 1986). And even among his staunchest defenders, the abstractionist nature of his theorizing "grossly oversimplifies political reality" (Kavka, 1986, p. 438). Seemingly on the Hobbesian view, methods derived from abstract first principles function, with the aid of reason, to determine normative behavior. In context, individual rights related to such behavior and the obligations to which they give rise originate in the natural right of self-preservation linked inextricably to "the endeavour for power." Accordingly, all psychological states are derivative from this source: Repentance is the remorse emerging when one's action is frustrated or thwarted; shame is the embarrassment on discovering some self-limitation of defect of personal ability, and so on.[1] For the historicist approach, lived experience constitutes the *terminus a quo,* the starting point from which such determinations must begin. Knowledge and social meaning are socially constructed.

The choice between these two major armatures, around which competing models of world societies have been constructed, takes us more closely to the forces against which globalism is directed. In a world of diverse nations and cultures, the rationalistic strain affects a posture of superiority that creates a network of disabling dichotomies. In turn, superiority and this disabling propensity are the product of a *reason* that its advocates suggest and even assert to be a peculiar European heritage. This reason bids and, more often than not, coerces the rest of the world to accept that truth demands nothing less than a "voluntary exile" on the part of the Other(s). For there is but a single path to human emancipation. As the disciples of the Prince of Peace were commanded to drop their fishing nets and follow, so are the non-European cultures commanded to throw off the burden of their worldviews and follow the Princes of the Enlightenment. The worlds of the Other(s) must be transformed into the world of the Self. The results have scarcely been happy ones, as the account in the previous chapters suggests. In 1949, President Truman declared war on the poverty of the "underdeveloped areas of the world"; in 1960, the metropolitan world was 20 times richer than this hapless lot; by 1980, the world of the Self was 46 times richer than that of the Other(s)!

A particular family of morality and ethics is integral to this posture. I use the term *family* because, as creatures of the Enlightenment, there is much scope for a variety of nuanced renditions to appear.[2] At the same time, it might not be an exaggeration to say that the morality and ethics especially evident in international relations are Hobbesian and Kantian in nature. Already, we have encountered the neo-Hobbesianism of the anarcho-Realists in the previous chapters. Recall, morality has no place in foreign policy. Thus spake George Kennan! For its part, neo-Kantianism is widespread in its appearance. In detail, the current renditions still hold to the a priori nature of rights and the elements that go into ethics and morality. "A purely empirical Philosophy of Right, like the wooden head in the fable of Phaedrus, is a head which may be beautiful, but which unfortunately has no brain" (Kant, cited in Vaughan, 1960, Vol. 2, p. 81). We are left to formulate ethics and morality from the somewhat first principles of Will and Justice; "out of such conceptions as that of the inalienable freedom of the will, and such abstract commands as 'Be just to all mankind' " (Vaughan, 1960, Vol. 2, p. 81). Duties of conduct to others are deduced from abstractions. This has led to a volley of arbitrary conduct, based on rights largely detached from sociality. Interpretation originates in the mind. The mind, in turn, is at the center of a reality where relationships are defined more by calculable self-interest than by any measure of "goodness." This inflection results from "a kind of priority of rationality over goodness" (Putnam, 1994, p. 176). In fact, rationality became the judge of what is good—a value—even though, as Putnam correctly asserts, rationality itself is overburdened by many unexamined cultural myths and prejudices. Indeed, the reader should most certainly recognize Hobbes here, except that, unlike Kant, he starts from the opposite pole, from the lowly passion of self-preservation. Contemporary expressions abound. Take Milton Friedman (1962). He advises business to reject any social responsibility other than to maximize profits, legitimately, for their shareholders. Anything else would profoundly "undermine the foundations of a free society" (p. 133). The "responsibility for the responsibility," to use Bauman's term, now tends to inhere in "putting one's bets on an ethical pattern likely to emerge victorious from the war of expert promises and/or popular ratings" (Bauman, 1995, p. 5).

Today, profound changes abound, influenced by the new realities of the times. *Theories of property,* to take one example, are being pressured into incorporating the existing global novelties of economic interpenetration and ecological interdependence; both phenomena raise intrusive issues relative to the distribution of control and benefit and about social responsibility, with the notion of national communities yielding ground to the idea of a "universal" community (Grunebaum, 1987; Reeve, 1987, 1991). As Andrew Reeve (1991) puts it, correctly, "the 'extension' arises because the external effects are no longer internal to a political community" (p. 112). *Transnational justice* is yet another instance of the new thinking. If "outsiders" were denied moral standing in the prior political and moral philosophies, such patterns of reasoning are now anachronistic. Global distributive justice is now an undeniable fact, as modes of discourse and ideologies shed their impenetrability and the self-sufficiency enticed by the dynamics of the sovereign state. Much of the argumentation related to the new theories of property mentioned above apply here, but, as Onora O'Neill (1991) has shown, the line of theorizing in evidence has a far way to travel.[3] Nonetheless, there is little doubt that the concept has taken on undeniable legitimacy and will find its way into status quo thought as its theories acquire cogency.

Today, the issue of transnational justice and other globally inflected issues such as human rights are not speculative but normative and programmatic. This is so because of the new globalization and interconnectedness in which economic, political, and ideological phenomena of the world's nations are interwoven. In the fight against drugs, poor producing countries, with much to gain from continuing production, join in the efforts to destroy cartels at home (Colombia, for example). Sovereign nations now interfere in the internal workings of their economies to fend off global economic dislocation.[4] The poverty, pollution, and environmental degradation of poor countries have been linked to activities in the major industrial economies, and the list goes on. And yet we are often confronted with truly anachronistic defenses of threadbare models of morality against which the natural ebb and flow of international relations simply revolts.

In short, we are presented with somewhat contrasting social systemic principles on which a global order is to be erected and by which the fortunes of interdependence are to be understood. Indeed both—and this is a source of the dilemma—are defined largely from the vantage point of the status quo—the "A" (Self) versus the "not-A" (Other[s]) framework addressed in earlier chapters. For what socioeconomic development *writ large* really demands, on this view, is the universalization of the "unencumbered" man. What is he?

Unencumbered Man owes much to Lockean notions of the free individual, unconstrained by the tyranny of the sovereign, whether monarch, government, or the majority. It is not a pure type, as traces of Hobbes remain, especially in the form of a system of obligations anchored to self-preservation. This construct is the pivotal point around which the interrelated subsystems of modernity revolve. From Kantian philosophy, it extracts notions of justice that are not partial to a particular definition of the good. The encumbered Man is said to originate in antecedently individuated principles, to use the language fashionable in the current debates (MacIntyre, 1984; Rawls, 1971; Sandel, 1984b). The unencumbered self is "not necessarily unaffected by the communally inspired particularisms, yet capable of cutting himself loose from the communal roots and loyalties" (Bauman, 1993, p. 39). He is supposed to be masterful at maintaining detachment from communal demands and pressures (p. 39).

On this view, the most serviceable world, one presumably reflected in the principles of the Self and the Other(s), should properly be populated by "antecedently individuated" people for whom a strong and productive sense of individualism is a key ingredient. The individual preexists community, for if this were not so, enabling norms such as freedom and justice, which foster an economically creative and productive life (one conducive to self-realization), would be impeded. The "unencumbered" self takes its cues from objective, detached, principles. It is a self "who confronts a separate world of content and produces cognitive, moral, and practical order" (Seidman, 1983, p. 59). In the shadows, Kant instructs that morally we should act according to the maxim that our wills should approximate the principles of universal law. This mind-set finds agreeable the notion that if people—individuals or nations—do not measure up to universally generalizable social rules—rules often expressed in a utilitarian vein—it is quite moral and, indeed, societally responsible to let them fall by the wayside. This mind-set comes in direct descent from notions of the political life of humankind shaped less by actual fact than by fictions about the origin and nature of the state, social contract, and rights. This mind-set forms one of the main theories of international relations—Realist theory—against which the forces of globalism are directed. For among its principles is the firm commandment that a nation should trust no other and be guided only by the rightness of its own national cause (Gurtov, 1988, p. 13). Likewise, it invites the view that rich countries should transfer nothing to poor countries, as such largesse would only promote population growth and overall economic unsustainability (Hardin, 1974). In the spirit of Hobbes, a nation, if it does not have a natural reciprocity in the relations with another, has no *moral* obligation toward the latter. If it acts, nonetheless, it has merely exercised a *prudential* obligation, an option whose display may win praise and approval, but whose avoidance does not justify moral ostracism. In other words, individuals come to live not so much in community as in civil society, where lives are lived in the context of legal relations among strangers; where the individual is bound mainly to rights-based duties that are not obedient to any other definitions, especially, per Kant, his or her duty is to obey the law even though it might clearly be unjust: "In such a case an action of this kind, however dutiful and amiable it may be, has nevertheless no true moral worth" (Kant, 1981, p. 11). Rights are theoretically open to all, but their content is never truly defined; *ergo* a citizen is no less a citizen for embracing white supremacist ideologies than he is for adhering to the principles of racial equality. In the end, sympathy and caring must take their cues from morality as a universal law. In the contemporary context, where Kant's categorical imperative and Adam Smith's "invisible hand" make common cause (i.e., in the realm of rational choice formulations), those cues are to be extracted from market forces. We will leave the forces of supply and demand to determine questions of distributive justice and be guided thereby, irrespective of the consequences. Throughout it all, the watchword is reason, one that has not become a slave to the passions. The stress is on intentions, not results.

The historicist limb of humanism takes objection to the very narrow conceptual and programmatic definitions attributed to reason. It is also unhappy with its ahistoricity. To get a sense of the reason expressed in the opening paragraphs above, we must probe Enlightenment thought to pick up the trail. The path leads us to two huge dissenting figures: Giambattista Vico (1668-1744), whose magnum opus is *Scienza Nuova,* and Montesquieu (1689-1755), whose *Esprit des Lois* is widely considered the precursor to modern social science. Both attacked formulations about society that artificially introduced dichotomies among people and, ultimately, nations, based on fixed, stationary laws. The full force of dissent comes through Vico, who weighed in against such Cartesian edicts by denouncing their abstractions and ahistoricity. He rejected the concept of innate ideas of that tradition, arguing instead that "thought was inherent in all men no matter where and when they were born" (Grimaldi, 1958, p. 1). That thought plays a far more central role. For Hobbes, Locke, and Hume, there is no a priori ethics, but at least in some fashion, human thought operates as a point of reference (although Hobbes often plays havoc with its content, due to his use of rationality). For Vico, human thought and lived experience are central.

Vico also prepared a solid groundwork for the primacy of history in the determination of truth. As the stuff of history was sedulously rejected by the *philosophes* (Descartes's successors) as the basis of truth, non-European thought, which was seen to rest squarely on this bed of unreliability, was discarded as primitive and barbarous (Collingwood, 1969, p. 86). In Vico's work (and in Montesquieu's, too), the stuff of which the primitive and barbarous is supposed to be made is given clear, compelling, and internally consistent expression. Instead of depending mainly on an apodictic application of reason, one in which, thanks to Kant, ethical questions originate and are answered largely from a subjective morality, this approach, broadly speaking, is more anthropological. Moral rules that are so central to an understanding of first-order human and social relations—the individual vis-à-vis other people, the interaction between nations, for example—originated in a culturo-historical context. For Vico, reason, in its comprehensive understanding, is not logic; it is faith and history born of the lived experiences of peoples that precede the ruminations of "academies and philosophers" (Vico, 1744/1984, p. 14). Parenthetically, the reason evolved by Descartes appears as a kind of "situational rationality." The political agenda of the Enlightenment might have induced the belief that its supreme function was to extinguish Other(s): "The Orient is there to enable the Occident, Africa is there to enable Western civilization to fulfill its mission, the woman is there to help man actualize himself in her womb, etc." (Benhabib, 1992, p. 15). But there are prominent reasons why such extinguishment will not occur in accordance with this plan. The Other(s) are not modernity's own presuppositions on the way to fulfillment; they are crucial elements in a more diverse and qualitatively different set of calculations from which reality cannot be separated.

This rebuttal begins life, in some fashion, within the inner logic of rationality itself, both as method and in its epistemological moment. More of this latter aspect will be developed in the context of the historicist perspective below. It should suffice, however, to state that the difficulties inhere in a rationalist approach that comes up against a perspective on social reality that confounds the notion that such a reality is *out there,* preformed, merely to be assembled. Closer to the truth is the linguistically derived epistemology that "we can and do make contact with each other, and with our surroundings, in a whole multitude of *self-constructed ways*" (Shotter, 1993, p. 59). This being the case, it is pointless speaking of knowledge as situated within "well-established, systematic discourses" (p. 59). Even so, established discourses do not foreclose the role of the dialogic dimension. For even though there may be universal rules, it can be offered that "argument and debate is the best way to discover them" (Lash, Szerszynski, & Wynne, 1996, p. 115).

Now let me get to the methodological issue. The cardinal principle here is the often self-expressed notion that reason is inseparable from its intrinsic duty to be self-critical—a point forcefully insisted on by Kant and others. If the rule is sedulously followed, we can immediately identify three major confounding developments. First, applying a rationality of Cartesian bent creates and sustains rather than eliminates the nonmodern in which Other(s) is situated. I sketch the conceptual basis for this proposition in Chapter 2 and address it further in this and subsequent chapters. A telling point in the explanation is that reason infers, indeed commands, that everything be open to criticism, if dogma and like impedimenta are truly excluded from it (Radnitzky & Bartley, 1987, p. 205). Contemporary applications of reason have not been freed of such dogma, hence the revolt of Other(s) whose definitions are caught by a reason more universal than situational in import. Second, reason is not itself above the imperative of critique lying at its core. Especially in its "instrumental" aspect, reason has often sided with the hegemon. Third, a reason that professes to serve a human and social world can only pretend to act neutrally. Reason and its powerful products—science and technology—have no extra-anthropological, no Archimedean, point of reference. Knowledge is linked inevitably to identifiable human interests—interests that are often suffused in power relations. The West (the metropolitan world) and the Other(s)—the latter, consisting, as it does, of subsets defined by the same overarching dichotomizing principles (Nature, women, indigenous peoples, for example)—are locked into new power relations caused by the dynamic interplay of these diverse interests. The interplay is not situated within predefined universes of discourse; rather, it is located within parameters of inequality where the dominant controls the negotiation process. Often it is not so much that the conversational dimension is not engaged; the difficulty lies repeatedly in the quality of the arguments marshaled. This is somewhat akin to the Marxist notion of "false consciousness," where arguments can be animated and sustained but ineffective on account mainly of the suitability of content.

The historicist approach gives priority to historical reason as against quantitative, "situational," reason. This is not to suggest that it excludes the quantitative; rather, it "decenters" it. As is widely known, Cartesian rationality expresses itself mainly as an instrumental form of rationality, one where reason is applied in narrow analytic terms. It is to be regarded as situational in scope. Cartesian perspectivalism is "scopic" in nature (Edgerton, 1976; Metz, 1982, p. 61). For it privileges vision over all the other senses. It is the master sense, one that is exclusionary, to boot! The scopic vision does not acknowledge the many other operations of human intelligence, those that are nonscopic, let alone subjecting them to its analytic method. If it does not fit, leave it out! Herein lies partly the domination and neutralization of the negotiating efforts of the Other(s) that are often scorched but never killed. For the process of negotiation comes to a virtual standstill, if the arguments to be marshaled by one side are denied legitimacy. (But this impasse might be formal only in nature; negotiating positions with powerful undergirdings will find ways to make themselves felt, as we saw in the case of the demise of the Soviet empire.)

The point at issue is hardly that vision is not crucial. After all, seeing is believing; it goes to the core of what constitutes reality. But the structure of reality embodies much more than the vision can communicate. If vision dominates, it preempts the terrain of knowing and understanding, which a scopic vision succeeds in achieving. Its reality becomes institutionalized and defines part of ongoing socialization via the physical and symbolic instruments lying at the heart of its ontological and epistemological "facts." It is small wonder that printing, the telescope, the microscope, and so on are so central to modernity; they are definers of an "ocularcentric" reality, as Martin Jay (1992, p. 178) refers to it. In other words, these devices "[graft] a Euclidean spatial perception onto scientific inquiry" (Fuller, 1991, p. 126)—a perception quite adept at leaving out what does not fit, especially where patterns, situated in an "epistemology of numbers," are not evident.

This regime does not, as Collingwood (1969) suggests of historical enquiry, "put [the] authorities in the witness-box, and by cross-questioning extorts from them information which in their original statements they have withheld" (p. 237). Even in the climate of Kantianism, where *sapere aude* is the watchword, the prospects are poor. Vichian reason, originating mainly in the stuff of history, will not get beyond Kant's barricades, as history is "value" not "fact." The ontological dimensions of language are also kept outside of the barricades. No, a thousand flowers will not bloom!

On the other hand, the historicist approach attempts, in some fashion, to incorporate into the structure of knowledge the defining phenomena from which social meaning is derived (language, poetry, intuition, myths, and so on). The approach does not reject logic and precision in arriving at answers.[5] Rather, it challenges the extent to which they can and should answer the broad, recurring questions of life. Language, poetry, myths, and the like are integral to the morphology of those large questions. Building on the historicist ideas of thinkers like Vico, we now know that these phenomena establish the principles by which human beings are united socially and become aware of their connectivity. For Vico, reason and truth are bound up with lived experience, with expediency, as determined by the interests and interactions of people and by the circumstances in which they are placed. John Shotter (1993), using hermeneutic-constructivist language, put it this way: "Primary human reality is conversational or responsively relational [which situates] one's 'person-world' dimension of interaction or being [within] a whole melee of 'self-other' relationships or dimensions of interaction" (p. 161). (A clear implication here is the undermining of the traditional notions of the individual, complete with his rights anchored to the principles of negative liberty. In its stead is the idea of citizenship in which inclusiveness operates as *positive* agencies in forging consensus.)[6]

Against a Cartesian penchant for spawning dichotomies in the self-other, or A-not-A mode—where, as we saw in the case of Hobbes above, first principles construct the Self—Vico counterposes the empirical picture of "the political life of man, as it shaped itself in actual fact" (Vaughan, 1960, Vol. 1, p. 204). It is a life, not shaped by such abstractions as the individual, rights, and contract, but by experience. These abstractions have their origins in historical processes. The famous dictum of Descartes—*cogito, ergo sum* (I think, therefore I am)—is claimed to be antecedently defined, ahistorically, away from, but related to, community. For Vico, "the mind develops in conformity with the laws of nature, the laws of becoming, its logic; and the thing that produces history is precisely this becoming" (cited in De Santis, 1959, Vol. 2, p. 806). This contrasts vividly with Descartes's and, later,

Newton's principles where, as the late Charles Frankel (1956) states it rather nicely,

> [Reason is] regarded as something static, detached, and timeless, and is set as the goal of human thinking in pursuit of an objective truth from which all the bias and partiality of an historical creature struggling with practical affairs are removed." (p. 122)

Vico's approach departs markedly from the historiography of the philosophes. First, their history—notably in the cases of Hume and Voltaire—does not get beyond the 15th century and Voltaire, in particular, commands that all that deserves to be known are "the genius, the manners and customs of the principal nations, supported by facts" (Voltaire, cited in Seidman, 1983). In turn, Vico places the burden of historical definitions on the "sapienza volgare"—"the wisdom of the crowd"—drawn from the collective sense of peoples, giving particularity to their experiences (De Santis, 1959, Vol. 2, p. 804). It is here that truth is to be found: "As God's truth is what God comes to know as he creates and assembles it, so human truth is what man comes to know as he builds it, shaping it by his actions" (quoted in Anderson, 1992, p. 67).

For his part, Montesquieu, largely through the use of sociological, anthropological, and travel literature, did much to cast doubt on the supremacy of abstractions by showing that different geographical and natural factors lead to different types of cultures, institutions, behaviors, and the like.[7] This feeds rather nicely into Vico's observation that each nation is thereby tied to its own history and a changeable one at that.

Both of the figures, along with others in the Romantic movement, were attempting to effect the required dialectic between logic and rhetoric on which a civilized and humane Enlightenment project should be constructed.[8] Vico systematizes and foreshadows:

> The will of man, by its very nature wavering and uncertain, finds assurance and determination in the common sense which in all matters of man's necessity or convenience—and these are the only two sources of natural Right—is the guide of the whole race. This common sense is a judgment formed entirely without reflection and shared in common with a whole Order, a whole Nation, the whole Race. . . . This common sense of the whole race is the organ of judgment which divine Providence has granted to all nations, so as to make them capable of arriving at certitude in all that concerns the natural Rights of men. And such certitude is attained when men discern the substantial points of agreement in which, despite variations of detail, all nations are at one. (quoted in Vaughan, 1960, Vol. 1, p. 247)

He also strikes a blow for the brand of communitarianism that I indicated earlier as lying at the base of globalism:

> There must in the nature of human institutions be a mental language common to all nations, which uniformly grasps the substance of things feasible in human social life and expresses it with as many diverse modifications as these same things may have diverse aspects. A proof of this is afforded by proverbs or maxims of vulgar wisdom, in which substantially the same meanings find as many diverse expressions as there are nations ancient and modern. (Vico, 1744/1984, p. 67)

In terms of foreshadowing, he lends support to the contemporary struggle of the Other(s). He makes the case inter alia that there can be no single history (*pace* Marx), only accounts of the past presented from diverse viewpoints. To the extent that his account of historical reason consists mainly of the stuff of rhetoric ("Philosophy contemplates reason, whence comes knowledge of the true; philology observes that of which human choice is author, whence comes consciousness of the certain" (Vico, 1744/1984, p. 63), it enables us to understand why the present project of constructing some form of post-Enlightenment science (see the efforts of McCloskey and Brown) draws much inspiration from this source (see Chapter 10).

Although the lines of demarcation are not as distinct, we appear to be in the presence of two types of human end products fashioned by these two types of reason. The distinctions are captured interestingly by Michel Foucault's interpretation of Kant's notion of *mankind* (in Rabinow, 1984, p. 35). In the first type, the Enlightenment could mean "a change affecting what constitutes the humanity of human beings." Here, it appears that the narrow, individualistic notion of mankind is one that begs the question. The other type involves the Enlightenment in a process by which the entire human race is caught: "In that case, we must imagine Enlightenment as a historical change that affects the political and social existence of all people on the face of the earth" (Ranibow, 1984, p. 35).

In the analysis to follow, it will be seen that these two interpretations that are not necessarily separate and apart but diverge mainly in terms of the assumptions with which they begin, have been jostling each other most vigorously since the Enlightenment. I will now turn my attention to a more studied view of Cartesian rationalism that provides our first important point of departure.

## ❖ Notes

1. Hobbes's theory of human nature is termed *psychological egoism,* the doctrine that all human action is motivated by selfishness. Mired in the complex tensions revolving around rights versus

the good, individual versus community, and so on is a specific ethical commandment: "When all motivation is reducible to an interest in self-preservation, then the only reasons for acting in the interests of others will be prudential ones: it will only be rational to serve the interests of others when one stands to increase one's own chances of survival by doing so" (Mathews, 1990, p. 25).

2. This family can be traced from Descartes, through Hobbes, on to Kant. Contemporary versions appear in Rawls (1971), Nozick (1974), and Dworkin (1977) (see Botwinick, 1993, for a good account, especially of the first two). Individuals here are treated as ends, where rights take precedence over the good. The first two are particularly suspicious of the notion of community, in the broad sense, thereby limiting the role of the Other(s). They favor the *public sphere,* the realm of the decontextualized, disencumbered self and think little of the *private sphere* as the locus of definition and meaning. Their application is increasingly problematical, especially the neo-Hobbesian inflection (see George, 1995; Rosenberg, 1994; Walker, 1988).

3. She directs her critique at problems in the two prominent theoretical bases in which the main arguments inhere: the "consequentialist" and the "action-based reasoning." The first focuses on harms and benefits, the latter on moral constraints on action (see O'Neill, 1991, pp. 282-288, for her arguments).

4. Examples in Chapter 3. See also Mastanduno (1993) on the cases of the United States and Japan.

5. The "historicist" position is not the antithesis of the "rationalist" one. Some forms of historical materialism (that of Engels's *The Dialectics of Nature*) can be just as mechanistic and decontextualized as Cartesianism and Kant. A more apt definition is one that grafts Vichian historicism with the social constructivist, hermeneutic approach(es) in which the self is "negotiated." The historicist is also situated within the communitarian realm, itself a mixture of different strains (see Benhabib, 1992, chap. 2; Frazer & Lacey, 1993; Mulhall & Swift, 1992). In any case, it inhabits a sociocultural "space" that many vying to define it will agree represents its logic (i.e., the attempt to situate the self in a network of relations and narratives consistent with its origins and indispensable to its continued existence; as Michael Sandel (1984a) puts it, "We are partly defined by the communities we inhabit, [and] must also be implicated in purposes and ends characteristic of those communities" (p. 5). Forming part of this ethic is a particular type of rationality—"expressive rationality which stands for a universal human concern with understanding the world in which we live" (Heap, 1989, p. 148). This rationality that inheres in a self attentive to diversities of experience and voices, which phenomena then emerge as strategies embodying a variety of "ethics" such as care, solidarity, liberation, and difference—most of which grate against the apodictic reason in which the structure of the "rationalist" self inheres.

6. This inheres in the concept of community. An encouraging version is Sarah Conn's (1990) notion of "individualism within the context of connection," in which "the world is all of a piece, coherent and connected" (p. 166). Alan Wolfe (1989) also calls for a like approach that avoids the market and the state and fixes on "common sense, ordinary emotions, and everyday life" (p. 101) (see also Lasch, 1995, especially chap. 5); for the more dominant factions within feminism, the call is for a communitarian ethics that enables "the *renegotiation* of our psychosexual identities, and their *autonomous reconstitution* by individuals as essential to women's as human liberation" (Benhabib & Cornell, 1987, p. 13; McClure, 1992). The same spirit infuses transnational justice (O'Neill), transnational migration (Barry & Goodin), transnational ethics (Frost), and the international imagination, a main purpose of which is "to educate moral choice by drawing out the real human relations involved—not to replace with philosophical guarantees or technical formulae" (Rosenberg, 1994, p. 105).

7. Examples of the respect for difference abound in Montesquieu (1906), who called for careful distinctions, "lest I should miss the difference of those which appear to be alike" (Vol. 1, p. xliv). On the law of nations, he was quite critical of Hobbes and Grotius. He rejected Hobbes's self-preservation principle, preferring the idea that mankind have a primary motive to live in society; against Grotius, he argued the falsity of a natural law principle that would bestow sovereignty on seeming none but European nations. He offered, with qualifications, that "all

nations have a law of nations, not excepting the Iroquois themselves, though they devour their prisoners" (Montesquieu, 1906, Vol. 1, p. 4). Montesquieu identified four laws governing conquest: (a) the law of nature governing preservation of the species, (b) the law of natural reason commanding that we do unto others as we would have them do unto us, (c) the law that forms political societies, and (d) the law derived from the nature of the thing itself. All these enjoin preservation, not destruction (Montesquieu, 1906, Vol. 1, pp. 144-145). See Pangle (1973), Berlin (1982), and Jones (1994) for excellent accounts.

8. The Romantic movement, while somewhat predisposed to a return to an idyllic age of innocence, indirectly (if not pointedly) supported the claims of difference and the place of rhetoric forms (versus logic) as the basis for understanding social reality (see Cassirer, 1966; Collingwood, 1969; Seidman, 1983). Such branches of environmentalism like deep ecology and ecofeminism find much agreeable in their respect for Nature and its collectivist orientation.

## Chapter Five

# Enlightenment, Rationalism, and the Attack on History

*The philosophical theory underlying [the Enlightenment] is that certain forms of mental activity are primitive forms, destined to perish when mind arrives at maturity.*
R. G. Collingwood (1969, p. 76)

This chapter begins by drawing attention to general features of the Enlightenment, or more pointedly, rationalism. It revisits a number of conceptual issues raised in the previous chapter. The body of thought forming the basis of this chapter is quite huge; consequently, my approach is to select typical Enlightenment concepts and then relate them to the defining parameters of the book.

The analysis is preceded by the prior debunking of certain claims made on behalf of the Scientific Revolution. It is necessary to do so, as a crucial part of the overall strategy is to elucidate how false claims are employed to exclude and marginalize the one, and lionize and make exclusive the other. We are unable to recount the many sins visited on the Other(s) because of an alleged incapacity to think "scientifically." This strategy fits rather snugly into the Enlightenment tradition, itself displaying that mind-set made even more potent and pervasive by its immense success as the destroyer of obsolete thought.

The second segment of the chapter locates rationalism in a historical context. My purpose is to show how its principles were systematically detached from the stuff of lived experience. In his *Discourse on Method,* Descartes reflects glowingly on the clarity of mind that overcame him as he sat enveloped in the agreeable warmth of his room "to converse with myself and my thoughts" (Descartes, 1984, p. 27). In a sense, Descartes's detachment is explicable on other grounds. He was deeply involved in a philosophical engagement with classical philosophy and revealed religion. But these thoughts had a concrete rootedness in the hurly-burly of his times, even though as one who had scant respect for the explanatory force of history, Descartes would scarcely have acknowledged its role in that engagement. Nonetheless, the truth is that Europeans were slitting each others' throats in the name of religion (in certain regions of Germany, as much as 60% of the population perished for these reasons); the middle classes were straining to break the bonds of absolutism, eager to secure their moment to shine; those European nations then forming a charmed circle of privilege were preparing to become the "idols of the tribe"; science was enlisted to create a new world that would turn out to be one of "haves" and "have-nots"; and so on. No, Descartes's thoughts were not situated in a pure, uncorrupted realm, one unmarred by the influence of the social and the historical. The final segment sketches the tension between logocentrism and emotivism that formed a major underpinning for the Self-Other(s) interplay. Let me now turn the focus on the main aspects of the chapter.

The Enlightenment—the basis of a fundamentally Europeanized world-view—is the source of unending research and commentary (Berlin, 1982; Cassirer, 1946, 1953; Gay, 1966; Schapiro, 1963). The constant flurry of intellectual activity it excites results as much from its peculiar features—*freakish* is a term often used—as it does from contentious claims made on its behalf, resulting, in part, from those peculiarities.

The peculiarities are largely two-dimensional. The first is culled from a claim that sets the Enlightenment and its world apart from all previous worlds. The elements of the claim involve the Scientific Revolution, which draws on the Renaissance and, later, the Enlightenment. Is this impressive revolution the product of a single mind-type, the European Mind? Quite preposterously, many variations on the claim exist. We may begin with the claims of the Enlightenment on the subject. For the *philosophes,* history begins with the rise of the scientific spirit informed by rationalism. If that is the case, which seems to be substantiated by a very limited historical vision—the very best of them, Hume and Voltaire, scarcely looked backward beyond the 15th century and the European arena—then we are in the presence of something startling. As the reason of the Enlightenment—"pure reason"—allegedly is unconnected with a past, let alone a non-European past, as "pure reason cannot come into existence out of pure unreason. . . . The sunrise of the scientific spirit . . . was a miracle, unprepared in the previous course of events and uncaused by any cause that could be adequate to such an effect" (Collingwood, 1969, p. 80). Much closer to our time, the distinguished historian, Arnold Toynbee, indicates, for example, that the historical records support the view that Western mechanical mind-set is peculiar. In another context, he volunteers that, for peoples inhabiting lush, bountiful, environments, scientific creativity is superfluous, and that exceptions were mainly "under colonial guidance" (Blaut, 1993, p. 71). Others take refuge in dualism. Thus, Stephen Marglin (Marglin & Marglin, 1996) develops the theory in which the Western mind attaches to science (*episteme*), whereas the non-Western mind is predisposed to technique and art (*techne*"). In his turn, Eric L. Jones (1981) speaks of the "European miracle" set off by what appears to be a peculiar mind-set. Such explicitness is matched by conspicuous silences in the volumes adjudged definitive histories of science and technology. The watchword is that if certain quarters of the world cannot produce science and technology of any sophistication, then one should not go chasing shadows!

Indeed, much that has been presented as original features and inventions of the Scientific Revolution has long existed in China and India: "nothing in the conditions even of Europe in the 16th century justifies thinking of the Scientific Revolution [as being due] at a certain point of maturation" (Graham, 1992, p. 141). The recent, highly regarded research of Steven Shapin (Shapin & Schaffer, 1989; Shapin, 1996) is even more critical of the claim to this revolution. In fact, he states that there was no such thing as the Scientific Revolution. Scientific thinking was based more on confusion, erratic twists and turns, rather than on clarity, certainty, and clearly defined courses of action. In fact, "the discovery of how to discover" emerged from a mix that included Islamic, Greek, Indian, and Chinese sources.[1] Contrary to a widely held belief, Indian philosophy is not predominantly religious, having little to contribute to logic, ethics, and metaphysics. Gautama (circa 400 B.C.) and Kanada (circa 400 B.C.) practiced philosophies with distinct epistemological and logical bases (Vaisesika, in the latter case) before Aristotle (384-322 B.C.) (Raju, 1971). The crucial point is not whether human beings the world over are capable of scientific thought. It is rather the assumptions to which those exercises are anchored and the social, economic, and political ends they serve. This *is* the litmus test.

In richly detailed studies, more information is now being revealed about the sophisticated technologies of Korea (complete with details on astronomy, the measurement of time, meteorology, printing and cartography); of Africa (complete with details on metallurgy, printing, and other contributions); and of the Aztecs, Mayas (Mexico), and the Incas (Peru) (complete with their knowledge of the precise measurements of the calendar, of the cosmic revelations about the earth, their awesome architectural feats, and so on). The list is truly immense.[2] Indeed, the only plausible explanation that has been offered for the rise of modern science is "capitalist profit" (Graham, 1992, p. 154); military superiority appears to lie at the heart of the formula (McNeill, 1967). According to Francis Bacon, the key elements of that formula are gunpowder, the magnet, and printing. All three originated in China. In truth, the records show that contemporaneously with early classical Hellenistic Greece, the Chinese, from 480 B.C. to 200 A.D., had produced "a variety of philosophical systems, complex medical theories, sophisticated mathematics and a technology far in advance of that in the West" (Lloyd, 1992, p. 54).

This greatly abbreviated account serves eminently the purpose of correcting gross inaccuracies and flagrant omissions. Of course, these were not innocent lapses. On balance, they were part and parcel of the twin purposes to privilege the cognitive stock of the European, while debasing that of the Other(s). But this alert serves a far larger purpose than the squaring of the records. It is to assist in preparing Self and Other(s) to walk toward each other across Descartes's Big Ditch. Hegemonic ideologies and spurious counterideologies have been the result of such inaccuracies, as the Self takes on an overblown superiority, while other non-Western cultures, excepting a short list—prominently China and India—tend to wallow in inferiority complexes and become easy prey to metropolitan dependence. The historical truth is that the respect Voltaire grudgingly extended to China and India "[in] awe of their Oriental sagacity" (Gay, 1966, p. 34) is justified for other cultures. Voltaire was deliberately shortsighted, being a prisoner of his times.

The second aspect of its freakishness—more a genuine peculiarity—is reflected in much that distinguishes modernity from other inclusive social formations. Among others, some of its main peculiarities are rationality as the key human organizing principle (Weber, 1968); commodification of social relations (Marx, 1975); progress as a rational strategy and an end in itself (Bury, 1932); the role of the nation-state, by which the world is carved up into anarchic units (Held, 1991); and the play of objective, impersonal, market forces dispassionately ordering human affairs (Friedman, 1962; Smith, 1776/1937). These are but a few of the congenial companions of the increasingly potent and pervasive image of the machine (Gergen, 1991). From modernity's perspective, all the crucial elements and institutions of society must take their cues from the "machinist" regularities displayed by matter and energy. If they both behave in accordance with simple rules, so should our social universe. Machinist thinking is not what is peculiar to the Enlightenment, traces of such thoughts intermingled with the ideas of classical philosophy (Harris, 1954, p. 56). Its peculiarity lies in separating these strains and attempting to erect a universal philosophy exclusively on those principles.

Insofar as the challenges are concerned, one should simply reflect on the responses evoked when a single worldview proclaims itself to be, not merely first among equals—a claim which, as it is, brims with conceit—but as *the* beacon casting light on the path that all humanity must tread: *In arce sitam quis occultabit* (A city set on a hill cannot be hidden). The challenges become even more severe, given that contemporary research has truly put in doubt the lavish claims of exclusivity. They are further intensified by fear, reflected, for example, in Islamic fundamentalism. It is the fear of extinction. For modernity's motto is a constant, captured actually and symbolically in Marx's apt phrase, "all that is solid melts into air." Nonmodernities are quite fearful of such ignominious eclipses. What, then, are the main contours of the system that so abhors the nonmodern and by which he/she is pursued like the Hound of Heaven?

The Enlightenment was distinctive in the way it approached theory and practice. In turn, this approach, which Zygmunt Bauman (1992) describes as "the intellectual model of an orderly universe blended with the ordering bustle of the politicians" (p. xiv), was intimately bound up with the other crucial aspect—the Enlightenment's epistemological exclusivity.

On the first point, Ernst Cassirer (1946) correctly interprets the approach as one in which the formalization and internal consistency of metaphysical and moral systems was overtaken by the practical realities of social life:

> Its whole energy was concentrated upon another point, not so much an energy of thought as of action. "Ideas" were no longer regarded as "abstract ideas." They were forged into weapons for the great political struggle. The question never was whether these weapons were new but whether they were efficient. (pp. 176-177)

Captured here is the shift from revelation to agency, from status to contract, as the new rationalistic principles a la Descartes took significant shape. "Souls" gave way to "forces"; light as divine *lux* became light as *lumen,* with the onset of the mind-matter dualism, one in which mathematical regularities eclipsed all that heretofore passed as knowledge (Edgerton, 1976; Jay, 1992; McMullin,

1978). Souls, to return to that concept, were shaped by mythical thought and superstition, "a strange and uncouth mass of ideas . . . a mere monstrosity," on this view (Cassirer, 1946, p. 182). Anthropomorphic explanations gave way to rationalism as a specific methodology. It was not as though these ideas were a novelty. Mythical and critical thinking had been part of the twofold formula even during the Middle Ages. "Mythos" is inseparable from critical and rational thought, as is viewed in the rational exercises of a Descartes or a Bacon (Daniel, 1990; Kolakowski, 1989). What was strategically crucial for the Enlightenment project paralleled that which was required of the natural law vis-à-vis the law of God, as I stress below: It is to stretch the opposition between critical thought or rationalism and mythical thought in a fashion that implied incompatibilities that were real and irreconcilable.

Underlying these new formulas are principles drawing their very lifeblood from rationalism. The habits of rationalism are intended to protect against the riddles, ambiguities, and confusion that Nature—Man's eternal nemesis—visits on social life. Indeed, the ruthless subjugation of Nature has been one of the first orders of the rationalist/empiricist project (see Chapter 3). The tack rests not so much on exhaustive probings of Nature; E. F. Schumacher correctly states that much of reality was simply abandoned out of the apprehension that all could not be known. To modify this view, it appears at times that members of the school do not think that what is excluded is worth knowing. And to know is to place our faith in numbers, whose magic was supplied by the Pythagoreans and, later, by Plato. Morris Kline (1980) deserves to be quoted fully on the point:

> The Pythagoreans were struck by the fact that phenomena most diverse from a qualitative point of view exhibit identical mathematical properties. Hence mathematical properties must be the essence of these phenomena. More specifically, the Pythagoreans found their essence in number and in numerical relationships. Number was their first principle in their explanation of nature. All objects are made up of elementary particles of matter of "units of existence" in combinations corresponding to the various geometrical figures. . . . [S]ince number is the "essence" of all objects, the explanation of natural phenomena could be achieved only through number. (pp. 11-12)

(Parenthetically, Pythagoras derived his science of numbers from astral mythology. In fact, it has been suggested that Pythagoras was driven more by religion and emotionalism than by any craving for rational explanations; Kirk & Raven, 1957, p. 216.)

For the Cartesian tradition, the stuff of the senses is chaos "out of which a world is to be fashioned and upon which . . . claims of certainty and truth can be made" (Daniel, 1990, p. 76). Man must make conscious choices, if a stable social and political order is desired. And it must be desired, as such is the command of reason. Methodologically, we must reduce phenomena into their simplest elements and, with the aid of these laws, reassemble them into laws having universal validity. Such a result is achieved, as I indicated in the preceding chapter, by the Subject as a rational being standing outside the world of objects and controlling them. The Subject and consciousness are the definers of reality. This process of reduction cannot draw initially or even substantially from lived experience. As I briefly touched on in the preceding chapter and will explore more fully in Chapter 6, the human body was not considered the appropriate locus of truth; it was irretrievably disqualified by its defects. Despite a pervasive Christian view that matter is the creation of God who does nothing in vain, the body was still seen as being defective (McMullin, 1978, p. 20). But if God did nothing in vain, he had clearly posed human beings with a dilemma that tempted explorations where mind and matter come to be viewed in terms of superordination and subordination:

> The human mind is the apparent possession of a finite creature. It seems to be somehow attached to an animal organism with a material body that is one entity among innumerable others in a world of finite things. Yet the mind has a character that seems quite incompatible with these facts of its existence, for there is nothing in the universe that is not at least a possible object of its knowledge, and while, in one sense, it appears to be confined to a single finite entity among a multitude of others, in another sense it claims to be able to possess and comprehend in knowledge the whole of the universe. (Harris, 1954, p. 43)

In a marked sense, man is a demigod who is linked, through commonalities displayed by the mind, to an infinite God. A clear option and pressing temptation is for him to attempt to jump out of his skin, to distance himself from his body. And as the field over which the Mind exerts itself is largely Matter, the body is accordingly placed in the category of all phenomena bearing that label, with its control and subordination, like all that is designated Matter, occurring incontestably. It is a conscious effort to break asunder the dialectical links relating one sphere to the other. There was a drift away from those tendencies, first sketched and magnified by Heraclitus, which attempted to bring the two realms into some semblance of dynamic connectivity: The principle "is that subject and object are, in the end, the same, and the mind knows the world because the world is no more or less than the generation of the mind, as it is itself generated out of the mind" (Harris, 1954, p. 73).

Universal validity necessarily obtained in extramaterial causation. It was fundamentally cognitive and rejected lived experience as the bases of knowledge. Thought preceded all notions of corporeal things and is the most reliable; "since we will doubt whether there are many things in the world, while we already perceive that we think." (cited in Harris, 1954, p. 121). "Motion and sensibility I refer for the most part also to the body, and ascribe nothing that belongs to them to the soul, save only as much as consists in thinking" (cited in Harris, 1954, p. 121). For Descartes, there is Mind (or the thinking soul) and that which is extended, elements from the world of Matter (imagination, sensations, and so on). Mind or soul is the world of consciousness, cognitivity, from which Matter is logically excluded. Matter represents mere extensions of the senses whose unstable natures are not (and cannot be) consistent with truth, as precious little should be placed on our experience of things. Descartes also rejected the sensations and expressions of Matter because they foisted themselves on his consciousness without his assent or cooperation. And just how are we to be assured that ideas are and will remain the product of reason? Descartes appeals to God's identification with the power and purity of the products of the mind. After all, this is the source—the interplay of mind and pure reason—from which God exercises his power over the Universe. Consequently, "God as the most perfect being would not allow intuitions of such ideas to be deceived" (Wallace, Vol. 2, 1974, p. 6). Malebranche implicates God even more directly in the fortunes of rationalism: "Ideas are archetypes in God's mind" (Brodbeck, 1972, p. 9). In his turn, Geulincx (1625-1669) advocates a total independence of Mind from Matter; neither one acted on the other—that is God's doing.

The stance against a central role for lived experience was uncompromising. The principles of validity avoided studiedly human sources of explanation of which history is perhaps their main repository. (Parenthetically, Hobbes, whose influence on contemporary morality has been acknowledged, abandoned history after translating Thucydides; he found a better method in science.) The search for truth must begin as closely as possible with first principles that form the bases for human nature and its essence. It is the only way to discover the abstract and, therefore, impartial principles of justice. On an aside, what passed as history rightly drew the bile and induced the contempt and suspicion of many scholars. Consider Laurance Eachard, who had set himself the task of writing the history of England from the time of its conquest by Julius Caesar. This historian "deems that in an age of refinement like his own, it would ill become him to go rummaging about among a lot of crude monkish records" (Hazard, 1963, p. 33). The animus such flippancy and ineptitude excited during the 16th to the 18th centuries had deeper roots than the suggested lack of dedication implies, for the ahistoricity of geometry and first principles was on the upswing. Nonetheless, it provided the opportune moment for Hobbes to intone that "experience concludeth nothing universally" (*Leviathan*, cited in Wallace, 1974, Vol. 2, p. 19).

Human nature and essence are a priori, resting on the power of pure reason that lies above any possibility of contamination by history and psychology. In fact, Descartes remarked that although he found the reading of history a pleasant diversion, it had nothing to impart to the pursuit of truth. As for psychology and the place that dreams and myths play in that realm, Descartes was contemptuous. Basically, he took refuge in a rule implicit in his famous motto (*cogito, ergo sum*) that nothing or no one can induce him to believe what cannot happen. So, too, were the opinions of the philosophes (Voltaire, Holbach, d'Alembert) whose minds Descartes had irretrievably influenced: These expressions—myths and legends, for example—"were merely obsolete relics of a barbarous past or a mass of obscurantist hocus-pocus" (Berlin, 1982, p. 99). This interpretation contrasts vividly with the historical approach of Vico. From myths, Vico extracts valuable data on the way Graeco-Roman people lived their lives and from which diverse cultures grew. In contemporary Nigeria and Ghana, there are parallels to the Vichian interpretation. In the first country, Bolaji Idowu (1973, pp. 5-6) states clearly that the theological and philosophical thoughts of the Yoruba people are given vitality and meaning by Odu myths. In the case of the Akan in Ghana, the noted philosopher Kwame Gyekye (1987) draws much of the materials to ground its philosophy from myths as the basis for abstract thought. This approach tends to keep intact what R. D. Laing finds missing from Descartes and Galileo—"sight, sound, taste, touch and smell and along with them have since gone esthetic and ethical sensibility, values, quality, consciousness, spirit" (cited in Capra, 1996, p. 19).

For the rationalist, generally speaking, there is intrinsic to the process of knowledge "an apodictic certainty; that is to say, absolute necessity, not based on experience, and consequently a pure knowledge" (Kant, cited in Cassirer, 1966, p. 23). This framework facilitates a *logical* as distinct from a *historical* characterization of man, then establishes, through deduction, all the necessary properties of this abstract, unencumbered Man. There was a specificity and symmetry to the affairs of unencumbered man, exemplified by Spinoza, whose approach to any question—mathematical or historical, religious or lay—nearly always concludes with the Pythagorean *quod erat demonstrandum* (which was to be proved). (His major work on morality is titled *Ethics Demonstrated in Geometrical Order.*) Likewise, the philosophes became infatuated with the idea of the social world as a a machine: Helvetius, for example, volunteered that one should solve moral problems via the approach of experimental physics; as Spinoza suggests, "what is the best government for men is in principle discoverable by anyone, anywhere, in any circumstances" (Berlin, 1982, p. 87). The high-water mark was probably reached with Kant's *categorical imperatives*, the wellsprings of apodictic reason. In sum, the a priori principles supporting reason command that experience is posterior to a knowledge of reality that is earlier apprehended in the mind. These a priori principles of knowledge do not inhere in sense data; they structure our experiences. The snow exists in our minds before we actually visualize it on the slope. If the forthright declaration of the geometricization of human behavior and affairs is somewhat muted in our time, it was hale and well up to the 1950s. In fact, Bertrand Russell (1956) speculated about human behavior conforming to the precision of "the mathematics of the machine" (p. 142).

R. G. Collingwood's (1969) reflection—expressed in the epigraph appearing at the beginning of this chapter—draws our attention to the epistemological exclusiveness of the tradition. For while much is made of the autonomy of the individual, a pluralist approach to interpreting social life is pointedly outruled. Ernest Gellner (1992) states the position with his usual candor:

> What Descartes and his successors said, in effect, was that there are an awful lot of meanings and opinions about, that they cannot all be right, and that we'd better find, and justify, a yardstick which will sort out the sheep from the goats. For Descartes, the yardstick involved the exclusive use of *clear and distinct* meanings, so clear and distinct as to impose their authority on all minds sober and determined enough to heed them, irrespective of their culture. The path to truth lay through voluntary cultural exile. (p. 38)

This exclusivity gives rise, naturally, to patterns of stratification as well as to hierarchies, both of which are influenced and conditioned by power relations. It is best that we get a glimpse of the underlying conditions that are so often obscured by internally consistent concepts and the symmetries of universal harmonies. Marx's caveat that one make the crucial distinctions between essence and appearance is well taken.

## ❖ Rationalism and Its Historical Context

Epistemological exclusivity merely expresses a *part* for the whole. In general terms, this exclusivity resides in what I have designated "logocentrism versus emotivism," to be discussed in the next segment of this chapter. But before proceeding with that discussion, let me provide a badly needed historical context. Indeed, the *whole* of which epistemological exclusivity forms a part is situated squarely in the rise of modernity and capitalism. The account provided below is not chronologically ordered and thematically exhaustive; in fact, many related themes will appear in the next chapter. It is to provide a suitably coherent orbit of discourse linking historical and experiential forms of lived experience to rationalism.

First, the insistence that there is but one way to discover how to discover (i.e., *the* scientific method) was primarily about the replacement of religion as the force that defined the world. It was religion that fueled the Thirty Years' War—a debilitating carnage that convinced the thinkers of the day of the urgency of such a course. As the ideas and insights of the rationalists (Descartes) and the naturalists (Grotius, Hobbes, Pufendorf) have shown, the task at hand was to marginalize religion in order to eclipse absolutism and promote individual agency (Schlatter, 1951, chap. 6).

The process of displacement was understandably complex and plagued by contradictions. Indeed, this was so because of what was inherent in the task of neutralizing religion. In fact, much that represented the essence of natural law appeared as a twofold phenomenon during the Middle Ages. The difficulty arose in separating the law of God from the law of Nature "in the no less evident tendency to stretch their opposition; and then in an attempt to reconcile the two, which of itself implied the rift was a real one" (Hazard, 1963, p. 271). It was a risky undertaking, as the fates of Giordano Bruno and Galileo clearly testify. These complexities were also compounded by the forces within the historical conjuncture. In truth, the imperative to abandon, displace, or construct social theories went beyond the relatively narrow injunctions of the Thirty Years' War. The perennial conflicts between Catholics and Protestants were now ensnared in a web of synergistic forces. At one level was the secularization of religion—the natural law—which was to prepare the ground for the emancipation of the individual; its point of greatest deviation from classical religious tenets was the severance of morality and ethics from narrow religious hegemony. The ensuing movement from dogma to reason introduced a freedom that was, nonetheless, problematical, as reason conjured up, as I showed in Chapter 2, a variety of definitional nuances for the grounding of a new ethics, morality, and conception of Man.

At another level, natural law tenets began to provide legitimacy for the principle of utility. That principle is prominently enshrined in the ideas and insights of Sir Francis Bacon: The duty that human ingenuity must now assume is to provide material bounty from the storehouse of Nature. In the hands of Hobbes, the selfish and rational-choice dimensions of utility appear as a fleshing out of materialism; festooned with the trappings of egoism, the individual was set on the course of self-satisfying morality to become "the calculator of his own interests" (MacPherson, 1962, p. 2).

At a more complex level at which many of the preceding ideas became integrated, the secularization principle nurtured by natural law and the force that would so successfully support Baconian utility—science and technology—ushered in a new era dominated by the principles of Political Economy. It is in this context that colonialism and, later, imperialism are to be understood. For the "discovery" of new lands now became sine qua non to Bacon's marriage between science and materialism. Here natural law was to contribute handily to the doctrine of *territorium nullius,* as labor productivity became the dominant means of increasing social surplus, indeed, the raison d'etre of the capitalist system. Locke used the doctrine to good effect in his *The Second Treatise of Government,* thus justifying European settlers' acquisition of Other(s)' lands. His labor theory of value, in which the doctrine is encased, is rather a clever way of perpetuating this heinous species of theft. His notion that labor contributes the lion's share ("ninety-nine hundredths" of the *use value* of things) and Nature the rest gets translated into the principle that any land that was not so reduced is territorium nullius. Land would, then, yield proprietary rights to those who so transformed it and there could not be prior "ownership" outside of these parameters, wherever that land might be and whoever traipsed across it and even had their being on it. Thus, labor, in the state of nature, gave a right to property. The implications of the concept for dependence are analyzed in the next chapter.

Topping it all off, and rather intricately interwoven into the concepts, principles, and justifications of the new order are claims for grounding Europeans as the new *idols of the tribe.* As historical accounts show, the successive dominations, to which different segments of the human race have been subjected, have scarcely been accomplished without some claims of authority from some power from the Ethereal Realms. Europeans were no different. But their brand of narcissism, for which rationalism formed the armature, had to integrate and synthesize all of the major new elements required by the new paradigm. Accordingly, it became qualitatively different, more widespread in its application but very narrow in conception, as a new mode of production began to take shape. Rationalism and its subsequent refinements after Descartes were required to reconstitute the theory and practice of race, institutionalize domination around the principle of the negated double, and so on partly to meet the requirements of the modern project. Let me focus on these dynamics.

We know from history—from Herodotus through to Toynbee and beyond—that this privileged status is as old as the hills. Vico (1744/1984) refers to this passion as "the conceit of nations" and points chidingly to the part played by their scholars "who will have it that what they know is as old as the world" (p. 61). This passion, with which rationalism is implicated, extracts its peculiarity from contrasting logics of domination. The Sumero-Akkadian and Indus civilizations (circa 1730-1250 B.C.) were not exempt from the pursuit of conquest, but xenophobia appeared to have dampened any enthusiasm for occupation and hegemony (Toynbee, 1976, p. 75). Likewise, up to the 13th century, conquerors and "discoverers" would take the usual bounty (precious metals, spices, and so on) but were not generally given to destroying or transforming other peoples' cultures (Abu-Lughod, 1989).[3] We noted in Chapter 2 that hegemonic internationalism, whose roots are being sketched here, exercised destruction and alteration as part of its civilizing mission. But Europe's thinly disguised task was to situate its new tribal claims in fresh, epochally appropriate contexts: Freedom, liberty, private property, and the like must now integrate, say, race and a socially constructed deformity—the negated double—into agreeable formulas by which, at least, theoretically, the inferior and the deformed can be rehabilitated. Those formulas are mainly of a piece with Progress, the grand narrative of modernity.

The consequences occupied huge spaces between the principles embodied in a new species of utterance and the realities of performance. New claims to be the Chosen of God were contradictorily bound up with a truly extraordinary synthesis of science—to which the soon-to-be Chosen laid exclusive claim erroneously—and a new mode of production appropriating precious metals and forced labor from other people's lands (Blaut, 1993; Hobsbawm, 1975), based, in part, on their alleged nonhumanity (Genovese, 1965; Williams, 1966) and, ultimately, their underdevelopment (Amin, 1976; Frank, 1968; Rodney, 1972). The interpenetration of these two forces brought profits and principle into irreconcilable conflict. In sum, the emerging order was rearranging old private vices into new public virtues. The institutionalization of private property, for example, legitimized the old private vice of greed via the joint stock companies; racism was the translation of the private vice of ethnocentrism and xenophobia into the public virtue of racial superiority, linked to the salvation of the feckless and the misbegotten. Involved here is that custodial function, the assumption of God's duty, which the Enlightenment arrogated to itself with His incremental, but inevitable, death (Chapter 2).

The pressures to install a system to justify a new regime of domination clearly resulted from the interplay between a nonrational constant (i.e., the stuff of our eternal narcissism)—a seeming admixture of ethnocentrism and xenophobia—and reason, as the epitome of fairness and justice. In a very real sense, what Enlightenment reason entails is an inversion of the old patterns of domination. Previously, it was the nonrational constant that dictated. Paul Feyerabend (1987) captures its expression rather well: "There is no argument; there is no attempt to understand; the form of life that has the power imposes its rule and eliminates behavior contrary to it" (p. 25).

Now, reason was assuming (or was expected to assume) a consistent coordination of theory and practice. Its principal charge was to outlaw or mitigate the corrosive tradition of the nonrational and its usual consequences (barbarism, the reign of force, and tyrannies of all kinds). In time, it would just not do to proclaim, as the Sun King (Louis XIV) did, that *l'état c'est moi.* Reason, as cause and effect, which, according to Orlando Patterson (1991), added the peculiar human right—freedom—was, along with a broadening democracy, creating a generalized, universal normative code. For, at bottom, the import of democracy and freedom is really to prepare the stage for minoritarian challenges and diverse views, based, mainly, on the constructive application of reason.

Reason was to impose its own constraint on its savants. But the results were not always satisfactory. Primarily, its limited interpretation contributed to growing difficulties. The stark truth was that reason could not be confined to the mind supposedly detached from lived experience. A more expansive reality exists outside of, but connected to, this sphere, one whose laws cannot be prescribed a priori *in toto.* Next, the supreme rationalists were proving themselves to being anything but machines. Wisdom found it difficult to disengage itself from ideology, from power. Indeed, we may, again, repair to the explanations of Pierre Bourdieu. Think of the case of the exquisitely civilized John Stuart Mill. Grasp the gist of the present statement: "The sacred duties which civilized nations owe to the independence and nationality of each other, are not binding toward those to whom nationality and independence are certain evil, or, at best a questionable good" (Mill, 1875, pp. 167-168). Why should such a broad and embracing humanism not extend to all members of the human race? Is this not the identical reasoning used by the discoverers to appropriate the lands of other peoples—precepts of which flourish in Grotian international law? Much has to do with the "collective unconscious" often directed against forces such as reason. In the case of the interface of power and reason, think of Locke and Grotius. The first was in the employ of Lord Shaftesbury of imperialist inclinations; the latter was a diplomat in Sweden who also represented the interests of the Dutch East India Company (1613). In both cases, there exist interesting contradictions. There is much currying of favor here; we are especially familiar with Locke's stance on private property and slavery. But there were distinct antitheses in both cases. Grotius's work was to have the principal effect of serving the interests of the ascendant middle classes against absolutism; the larger impact of Locke's work resides, perhaps, in his contributions to liberal-democratic principles. Reason would appear to have won the day. Grotius's employment as well as Locke's would merely confirm the proposition that men, including themselves, are not the machines their own systems would have them to be. The most profound decisions on questions of great import, such as justice, are often taken in a social context, usually institutional contexts, not individually, as Mary Douglas (1986, p. 124) insists. The examples of Grotius and Locke clearly depict reason's appropriate bounds extending beyond the individual. It cannot be acceptable to justify such potential for mischief intrinsic to Grotius's or Locke's dual role on the basis of self-interest or self-preservation, or the disjuncture between word and deed, which prompted Kant to state that the philosophes did not live in an enlightened world but rather in the Age of Enlightenment. Yet the broader conception of reason, to which I refer, does install canons by which the employment of a Grotius may be rationally assessed. It could be done, via the expedient of establishing rules that make clear those behaviors likely to result in a conflict of interests. Such a regime presupposes, at least in principle, an equal forum for the "haves" and the "have-nots." But alas, *l'état c'est moi!*

If the application of reason was to be so narrow, reason did become a victim of its own diverse nature. Because it is expressible in many forms—at times working quite diligently at cross purposes, as one detects in the conflict between substantive reason and instrumental reason—confusion abounds. Reason became prone to a form of relativized selectivity, due to the absence of suitable ethical definitions. What slipped or were pushed from the definitional orbit of social knowledge were the irrational and the nonrational—two measures that were to figure so prominently in the metropolitan grounding of dependence. These phenomena often represent the reality existing outside of the narrow, apodictic reason of Cartesian and Kantian derivation.

And so to ground a European intellectual originality and superiority, an elaborate ruse was fabricated to show a lack of continuity between the so-called inferior peoples (who are the carriers of nonapodictic reason)—Egyptians, Africans, Jews—and a Greek-centered civilization from which the superiority of the European Mind springs. The ruse was to illustrate as well that the Scientific Revolution was the logical extension of this peculiar mind-set. In effect, the nonrational—namely, the compulsion to be idols of the tribe—now became the core of a rational project in which science and reason served biased ends.

In both cases, the centerpiece is race. The distinctiveness of people by now had taken on biological connotation, clearly different in implication from the earlier Jewish approach or the environmental explanation associated with the Greeks (Appiah, 1992, pp. 12-13; Snowden, 1970). There is no mistaking the often huge animus stirred up when the differences of people confront each other. It is a matter of common knowledge that Aristotle looked askance at any culture that was not Greek—indeed, he had a most unflattering comment on England—but "it was a feeling qualified by the very real respect many Greek writers had for foreign cultures, particularly those of Egypt, Phoenicia, and Mesopotamia" (Bernal, 1987, p. 28). Then perspectives began to change. Rationality assumed new guises, but the force of its much larger project could be detected. Take the issue of race. Thinkers like Leibniz, Locke, Hume, and Hegel, among others—many of them shining stars of the Enlightenment—did support some form of polygenesis. There is not, the argument went, a single race but several different biological species, with their colors arranged in descending order from white to black. In the United States, a certain Lord Monboddo, seemed, sometime between 1700 and 1755, to have provided "scientific" proof of black people's descent from orangutans: He appeared to have brought an eyewitness's knowledge of black African females copulating with apes (Jordan, 1974, p. 106).

It is not clear whether the plethora of disabilities visited on the lowly is fixed, variable, or transitional. Interesting and encouraging ambiguities are, however, on display. There are indications (in the cases of Hume, Hegel, and Jefferson, for example) that the reason to which they were so passionately committed did subject their racism to certain ambiguities. Take, for instance, Hegel in a quote from *Lectures on the Philosophy of World History.* What appears to be at work here parallels the contradictions mentioned earlier in the cases of Grotius and Locke. If the emotional side of Hegel displayed racism, his devotion to reason compelled him to oversee its application dispassionately (although one finds unequivocally racist statements occasionally). In other words, if Hegel and other prominent savants of reason expressed racist sentiments against peoples of color, such expressions were not necessarily a feature of reason.[4] Below are Hegel's observations:

> The characteristic feature of the negroes is that their consciousness has not yet reached an awareness of any substantial subjectivity—for example, of God or the law—in which the will of man could participate and in which he could become aware of his own being. The African, in his undifferentiated and concentrated unity, has not yet succeeded in making this distinction between himself as an individual and his essential universality, so that he knows nothing of an absolute being which is other and higher than his own self.[5]

Of course, these Hegelian formulations have spawned a rash of theories, notably those advanced by Lucien Levy-Bruhl (1949)—namely, that the African mind exists in a "prelogical" realm. This sphere is juxtaposed to a "logical" realm occupied by the modern, European Mind. The mystical undergirding of the prelogical realm does not allow its user to comprehend and manipulate the niceties of reason's favorite child, logic. Indeed, these formulations, along with like notions of Hegel, have been roundly criticized for their logocentrism (see Appiah, 1992; Masolo, 1994; Outlaw, 1991), but that is hardly the point here (important, as it is). In truth, what Hegel seems to infer is that there are no inherent barriers to the black man's also appropriating a Europeanized notion of Reason. It is clear, as Masolo argues, that, for Hegel, Africa has lacked the civilizing ingredient, but this deficiency is not fatal, as its peoples can be led along enlightened paths. Perceived inferiority does not appear to be biological but cultural. His studied application of reason appears to foreclose any *rational* identification with theories of racism. On this reconstructed account, reason is not the monopoly of the superior race. But while seemingly abolishing the cognitive inferiority that is perhaps the hardest pill for the victim to swallow, are we not facing the dynamics of the negated double here?

Indeed, we are really witnesses to two main orders of discrimination, the one more deadly than the other. The first, purporting that the African mind is capable of the niceties of reason but only if it is inserted into favorable milieux (read, European). This first version is still with us, as Richard Hernnstein and Charles Murray's (1994) *The Bell Curve* attests. One of its central theses is that cognitive performance is positively correlated with race, with whites being cognitively superior to blacks. But its fate is proving to be identical to that of the suspect claims advanced on behalf of the Scientific Revolution.[6] The second version is the message showcased by modernization theory. An adjunct of this thesis is the saga of the "white man's burden" that Carlyle and Kipling accepted as part of the custodial function incident to the responsibilities of modernity (Chapter 2). Profoundly implicated here is a civilizing process, where the "mother surrogate" bends the "child" to rectitude of thought, word, and deed. In truth, the child is capable of sophisticated thought; it has merely wandered on to the wrong side of the tracks, or, perhaps, it was born there, but in any case, it can be rehabilitated. Nonetheless, it appears to be the experience that for the Other(s), metropolitan cultural criteria rapidly become unattainable, as the rules of the game were often unilaterally and arbitrarily made and changed.[7]

The translation of difference or inferiority took a curious turn. From as far back as Pliny the Elder (23-79 A.D.) and earlier, a taint of mystery has followed the "monstrous races" among whom peoples of color are significantly represented. More an expression of mythological excesses than an exercise in fact (although returning sailors were notoriously fond of peddling inaccurate tales about exotic lands), Pliny would use the grotesque to describe these races: hairy and horned, with lips ample enough to serve as umbrellas when it rained; Amazons amputating their right breasts to facilitate their use of the bow and arrow; Libyans whose heads were situated in their chests; females of five years of age giving birth, and so, *ridiculously*, on.

But for all their flights into the grotesque, Pliny and the premoderns, generally speaking, did not categorize people into races. They had certainly provided "models that modern racism would assume and transform according to its own lights" (Goldberg, 1994, p. 23), but there was no thinking of people in explicit racial terms. Those models were aided, in part, by an explorer of some distinction who reported during the 16th century to have seen Pliny's people in Africa or Lord Mondobbo, who, two centuries later, helped to create a race based on the mating habits of apes and African women. In larger part, much of the impetus for model building came earlier with rationalism's passion for apodictic reason: first, with Newton and the social extrapolations to which his laws of the universe would be put (Chapter 6); second, with the passion of the encyclopedists whose penchant for neat classification was a spur to the establishment and consolidation of hierarchies (Bury, 1932; Draper, 1904) and like classifications in biology and botany by Linnaeus, "one of the greatest scientific triumphs of the class concept" (Cassirer, 1966, p. 124); third, with linking the alleged inferiority of non-European peoples with an alleged noncognitivity of Matter that attaches to bodily emanations such as sex, emotions, love, and so on.

While the reasons for racism did collectively entrench it during the 18th century, the third reason given above was perhaps the most effective. In the 13th century, the Franciscan monk Giacomino di Verona could present the case against the human body with a vehemence from which the more secular and rational view of a Descartes would benefit:

> But if you have a bit of sense, you will know
> That the fragile body in which you lived,
> Where you were tormented eight months and more,
> Was made of rotting and corrupt excrement. . . .
> You came out through a foul passage
> And you fell into the world, poor and naked. . . .
> Other creatures have some use . . .
>
> (cited in Stannard, 1992, p. 159)

Influential rationalists and other Enlightenment figures, with a few exceptions like Condorcet, adopted the spirit of di Verona's "antibody" perspective but chose the more secular and scientific characterizations. The concept of the *Savage Man* was eminently serviceable: violent, sex-driven, subhuman, the Other(s) (Goldberg, 1994, pp. 23-26; see Mudimbe, 1994, pp. 5-15). They would hardly have recourse to di Verona's sentiments, expressed above. Instead, we witness a transposition of sexual license, absence of morality, and a host of other negatives, including those attached to love: "It is the sublime idea we are apt to form of it. But to speak the truth, love, considered as a passion, is nothing but blind instinct that one must know how to appreciate properly" (extracted from Graves's *Symptoms of Love,* cited in Gergen, 1991, p. 29).

It was mainly in this context that Hume proclaimed black people's lack of any evidence of practical and intellectual distinction. In a major essay, "Of National Characters" (1748), he could not bring himself to accept the intellectual accomplishments of the black Jamaican poet Francis Williams, who wrote splendid verse in Latin. Rather than accepting the stubborn fact of black cognitivity, he took refuge in an avarian metaphor: "'Tis likely he is admired for very slender accomplishments, like a parrot who speaks a few words plainly" (cited in Gates, 1992, p. 60).The venerable Kant even forged color and "stupidity" into "a strictly causal relation," based on nothing more than the rehashed, ill-considered pronouncements of Hume (Goldberg, 1994, p. 32)—ill-considered because more measured conclusions could clearly be derived from widely available data and methods of evaluation that counted Hume and Kant among their high priests (Bernal, 1987, chap. 5).

Of course, the historical inaccuracies from which such mischief derives have been systematically undermined. Many scholars such as George M. James (1954), Anta Diop (1974), and, notably, Martin Bernal (1987) have done much to put in disrepute the alleged correlation by showing that the Greeks did borrow from Egyptians and Africans. What is more, they did acknowledge their intellectual debts to Africans—a point that is conveniently excluded from historical accounts on which many of these theories depend: that Danaos, the black Egyptian, was instrumental in founding Greek society; that Copernicus did, in all probability, derive his model of planetary motion from the Egyptians. So, the key ingredient that, by European definitions, gives status to peoples—the cognitive component—was present among the "inferior" and formed the direct basis for what was later to be trumpeted, falsely, as a European peculiarity.

When we get to the British conquest of Egypt in the late 19th century, the genealogy is practically expunged. Now, the Egyptians are children, *in statu pupillari,* recipients of Europe's civilizing legacies. In the considered opinion of the colonizers (Lord Cromer, for example), Egyptians were childlike, lacking in the niceties of reason, gullible, and deceitful (see Said, 1978, chap. 1). In the case of India, Lord Macaulay, during the same century, remarked scornfully that all the books written in the Sanskrit language were of less value than those to be found in libraries of any preparatory school in England.

And yet such has been the historical nature of vying for leadership of the human race(s). Indeed, even when the Greeks were situated at the center of European civilization, their bona fides were also called into question. Listen to Bacon (1994), after he has roundly accused Greek learning of being disputatious—a quality inimical to the search of truth—and comparatively childlike. (The notion of "childlike" is particularly significant, because it brings into play the custodial function of "mother"): "Certainly they are like children: they chatter readily, but cannot procreate. Their wisdom appears full of words but is barren in works. Thus, the signs we get from the fount and birthplace of present-day philosophy are not good" (Aphorism 72). These strictures were reserved mainly for those thinkers, excluding strict logicians such as Leucippus and Democritus (but not Pythagoras), whose thinking included superstition, myths, and those ingredients the rationalists find so abhorrent.

This brings me to the end of a rather abbreviated sweep across a wide expanse of history and thought. It is this general picture that should be kept in the background as we discuss the expansive role of rationalism in its formative period. Truth determined mainly from abstractions usually results in concepts that, dangerously, take on lives of their own. In fact, concepts were more than responding to the principles of logic. They were, and had to be, extracted from lived experience; in turn, lived experience should hardly be the source for selective use in substantiating a priori first principles. Snippets from Vico in the earlier chapter allude to this fact. In the end, these concepts are hard-pressed in supporting the proposition that the truth they purport to convey rises above the stuff of lived human experience. What follows brings us into contact with the marginalization of other "truths" often heavily dependent on the lineaments of Matter.

## ❖ Logocentrism Versus Emotivism

In his much-heralded book, *The European Mind,* Paul Hazard provides us with a snippet of a fateful encounter between the champions of two competing philosophies that would have a direct and an indirect bearing on the role of logic and emotions as the foundation of the new social order to rise from the ashes of the Thirty Years' War. Cartesianism confronted the quaint Epicureanism of Pierre Gassendi, by now "pinchbeck and threadbare" (Hazard, 1963, p. 128). To begin the debate, the redoubtable Gassendi proclaims, "O *mens!* O spirit pure and immaterial!" "Say rather, I beg you, O flesh!" countered the pugnacious Descartes (Hazard, 1963, p. 120). Of course, Descartes's reference to the flesh was principally as the material locus in which the mind resided!

So much of contrast is captured in this anecdote. In its broader interpretation two Ages stood face to face: the Age of Faith and the Age of Reason. Gassendi and his now quaint philosophy would be rebuffed ("Gassendi got the worst of the encounter"), as the reign of reason was installed. What is captured here is the encounter between logic and emotion as foundational bases for society. For one thing, Gassendi and the Epicureans were prone to surrendering the human enterprise to chance. The rationalists and their heirs would have none of it. There is no doubt or error in geometry!

Within the narrow definitional context of epistemology, critiques and contentions take place in a clearly defined orbit, first mapped out by Descartes, then sedulously built on by Locke and a diverse but paradigmatically faithful exegetes. This school of epistemological innovators counted in their numbers the skeptical David Hume, who found Cartesian cause-and-effect relationships unacceptable, a Diderot whose strongly religious temper was not taken as being at odds with the largely implacable anticlerical Deism of the philosophes. In other words, we may say that the Enlightenment was fed by thoughts from different though connected reservoirs. Cartesian rationalism, with its stress on the innateness of ideas, together with Lockean empiricism, for which the secrets of the world are revealed through the physical senses, formed the synthesis providing *the* method for discovering how to discover. Reason, on the one hand, and observation, on the other, crafted the exclusive framework for solving social problems. Residing here is the kernel that Richard Rorty (1989) refers to as "a permanent framework for inquiry" (p. 380) for all times, one in which the alterity of other cultures would be subsumed or relegated to an inferior status.

Patterns of stratification and hierarchies *between* social systems do also result from this exclusivity. Well-grounded systems of thought and action that stood other cultures in very good stead were treated as epistemological lepers. As E. F. Schumacher (1977) observes of that process, the rationalist methodological injunction is, "If in doubt, leave it out" (p. 3). As Descartes directs, if "intuitive cognition," the measure of truth, is blocked in an inquiry, we must stop forthwith and "spare ourselves superfluous labor" (cited in Schumacher, 1977, p. 9). Philosophical systems based on faith and revelation were "supplanted by a religion of reason whose only aim is to know what there is" (Aiken, 1984, p. 23). These are the systems that Locke modestly speaks of as the "underbrush" that should be cleared away. Pushed aside and systematically marginalized were the richly contextualized spheres of history and poetry. Reflections on the detailed circumstances of the human condition—its lived dimensions—were contemptuously brushed aside. To the mind of the philosophe, "the clergy, old wives and folk proverbs [were] responsible for the lamentable state of popular habits" (Bauman, 1992, p. 9); the first reeks of faith and revelation; the second suffers from those crippling deficiencies that women ("unfinished men," "walking wombs") negatively inflict on the project of emancipation, as manifestations of the world of emotions, of Matter. And the third inhere in the hocus-pocus of history, culture, and the universe of "value."

The point is supported by several comments, principles, and observations of prominent Enlightenment figures. Thus, Voltaire, with his penchant for viperous utterances, made a mockery of the fact that in one German township the law is one thing, and, indeed, quite another in a neighboring township. The abuse was clearly intended to stress the absence of certainty that rationalism would provide; likewise, such raillery embodied a dualism defined by the principles of superordination and subordination. Another point of no small significance involve the question of language. So as to remove the influence of historical context on the individual—it supplies the impedimenta of culture, imagination, and the stuff of myth—Voltaire and, moreso, Leibniz worked vigorously to create a universal language to bear witness exclusively to the two axioms of the supremacy of reason and the invariability of the laws of nature.[8] From the Cartesian perspective, to which the support of d'Alembert and Condorcet are added, words "designate" and are "the signs which provide the representations of reality that exist only objectively" (Garver & Lee, 1994, p. 63). Another factor, too stubborn to be disdainfully brushed aside, was religion. A number of philosophes, Helvetius prominently placed among them, felt that it, like language, could be reduced to the principles of geometry and made a matter of objective demonstration. The Scotist, Papist, Calvinist, and Jansenist are sects whose functioning is inseparable from "doubt and error." "There are no sects in geometry" (Voltaire, 1924, cited in Manuel, 1982, p. 24).

What accounts for this totalitarian approach to the general scheme of things? Was it, primarily, the inviolability of the method? From the perspective of the Enlightenment, such attempts at disembodiment can be attributed to a couple of causes. The first is that reality itself is doubted. The seeds of the doubt, a schizophrenia even, are reflected in Errol Harris's insightful quote cited earlier. If man chooses to compete with God for the control of the Mind, of ideas emanating from "pure" reason, then doubt and schizophrenia are predictable. Recall the earlier observation relative to Turgot's detachment from God's contribution to the human project: God could just as easily disappear from the Enlightenment project without affecting the proceedings (Chapter 2). The other major point is that there is a fundamental lack of confidence in human ability to trust the senses and reason. "All we need, Descartes sometimes implies, is a starting place in fact, and geometry will carry us the rest of the way" (Stromberg, 1966, p. 46). This suspiciousness also flows from the explanation of her first point. In the case of reason, we have concrete justification for its nonconfidence in Dependence II. In fact, Horkheimer and Adorno remarked in their *Dialectic of Enlightenment* that reason is infected by the disease to dominate Nature and humankind.

From the above, we are presented with the stuff of a new paradigm, one whereby reality would be determined from without. Its main contours will become evident in the discussion of Newton's heliocentric model in the next chapter.

Where emotivism and Africa were concerned—Africa because its peoples are, without question, *the* principal negated double—the color-stupidity correlation expressed by Kant motivated the benevolent and the supporters alike. There was much to defend or to continue to denounce, as this vast continent and its peoples, many of whom have been scattered to the four winds, simply flourished as rationalism's uneasy antithesis: emotivism. The ethnophilosophies and epistemologies of Africa were surfeited by what the rationalist despises: belief in the supernatural power of words, essentialism, myths—all of which fit the description of Locke's underbrush.

My earlier references to the continued existence and power of myths in the African context should be recalled. Myths, along with legends, storytelling, proverbs, and other distrusted manifestations of Matter, are not disappearing under the onslaught of modern epistemology and science. In fact, it is quite common for African social and philosophical systems to review and reject or accept. Such is implicit in the thought of Kwasi Wiredu (1995, *Conceptual Decolonization in African Philosophy*). The issue is Cartesian "certainty" versus the Akan (a Ghanaian ethnocultural entity) conception of the term. Whereas the Cartesian conception aspires to infallibility, not so that of the Akan. For infallibility for the latter is impossible and an absurdity. What appears to occur in such circumstances (and to be greatly urged by Wiredu) is a rejection of Cartesianism, but not before it as well as other like foreign concepts work their way into the Akan culture. The concept of reason also highlights many of the tensions consequent on the modern-nonmodern interplay. A representative quote from Leopold Sedar Senghor, the distinguished Senegalese poet and philosopher, is presented less as a reflection of the common or substantial scholarly and intellectual mood throughout Africa than as a capsule of the tensions implied in different approaches to the concept of reason:

> The life-surge of the African, his self-abandonment to the other, [is] thus actuated by reason. But here reason is not the eye-reason of the European, it is the reason-by-embrace which shares more the nature of *logos* than *ratio*. *Ratio* is compass, set-square and sectants, measure and weight, where *logos*, before its Aristotlean tempering, before it became diamond, was living speech. Speech, which is the most typically human expression of neosensory perception, does not cast the object untouched, into rigid logical categories. African speech, in raising itself to the Word, rubs and polishes things to give them back their original colour, with their grain and their veins, shooting their rays of light to restore their transparency penetrating their surreality, or rather their underlying reality, in its freshness. Classical European reason is analytical and makes use of the object. African reason is intuitive and participates in the object. (cited in Reed & Wake, 1976, pp. 33-34)

There is little doubt that these two conceptualizations of *reason* are different. What is also quite obvious are the strongly rhetorical dimensions to Senghor's reason. In a number of his reflections on the philosophy of *negritude*, Senghor certainly implied essentialisms to be claimed by both sides—namely, reason by the European and emotion by the African (the black). Now, there is less patience with such a dualism, as the notion of epistemological diversity takes root. In any event, these examples indicate nothing in the nature of Cartesianism and Enlightenment rationalism riding a coach and four through nonmodern and so-called primitive and backward societies. Reevaluation and reinstatement appear to be highly visible procedures in the broad areas of theory and practice.

As this chapter has shown, the philosophical engagement between Descartes and classical philosophy as well as revealed religion ran far more deeply than the hostilities engendered by a war of ideas. The debates and the new paradigm to result carried important implications for the world community. Those implications have their origins in the dynamics of Mind and Matter. How each was to be defined and applied to concrete situations—animate and inanimate—had enormous significance for the phenomenon of dependence. And yet if Descartes and his school and fringe supporters could take the process only part of the way, it was left for another thinker and scientist, Newton, to fill in the missing gaps in that framework. This analysis will be undertaken in the next chapter.

## ❖ Notes

1. The impressive work of Joseph Needham and his collaborators, resulting in six volumes, remains quite unchallenged in this assertion (Needham, 1954-1984).

2. For a good overall account, see Claude Alvares (1991). Other important sources are White (1962), Wai-Andah (1981), Pacey (1990), Gies and Gies (1994).

3. This is exemplified in Europe during the Age of Dynasties (1400-1559), where the motive was not direct control or securing revenues but "overlordship," the lust for homage (see Luard, 1987, pp. 135-144).

4. My impression in sketchily situating racism in the general framework of these philosophers is that a deep tension exists between reason and rationality, on the one hand, and ideology, on the other. Jefferson, Mill, Hegel all struggle, with the ideological often overcoming the rational.

5. See Hegel (1989, p. 177). Other statements betray the ambivalence mentioned in the above note.

6. See Fraser (1995) and Jacoby and Glauberman (1995) for ample verification of this point.

7. African Americans complain that these standards are changed as soon as they are approached. Women complain that the undermining of patriarchy (as the domination of the fathers) is merely replaced by fraternity (the rule of the brothers) (see Pateman, 1988, chap. 2).

8. Identical traits are found in Bacon, Galileo, and Bodin (see Reiss, 1982b, for a revealing account of this changed perception of language.

# *Chapter Six*

# NEWTONIANISM AND THE HELIOCENTRIC FRAMEWORK

*Nature and Nature's laws lay hid in night.*
*God said, let Newton be, and all was light.*
Alexander Pope

The process of systemic domination of non-European peoples, first enacted by colonialism and followed by imperialism, can be traced to the agreeable interplay between Grotian natural law and the social, political, and psychological applications of Newton's heliocentric system. Of course, many of the features of domination were represented quite sharply in classical philosophy (in the writings of Plato and Aristotle, for example) and in Judaism, where the notion of a Chosen People supplied the license to chastise, mercilessly, even the slightest transgressions of the Gentiles. In the case of women, domination inheres in like sources, heavily complemented by centuries of "scientific" support undergirding at once their alleged inferiority and the necessity of their control by men—their nature being inherently threatening to civilized social order. It is the virtue (or misfortune?) of Newtonianism, however, to encompass within it a regime of scientific justifications that apply at one and the same time to the domination of nonmodern peoples, women and Nature. The entire project is subsumed under Newton's famous maxim, one based on immutable laws standardizing the principles by which the physical and social worlds are governed: Nature is always in harmony with itself (*Natura est semper sibi consona*).

Newton's model, in which "Nature's laws lay hid in night," now surfaced as scientific proof of a natural pecking order of nations and genders. On the broader canvass, those crippling limitations of matter referred to in the previous chapter would come to define an exclusive and exclusionary politics of cultures and of nations. To the predictable extent that these nations fell short, due mainly to the abuse or nonuse of apodictic reason, they were placed, along with their cultures, in the matter column of the Cartesian ledger.

The first segment of this chapter analyzes the politics of the mind-matter dualism and illustrates the ideological ballast it provided for the initial Cartesian project. This project relates specifically to Descartes's immense contribution to the modern project. For many of the dualisms on which his system is erected had been anticipated by the classical philosophers, notably Plato, in whose *Phaedo* the clear precursors are displayed. In the second segment, I take the analysis backward from Newton to pick up the trail of natural law and its influence in the hands of Grotius and Pufendorf, the first major exponents of international law. A key purpose here is to establish the links between these formulations and dependence. The final segment analyzes the manner in which the two moments combine to produce, in broad relief, the contours of dependence. Throughout the analysis, frequent references are made to the construction of two additional Other(s)—women and Nature—as they are really of a piece with dependence. A portion of the analysis of Nature has already been undertaken in Chapter 3.

## ❖ The Politics of Mind-Matter Dualism

If Newtonianism was urged into the service of creating the First World-Third World dichotomy, other dichotomies, often directly related to it, were likewise endemic in that process. These latter dichotomies would surface, in time, with the contradictions of the First World-Third World dichotomy. Just like these contradictions, their emergence is induced mainly by a common phenomenon: the unavoidable rise of *equality*. Despite the huge discrepancies between creed and deed that modernity so often displays, it is committed to such democratic principles as rights, equality, freedom, and the like. Such commitments are linked directly to the emancipatory strains of agency and reflexivity that, at once, cause, and are caused by, equality. Clearly, major contradictions are close at hand that, at the time of maturation, force the system to turn on itself via the logic it embraces (Schumpeter, 1943, p. 14) and to act like the proverbial snake "chewing at its tail" (Bauman, 1993, p. 209).[1]

Two such dichotomies involve Nature and women. And while their implications for interdependence are partly analyzed regarding Nature in Chapter 3, and will be further addressed in Part III, in the case of women, I will trace their origins here. For the mind-matter dichotomy on which Newtonianism is heavily dependent explains much that vests these two entities with the status of Other(s). The gravamen of the dichotomizing process is *monopoly* in defining reality rather than *negotiation*. The Self, Newton's superordinate entity, whose characteristics constitute an A, does not relate to the Other, based on differing qualities of the latter that legitimately vest it with its own particularity, its appropriate label as B. So, African epistemologies, for instance, are not defined in their own terms but in relation to their failure to measure up to the Western model. As we shall see, these displays of knowledge appear in the matter column of the Cartesian ledger.

The mind-matter dualism is the final arbiter of what qualities are appropriate in the relations between the A and the not-A, in the Self and the Other, respectively. In fact, this generic dualism actively functions as two related types—the mind-body dualism and the mind-Nature dualism. The burden of the first is to create "negated doubles" of women, Third-World peoples, and so on, while the mind-Nature dualism targets mainly Nature. Categorial overlap is predictable, as logic in both cases varies only slightly. Thus, Carolyn Merchant's (1980) widely read *The Death of Nature: Women, Ecology and the Scientific Revolution* does well to link Nature and women to a common form of domination.

The parent dualism—mind versus matter—receives its systematic explication from Descartes, to whom I shall return, but its origins can be traced to the classical philosophers and to medieval religious thought, as I hinted in the preceding chapter. Aristotle is well-known for his disparaging remarks on the naturalness and expediency of a number of iniquitous dualisms: man over Nature, man over animal, master over slave, man over woman. For instance, "The relation of male to female is by nature a relationship of superior to inferior and ruler to ruled. The same must of necessity hold in the case of human beings generally" (Aristotle, 1984, Book 1, chap. 5). The Gnostics of the second century had serious fears that the Divine Light could become irretrievably trapped in the recesses of an unworthy human body:

> Humanity's true or higher nature was not of the sensible world, but of the spiritual one. It originated in heaven, and the sensible realm of the body and nature where

> humans must live, as in a prison, was the creation of the devil. (Plumwood, 1993, p. 105)

Likewise, as I indicate in the previous chapter, the imputed abject quality of the human body was mercilessly vilified by Friar di Verona, who commented disparagingly on women through whose "foul passage" men entered the world. *Inter urinas et faeces nascimur* (we are born between urine and feces) is a confession unrivaled in ignominy by one who must be a demigod or the personification of the Divine Spirit! The goodly Friar joined a long list of prominent men of the cloth, including Tertullian, who enjoyed "cudgel[ing] of their brains for terms evil enough to describe the daughter of Eve" (Wright, 1935, p. 465).

The Divine Spirit's abhorrence of the body is dramatized in the religious ethic of *contemptus mundi.* The path to Paradise must be paved from an assortment of venal cruelties to the body, partly as expiation for the unworthiness to which the Spirit is exposed on account of its indwelling. Self-flagellations, mutilations, self-inflicted injuries and diseases (leprosy, for example) were among the expressions of atonement. Of the other part, these behaviors and displays were indulged either as a deterrent to erotic inclinations or as acts of repentance for even the mere thought of the pleasures of the flesh. God's will is "holiness," which is counterposed to "impurity," the lustful passion (*porneia*) germane to the pursuit of the flesh (Meeks, 1993, pp. 151-152; Stannard, 1992, p. 160). In context, the illustrious Tertullian (160-230 A.D.), a foundation stone of the Christian Church, had himself castrated; in turn, the Valentinians, a Gnostic sect, imagined that Jesus did not defecate (Meeks, 1993, p. 137). Such is the price to be paid as a result of the Fall.

It is against this backdrop that Descartes's ingenious mind-matter dualism is to be viewed. It was the secularization of the religious canons of his day. In the first case, Nature must be exploited, first, via Baconianism, through a combination of instrumental philosophical injunction and Puritanical religious directives, aligning such exploitation directly to "God's purposes" (Taylor, 1989, p. 232). That process, in its passage to mature modernity, would still be blessed with divine dispensation but the instrumental philosophical would become the instrumental rational, accordingly as philosophy yielded ground to science in the quest for certainty. Such was the quest, as the individual qua Man (really, white man) became the measure of reality. As we shall see below, Nature was without social and ethical significance: In Cicero's words, "We do not talk of the justice of horses and lions" (cited in Grotius, 1903, p. 23). Nature is merely the means to human ends "via the application of a moral dualism that treats humans as the only proper objects of moral consideration and defines 'the rest' as part of the sphere of expediency" (Plumwood, 1993, p. 69).

In the Cartesian framework, if mind and matter were largely defined to be separate and controlled by different principles, and if the mind generates ideas innately with the aid of reason, by what measures, principles, rules, and so on is matter to be understood? Let me record some of the main ideas of the above dualism whereby, "the other is made serviceable to the self, a creature constituted by the dominant self to represent what it is not" and then discarded (Sampson, 1993, p. 5).

In the end, what results from the pride of place given to the mind is that matter is reduced to an inferior status. Matter, unlike the mind, was seen as "fully in being, incapable of becoming, therefore without capacity for internal development and equally incapable of having its essence as matter changed from without" (Grier, 1990, p. 230). This essential quality of matter indicated that, as a phenomenon incapable of progressing toward perfection, its value to the search for certainty was highly dubious. One cannot build durable castles on the sand!

The implied dualism of a mind anchored to defining principles of certainty and matter as not-A is supported by reason and the concomitant laws approved by God. Already under the particular influence of Galileo, its theoretical aspect convincingly intuited universally generalizable axioms about the world of nature; by extension, its practical aspect intuited equally universally accurate propositions about epistemological and moral principles arrived at with the selfsame objectivity. Relative to the issue of authoritative sanction, these concomitant laws were God given; for the rationalists' attack was not directed against God and religion as such but took its aim directly at their corrupt and misguided expressions. The *philosophes* were, for the most part, good anticlerical deists. Newton, himself a deeply religious man, wrote a commentary on the Old Testament book of Daniel (Manuel, 1982, p. 25)—an act that of itself suggested God's approval of the ends to which Newton's momentous discoveries would be put. Indeed, Newton would gently, but distinctly, redefine God's role: "He governs all things, not as the soul of the world, but as Lord over all" (Newton, cited in Bricker & Hughes, 1990, p. 13). Not only does God delegate, but the "delegatee" enjoyed significant autonomy. This God was pledged "to endorse the findings of reason" [as] "the God of Descartes, Hobbes, and Spinoza" (Caton, 1988, p. 166). Indeed, their predecessor Francis Bacon used, ostensibly at God's rational insistence, geometric laws in his *Opus Majus* to reflect "God's manner of spreading His grace throughout the universe" (Edgerton, 1976, p. 16).

The mind/reason alliance bestows on human beings their humanity. Its locus is exclusive. From as early as Plato, it is explicitly stated that the human body and its inevitable passions must be relegated to an inferior level: "Then when does the soul seek truth?—for in attempting to consider anything in company with the body she is obviously deceived" (Plato, 1969, p. 94). Furthermore, although the body is undependable, it must be subject to the control of the mind/reason alliance, as part of a necessary hierarchy, as its contribution to truth is usually deception. In Chapter 5, we detect similar ideas in Descartes. Mind/reason and that of matter are arranged hierarchically. Such a hierarchical arrangement, one anchored to God-given laws, is the basis of the stability of the natural and, by extension, the social worlds. Its efficacy came to depend largely on ingeniously fabricated rational and linguistic explanations.[2]

The body is, by these terms, defined as matter. As matter, it takes its inferior place in the hierarchy mentioned above. Like the impediment the body presents for the Spirit or the Divine Light in religious terms, it does likewise in secular terms. It impedes the mind against which evil it must be protected. As a result, most of the bodies organic manifestations related to sexuality and its carriers—women, for example—as well as others considered essentially bodily (emotions, myths, nurture, and so on) are regarded irretrievably as matter. The taboo that modern culture attaches to the practice of men weeping in public—a fairly common practice in Third-World cultures—has its supreme model in Socrates. Here he dismisses the crying women from his deathbed and chides his male disciples for displaying that emotion: "I have sent the women away mainly that they might not behave in this way, for I have been told that a man should die in peace" (Plato, 1969, p. 152). Death favors the exercise of reason over a display of emotions. Phaedo and Apollodorous could, as men and the paragons of reason as well as the guardians of the mind, heap no greater disgrace on reason than by yielding to such frailties of the flesh.

Likewise, sex neutrality and other attributes of the mind are anchored to reason. In fact, Philo, the first-century Jewish philosopher, asserts that God's reason for creating man (Adam) and then woman (Eve) was to ensure the perfection of man's faculty of reason (Lerner, 1993, p. 142; Tuana, 1993, p. 11). Man's existence and purpose were totally independent of any major contribution from women. Indeed, it was necessary to create him first to avoid the destructive contagion of a more synthetic relationship. A derivative notion is that reason is mental, existing on a higher plane than emotions and sexuality, which are base and sensual. Reason was "autonomous and self-dependent," without the need for any "external help" (Cassirer, 1946, p. 172).

Indeed, the late, well-known author of *I, Claudius,* Robert Graves, compares love in typically Enlightenment fashion to a migraine that impairs the efficacy of reason.[3]

The world of matter, whether animate or inanimate, was seen to exist largely for the use of mind and spirit, which, in turn, is not bound by any moral or ethical duty to that world. For the Other(s) are external, "insensate, brute, blind, inert, formless" (Mathews, 1990, p. 32) and are really outside of moral reckoning. In addition, the process creates an atomism, a discreteness that fosters an alienation from the Other(s) and, with time, self-alienation. In phase, the approval of God was always ensured in some fashion or another. The earlier Latitudinarians had preached that God interacts with human beings "by reason and argument" (Marnell, 1968, p. 18).[4] He has graduated from being the God of revelation; now he provides human beings with the tools to reveal his purpose. And this God must even stand corrected by the reasonableness of these laws, as Hugo Grotius informs us later. Now, to the case of women.

Woman as Other, as a reincarnation of matter, of the World, comes, of course, through an imputed "naturalness of the form and capacities of the female body" (Gatens, 1991, p. 25). Woman as Other springs from a variety of sources culminating in the abject quality of "naturalness." Woman and Nature became joined, for as matter that is "fundamentally disorderly and morally wanting, [they could be redeemed] only to the extent that rational order transforms [their] wanton and mindless chaos" (Plumwood, 1993, p. 94). The Spirit that lived in Nature in premodern times now resides in the mind, in Man. It is the mind that propels inert matter into action, so Man rationalizes and controls (Contrucci, 1988; Griffin, 1980; Merchant, 1980).

First, there was a basic distrust of the human body as a reliable source of knowledge and truth. Beyond cure were the plethora of weaknesses that affected the body, including its "dangerous appetites," of which sexuality is primary (Stannard, 1992). Women's role in this hideous fiasco is huge. For men, it is bad enough that their bodily equipment is outside the pale. But women, their creator and provider of their sensuous dross . . . woe betide! During the Middle Ages and down through the Renaissance, women were openly regarded as "walking wombs." Indeed, Manicheism opposed marriage and procreation, as these sexually and sensuously underpinned expressions would only clutter the world with more bodies to impede the passage of the Divine Light. Second, women were also seen as incomplete and "imperfect" males. Thus spake Aristotle and, later, Freud, whose "phallocentric" theory has its origins in this long tradition (see Cixous & Clement, 1986; Irigaray, 1985).[5] For Hegel, for whom women lack "a universal ingredient," the ensuing disability forecloses any real prospect of higher creative thinking involved in science and philosophy. For Edmund Burke, a woman "is an animal, but not of the highest order," while Jonathan Swift saw her as "a species hardly a degree above monkeys" (Morgan, 1989, pp. 62, 187, 191).

These two disabilities—namely, walking wombs and imperfect males—are the primary sources for much of the abuse directed at women even to this day. First, women as walking wombs: The female reproductive organs were uniformly seen as the site for what was dangerous, different, and inferior to the positive attribute of man *qua* the supreme architect of the world—namely, reason. From Hippocrates (460-360 B.C.) down to the late 19th century, women were the twin objects of ridicule and pity—objects to be brought within civilized order.

Women's sexual organs were the veritable hornet's nest from which all hell broke loose. Vaginas and uteruses were the centers of mental diseases, dramatizing their opposition to man's embrace of reason. In the cases of certain non-European cultures—the Baruya of New Guinea and the Maori of New Zealand—feminine sexual secretions become associated with the forces of evil. Accordingly, one should avoid sexual contact with women when certain crucial activities were to be engaged—making a house, preparing for the hunt, to prepare the soil for cultivation, and so on (Badinter, 1989, p. 102). As a wide compass of historical and comparative cultural evidence suggests, the widespread notion was that huge social pathologies and disharmony have their origins here. The Maori, for example, attribute the origin of death to a legendary scenario involving a woman's vagina; in Muslim scholarship (Ait Sabbah), a woman's seemingly uncontrollable acquiescence in the demands of "the quivering muscles between her legs" leads to liaisons with men of the lower social orders, thereby "reversing the system of values" (Badinter, 1989, pp. 103, 110). Likewise, "women's nature, her supposedly greater role in reproduction, makes her more vulnerable to insanity. But any attempt on her part to defy her 'nature,' perhaps by striving for an education equal to that of man, will also bring about a mental breakdown" (Tuana, 1993, p. 100). Not only does woman visit social disorder on society via her abnormal sexual excesses but her sexually derived cognitive inferiority renders her the subject of care and rehabilitation. Thus, properly, she should be domesticated within the orbit of the family where the control of a husband is paramount. Here, her excessive sexual appetites will be honed to the constrained and edifying sexual example of her husband; the rationale is that much of the pernicious excess will be diverted to the socially significant role of rearing a family and catering to her husband's needs. Ergo, a woman's place is in the home.

Excessive sexual appetite was inimical to reason and morality. From classical thought down to the Enlightenment (see Kant, Hegel, and Schopenhauer, for example), the thesis has been that a woman's unlimited capacity for sexual gratification precludes her from grasping the sublime as well as the subtleties and complexities of justice. Schopenhauer, for example, volunteers that women's frailty results from their paying no heed to the past or the future, the absent or the remote. In other words, women are moved by emotions, not the preferred logical reasoning: "They tend to show more sympathy for the unfortunate than men do" (cited in Agonito, 1977, p. 53).[6] Indeed, Freud develops his antiwomanist sentiments around like arguments, stating specifically that a woman is prevented by her psychological inabilities to fashion a healthy superego required for leadership roles in society—a role to be performed permanently by men (Freud, 1962, p. 50).

Medical theory merely followed the prominent formulations presented by a long tradition of scriptural and philosophical thought. The womb and later the uterus were "the seat of disease and derangement" (Tuana, 1993, p. 104). So great was the danger that the clinical removal of women's sexual organs acquired the status of a public policy; hysterectomy and clitoridectomy—practices in which many of the victims acquiesced—were employed to rid women of their nemesis.

If the notion of walking wombs did much to "naturalize" women, the idea that they were imperfect males provided grist for rendering them dispensable. This weapon was supplied by varieties of the "creation principle." Whether in Hesiod's account in the *Theogony* or the Judaic version in the Book of Genesis, the role of women in procreation is marginalized. Strong currents of parthenogenesis permeate these myths—currents that have been used effectively to fabricate dualistic distinctions between the sexes and to reduce women to the control of men. Myths thus inflected are certainly not the monopoly of Western culture; Islamic culture, for example, partakes of the need to induce a regime of female sexual control (Badinter, 1989, pp. 91-92), as do other near-Eastern cultures (Carmody, 1992).

As Nancy Tuana has shown, the creation of the world, according to the Greeks (see Hesiod's *Theogony*, for instance), was at once parthenogenetic and reflective of a process accomplished by the art and craft of the male. After the principal gods arrived parthenogenetically—such gods as Erebos and Pontos—subsequent creations resulted from mating involving female gods but the primary act of creation excluded women. (One might also note the myth of Deucalon and Pyrrha in which men were created from stones; see Cassirer, 1955, Vol. 2, p. 22.)

In the Genesis version of creation, woman also appeared as subsidiary. First, Eve was created from a rib of an antecedently complete Adam. This account carries important implications. Initially, it reverses the natural biological process as we know it. With that has evolved the idea of man being capable of independent existence. Adam was not born via the natural biological process; he was crafted through the imposition of form on matter. Here we begin to glimpse the initial shape of a cosmology that graciously accords a marginal role to women in the creation of the world. And where she was directly involved, one could only expect mischief—such is the implication of Lord Mondobbo's theory of the rise of the black race—namely, African women mating with apes (see Chapter 5). The mischief is that the entire black race emerged as an inferior group.

As this version continues, God did not create Eve because of a pivotal requirement of his Grand Design. Man was not of, nor created for, woman, but woman was created for man (Lerner, 1993, p. 140). She was required to relieve the life of tedium Adam was destined to experience. There was, then, no need to invest her with the qualities of reason; she provides "backgrounding" for men, the "environment" and conditions against which male achievement occurs (Plumwood, 1993, pp. 21-22).

The secularization of this story of superordination and subordination received much of its impetus from medical science. There was a certain fascination associated with the respective functions and importance of the male's sperm and the female's ovaries. If the tales of creation told by the Greeks, Judaism, or even Zoroastrianism suggest man's existence to be independent of woman; if women were "painted with fair colours" but were, nonetheless, "an evil of nature" and seemingly unnecessary for the agenda of life, can science provide the required proof?

Starting with Aristotle, the male sperm began to receive a depiction of superordinacy displaying a kind of existential autonomy. For him, women and their ovaries were the mere receptacles providing nourishment to the sperm; the tandem contributed very little of vital significance to the creatures to which they give birth: "The purpose of the male sperm is to give form in the likeness of that from which the sperm comes. From the male sperm, therefore, come spirit and creative power and form; from the female sperm come foundation, generation, and material" (Ricardi Anglici's *Anatomia Vivorum,* cited in Tuana, 1993, p. 137). Foundation, generation, and material, while important for the health and development of the child, could be located elsewhere. Female sexual organs were viewed and presented in medical quarters as partial, arrested, or undeveloped male organs. Indeed Aristotle and Galen (130-200 A.D.), the Greek physician, did much to vest female inferiority, their not-A status, with scientific authority. For Aristotle, a female would have been a male if more heat were generated during the reproductive process. Galen saw the female's inferior status to be linked to her genitals, which, although quite identical to those of the male, were situated *within* and not *outside* her body; the internal location is evidence of their (and women's) arrested development (Tuana, 1993, pp. 21-25). There was but a short step from this thesis to Freud's "phallogenic" notions of penis envy! The crucial factor here is that the male sperm arrives with a complete blueprint; it penetrates the female ovaries fully formed, as the only bearer of the "primary creative force" (Tuana, 1993, p. 137). In fact, Paracelsus (1493-1541), the noted physician and alchemist, claimed to have created human beings ("homunculi") outside of a woman's womb:

> If the sperma, inclosed in a hermetically sealed glass, is buried in horse manure for about 40 days, and properly "magnetized," it may begin to live and to move. After a time, it bears the form and resemblance of a human being, but it will be transparent and without a corpus. If it is now artificially fed with *arcanum sanguinis hominis* until it is about 40 weeks old, and if allowed to remain during that time in the horse manure in a continually equal temperature, it will grow into a human child, with all its members developed like any other child, such as may have been born by a woman, only it will be much smaller. (*The Prophecies of Paracelsus,* cited in Tuana, 1993, p. 146)

Ergo, the internal organs of woman are like horse manure! There was a pervasive notion, shared by the religious, philosophical, and medical communities, that man did not really need woman in his life. Her presence operated more as a hindrance to society than a benefit. And when her multiple limitations were not suitably brought to heel, especially her deleterious sexuality, the well-being not only of men, but entire humanity, was at risk.

In time, these strains of antifeminism would be reinforced, philosophically and socially. Added dimensions of a woman's disabilities were to deepen her inferiority, which—as expressed in antitheses intrinsic to the domesticity thesis—made her suited only to bear and rear children, take care of her husband, and maintain the home. Such is reflected in countless utterances of Enlightenment philosophers such as Rousseau, Kant, and Hegel, all of whom saw women as ill equipped for public life and a life of the mind. Freud, as we say, would join the chorus by adopting some version of Hegel's charge that women "pervert the universal property of the state into a possession and ornament of the Family" (cited in Tuana, 1993, p. 166).

Through a variety of permutations—philosophical, religious, scientific—conditioned by the ebb and flow of history, the alleged disabilities of women moved to a point of "naturalization." As men resided increasingly more comfortably within culture, women became inextricably bound to Nature. This latter tandem was destined for an identical, negative treatment (Merchant, 1980; Mies & Shiva, 1993; Plumwood, 1993). It is hardly a coincidence or a famine in appropriate verbiage that precipitates the interchangeable terminology developing around these Other(s). Terms such as *ravage, violate, conquer,* and many others, harness women and Nature to a common fate originating in a common conception of an evil. Women, through Eve, are responsible for having death introduced to the world, states Tertullian (Lerner, 1993, p. 141). They are the source of the major problems of the world "from which mankind was never afterwards free," á la the Pandoran myth (Murray, 1995, p. 208), of ills sharing common origins with Nature. As one writer muses, we are reminded "of man's 'God-given' vanquishing power over woman, and the natural and potentially dangerous forces with which she is associated" (Weisman, 1994, p. 21). As for Nature, Francis Bacon stipulates (and contemporary capitalism continues to concur) that *she* has valuable secrets from which mankind will benefit, but like Proteus, these will not be divulged until she is straitened and held fast.

In the foregoing account, I have sketched the dynamics of the mind-matter dualism as it relates particularly to women and, less so, Nature. What follows is an account of the specific relationship Newtonianism as cosmology bears to the dependence of nonmodern peoples. One must comment, in passing, that the current thrust of feminism is not without severe provocation.

## ❖ The Power of the Newtonian Cosmology

Newton's heliocentric model has its central importance in the fact that planets revolve around the sun in accordance with stable, predictable laws. His laws of gravitation verified relationships in which the sun's superordinate powers predominate, placing planets in a *stable* solar system, with the lesser ones operating in response to the determinate power of the sun. As certainty was the elusive power sought, the men of the times subsumed the operations of the physical as well as the social under a single, machinist, set of calculations. Nature was always in harmony with itself. Note that this certainty—a strategic retreat from chaos—is based less on observation and the stuff of lived experience than on the intuiting of spatial relations.

The reinforcement of Cartesian rationality, the atomism it insinuated, was provided by Newton's mathematical precision via laws. Cosmologically, the structure and function of the solar system confirmed that "higher and lower things are linked so that motion in nature, and action in society, flow from 'higher' to 'lower' creatures" (Toulmin, 1992, p. 112). Herein lies the foundational principles on which the relationships of Self and Other(s), in part, rest. It has mainly to do with reality *in toto* obeying, in *all* its expressions, the principles of the machine. The problem, from a comparative humanistic point of view, is that it gave added vigor to a slate of groundless "theories" of differential superiority. It did so on two bases. First, by virtue of analogy, often superficial—thanks in no small part to the dualism that automatically accompanied comparative thought. Second, history shows that these theories, which were animated more often by prejudices than science, were carried via their various incarnations across the historical conjunctures. For instance, prejudice, through ethnocentrism (Greeks and Romans), transmutes into prejudice through race and gender (biological and sexual inferiority). In every cycle of such change, whether it was spurred on by expediency and/or informed thought or science, intense politics were involved. Indeed, Newton became implicated in the cycle of his times: He was to freely concede Europe's debt to Egypt and Africa only to retract it when the authorship of rationalistic knowledge became the linchpin in establishing the supremacy and peculiarity of the European mind (Bernal, 1987, pp. 167-168). In a convenient change of mind, he locates the Egyptian civilization *after* the biblical tradition. Such was the politics of model building, as Aryanism tried desperately to supplant the Ancients (Egyptians, Phoenicians, Africans) as the originators of what lies at the core of the Scientific Revolution.

To get at the nature and impact of Newton's model, as well as its metaphorical usage, we need to analyze, to deconstruct, the subtexts involved and endemic in that model. I will follow Professor Toulmin's surefooted leadership, which dramatizes the importance of relating context to these developments.

Toulmin joins others in drawing attention to the social and political conditions prompting the search for a new order (Buchdahl, 1981; Jacob, 1976). It was the Thirty Years' War of carnage that resulted from deep religious differences. As I stated in the previous chapter, the war claimed the lives of 60% of the population living in certain regions of Germany. Descartes's unitary system of rationality was intended to create a framework that could at once provide a philosophical perspective around which all the warring Europeans could unite and neutralize, once and for all, the divisive tendencies of religion. That *emotion* was so carefully conceptualized as "bodily," "carnal," and "of matter" had much to do with this project. This conceptualization meant that sexual behavior, real or conjured up by the imagination, was a positive mark in favor of Otherness. The 5-year-old mothers from the "monstrous races" in Pliny the Elder's famous tables shaded neatly into this perspective. In fact, this association is hale and well in contemporary claims of national superiority. Sexual behavior is correlated with rationality and accounts, in part, for "the quality of Europeanness." That appears to be a thesis of Eric L. Jones (1981, p. 219) and John A. Hall (1985, p. 131). The Chinese, in both cases, would be found lacking on two related fronts. Their excessive population is clearly the result of an irrationality to which sexual activity as matter is prone. Taking refuge in the bed, accordingly, exacted the price of exerting too much pressure on limited resources. The second reproach is moral, with Kant only rather thinly obscured. For him, sex is the "gratification of an animal drive" that he judges worse than suicide, for "the obstinate throwing away of one's life as a burden is at least not a weak surrender to animal pleasure, but demands courage, in which there is always found respect for humanity in our person" (cited in Pangle, 1992, pp. 11-12).

Religion was still central, but it was of the kind one associates with a God providing the wherewithal for discovering the rational laws that define the stable nature of the physical and social worlds. As we saw earlier, Newton's deep Christian faith contributed, by association, to this new version of God. In tandem, recall Alexander Pope's epigraph at the head of this chapter. Indeed, the new perception of God was even more explicitly advanced by his predecessor, Johannes Kepler, who believed that God, working through "the Holy Spirit," incorporated in the sun the force from which these laws ultimately resulted (Fuller, 1991, p. 75). This version was not the kind that expresses itself as matter, as emotions. God relates to human beings through reason and argument. What must be abolished is the emotion-driven God of the Thirty Years' War and the earlier One Hundred Years' War, when his name was enlisted in the services of acts that unfettered human reason—the variety that God and human destiny uncompromisingly contemplate—could hardly countenance. This edifice of unfettered reason was to be constructed from chaos. In a way, it is not surprising that Descartes and his later disciples were not disposed to taking a studied retrospective look at the path the peoples of the world had trodden. The model identifies a reason that renders the stuff of what is now "prehistory" relatively insignificant. Focus on the prospects of the new society "often led them to ignore the variations in human conduct throughout the centuries" and a profound contempt "towards earlier forms of society" (Brumfitt, 1970, p. 1). In an approach that extracts its structure (method) from first principles or Euclidean geometry, empirical justification is superfluous: "To safeguard against empirical critique, Plato and Descartes have typically supplemented their account of the idealized rational knower with a story how he is continually undermined by his own deep-seated passions" (Fuller, 1991, p. 17). The mind should never be enslaved by the passions.

When we, then, bring these restructurings of reason into their logical and necessary associations with the social world, we begin to recognize the tensions between abstractions and concrete reality. It is readily recognized, for example, the social significance of all those theorems having references to hierarchies, dualisms, and the like, at their very core. Central to the process is the role of the machine as the model of both natural and social realities. "For if only material world can be observed, then the knowledge of persons we seek must be the knowledge of the material" (Gergen, 1991, p. 40). In truth, the entire universe of matter, of the Other(s), could not be reconciled within such a framework. If it did not fit, leave it out and destroy it if its perniciousness is too threatening!

Predictably, these fictions did come down to earth. As the heliocentric model was universal in scope, it crept into social and political life. Socially, the enthusiastic beneficiaries in British society of this new order—the middle class—were quickly rebuffed for attempting to cast the "lower orders" as "inert matter" that must be set in motion by "a higher agency" (Toulmin, 1992, p. 121). Would we also suspect that the structure of the nuclear family had much to do with the planetary figuration of the universe—father at the center and the family rotating around him? This is an example of the principle of a "higher agency" at work.

Indeed, Grotius and Pufendorf, noted jurists, had begun to use the natural law as a carrier for these ideas quite some time before the publication of the *Principia.* In fact, Grotius, whose jurisprudence had already taken on the abstract, fictive, decontextualized, form, had published his magnum opus—*On the Law of War and Peace* (1625/1903)—before Newton was born. I will return to them later, as their role in creating "the colonizer's model of the world" is quite marked.

In terms of political theory, though, the principles of the decontextualized approach via natural law were taking root in the ideas of Hobbes and others who peddled contract theory in some fashion, even Grotius himself. A Newtonian cosmology, which came after Hobbes, was really to reinforce the existing a priorism with the license of mathematical precision. Reality, whether physical or social, bowed to the huge intimidation Newton introduced with the concept that all about the universe functioned like a machine. Generally speaking—and Hobbes exemplifies the tradition—political and moral obligation did not inhere in historical and anthropological methods. His sketchy "empiricism" was the commonly "known natural inclinations of mankind" (King, 1974, p. 312). Which "mankind"? Obviously, the British and the Europeans, perhaps, since Hobbes abhorred history. The method was to deduce, ahistorically, society's fundamental duties and obligations. From these fundaments, there are three of cardinal importance to stable social order. The first is our submission to a sovereign power; the second relates to the pursuit of self-interest; and the third adverts to a moral obligation to act toward others self-interestedly. The morality involved is adjudged according to the benefits and the detriments to be received or suffered by the individual by whom the act was made and for whom it is the right to make that judgment. In confirmation, Helvetius pandered like ideas to his 18th-century audience: "Moralists might succeed in having their maxims observed if they substituted . . . the language of interest for that of injury" (Helvetius, *De L'Esprit,* 1758, cited in Hirschman, 1977, p. 48). Hobbes states that without this arrangement, life would be solitary, poor, nasty, brutish, and short.

There is, then, no real justification to see society as being fashioned and dictated by lived experience. It is to be fashioned from first principles extracted from laws. The method for ascertaining truth was not historical and psychological but analytical and deductive. In fact, Hobbes remarked that he required nothing more than geometrical and physical first principles derived from matter and motion to explain the structure of society. From these principles, the "ought" originates in personal interest ("psychological egoism"). Hardly an aberration were these notions as they quickly inspired poet and worker alike. Listen to Alexander Pope: "Thus God and Nature link'd the general frame/And bade Self-love and Social be the same" (cited in Mansbridge, 1990, p. 306). Like sentiments were expressed by the Levellers (1646-1650), whose strong socialist inclinations rendered that stance somewhat contradictory. More on this issue later.

Hobbes confined his ideas mainly to the nations of Europe, but they were to have incalculable consequence on international relations. For his approach to natural law, as we shall see, encourages the pillage of those nations not caught by the principles of this legal tradition. His concept of self-preservation does lead to the brand of morality that Helvetius, earlier, favored. Moreover, he stated by way of extension that "as the physical world is ruled by the laws of movement so is the moral universe ruled by the laws of self-interest" (Helvetius, 1758, cited in Hirschman, 1977, p. 46).

The philosophical significance of the heliocentric theory, according to John Draper (1904, Vol. 2, p. 268), was that it represented "a most important step to the establishment of the doctrine of the world by law." Shortly after the publication of Newton's *Principia* in 1686, the mood was one of euphoria and rapid adoption. John Draper (1904) captures the ineffability of these discoveries:

> What, therefore, now becomes of the doctrine authoritatively put forth, and made hold its sway for so many centuries, that the earth is not only the central

> body of the universe, but, in reality; that the sun and stars are mere ministers or attendants for human use? In the place of these utterly erroneous and unworthy views, far different conceptions must be substituted. Man, when he looks upon the countless multitude of stars—when he reflects that all he sees is only a little portion of those that exist, yet that each is a light and life-giving sun to multitudes of opaque, and therefore, invisible worlds—when he considers the enormous size of these bodies and their immeasurable distance from one another, may form an estimate of the scale on which the world is constructed, and learn therefrom his own unspeakable insignificance. (Vol. 2, p. 279)

But the "unspeakable insignificance" is really, at bottom, the source of a new power. For this insignificance—Man vis-à-vis the Universe—meant that he could dispense with the Platonic and Aristotelian "great chain of being" and final causes and dedicate himself to self-assertion. This self-assertion, as we have seen, now translates into inter alia man-made morals. It is one that would make of morality exercises of individual conscience, one whose relations with other people are defined by self-interest and a utilitarian ethic. Following Hume's lead, the rationalist had little difficulty disposing of the "abstruse" questions directly related to global interdependence and unity; questions such as Am I my brother's keeper? What is virtue? What is happiness? are left to individual conscience. Freedom and contingency fill the apparent vacuum. Such is a prominent theme communicated by the realist theory of international relations—a theory cast somewhat in the mold of Social Darwinism. It is small wonder that some have been encouraged to declare that what Hobbes said in the 16th century the realists are saying in the 20th, as the world approaches the 21st century (George, 1995; Rosenberg, 1994).

## ❖ About the Laws of the Universe and the Law of Nations

Newton remarked that his accomplishments were achieved by his standing on the shoulders of others. We might quite rightly think of Descartes, Kepler, Copernicus, and Galileo. These figures are associated with Newton, the physical scientist. But there is another group—jurists, more particularly—whose ideas, extracted primarily from the natural law, served to insert Newtonianism prominently into the field of international relations. Preeminent among these are Hugo Grotius and Samuel Pufendorf. To this short list must be added Thomas Hobbes, for while he was no jurist, his use of the natural law was to prove quite agreeable here. A significant difference must be recorded, however; Grotius and certainly Pufendorf tend to base their natural law on sociality, and Hobbes was partial to the compulsions of self-preservation. Natural law may be defined as those principles governing the development of the world community. These principles, it is said, derive from the fundamental nature of man and are common to all people the world over.

Let me first address Pufendorf's contribution, even though it follows those of Grotius and Hobbes. His ideas, mirrored in the *Law of Nature and Nations* (1672), were published twelve years before the *Principia.* While it was Grotius whose juristic notions brought God, natural law, and the nation into tolerable balance—with natural law taken to supersede God in certain circumstances—it was Pufendorf who provided for its practical acceptability. He is regarded as being responsible for translating natural law principles of governance into social theory. Of special note are his formulations on property within the context of community, with the clear intention of bringing the issue of property squarely within a liberal perspective. In the end, his favored model of community was the "negative" as opposed to the "positive" version. Negative community, which characterized the state of nature, betrayed the concept of property presented below in an often-cited quotation:

> [The things existing in a state of negative community] are said to be common, according as they are considered before the interposition of any human act, as a result of which they are held to belong in a special way to this man rather than to that. In the same sense such things are said to be nobody's, more in a negative than a positive sense; that is, that they are not yet assigned to a particular person, not that they cannot be assigned to a particular person. They are, furthermore, called "things that lie open to any and every person." (Pufendorf, 1672, cited in Schlatter, 1951, pp. 145-146)

In short, Pufendorf's forays into the sphere of private property served to install the principles of rights under law. He was to aid in the pillage of non-European lands, but it was clearly not a premeditated act. The agenda formed part of the larger rationalist purpose to improve on God's performance, as the natural law was intended to do. There were simply too many mistakes made by One who was supposed to be Omnipotent. Natural law would avoid those ignominies—war, violence, cunning—to which property was exposed and that the Law of God seemed to tolerate. The problem is that the logic to private property came with its own ignominies via its principal role in a new mode of production driving and being driven by competition for profits. Property now signified progress: Captain Cook and Sir Joseph Banks thought the Australian aborigines "backward because they showed no signs of personal ownership" (Young, J., 1990, p. 28).

This effort and those of Grotius and Hobbes before it were animated by a social context that allows us to recognize the absence of a conspiracy theory against non-European peoples, as such. In the context in which these initiatives were inserted there were already existing approaches to property that fell outside of the canons of the rational order, where laws of certainty were expected to eliminate the chaos and immorality in view. The prevailing approach to property was one of utility. From the pen of such Restoration writers (Thomas Sprat and James Harrington, for example) the manner in which property was acquired seemed to be secondary to the subsequent productive use to which it could be put. "Private ownership, they admitted, may well have been instituted by chance, war, or the cunning of the wiser and the violence of the stronger. It should be maintained now because it is useful" (Schlatter, 1951, p. 144).[7] The mischief that Pufendorf's theory was to unleash against the interests of the non-European nations came in the statement that men in the state of nature had no property rights. We will see later how simple a matter it was to locate the nations of Africa, the Americas, and Asia into the state of nature or outside of it. For either locus would generally induce the same results. Indeed, Grotius's theory of property originates in the notion of community agreement, yet this did not prevent its role in the pillage, for "community" had a curiously European ring to it.

Let me now take the analysis back to him. It is in his work that an internally consistent theory of international law has its origins. Grotius, with a deluge of support from Antiquity, was to package the law (contract, treaties, equity, tort, the justness and unjustness of war, the legality and illegality of certain statuses [slavery, for example], the defense of person and property, and so on) into a neat bundle, originating in, and sanctified by, natural law. The natural law even, at times, challenged God: "[The] Natural Law is so immutable that even God Himself cannot change it. For though the power of God be boundless, yet it may be said that there are some things to which it does not extend" (Grotius, 1903, p. 41).

Such a clever formulation was really to appease the Man of the Cloth and the Man of the Sword at one and the same time. When the *conquistadores* went on their imperialistic jaunts, they would often have accompanying them "chaplains and missionaries . . . and learned notaries" (Schwarzenberger, 1964, p. 35) with complementary roles. In a typical enactment of this collaboration, a proclamation was read explicating the papal or Iberian claims to the "discovered" lands, "with the alternative of acknowledging the supremacy [of these claims], or enslavement and confiscation of their property. When the ceremony was completed and the [natives] proved recalcitrant, the way was free war or annexation of their territories" (Schwarzenberger, 1964, p. 36). If

Thomas Sprat and company linked violent acquisition to *utility*, the tack here is to link it to *religion*. The Fall provided a flexible body of justification for religion to exact vengeance on a segment of humanity existing perpetually outside of its purview. On another front, it did also provide a veneer of sorts for a Machiavellianism that, despite its empirical basis, would simply not be in accord with the encroaching Enlightenment: "The desire to acquire possessions is a very natural and ordinary thing, and those men do it who can do it successfully, they are always praised and not blamed" (Machiavelli, 1935, p. 13). Utility, habit, and custom needed to be draped in principles consistent with a perceived civilizing process: *Force and right are the governors of the world; force till right is ready* (C'est la force et le droit qui reglent toutes choses dans le monde; la force en attendant le droit)—an apt aphorism from Joseph Joubert (1754-1824), carrying distinct Enlightenment connotations. Machiavellianism, though pragmatic and realistic, was now becoming insupportably crude!

This formula, which bent to contingencies, was gradually institutionalized. It was, first, to form a basis for European peaceful coexistence on principles other than those of a religious nature and, second, to make a civilization based on natural law preeminent. We shall see, on this last count, that although Grotius spoke in the general tone of justice, his proffered legal principles were the seeding bed of planetary hegemony. Indeed, we may gather as much from one of many like statements in his works. From the statement, we can infer that such is sanctioned by the natural law: "It is established *a posteriori* when by certain or very probable accounts anything is found to be accepted as Natural Law among all nations; or at least among the more civilized" (Grotius, 1903, p. 11). An important question here is what is the fate of the "uncivilized" nations? We will mine Grotian thought later, as it relates to the reality of planetary hegemony discussed below.

These two jurists were, unquestionably, guiding the rays of the European sun through natural law prisms. So, too, was Hobbes, whose kindred ideas will be linked later to First World-Third World hegemony. Nonetheless, the rays of the sun had been moving centripetally from Europe: In 1564, Vasquez, the Spanish theologian, said that states within the region were bound reciprocally and regulated by the *jus naturale et gentium*; in 1612, Suarez adverted to a customary law that created independent states bound by fundamental principles of justice; Conrad Brutus, the German jurist, did, in 1548, speak of laws and duties guiding the action of ambassadors of states; and Albericus Gentilis, the Italian, published influential treatises (*De Legationibus* and *De Jure Belli*) on matters of international law in 1583 and 1589 (Grotius, 1903, p. 3).

In Pufendorf's hands, a social order underpinned by natural law started taking shape. The Hobbesian application of this tradition coupled with a mechanistic, ahistorical methodology as well as reason were the main ingredients. Newton's contribution was to supply the missing link. By applying the laws that establish constant and generalizable relationships between matter, the "establishment of the doctrine of the world by law" was set in place (i.e., the sun [the European civilization] with the other planets [the non-European cultures] revolving around it). Another way of representing the theory more in keeping with dependence is to state that all nations and cultures are enmeshed in superordinate/subordinate relationships with a center, and that these relationships were based on irrefutable laws that promoted certainty against anarchy. And as Grotius repeatedly stresses, they were common to all nations and rooted in reason; it was a form of apodictic reason, for Grotius, like Hobbes and Pufendorf, worshiped at the shrine of Euclidean geometry.

That the nations of Europe would, in time, come under the sway of the evolving orthodoxy seemed evident. The requirement that Newtonianism would fulfill was that of removing "the stubborn *residuum* that gives to the Englishman or to the Italian his unmistakeable national character" (Hazard, 1963, p. 130). We can, likewise, add the Spanish, the German, or the Dane. Indeed, Enlightenment thought had traversed Europe, as the poverty-striken English poet playing a flute for his meals throughout France, or the British philosophes making frequent visits to Paris or their French counterpart visiting England to look closely at the democratic institutions of that country. There developed a European consciousness, a kind of cosmopolitanism, which emerged as the global center vis-à-vis the lesser planets represented by the non-European world. "The sovereign states followed their ordered paths in a harmony of mutual attraction and repulsion like the gravitational law that swings planets into their orbits" (Wight, 1973, p. 98). (Such are the words of a noted realist who provides much ballast for the contemporary realist theory.) He had little difficulty in the 1970s fully accepting Newtonian extrapolations.

Empirically, even the earlier wars, the wars of the Middle Ages, for example, bore marked orientations toward some sense of unity. First, this was evidenced by various ambitious leaders entertaining the idea of a united Europe: Henry V thought he could use the notion of a united Christendom; Gustavus Adolphus (of Sweden) sought to do so in the name of Protestantism (Wight, 1978, chap. 2). Second, as Georg Schwarzenberger (1964) notes, "European states still shared a vast fund of values, cherished by Roman Catholics and Protestants alike" (p. 30). The notion of "Europe" was a commonplace: "It was something like the air they breathed" (De Rougemont, 1966, p. 75). In fact, the region had markedly abandoned its appearance as "a confused heap of detached parts," and at the same time embraced the doctrine of the balance of power, "equilibre europeen," which came into existence about 1700 (Manuel, 1982, p. 113).

Newtonianism was to fit these defining strains within its cosmological vision of the universe. What one should observe is a form of consolidation of systems of certainty that had been dictated as much by political expediency (European unification) as by economic expansionism (structurally inherent in the Age of Discovery). The natural law provided a kind of anthropological certainty linking God to the historically verifiable regularities of human behavior; Euclidean geometry began to make suggestions about the systemic nature of reality, as a whole; and then to Newtonianism, which aligned these systems of certainty to a machinelike precision and its cosmological vision. There were also longstanding "certainties" from other narcissisms to be so sanitized. If the new *substance* could not be appreciated or agreed, the dichotomous *form* universal to these definitions kept old prejudices intact, in accordance with the *justification post festum* principle. Old prejudices and oppressions stored up in old dualisms hardly disappear with the rise of the new, however scientific the latter are touted to be.[8]

It was quite another story in the case of nonmembers of the club. Their fate would become intertwined with a Europe in which domination would become conditioned by an intricate network of theories, prejudices, and dogma having their legitimacy in the power of a new cosmology. It was a cosmology in which the principles of the negated double gathered impetus.

## ❖ From Planetary Laws to Laws of Planetary Hegemony

The domination of the non-European world by a Newtonianized Europe appears to obey a "theory" of international relations defined by two major tendencies. The first approach may be labeled "domination-with-altruism"; the other, "domination-without-altruism." The notion of altruism has primarily to do with the nature of justification for such domination; here religion is deeply implicated. The absence of altruism brings into play a Hobbesian nonrealism. In the international realm, anarchy reigns, and the way to survive is to play by the basic rules of the game. Notions of right and wrong do not exist as determinants of conduct, if they are not defined laws enforceable by sovereign power: "Where there is no common power, there is no law, where no Law, no injustice" (Hobbes, 1962, chap. 13, p. 101). As Hedley Bull (1981) states forthrightly, "All of what Hobbes says about the life of individual men in the state of nature may be read as a description of states in relation to one another" (pp. 720-721). In a similar vein, Donald Hanson (1984) speaks of Hobbes as the "quintessential realist" and the founder of the "Hobbesian tradition."[9]

Generally, the two strains of domination are not separate and distinct, as they often overlap considerably. We do find, for example, that many justifications are common to both tendencies. Race provides a good example.

### *My Land Is My Land, Your Land Is My Land (I)*

It is widely agreed that the place of "discovery" and conquest is central to the Scientific Revolution, which provided the fulcrum for European hegemony. But quite obviously, the appropriation of other peoples' lands preceded the particular venality one comes to associate with that Baconian project of empire. The annexation of other people's lands has run a predictable gamut from the use of naked force backed by tyranny and the arrogance of power to the spoils of war—even a just war. In history lands are invariably appropriated because of their value to the takers. Accordingly, the burden of justifying the act of appropriation becomes more onerous when the appropriating nations (a) profess civilized mores and customs and (b) when the lands in question are of demonstrable benefit to the appropriator and/or when the curtailment or usurpation of their uninterrupted, sovereign, use exerts a huge detriment in the dispossessed.

Most accounts covering the activities of Europeans during the Crusades and up to the Thirty Years' War make it difficult to believe that, even though God was in the midst of these carnages, altruism could ever exist. The Chosen had affected a self-righteousness that justified grinding the infidel into the dust—equally on the authority of politics (remember Machiavelli and Richelieu) and religion (there are the Spanish clerics [Molina and de Valentia] in their counsels to the Spanish conquest of the New World). Such was the fate of native peoples under Spanish colonization (Luard, 1987; Stannard, 1992) and during the expansionist period in U.S. history (Wilmer, 1993).

But there were always the scattered, yet powerful, voices—that of Augustine, among them—that acted as moral yardsticks. One may recall his widely cited lament that empires are nothing more than great robberies, unless erected on the foundation of justice. Justice is the due of all men, even though they may appear strange "to our senses in bodily form or colour, or motion, or utterance" (cited in Stannard, 1992, p. 168). Similar traces appear in Cicero's definition of natural law, while Francisco de Vitoria (1480-1546), a founder of international law, joins this company when he resisted Charles V's (of Spain) activities in the New World (Luard, 1987, p. 341)—a resistance that "at least prick[ed] the conscience" of his government (Schwarzenberger, 1964, p. 35). (Vasco da Gama's name could be added to the list, even though he pleaded for the Natives' lives and not for a return of their possessions.)

Domination-with-altruism took Augustine somewhat seriously and enlisted religion to its service. Beginning with the territorial exploits from the Iberian peninsula, which effectively introduced the era of dependence, history provides us with examples of the ruses used to link territorial robbery to God's grace. The use of papal bulls describes an approach that existed up to the Peace of Westphalia (1648), when the nation-state was established. Papal bulls, like the well-known *Romanus Pontifex* (1454) and *Inter Caetera* (1493), were used to appropriate other peoples' lands via the doctrine of *territorium nullius* (nobody's land). The natural law doctrine was to later provide some legal basis for this travesty, but before then, the method was the use of fictions. Two of them are central to the ritual of robbery.

First, the Pope or King as the earthly representative of God would act on His behalf. The second fiction was that heathen nations were outside the pale and existed by leave of Pope or King. Such dominion ran the gamut from the confiscation of land to the reduction of its inhabitants to slavery. By divine dispensation, non-Christians had no political, legal or property rights. The hapless, who were sometimes referred to as the "monstrous races," inherited these crippling disabilities from Cain. As the Old Testament was conveniently interpreted, the slaying Abel justified inflicting the most inhumane treatment on Cain's seed. Within the papacy or the kingdom, Christianity acted as judge, jury, and became the beneficiary. In 1578, for example, Queen Elizabeth of England conferred on Sir Humphrey Gilbert the power "to inhabit and possess at his choice all remote and heathen lands not in the actual possession of any Christian prince" (Schwarzenberger, 1964, p. 202). Note the respect extended to other European members of this exclusive club.

Where, then, is this altruism to be found? This is a good question, especially as the clergy's avarice was, in noteworthy cases, the equal of the explorer's (Hale, 1971, p. 145; Mudimbe, 1994, chap. 1). Its application was indirect. Altruism was not bound by any specific duty to the heathen. Rather, the conqueror might expose the vanquished to the wisdom of his ways, to a kind of apprenticeship, from which the latter would learn civilized conduct and practices. Such altruism was unevenly and indifferently applied, as the contrasts between Iberian and British colonialism illustrate. In the case of the one, its lack of altruism, its unspeakable barbarism, has passed into a proverb;

*reform* is the forte of the latter, albeit self-serving in the majority of cases. Indeed, there were even cases of "reverse acculturation," through which control is achieved—exemplified by the period of Warren Hastings's stint as governor-general of India (Viswanathan, 1989, p. 28). The practice of apprenticeship, as I have sketched it, is a centerpiece of British colonialism.

David Theo Goldberg (1994, pp. 25-27) also makes the interesting point that the famous debate (1550) between Father Sepulveda, the Aristotelian scholar, who stuck resolutely to his mentor's chain-of-being thesis, and Bartolome de Las Casas, the Dominican priest, also introduced the first glimmer of "the modernist value of individual liberty" (p. 25). Of course, this very early view of individual liberty, aligned to a communitarian-oriented humanism, became progressively rationalized (and personalized) through Descartes, of which Grotian jurisprudence is representative.

### *My Land Is My Land, Your Land Is My Land (II)*

Domination directed along this secular path placed only marginally direct emphasis on religion. Such is apparent from the formulations of the natural law advocates, as they fashioned the doctrine of *raison d'etat*—a space in which politics could operate without much interference from religion and morality. Related legal exigencies were also a causal factor: Did the doctrine of a just war apply to the natives of the New World? Was it legal to reduce them to slavery and confiscate their possessions?

Grotius, it is true, invokes the name of God repeatedly, but He was formally subordinated to the injunctions of the natural law. Hobbes, on the other hand, was an atheist. At the same time, we should not lose sight of the role of expediency here. In the spirit of expediency, all of this effort of pure knowledge building was tied, concretely, to basic interests. Grotius cites approvingly Cicero's comment on law as "a preeminent science," but the practical concern with what would be required to bring peace and stability to Europe was prior in time and importance. Indeed, as events would confirm, the law was not averse to creating a patina of legitimacy for the forces of domination. Let us see how these ideas became the agent of this species of domination, bearing in mind that while our attention may be immediately riveted to variants of natural law and Euclidean geometry, their ultimate impact occurred against the backdrop of Newtonianism. It was a filter crafted from cosmology and scientific precision.

Governance, which begins with the natural law, is really the attempt to impose a regime of universal reason. Whether one views it from the more prosociality stance of Grotius or the a priorism of Hobbes, social order is imposed with a clear message. It originates in human experience—from Grotius and Pufendorf, for reasons of sociality; for Hobbes, due to the imperatives of self-preservation, requiring "a powerful sovereign to keep [man] at peace with his fellows" (King, 1974, p. 165). In either case, the specific rules of operation are clearly circumscribed, for while the corpus from which the code would be created was general to all people, the formula was particular. Indeed, it should be stressed that even those nations not actively practicing the natural law still became subject to its commands, better still, its negative consequences.

If Grotius is read and interpreted principally within a European context, there is much reasonableness in evidence, albeit of the "situational" kind. Natural law is merely the systematization of human reason on the question of social order drawn from the wisdom and insights of European experience. In the Prolegomena to his magnum opus, he sketches parts of a society under natural law as one that strives for sociality and for a life of tranquility, one tempered with *rationality.* When we look at the institutions within that society, we see much that reflect the trappings of European societies. There is little, for example, to separate his notions of the family from those of Hobbes. Grotius did speak in expansive terms of the nations of the world, but his expansiveness is often undermined by his frequent references to "uncivilized" nations. Perhaps as a form of redress, he would, in the spirit of natural law proper, invoke compassion! Biases also proliferate. Greek and Roman philosophers and the Bible appear to form the bulk of his sources and references.

When Grotian formulations are applied to the non-European world, we witness a tension between the demand for uniformity and the certification of contingency. The insistence on uniformity relates to intra-European dynamics—a uniformity sanctioned and defined by the natural law. The spirit of contingency, on the other hand, would apply to situations (and nations) where the natural law does not exist. In other words, as laws are fundamentally about the rule of rights and obligations, those nations operating outside of a specific jurisprudential regime are often without legal and moral protection.

First, this nation is free to exercise domination on one that functions outside the bounds of natural law. Grotius, although focusing on the question of necessity, seems to cite Cicero approvingly on a related matter of land ownership. Here the case of Cassius's campaign to Syria makes the point. He would be free to take Syrian soil as his own, by natural law, if Syrian laws are *unwritten,* or if written, were abandoned! (Grotius, 1903, p. 92). What follows from this rule is, of course, the *territorium nullius* principle with which Locke's name has become synonymous. For this thinker, who would embolden Teddy

Roosevelt to justify the seizure of Native Americans' lands on account of their nonhumanity and "savage" nature, it is enough to expend one's labor on land existing in nature to render it their property: "It being by him removed from the common state nature has placed it in, it has by his labor something annexed to it that excludes the common right of other men" (Locke, 1952, p. 17).

Although there is a condition—namely, the input of labor and a derived process of transformation, unacceptable that it is for non-European peoples—Grotius's proposition seems even more objectionable. On Grotius's view, is this not a temptation to capture other people's lands under the pretext that their customs were outside the pale?[10] Would it make any real difference to a James Harrington, who thought the acquisition of property was justified by utility by whatever means necessary, that the natural law existed and was codified? Seemingly not. Indeed, Grotius justifies these forms of pillage with a citation from Xenophon: "There is an ancient law among men that when an enemy town is taken the property and money come into possession of the victor" (cited in Tunkin, 1974, p. 408). Second, Grotius appears to be suggesting that the sovereignty eventuating from natural law entitles the conqueror to impose his will on the property and person of the vanquished. In the latter case, the reference is to slavery. On this point, his formulations, like those of Hobbes, have little patience with ethics. On display here is the absence of altruism, as there appears nothing in natural law that specifically enjoins the conqueror to provide the kind of welfare for the vanquished as he would for himself. The conqueror does as he pleases; the might is right. Third, the natural law enables a nation to impose, through conquest, what it considers the proper regime on the vanquished. Fourth, even where hostilities are not exercised, it seems clear that natural law is guided by a specific definition of what is supposed to be general to all peoples. That specific definition does not allow diverse peoples to apply reason to interpret and actualize these truths in keeping with the traditions and peculiarities of their own cultures. If there are universal human ends, it must follow "all men are free to exercise their reason in determining what the application of these fundamental and general truths to their situation is and in deciding how their positive laws and their institutions are to reflect and exemplify these truths" (Hutchins et al., 1966, p. 33). From this terse rendition of the father of international law, we see the makings of the theory of realism. There are still traces of the conqueror laying claims to the land of the vanquished and legislating on its behalf, even though, since the movement to self-determination following the First World War, this practice has been losing favor (Korman, 1996).

Hobbes, for his part, contributes to the tradition of dependence by the formulation he offered in support of what he considers to be our innate propensity for self-destruction. His formulations on property are not what are specifically contributory to the pillage of the property of non-European peoples. In fact, Pufendorf took issue with his formulation that each member of society has a right to everything. Hobbes discusses a number of contributory factors (the lust for personal honor and dignity and diffidence) but the burden of his argument turns on the role of competition. Competition becomes natural, as the natural inclinations to pursue wealth and the reality of scarcity collide. In Hobbes's (1962) words, "Material desires maketh men invade for Gain" (p. 63). The kind of constraint, which only a sovereign power can be expected to provide, supplies the assurance of a productive social life, replete with material possessions, and kept intact by the principles of law and order. Nations whose systems of governance are without this model are really in a state of anarchy. In such a state, there is no law; where there is no law, there can be no injustice. This opens the way again for the advocates of James Harrington's utility principle.

If there is no injustice, then the contingency factor I mentioned in the case of Grotius becomes operative. By deduction, the nation bound by the natural law can intervene without moral qualms. He speaks of this condition as "Independency," one clearly linked to a lack of constraint because of the absence of laws. Reducing non-European, nonnatural law-oriented nations and cultures to dependence is consistent with other aspects of Hobbes's theory. If his theory sees all social structures as "essentially a matter of command and obedience" (King, 1974, p. 181), then hierarchies are fundamental to it.

From the perspective of the hapless, it is the nature of the relationship of command and obedience, just as it would be for the wife in the family, subjects vis-à-vis sovereign, colonies vis-à-vis colonizing power. It is imperative that the first member of each tandem accepts its dependence as the price for self-preservation (King, 1974, p. 181). Quite evident also in his thinking is the importance and centrality of a chain of command.

In both cases, there are broad outlines of an international law in which the relations between Europe and the rest of the non-European world are characterized by anarchy and the application of a natural law that is not only riddled with inconsistency and ambiguities but displays a reckless disregard for the culture and interpretations of reason of other peoples.

In the end, what can we reasonably adduce from the foregoing? Newtonianism, as the chapter illustrates, was quite instrumental in grounding the "scientific" conditions for dependence to take root. While it had clearly, in alliance with Cartesianism, created Other(s) of women and Nature, there was a larger project—a project of empire—that was also aligned to that process. It was the forging of non-European cultures into dependence. As in the cases of women and Nature, it was a confluence of two scientific systems of superordination and subordination—the mind-matter principle from Descartes and the heliocentric system from Newton—that resulted in an agenda of systemic dependence.

The agenda has been constantly eroded with the growing insupportability of its foundational premises. In the next chapter, I summarize the main arguments of Part II before the analysis of culture.

## ❖ Notes

1. Democracy provides a good example (see Hannam, 1990; Mouffe, 1988b). Fox-Genovese (1991, pp. 176-178) sees the contradiction also in Hobbes (1962), who, despite his antifeminism, provides the "ideological categories in the name of which successive struggles for fuller social and political participation would be waged" (p. 178).

2. Playing word games was a common practice. *Vir,* the Latin word for man, was equated with *virtus,* or strength or rectitude; *mulier,* the word for woman, translates into *mollita* or softness, volatility, and evasiveness (Badinter, 1989, p. 90). Gobineau used the opposition of *white* and *black* with like deleterious ingenuity: The color black does not reflect light, ergo, black people do not reflect, do not think! (see Miller, 1985, p. 31).

3. From his "Symptoms of Love," cited in Gergen (1991, p. 29). Evelyn Fox Keller (1985) has some interesting things to say here. She finds that young men now devoted to the scientific ethos often choose to look to their minds for even those pleasures of an erotic nature. What exists below the head is inferior (see also Mies & Shiva, 1993, chap. 10).

4. A late 17th-century group of the Church of England who used Newtonianism to prop up Christianity.

5. The attack is distinctive. They do not refute Freud's notion of penis envy as another case of a negated double or a not-A. Feminine reproductive organs were depicted as a B, as two lips, not a deficient penis (see Irigaray, 1977).

6. Feminists have used these deficiences as bases for their new theorizing: "standpoints." The weakness of compassion Schopenhauer comments on now forms a theoretical fragment of "caring" (see Noddings, 1984). Schopenhauer is turned on his head!

7. Even the most visible opposition to aristocratic privilege of the day—the Levellers (1645-1650?)—to which democracy as well as socialism have laid claim, carried within it a huge contradiction. For while it meant "to destroy rank [and] subvert private property, particularly property in land" (Wootton, 1992, p. 73), the movement seemed hopelessly caught in the web of private property spun by Lockean ideas. See Wootton (1992) and MacPherson (1962) for accounts of these contradictions.

8. The legitimacy of the monarch is a good example. Sir Robert Filmer suggested that the kings of Europe should be obeyed because they are the direct heirs of Adam. In Spain, the monarchy was traced to Tubal, the son of Noah. Filmer extracted his *Adamist* thesis from the natural law (see Marnell, 1968, p. 14).

9. Other Realist theorists have reinforced this tradition with, first, the concept of *animus dominandi* (i.e., the will of the powerful to dominate). Morgenthau (1968, p. 31) defines it as an

"elemental bio-psychological drive" to be compared with "drives to live, to propagate" (see also Aron, 1966). A second supportive strain comes from Robert W. Tucker (1977). He holds that international relations are nationally unequal and to tinker with them in pursuit of a mythical equitable distribution will lead inevitably to anarchy.

10. A concession was made in 1801. "Non-Christian rulers might 'on some points of the law of nations, be entitled to a very relaxed application of the principles, established by long usage, between the States of Europe, holding an intimate and constant intercourse with each other' " (Schwarzenberger, 1964, p. 37).

*Chapter Seven*

# BROAD SKETCHES OF A REVOLT AND A SUMMARY OF THE ARGUMENT

*If your only tool is a hammer,*
*then all problems will appear to you as nails.*
Mark Twain

*Neither God nor tradition is privileged with the same*
*credibility as scientific rationality in modern cultures.*
Sandra Harding (1986, p. 16)

The last three chapters have—to revert to my architectural metaphor—pointed to wall joints not properly sealed, poorly made bricks, and really suspect workmanship. In the course of the analysis, we were also made aware of the shadows cast by the oncoming revolts. I drew attention to the ways in which the system of the Enlightenment, particularly its modernist dimension, was crafted. The collaboration of Cartesianism and Newtonianism resulted in a host of Other(s), of "negated doubles" ostensibly existing in predetermined inferiority. Like the planets revolving around the sun in the solar system in accordance with laws "presiding over [them] to be other than they are" (Draper, 1904, Vol. 2, p. 276), non-Western societies (particularly those inhabited mainly by peoples of color), women (without distinctions made between First World and Third World women), and Nature revolved around a European sun, with "laws" of superordination and subordination extrapolated from the Newtonian model. Other related systems of thought—Hobbesianism, the ideas of Locke, and Kantianism—bore down heavily, through different thought styles, to construct a rational ethics coextensive with the demands of the machine. An ethics based on duty, such that Kantianism presents, manages to avoid the taint of lived experience, as "duty" does not inhere in "values" that the rationalist abhors. Duty inheres in our faculty of reason, a "hyper-rational" conception of morality, as Stjepan Mestrovic (1991, p. 109) refers to it. Overall, the prior chapters have hinted at some of the essences of an Other-driven revolt against this system, which will acquire greater specificity and pointedness in the remainder of the book. This should become more evident as the later analyses identify the newly combative features of culture and the multifaceted revolt of reason.

I would like to use this chapter to revisit, somewhat selectively, two major aspects covered primarily in the previous three chapters. The first segment will address the inherent limits of Enlightenment historiography, the type that is evident in Voltaire's work, and to indicate a qualitative shift that releases history from the severe grip of Euclidean geometry and the tyranny of first principles. The second segment reviews some key aspects of rationalism that are discussed as epistemological fractures. In both cases, I will draw attention to those areas where things are falling apart and useful reconstructive activity appears to be taking shape. In neither instance will any attempt be made beyond capturing the essence of significant trends.

Finally, I will be partial to the case of Africa, even though scholars like Moira Gatens (1991) and Jane Flax (1990) have argued for women as the principal Other. While one can appreciate biases on either side, I do not really think that my selection does violence to the position of women. In truth, Africa, the "invention" that it is, appears mainly as a synecdoche, as much of the argumentation for its dependence applies equally to all of the Other(s). By *invention* is meant "a Western style of dominating, restructuring, and having authority over [the Other(s)]" (Said, 1978, p. 3). In the African context, it surfaces as three "speeches" (to use Foucauldian language) as (a) an exotic representation of savages, as (b) philosophical representations, based on a hierarchy of civilizations, and as (c) the anthropological search for primitiveness—all of which combine to create "the Western consciousness" (Mudimbe, 1988, p. 69). To the other Other(s) like women, the above definitional frame applies, subject to the substitution of appropriate parallels. Look at the history of the Aztecs, of the Incas, of the Mayas. Here we observe the dynamics of the negated double at work. For women, I might direct our attention to a short list of sources from which the frame can be empirically constituted: Wright

(1935, especially chap. 13), Schapiro (1963), Okin (1979), Merchant (1980), Harding (1986). Of course, one must make allowances for the tensions between, and the peculiarities of, the various "standpoints" of each Other, those conceptually defensible "essentialisms" and/or "affinities" that sustain the various claims of *difference*. Nonetheless, it can hardly be disputed that the Other(s) are, in general, cut from the same cloth.

The choice of Africa has another factor in its support. There is growing recognition from key metropolitan scholars that African languages and art embody dimensions of ontology and epistemology not readily evident in Western thought. The significance of these developments for the omnibus project of difference is obvious, whether the focus is the reconstruction of the Self (and the Other), or the formulation of the standpoints of the Other(s) in grounding difference.

## ❖ Because History Begins With the Enlightenment . . .

It is no exaggeration that the tales of explorers and navigators as well as colonial reports have greatly savaged the realities of those people living in Newton's satellites. It is true that colonial reports and administrators formed the backbone of the discipline of anthropology, which perhaps leads the way in correcting the falsities and misconceptions circulated about the Other(s). But this status of relative respectability was not achieved before these incipient anthropologists, like the priests who rubbed shoulders with Cortes and Pizarro (some of whom were later to become explorers themselves), rendered yeoman's service to the causes of colonialism and imperialism. From Herodotus's statement that black people have black blood to Pliny the Elder's monstrous caricatures in his *Natural History* (Chapter 6) and his assertion that silken fibers (introduced into Italy from China) "grew on trees" (Gies & Gies, 1994, p. 84) to services to the causes of colonialism and imperialism; from Linneaus's *homo ferus* (a four-legged, mute, and hairy wildman) and so on—all these representations are characterized by poor and, often, self-serving historiography and ethnography. Texts on Africa were, until way into the 19th century and certainly beyond, glorified hearsay, "allegory rather than realism." "And tended to repeat each other in a kind of cannibalistic, plagiarizing intertextuality" (Miller, 1985, p. 6). As one finds even down to the 1950s, the research was little more than "cultural curiosities perceived and analyzed not as rational systems in their own right but rather as exotic and primitive exempla" (Mudimbe & Appiah, 1993, p. 117).

These sources of knowledge were not given the degree of scrutiny required, largely because of the model of interpretation into which they were inserted. In truth, the Cartesian framework did not really require such scrutiny, because investigations of comparative cultures were not crucial to it. The major exceptions to the rule were, of course, the nations of Europe, given their imminent role as the metaphorical Sun. Another group of exceptions was the Ancient nations (Egypt, Greece, Ethiopia, Phoenicia, for example) whose studied derogation was needed to ground an Aryan model of the world. I have also alluded to the respect thinkers like Voltaire extended to the "sagacity" of India and China. It has been persuasively argued that this latter construct-in-being was nothing short of the Aryan model of the world. Its burden is that Western civilization, with its hub in Greece, was not influenced directly and substantially by Egyptians, many of whom were black, but rather by Indo-European-speaking Greeks of earlier "pre-Hellenic peoples." If Frederich von Schlegel (*Language and Wisdom of the Hindus,* 1808), and Hippolyte Taine (*History of English Literature,* 1860) allude to an Aryan race "scattered from the Ganges to the Hebrides" with its languages, religions, and literature rather kept intact and strengthened by "thirty centuries of revolutions" (Taine, 1897, cited in Appiah, 1992, p. 51); if our accounts of history point to an implausibility, we are in the presence of the politics of grounding the exclusivity of the European tribe. *Mirabile dictu,* Europeans must indeed be a special tribe, blessed with the magic to fend off what other tribes have not been able to do—namely, to avoid acculturation and the multiple forms of hybridity incident to contact. Such was the inevitable myopia to result from the pronouncements of as stellar an historian as Edward Gibbon (1737-1794). This revered author of *The Decline and Fall of the Roman Empire* declared, carelessly, that the medieval period and earlier were the Dark Ages, "the triumph of barbarism and religion" (Edward Gibbon, cited in Gies & Gies, 1994, p. 1). In the case of Africa, John G. Jackson's (1990) *Introduction to African Civilizations* and Richard Bernal's (1987) *Black Athena* have revealed more illumination than darkness!

The non-European world was "enveloped in the dark mantle of Night" (to borrow Hegel's characterization of Africa). This Stygian Darkness, studded with the nations and cultures by which it is inhabited, could only be fashioned into enlightenment, "absolutely as the moon does with the light of the sun" (Gobineau, 1967, cited in Miller, 1985, p. 16). Blank darkness! Voltaire, as stated earlier, showed interest only in those nations whose arts and culture he approves. Hegel might have been brought to heel by the compulsions of the reason he worshiped, but his erasure of African history is well known: "Africa proper, as far as History goes back, has remained—for all purposes of connection with the rest of the World—shut up" (Hegel, cited in Outlaw, 1991, p. 26). And yet, despite himself, Hegel was to make his own contribution in extricating history from geometry and first principles. This results from the direct role he accords to history as the engine of social change *writ large.*

"The clear mantle of Day" (to indulge a play on Hegel's earlier characterization) was, on the other hand, the beginning of history. Isaiah Berlin (1982) gives us a crisp reading of Monsieur Voltaire's approach to the subject:

> Voltaire interpreted [the principles of the Enlightenment as they relate to history] not as the deductive method of logic and mathematics, which was too abstract and unrelated to the facts and needs of daily life, but as *le bon sens,* the good sense which, while it may not lead to absolute certainty, attains a degree of verisimilitude or probability quite sufficient for human affairs, for public and private life. Not many men are fully armed with this excellent faculty, for the majority appear to be incurably stupid; but those few who do possess it are responsible for the finest hours of mankind. (p. 88)

Voltaire was prepared to acknowledge only four such civilizations in history: Alexander and the classical age of Athens, the Roman Republic and Empire under Augustus, Florence during the Renaissance, and France in the reign of Louis XIV. This is the core of the European Sun! As Berlin (1982, p. 92) remarks sharply, Voltaire ignored "the multiplicity and relativity of values of different times and places, or the genetic dimension of history." The ages were either bright or dark, the latter being the result of the "crimes, follies and misfortunes of men." Indeed, "the central point of history is the sunrise of the modern scientific spirit" (Collingwood, 1969, p. 80). African history began with the arrival of the Europeans.

But history was to be given "the notion of change and growth" by Hegel, whose earlier swipe at Africa would hardly suggest such a possibility. Nonetheless, he aided in rescuing history from mechanics, geometry, and first principles so clearly mirrored in Voltaire and endorsed by the Cartesian and Hobbesian traditions as well as Kant. The effect of constructing the world along the lines of a machine is the nullification of history, or its constriction by mechanistic rules (Collingwood, 1969, pp. 61-63). On any account, whether epistemologically or in terms of history, the perspectives of the Other(s) remain marginalized, while the Cartesian framework appeared dynamically static and nonevolutionary (Datson, 1994).

The Political Economy model ushered in by Hegel (see Chapter 2) has really broken the stranglehold of the above dynamism through the dialectical role it accords to history. Moreso in the hands of Marx, history has become the site of a plethora of social relations with their engine driven by some form of conflict, exploitation, or oppression. In short, the recognition of these relations has been the precursor of class analysis and, later, racial, ethnic, as well as other, analyses—investigations that, by virtue of specific class, racial, ethnic, and other interests, revealed as being threatened, exploited, or destroyed, animate challenges to the deterministic and evolutionary theories implied by the heliocentric model. Knowledge and its development as well as emancipation are all intrinsically historical.

Spasmodically, but especially from the 1920s or so, a steady revolt has been directed against domination and its ideologies. Quickly, the literature and efforts in theory and practice can be captured through a loose periodization. There was a first group that embraced what might be broadly termed the *tu quoque* position. This was a reconstructivist approach to restore the black race to a position of equality vis-à-vis its white counterpart. Within this approach were two distinct tendencies: One, which included a mixed body of advocates, sought to right the wrong by pointing to the undisclosed information about positive black contribution to Western civilization (George M. James, Cheikh Anta Diop) and on an impeded development through colonialism and/or the failure to initiate research and objective interpretations (Maurice Delafosse, Leo Froebenius, E. E. Evans-Pritchard); the second tendency attempted to settle the question of race through a form of benign polygenesis, based on the principles of *different but equal* (Edward J. Blyden and W. E. B. Dubois; see Appiah, 1992, chaps. 2, and 3, for a nicely integrated treatment).

The issue of cognitivity is a crucial pivot. From Hume and Kant (in philosophy) and Voltaire (in history), the African was "unqualifiedly lacking in rationality" (Blaut, 1993, p. 15). In the early 1930s, noted French anthropologist Marcel Griaule (1965) used his dialogues with a Dogon sage, Ogotemelli, to show that the African was no less capable of indulging in highly abstract intellectual exercises. Quite the same conclusions are drawn from careful research on the thought systems of the Yoruba people of Nigeria (Hallen & Sodipo, 1986).[1] In 1927, Maurice Delafosse's study of West Africa led him to compare the African medieval age with that of Europe. It was an age of great learning and philosophy, literature, and architecture, among other areas of scholarship that flourished in centers such as Timbuktu and Gao. His research led him to dispute claims of African intellectual and cognitive inferiority made by Levy-Bruhl and others. In fact, Levy-Bruhl (1949) was to retract in his *Les Carnets* where he now spoke not of an African "prelogicality," but of African systems of thought being different, yet possessing the qualities of logic and reason that had supposedly made it the grossly inferior binary opposite to modern, Western thought. The recantation had a liberatory effect: As Mudimbe and Appiah (1993, p. 118) indicate, it was part of a rupture leading to the abandonment of evolutionist and diffusionist models of a primitive Africa, a continent without a history. Disciplines and methods of study were correspondingly transformed, as, for instance, the study of African cultures and religions replaced earlier concepts of "primitivism" and "paganism."[2]

In chronological order, the foregoing was followed by the decolonization in the 1960s. To give short shrift without intending any diminution of this crucial period in African history, the stage was seized mainly by politicians, many of whom had pretensions to being philosopher-princes. They were liberationists, radicals of right and left ideological persuasions, Marxists, and so on. In the main, their initiatives were directed at economic development, with a few among them, Kwame Nkrumah, for example, having larger agendas such as African unity. Of that period, one is quickly reminded of other luminaries like Nnamdi Azikiwe (Nigeria), Kenneth Kaunda (Zambia), Julius Nyerere (Tanzania), Milton Obote (Uganda), and Ahmed Sekou Toure (Guinea).

But political economy, even though it was quite important for the founding of these new ex-colonial states, soon ran into two main types of difficulty. The first was the disaster that followed in the wake of the importation of inappropriate foreign models: modernization theories, Marxism-Leninism, Maoist Marxism, dependency theory, and, for Basil Davidson (1992), the curse of the nation-state—an anachronism as far as Africa's history is concerned. The second difficulty (derived from the first) was really a sin of omission. Indigenous practices and habits of mind were largely excluded from the developmental calculus. They are the backward and the primitive that metropolitan models of development, traceable in a direct line to the Cartesian perspective, dismissed as products of matter that were inappropriate for rational economic development. Marxism did not fare much better. It was "the greatest influence on African thought from the 1930s to the 1950s" (Mudimbe, 1988, p. 90), but although the system was to influence many leading political leaders (Kwame Nkrumah, Leopold Senghor and Sékou Touré), it really was no match for African cultures. Perforce, Marxism became "Africanized," and, as such, the rhetorical (as against the logical) bases of Africa's cultures took command. Thus, Leopold Senghor could call African Marxism, perhaps the Marxism influenced by Negritude, "existential and lyrical socialism." The distinctions between logical and rhetorical carriers of rationalities will be made more clearly in Chapter 10.

Progressively, these failures revealed the complex nature of the agenda. First, indigenous factors proved to be quite resistant to metropolitan market economics. Informal socioeconomic activities would in time provide higher levels of employment, despite recastings of the economies to meet the demands of the market. On the Marxist front, the resistance to socialism appeared as low levels of revolutionary consciousness or as economies in flux, labeled and analyzed as "articulated modes of production" (Cliffe, 1985; Foster-Carter, 1978). Briefly, as in the case of the proliferation of informal sectors activities, cultural factors tended to dominate. In an economy characterized by articulated modes of production, the traditional "modes," sections of which would yield to market principles ("modern sector"), appeared quite resilient, keeping alive (and being kept alive by) indigenous, traditional relations or, in some cases, "a fusion between [them]" (Cliffe, 1985, p. 127).

By the late 1970s and the early 1980s, the world economy started showing signs of shifting away from the determination of its dynamic processes by the forces of production and distribution. Increasingly, culture, as analyzed in this work, began to play a prominent role. To a considerable degree, the new cultural emphasis from the global sphere coalesces with like dynamics in African societies, giving added impetus to many of the culture-driven research, formulations, and practices forming the agendas of a new initiative addressed below.

A continuing rear guard action moves rapidly apace in the contemporary scholarship of Mudimbe, Appiah, Gyekye, Hountondji, Wiredu, Fabien Eboussi-Boulaga, and Ngugi wa Thiong'o, to cite a few prominent figures. These are members of what might be called the second wave of reconstructionists. For the most part, they move beyond the largely *tu quoque* position of the earlier reconstructionists.[3] Much effort is exerted on proving the cognitive capabilities of black people, but far more is directed at problematizing the diversity long impugned and suppressed by domination. Proof often appears derivatively, as products of critique or theory building. One thinks immediately of V. Y. Mudimbe, of whom Wyatt MacGaffey remarked that he has read everything and appears to have forgotten nothing. Mudimbe's work is associated with the concept of *gnosis*—an exploration in knowledge with huge implications for difference. The concept does not derive from the classical philosophical notions of *episteme* or *doxa:* "It embraces the question of what is or is not African philosophy and also orients the debate in another direction by focusing on conditions of philosophy as part of a larger body of knowledge of 'Africanism' " (Mudimbe, 1988, p. ix). His learned and revolutionary discourses focus on the intrinsic character of Africanism, a task given much encouragement by such illustrious guardians of the Western kingdom of knowledge as W. V. O. Quine (1975).[4] In sum, like Harvey Cox who places liberation theology in the forefront of a new postmodern religion, Quine invests African languages with the role of broadening Western notions of truth and knowledge.[5] *Gnosis*, of which Mudimbe is the most visible advocate—others flourish in the area of African art, for example, where a like metamorphosis is predicted (Hallen, 1995; Nooter, 1993)[6]—is caught within a zone of incredibly realizable epistemological inventiveness. For concessions of this kind are really admissions to certain systemic poverty of Western thought for which nonmodernities loom as possible antidote. Involved as well is the reality of epistemological "border crossing" in which knowledge becomes a two-way street (Marglin & Marglin, 1996).

It should be expected that the disengagement from the ontological totalitarianism of modernity will lead to a rash of theory building and political initiatives where controversies are a common place. One of these is the raging debate over African philosophy: Should sagacity qualify as philosophy? Must clear distinctions not be made between philosophy and ethnophilosophy (the array of proverbs, myths, and so on, guiding the life of African societies?) (see Appiah, 1992; Masolo, 1994; Odera-Oruka, 1983, for useful and enlightening accounts of these debates). Another reformulation of note involves the role of philosophy: Should it merely be a contemplative, detached, exercise in the classical sense, or should it not be enlisted in the service of basic social problems. Paulin Hountondji (1983) and H. O. Oruka (1985) have made steps in this direction. The task of philosophy is not to contemplate the world, but to change it.

Evidence of a global reconstructive ferment such exercises certainly appear to be. Indeed, one detects an identical *elan* in the complex, but encouragingly transformative, contortions of feminist theories. In view, as in the case of African theory and practice, is an undaunted initiative to make the 'spaces' yielded by old-style domination become the sites for emancipatory theory and practice. One thinks immediately of Ngugi wa'thiong'o's crusade to decolonize the minds of his people (Africans, in general, and the Gikuyu of Kenya, in particular) via a return to exclusive uses of native languages to their fullest extent (see Ngugi, 1986).

Let us now turn our attention to the epistemological fractures around which much of this emancipation is taking place.

## ❖ Some Deep Epistemological Fractures

Unhappy is the head that wears the crown! So goes a trite but true homily. Reason and rationality are no exceptions. Their combined history shows that controversies of some kind have always accompanied their journey across time and space. For instance, Hobbes, the paragon of reason and rationality, was pilloried in the following way: "Where [Hobbesian] principles prevail, adieu honour and honesty and fidelity and loyalty; all must give place to self-interest"

(John Bramhall, 1658, cited in Skinner, 1966, p. 316). Yet, on the view of Professor Brand Blanshard (1991), the two concepts were at no point in the past 2,000 years ever subjected to "a bombardment so varied, so competent, so massive and sustained, as in the last 50 years [prior to 1962]" (p. 26). Exemplary among the bombardiers are Freud, whose theories showed "that man was imperfectly released from his animal status" (Blanshard, 1962, p. 38), and Westermark and Sumner, whose work "was to show with the fullest documentation the diversity not only in men's outward behaviour but also in their moral standards and ideals" (Blanshard, 1962, p. 40). Overall, the drift was increasingly toward a rationality in which the judgments of human agents figured more centrally in rational procedures, with the falsity of these judgments igniting critique, evaluation, and replacement.

The scrutiny of reason and rationality has continued unabatedly. During the 1960s, any number of excluded and marginalized groups—gays, minority, counterculture movement, and so on—mounted conceptual offensives. In the overall, the result was an odd mix of recalcitrants, many of whom, if not influenced by Marxism, took to a limited version of Cartesianism and Lockean sensationalism (i.e., "limited rationality"). As W. W. Bartley, III (1988) defines the stance, "it is the making of a final, unquestionably subjective commitment to some particular authority or tradition or way of life" (p. 208). In short, the limited rationalist states or implies his or her subjective position, fully aware of its value-laden and bias-ridden nature, then aligns reason and rationality to that subjectivity. Some ecofeminists refer to their version of the practice as *conscious partiality*, "which is achieved through partial identification with the research objects" (Mies & Shiva, 1993, p. 38). It is not suggested that all aspects of comprehensive rationality will be discarded; mathematical knowledge still has its place, albeit in a reconstituted epistemological orbit, one bombarded by skepticism, by a rationality driven by human reflexivity, and by alternative paradigms like language. Donald McCloskey (1993) states the position quite well, using modern economics as his point of departure:

> The failure of modernism in economics and elsewhere in the culture does not say that it was a bad or stupid idea to try. And it certainly does not say that we should now abandon fact and logic, surface and cube, and surrender to the irrational. . . . It says merely that we should turn back to the work at hand equipped with the full tetrad of fact, logic, metaphor and story. (p. 73)

He has placed rhetoric (i.e., metaphor and story) into the new calculus. I will have more to say on this score in later chapters.

Limited rationality can be seen to good effect in the crucial area of scientific method. Three thought styles as distinct as those of Sandra Harding, Jurgen Habermas, and Paul Feyerabend make the point. In *The Science Question in Feminism,* Harding (1986) points to the manner gender difference as "the most ancient, most universal" (p. 17) of symbol systems influences the way science gets formulated. Against this backdrop, she attacks the notion of a value-free scientific method, indicating in the process the strong masculinist biases subtly built into standard research design. Adopting Willard V. O. Quine's (1975) persuasive argument that human beings cannot possibly determine whether they are responding to experience or the compulsions of their language—thereby gravely undermining the objectivity of standard scientific method—Harding places herself squarely within the limited rationality camp. But there is more. She moves well beyond Quine—since his constructive critique notwithstanding, he still adheres to classical logic—to a framework that incorporates much that orthodox science declares as "values" (politics, race, gender, ethnicity, etc.).

Jurgen Habermas's limited rationality emits profusely from his prodigious writings on this subject, along with a host of other related or unconnected topics. We know from his theory of communicative competence (Habermas, 1986) that rationality is diverse; from his analysis of the crisis of advanced capitalism (Habermas, 1972) that it is not neutral, especially as rationality serves directly the interests of the state and advanced capitalism. We have noted in his critique of the philosophy of consciousness (Chapter 2) his elimination of the knowing Subject, which effectively undermines the efficacy of comprehensive rationality; he argues, derivatively, that knowledge produced by reason and rationality serves specific human interests (Habermas, 1972). This is so, because science is socially constructed.

Paul Feyerabend addresses many key issues in the modern application of reason and rationality. On the specific question of method, the message is unequivocal and forthright: There has never been "one 'scientific method,' " but there is a great deal of opportunism; anything goes—anything, that is, that is liable to advance knowledge as understood by a particular researcher or research tradition (Feyerabend, 1987, p. 36). The other two philosophers are not anarchists like Feyerabend. Despite his flair for excesses, Feyerabend stands under the same umbrella as Thomas Kuhn, whose general and convincing position is that science, as a whole, is a social product acquiring its basic structure and significance from forces situated in the historical periods in which it is inserted.

The anti-Archimedeanism in evidence directs its main barbs at rationality. Comprehensive rationality, which lies either within the intellect or reason

(Descartes, Spinoza, Leibniz) or its Sensationalist inflection (Locke, Hume, Carnap), is widely adjudged to be irreparably flawed. This is the consequence, whether by a direct attack on the psychological and physiological impurity of empiricism—it is hopelessly theory impregnated, laden with bias and error; or a like assault on rationalism's irresolvable difficulties with the principles of justification, or the mutual exclusivity of reason vis-à-vis empiricism, leading to a marked tension lying at its core—comprehensive rationality has not been able to weather the storm (Bartley, 1988, chap. 9). As Robert Nozick (1993) reflects, there is a constant interplay between our view of the world and what is deemed rational: "Our standards were born with impurities, and philosophy's attempt to redeem us from this original sin has thus far been unsuccessful" (p. 135).

This demolition of the idea of a comprehensive rationality forces the compromise—limited rationality—or the major transformation, suggested by Harding and Feyerabend. Science, as a whole, is still obviously of immense value, but fixity of method, especially one standing outside of the epiphanies of everyday life, is abjured. Truth must be established as *process,* one in which foundationalism plays a minor role.

In terms of the framework's own internal logic, the definition and application of rationality have been seriously contested. By its own principles, the framework should view rationality as being impossible to confine within a single framework, especially as knowledge must be taken as always in the process of becoming (Kuhn, 1970; Popper, 1968, although their explanations differ). Methodologically, this state of affairs compels reason and rationality to take up a position contrary to their traditionally narrow, *comprehensively* rational, posture. But the processes are hardly as Popper would have it: If the processes of becoming are the direct influence of the subjective, then reason and rationality must, accordingly, be so influenced. In Popper's view, the analytic and evaluative processes that follow must be left to the principles of formal logic, untainted by the influence of the human agents responsible for the state of affairs. From a different position, Kuhn takes umbrage; for him, it is the community of scientists in power that determines, for the most part, what science is *tout court.* I think that Kwame Appiah (1992, p. 116) indicates the consequences of this stance rather well when he states that a realistic approach should be adopted. Rationality must be conceived as an ideal, but never realizable. Our task is to prepare our minds for change in the face of evidence and reflection that, if adopted, would make our changed beliefs more likely to be true. In truth, these are echoes from an Aristotelian past that speak of the intrinsic neutrality of rationality. As Richard Bernstein (1983) states in the context of defining truth, rationality should hardly be about establishing fixed points to judge the world, such points do not exist. Rather, it should be about creating dialogue based on respect and on the notion that one's view can be altered. Expressed another way, rationality has a variety of applications and care should be exercised in ensuring that a monopoly of usage does not occur (Meynell, 1991, p. 194). W. W. Bartley, III (1988) captures a sliver of this heterogeneous trend as "the ecology of rationality":

> Instead of positing authorities in terms of which to guarantee and to criticize action and opinion, we aim to construct a philosophical program for fostering creativity and counteracting error. Within such a program, the traditional "How do you know?" question does not legitimately arise. For we do not know. A different question becomes paramount: "How can our lives and institutions be arranged so as to expose our positions, actions, opinions, beliefs, aims, conjectures, decisions, standards, frameworks, ways of life, policies, traditional practices, etc.—whether justifiable or not—to optimum examination, in order to counteract and eliminate as much error as possible?" (p. 213)

The upshot of this perspectival shift is that objectivity now appears as intersubjectivity. What is now normative is less a function of a consensus conferred by society because of an intrinsic objectivity; it is normative (objective) because its defining elements are jointly accepted as a result of dialogue.

And yet there is a curious side to the difficulties in which reason and rationality are now immersed. The records indicate that much that bedevils the two today has a long, continuous history. Relative to the concept of "reason," Popper (1966) reminds us that Plato, the rationalist, would often express thoughts so irrational and mystical "that [they] nearly ousted the rationalism he inherited from Socrates" (Vol. 2, p. 353). In truth, he could be described as a rationalist "only if rationalism is allowed to encompass an intuitive, nonconceptual 'vision' " (Garner, 1994, p. 221). Indeed, this is precisely the point now confirmed by research on the nature of rational thinking. Coextensive with the widened base of rationality sketched above is a like and parallel widening of the bases of reason.

The role of myth has always been taken as the core of the irrational. Spinoza is known to have chastised Descartes for the "occult qualities" to certain aspects of his reasoning (Spinoza, 1982, p. 204). Myth, as we saw earlier, was impedimenta for the rationalist, yet he could not escape it. As it developed, it was not possible to avoid its intrinsic human immanence by the use of language as words bearing meaning imposed *ab extra.* Not only is language fundamentally outside the sphere of rational calculations in terms of its origins, but the epistemological basis it provides for structured cognitive exercises, such as rational and scientific discovery, is mythical in nature.

Today, myths are widely accepted as not only inescapable, but as vital to theorizing about the social world. The verification surfaces from two main sources: the cultural theory of deconstruction and "philosophical anthropology." Stephen Daniel (1990) is representative of the first approach. For some time, Jungian psychology, for example, has been effective in revealing the presence of the shadowy figures that stalk first principles such as those claimed by Cartesianism. Today, deconstructionism is used persuasively to uncover the shadowy forms that first principles *must* attempt to adumbrate. Daniel found these shadows in several mighty Enlightenment figures: Bacon, Descartes, Diderot, Condillac, among them. In Bacon's case, Daniel found "mythic thought [to provide] the context for specifying the prerational and the prephilosophic structures upon which a theory of discovery can be based" (Daniel, 1990, p. 46). In an exercise in deconstruction in which language is obviously implicated, he forges the dimensions of language, without which, for us, there is no reality, from the mythic and metaphoric "order experience and expression in such a way as to make possible a world to be known" (Daniel, 1990, p. 4). In philosophical anthropology, Hans Blumenberg, by pushing well beyond the early efforts of Cassirer's on the subject, does well to illustrate the mythopoetic as a constant in epistemology. In his *Work on Myth,* he argues persuasively that myth is unavoidably recurrent because of what appears to be limits imposed by our biology. It seems that when we, unlike other animals, stood upright and walked, our relationship with our environment became a schizoid affair. While reason and rationality now became central because of our increased frailty vis-à-vis Nature, they were not enough to dissolve or marginalize the central role of myth. The journey was hardly a direct one from *mythos* to *logos*. It seems, according to Blumenberg, that rationality and science had to be developed to compensate and protect against the dangers brought about by a poorness of fit now existing between us and a now alienating and alienated environment. Many of these dangers reside in fear, and that fear reveals itself in another expression common to nonmodern and nonrational cultures—expressions against which rationalism inveighs. The expression in question is the story. The main value of the story is its direct association with the ever present archaic that irretrievably suffuses our consciousness. The archaic that commands the story "is the fear not so much of what one does not yet know as merely of what [one] is not acquainted with" (Blumenberg, 1990, p. 35).

What Blumenberg has claimed to do by way of correcting Cassirer is to get rid of the idea that myths are things or states of mind to be surpassed and disposed of by science. What he does well to confirm, following Cassirer and

Kolakowski, for example, is the mythical nature of science itself. So, the "underbrush" that Locke was attempting to clear away in the interest of lucid scientific certainty merely constituted an exercise in futility. By extension, it is Blumenberg's view that the mythopoetic, the story, and the like ought not to be used as indices of primitivity or backwardness; such phenomena are anthropological, common to the habits of mind of all people.

The insights expressed immediately above find apt application in the dynamics of African religion and the scientific method. Myths, such as those embodied in sorcery and divination, are used by the African, the Azande, for example, in a fashion closely akin to the way a modern scientist formulates scientific ideas (Evans-Pritchard, 1976; Horton, 1967; Horton & Finnegan, 1973). The differences lie in the nature of metaphorical usages employed by each type of society (i.e., modern sets of images—those deriving from a technological culture—and a Nature-bound collection of images, reflecting strong and abiding associations with Nature). The clear message is that nonmodern people actually engage in rational and scientific thought. But this is not all there is to these conclusions. Myths, divination, sorcery, and the like are also conjoined to other worldviews, other epistemological systems.[7] What needs to gain greater acceptance is the fact that these worldviews are located, properly, within a wider definition of rationality, forged from hetereogeneous, yet compatible, notions unremittingly pushed by the likes of Putnam, Habermas, Bernstein, Bartley, Appiah, Mudimbe, and Odera-Oruka, among others.

What has been the specific consequence of this shift on the position of the Other(s)? First, it must be remarked that there exist outstanding dissenters who find the epistemological totalitarianism of reason and rationality a la Descartes and Locke unacceptable. Western reason and rationality are suspect, as they are understandably seen as extensions of the domination exerted by colonialism and imperialism. One thinks immediately of Aime Cesaire and Kwame Nkrumah. The first pleaded for an African Copernican Revolution from which an anti-Western, and pro-African, science would result. His antipathy toward Western-centric reason oozes from his celebrated poem "Cahier d'un Retour au Pays Natal" ("Return to my Native Land"). In turn, Kwame Nkrumah made it explicit when he opened the University of Ghana (Yankah, 1995). There is little evidence that these strictures did create enough of a critical mass. These were the voices of the proverbial John the Baptist, preaching, ineffectively, in the wilderness.

But the call from metropolitan sources has been gathering strength. There is a perceptible shift in the formulation of reason and rationality in which Other-derived variations are supported. One can think of the largely implicit, but, at times, quite direct, contributions of Paul Feyerabend. For in his unsparing attack on Logical Positivism and Critical Rationalism, his critique has championed a new scientific approach in which the nonrational and irrational of the Other(s) are central. In his *Against Method* (Feyerabend, 1979), that much is reflected in his new agenda for the scientist:

> The task of the scientist, however, is no longer "to search for truth," or "to praise god," or "to systematize observations," or "to improve predictions," These are but side effects of an activity to which his attention is now mainly directed and which is "*to make the weaker case the stronger*" as the sophists said, *and thereby to sustain the motion of the whole.* (p. 30)

Very much the same themes flow over into his *Farewell to Reason* (Feyerband, 1987). Noteworthy are the first three chapters ("Notes on Relativism"; "Reason, Xenophanes and the Homeric Gods"; and "Knowledge and the Role of Theories"), which bristle with support. On the matter of what the postmodernist refers to as "grandnarratives," he counsels that

> general ideas such as the idea of "humanity" or the idea of "freedom," or the Western ideas of "rights," arose in particular historical circumstances; their relevance for people with different past[s] must be checked by life, by extended contacts with their culture; it cannot be settled from afar. (p. 39)

He is also quite familiar with the principle of the negated double, which he chastises as a weakness in Parmenides's thought: "Parmenides's arguments take it for granted that 'it is different' is the same as 'it is not' so that the only 'real' difference is between Being and Not Being" (Feyerabend, 1987, p. 121). As I suggested above, Sandra Harding's work in feminist science moves beyond narrow structural issues to more fundamental disagreements. She speaks of a fundamental recasting of epistemology, one in feminist terms. Its implications for Other(s) outside of the narrow feminist context derive from the cultural phenomena that are now claimed to be at the heart of an alternative science. As these contentions run parallel to the notions of a rhetoric-driven science, I will discuss them in that context, with special reference to their role in rhetoric-driven theory and political practice in Chapter 9.

Such has been the thumbnail sketch of the trends away from a modernist interpretation of history and reason. The drift continues in other areas, one of which is culture, to which the analysis in the next chapter is directed.

## ❖ Notes

1. This is also common to the Songhay of Niger (private conversation with Paul Stoller).

2. This shift has important theoretical consequences for all disciplines (see Bates, Mudimbe, & O'Barr, 1993), a powerfully argued collection of essays on the transformative role Africa is having on all the main disciplines). An interesting observation is the ability of African scholarship to elude the tight disciplinary boundaries we associate with Western scholarship.

3. Just a cursory glance at the references made to these scholars in the text point to the renaissance in thought in which they are involved. A stellar example is Mudimbe's work, to be discussed later.

4. The prospects are exciting: More than a thousand completely different languages are spoken in Africa—76 in Ethiopia and Eritrea, 326 in Zaire (see Knappert, 1990, p. 12).

5. Similar concessions are made by "ecotheology" to many Other-inflected religions such as Native American religions. John Carmody (1983) states that Hinduism, Buddhism, and Taoism "offer rich reflections on nature that Christian theologians have yet to appropriate" (p. 126). See also Bruce Allsopp (1972), Jay McDaniel (1989), and Eugene Hargrove (1986).

6. In an interesting chapter ("Truth and Seeing: Magic, Custom, and Fetish in Art History"), Suzanne Preston Blier (1993) explores the added meanings these three concepts assume in African art vis-à-vis Western art. She volunteers that new methodologies in poststructuralism and in the deconstructionist vein "may be inadequate for the examination of the unique issues raised by African art" (p. 140). See also Biebuyck (1983), Adams (1989), and Ben-Amos (1989).

7. There is increasing appropriation of these especially in anthropology. Many have built the experiences of possession, mimesis, and so on into their operating epistemology (see Chernoff, 1979; Duerr, 1985; Taussig, 1987).

# Part III

# Chapter Eight

# CULTURE AND THE REVOLT AGAINST REASON

*Culture [is] praxis.*
Zygmunt Bauman, 1973

## ❖ The Relief

It should be evident from the previous quartet of chapters that the Enlightenment crisis would set caged birds free. Philosophically, as we have seen, it prepared the way for diverse epistemologies to flourish, as much from paradigmatic shifts as from the maturing of systemic contradictions.

Culture is the other caged bird of enormous importance that has been set free. Like philosophy, from which it can be separated only for analytic purposes—and that is what I have done here—it is symbiotically linked to the integrative agenda lying at the heart of globalism. Perhaps, a freed culture, above everything else, provides the stuff for theory building, which then informs a politics of action. Both elements are vital for an evolving project of *difference,* and for recasting a world situated in a political economic ontology. These elements are also extremely useful in eradicating or reducing the inferiority complexes traditionally suffered by ideologies and worldviews under metropolitan auspices. We observe the reversals in the pride of Black Studies and in the not-too-excessive boasts of feminists who claim that their theorizing is in the forefront of contemporary theoretical work.

This relief relates to Part III, which consists of three chapters that are designed to fulfill three complex tasks. The first is to outline the changing morphology of culture. Chapter 8 traces the main movements of culture from a frozen set of abstractions of Platonic provenance to culture as praxis. Within that framework, the analysis draws attention to the rise of cultural politics as well as to the different postures such a politics assumes in modern and nonmodern cultures. We witness a growing convergence of politics "from below," a feature now common to the two sets of cultures from the metropolitan and the nonmodern spheres caught within the new strains of globalism.

The next chapter (Chapter 9) takes up the analysis where a culture and politics from below begin to fragment. This fragmentation despatches waves of emancipatory energy within and outside of the metropolitan world. The carrier of this new, global energy is deposited partly in postmodernism; thus, its proclamations directed at the abolition of logocentrism form the basis of the chapter's contents. Postmodernism correctly, in my view, supplants narrow logic-driven forms with more expansive rhetoric-driven forms; these are forms more directly associated with lived experience. As postmodernism, perhaps more than any other intellectual current, is responsible for identifying the key epistemological adjustments needed to rehabilitate the Enlightenment—namely, a shift mainly from logic to rhetoric—a contextually appropriate analysis will be provided.

Chapter 10, the last of the trio, examines what is really involved in the contest between logic and rhetoric. Rhetoric and its momentary ascendance are pivotally situated within the difference on which many of the claims of the Other(s) rest, together with the more enveloping ethic of globalism. The chapter explores its implications for an emancipatory theory and practice. We discover that there are new theoretical and praxiological forms, which at once tend to eliminate the dichotomous tendencies of formal logic, to bring the endowments of the Other(s) more squarely in phase with global theorizing, and to make suggestive overtures regarding the manner in which an appropriate politics might be devised.

## ❖ The Changing Morphology of Culture

Culture passes through many mutations, even though the ease or difficulty of passage depends on the nature of social relations writ large. Consequently, the concept, as Raymond Williams volunteers correctly, is one of the three most difficult words to define in the English language. Culture runs a gamut of definitions with meanings quite clearly influenced by power relations and the changing configurations of social structures. In the end, it assumes a number of expressions: from a cognitive, cerebral, quality—the preserve of a few—to a state of intellectual and moral development of society, to a collective body of arts and intellectual work and, finally, to the whole way of life of a people (Jenks, 1993, pp. 11-12; Williams, 1977, chap. 1). The last expression of culture represents the pluralist inflection in which difference is situated.

Castelike social formations are more restrictive of cultural change, as one should expect. In its most dynamic and transformative aspects, culture has marched down a distinctly more egalitarian path; it progresses from being a divine essence or the product of an enlightened elite, to culture as the way of life of a people. Yet despite the rise in importance of the popular or mass culture in metropolitan societies, the shift stopped at the door of the cultures of the Other(s)—or so it appears.

At present, culture seems to be arriving at a new mutation that involves deeply the once-vilified and marginalized cultures of the Other(s): The shift is from culture as the way of life of a people to culture as the ways of life of people(s). The first is a dominant, hegemonic culture imposed on the Other(s), while the latter speaks to the pluralism characteristic of difference. This trajectory results from a symbiotic relationship between metropolitan culture and the culture(s) of the Other(s), a distinct feature of which is a reduction in hegemonic and dichotomous tendencies.

A certain bias is accorded culture in modern, industrial, societies. The fact is that the shifts I mention above are dictated by a movement in these societies from logic to rhetoric or an appropriate synthesis of both; at its core is the attempt to abolish the *fact-value* controversy by introducing *values* as a legitimate basis for scientific theory and practice.[1]

The task in this chapter is to provide an account that is at once a general framework from which the qualitative shifts in culture can be understood, as well as a specific and empirically verifiable rendering of the contents of these shifts. To set the stage, I begin with a discussion of culture in the current sociohistorical context; I enlist the services of the late Raymond Williams for such a task, moving beyond some of his insights, as required by current developments.

Following Williams (1966), culture is defined as "a whole way of life, material, intellectual, and spiritual" (p. xiv). This comparatively new interpretation of culture originating from a global perspective (as this definition applies equally to modern and nonmodern societies) is to be viewed from a "new convergence" (Williams, 1981, p. 12). As Williams (1981) stresses (and I agree), culture must now be seen as a "signifying system through which necessarily (though among other means) a social order is communicated, reproduced, experienced, and explored" (pp. 12-13). In other words, culture is not "simply derived" from a social order but is itself constitutive of that social order through "cultural practice" and "cultural production." One can clearly see the shadow of Vico stalking this definitional exercise, as for him it is within culture that we live, move, and have our being

> a truth beyond all question: that the world of civil society has certainly been made by men, and that its principles are therefore to be found within the modifications of our own mind. Whoever reflects on this cannot but marvel that the philosophers should have bent all energies to the study of the world of nature, which, since God made it, He alone knows; and that they should have neglected the study of the world of nations or civil world, which, since men had made it, men could hope to know. (Vico, 1948, cited in Williams, 1977, p. 16)

Conceptually, cultural practice and cultural production foreshadow culture as performing, in at least some autonomous fashion, with quite clear tendencies toward egalitarianism. For with the onset of industrialism in England, culture, represented mainly by literature, was now responding, in clearly distinct ways, to market forces. The reading public had expanded, bursting through the barriers erected by the elites and filtering into the spheres of the middle class, whose members were now establishing a market relationship with the writer of novels. Accordingly, cultural practice and cultural production were now caught in the sweep of production and distribution relations, as well as in that of democracy. Combined, market forces and those of democracy pry loose cultural features from the total control and domination of any social group or interests. In fact, writers like Sir Walter Scott began to treat the relationship with his readers in market-oriented terms, which meant pandering, to some degree, to their viewpoints, their modus vivendi, and so on: "The Waverly novels [reached] a multitude which never could have been reached by pamphlets" (Kirk, 1987, p. 119). Much the same tendencies were found in the novels of Charles Dickens. His *Hard Times*, for example, is read partly as a satire on the prevailing conservative ideologies of the times (Klingender, 1970, p. 198).

Empirically, there was evidence to refute the vulgar base/superstructure determinism advanced by certain segments of Marxist thought. The cultures of social classes were inextricably bound up with materialism, as Raymond Williams (1977) asserts after he researched the histories of the British social classes:

> The social and political order which maintains a capitalist market, like the social and political struggles which created it, is necessarily a material production. From castles and palaces and churches to prisons and workhouses and schools; from weapons of war to a controlled press: any ruling class, in variable ways though always materially, produces a social and political order. These are never super-

> structural activities. They are the necessary material production within which an apparent self-sufficient mode of production can alone be carried on. (p. 93)

Doubt as to whether culture forms part of the crucial functions of the base is no longer entertained in the contemporary period of "late modernity" (Jameson, 1984) or postmodernity (Featherstone, 1992) or within the new "mode of information" (Poster, 1990), as subsequent examples will substantiate.

Williams's contribution to this redefinition of culture is twofold. First, he succeeds in grounding culture on a materialist basis, without courting the economic determinism a good many Marxists extract from that famous statement in the Preface to *A Contribution to the Critique of Political Economy*, whereby the mode of production determines politics, social relations, and the spiritual processes of life. Instead, he shows that the notion of determination found in other works of Marx, like the *German Ideology*, is the proper way to relate culture to materialism: Here, life is not determined by consciousness but the other way round. Encasing culture within the more constitutive framework of language, Marx and Engels made this significant point on the issue:

> From the start, the "spirit" is afflicted with the curse of being "burdened" with matter, which here makes its appearance in the form of agitated layers of air, sounds, in short of language. Language is as old as consciousness, language is practical consciousness, as it exists for other men, and for that reason is really beginning to exist for me personally as well; for language, like consciousness, only arises from the need, the necessity, of intercourse with other men. (Marx & Engels, 1963, cited in Williams, 1977, p. 29)

Consequently, human agency plays a leading part and does not respond to economics, either directly or in the last instance. Action is not determined by the almighty *structure*, as suggested by Althusser and Poulantzas.[2] The subordinate classes have no need for legislators or a *clerisy* (to use Coleridge's term) to tutor them in the ways of "sweetness and light" (Arnold's, 1947, definition of culture). Indeed, the result would be the complicity in self-effacement of a pathetic kind, for the model was "the 'organic community' of a mythicised past, the 'University English school' " (Eagleton, 1978, p. 13).

The second contribution of Williams's work follows from the first. By providing a sophisticated theory of culture that remains grounded in a new understanding of its material derivation, it serves to undermine current attempts to reassert elitist views. These views, which have sparked debates over political correctness and the struggle over the validity of the Western canon (in which several contingents of Other(s) are implicated—see Bloom,

1987; Gates, 1992; Kimball, 1990), are really grounded in characterizations of culture derived *ab extra,* like those proffered by Samuel Taylor Coleridge (1772-1834) and Matthew Arnold (1822-1888). Williams's work allows our emerging understanding of culture to be grounded in the present, as opposed to a nostalgic return to the age of unquestioned idealism. This result is accomplished by a very persuasive neo-Vichian analysis of the language to which culture is unalterably bound. Culture is constitutively bound up with the rough and tumble of the world as we make and interpret it (see Williams, 1977, chap. 2).

Changes in the materialist perspective introduced by the postcapitalist features of the global economy led to extensions to Williams's theses. The examples of communication and aestheticization make the point. First, Klaus Eder (1993) declares that communication is not (and cannot be) perpetually bound to class issues. It will inevitably fix on nonclass issues, and when this occurs, "cultural dynamics diverge from class dynamics" (p. 2). In the case of aestheticization, the current determination of taste, styles, and other aspects of culture by popular class criteria does remove (or diminish) the traditionally determinate role of the upper class; there is "a general stylistic promiscuity and playful mixing of codes" (Featherstone, 1992, p. 267). Second, this newfound power allows the popular classes to use their growing influence in commodity production to articulate their political views and choices—the advent of "symbolic culture" (Hall, 1991; Lash & Urry, 1994; Wilson, 1991). Taste and style are part of a secret language expressing defiance, resistance to power, and forming the underpinning of political practice (Hebdige, 1979). As Peter McLaren (1991) notes agreeably, "conflictual social relations (society's social logic) are actively inscribed in human intentionality and agency without reducing individuals to simply the static outcomes of social determinations" (p. 161) such as Althusserian structures. Furthermore, the human body is actively and singularly implicated in this intentionality, resulting in a "politics of enfleshment."

Scott Lash and John Urry (1994) add a reflexive aspect to an already politically driven aesthetics. It is termed *aesthetic reflexivity,* where reflexivity, as defined by Hilary Lawson (1985), is the ability "[to] turn back on oneself, a form of self awareness" (p. 10).

> Whereas cognitive reflexivity has its origin in rationalist and Cartesian assumptions of the Enlightenment tradition of modernity, this other dimension of reflexivity is rooted in the assumptions and practices of aesthetic modernism, in another modernity—not of Descartes but of Baudelaire, not of Rousseau but Rimbaud. If cognitive reflexivity is a matter of "monitoring" of self, and of

> social-structure roles and resources, then aesthetic reflexivity entails self-interpretation and the interpretation of social background practices. (Lash & Urry, (1994, pp. 5-6)[3]

The outcome of increasing "reflexivity" and human agency, combined with other factors such as, paradoxically, the marketplace and the spread of Enlightenment principles, feed into the ethic of empowerment. Reflexivity aligned to agency is, as Anthony Giddens remarks, the recipe for power and the impetus for doing. We are speaking of "self-reflexivity and speech—[which] enter human experience as a concrete and lived possibility that overshoots and struggles against whatever is given as reality" (Brenkman, 1987, p. 160). Such is clearly the case with Third World women now strategizing to undercut a tradition of patriarchy and increase the frequency of cultural border crossings. Michel Foucault (1983) expresses it rather nicely, albeit in the context of social movements, where the two phenomena are mostly actualized. He speaks of a reaction in which the two are clearly implicated, which "attacks everything which separates the individual, breaks his links with others, splits up community life, forces the individual back on himself and ties him to his own identity in a constraining way" (p. 211).

The process of forcing the individual "back on himself," in turn, introduces a new dimension to agency and reflexivity: *personhood.* The basic human body has now become an arena of political contestation, as much a reaction to the tyranny of the mind-matter dualism as it is a revolt against the more nefarious aspects of the "negated double." In the case of the one, the release from constraints imposed by capitalist production, plus the growing acceptance of more bodily oriented truth-claims, make the body less of the object of disdain, less the unworthy repository of the crystalline ideas emanating from the Cartesian mind. Revolt, triggered, in part, by the related dynamics of the negated double, expresses itself in a prideful celebration of the body—the notion of "summadification" ("I am somebody") of the Rastafarians, which takes the body "as a terrain of the flesh in which meaning is inscribed, constructed, and reconstituted" (McLaren, 1991, p. 150); it is a notion that Charles Taylor (1991) approves as an expression of self-fulfillment consistent with a moral ideal, a striving for recognition (see also Levin, 1988, chap. 2).

The emergence and application of agency and reflexivity have moved our understanding of culture beyond Raymond Williams's formulations. For even though his ideas bristle with populist vibrations, they have not been suitably applied to the postmodern, postcapitalist aspects of globalism. His formulations extract most of their defining power from a political economy in which production and distribution predominate. The consequences are vastly different in a new global regime where consumption undercuts production in social importance (Felski, 1995) or one in which we can clearly speak of a "mode of information," with its focus directed at "the manner and forms in which cultural experience constitutes subjects" rather than objects and "configure[s] subjects as 'other' " (Poster, 1990, p. 16). It is, nonetheless, to Williams's (1986) credit that he sought to push "socialist democracy" to the recognition of difference. In a statement in which the centrality of social class is criticized, he indicates that "certainly the conflicts of interest have to be resolved, and the difficulties there have to be priorities. But nothing is gained by pushing a residual version of political monopoly so hard that the only place for others to go is into faction and enmity, or into an equally damaging apathy and cynicism" (pp. 56-57).

From the present account, we also begin to get a sense of the political spirit by which culture has become possessed. Let me now continue with the historical conspectus. Here we come to appreciate how culture arrives at this moment.

## ❖ Culture in Pursuit of Autonomy and Praxis: Modern Cultures

The materialist conception of culture formulated by Raymond Williams must be seen as the product of a historical conjuncture. Likewise are the earlier interpretations, including those that, exposed to Platonic conditioning, pursued ahistorical, universalistic strivings making of culture "the embodiment of ideas, spirit, beauty, and universal truth" (Griswold, 1994, p. 27), separate and autonomous from material and earthly life. It inhered in a "higher life . . . [in which] reason—purity, order, limit, the unchanging—governs the desires, with their bent to excess, insatiability, fickleness, conflict" (Taylor, 1989, p. 20). As the "highest good," supposedly detached from domination, culture is not situated in "the established material organizations of life" (Marcuse, 1968, p. 89). Indeed, Aristotle referred to the antitheses of these universalities—all of which inhere in work—as the "banausic" arts, defined in their relation to the earning of wages. Such activities served deeply "to degrade the mind."

This characterization was clearly the result of the prevailing notions of social life from which new definitional perceptions can be discerned. Indeed, culture, with any hint of the collective ways of life of a people, surfaced during the period of the Industrial Revolution in England. And this development, as Raymond Williams informs us, owed its impetus to conditions that transformed heretofore comparatively neutral terms such as *art*, *class*, and *democ-*

*racy* into divisive and contentious concepts. This was the result of a paradigm shift that I discuss further later. In any event, a retrospective look at culture does more to indicate the constraining conditions under which the great masses of people lived than to trace any sustained, activist inclinations of their cultures. For the most part, this exercise is an extrapolation from the present to the past, with fragments of key figures (philosophers, poets, dramatists) providing the materials for reconstruction. What follows, therefore, are pieces of related information from which we can capture the relevant impressions.

Take the classical Greek period. It is convenient here to view the Aristotlean perception: Work and production were merely necessary evils; definitions of freedom were hierarchically arranged qualitatively away from them, as work was tedious and degrading. Initiatives of the mind should radiate from self-knowledge. An important distinction was made between the use of reason as knowledge and the deployment of skill—*techne*—which was not knowledge; skill, or techne, implied that the elements that were regarded as the sum and substance of culture did not originate from these sources (Drucker, 1993, p. 27). In turn, knowledge was coextensive with morality, as was apparent in the case of the Greek, European, and Chinese civilizations, for example. The dynamics of economics and politics proved "insufficient by themselves to furnish the primary aims of society as a whole" (Feibleman, 1968, p. 235). In the last couple of centuries of the Chou dynasty in China, economic activity came under the sway of the Age of the Philosophers in which "social welfare [had] an economic base, but [had to] include a common moral outlook if it is to survive" (Feibleman, 1968, p. 237). The Chinese, by Drucker's account, had failed to move toward technological mastery because of the absence of the concept of techne in their philosophies.

Down to 16th-century Europe, as R. H. Tawney (1926) informs us, there existed "class divisions sharply defined by custom and law, and little affected by the ebb and flow of economic movements" (p. 65). The forces of displacement then on the ascendant drew attention sharply to the part played by a static traditional social philosophy. In truth, if work carried a negative connotation from the classical times, through the Medieval period, up to the edge of the Industrial Revolution, there were potent religious justifications to be aligned against it. An appropriate example is provided by the story of Adam and Eve in the Garden. God had commanded Adam not to eat of the tree of knowledge of Good and Evil, but through Eve's cajolings, he did. One of the condemnations Adam had to bear for such disobedience is the scourge of work: "Cursed is the ground for thy sake, in sorrow shalt thou eat of all the days of thy life. Thorns and thistles shall it bring forth to thee. . . . In the sweat of thy face shalt thou eat bread, till thou return to the ground" (Genesis 3:17-19).

But work and its handmaiden, economics, did not remain for very long a supplicant to morality. In fact, it was Aquinas (1225-1274) who was perhaps the first to take a pragmatic approach to the gathering forces of political economy. Strict Christian prohibitions in matters of trade, commerce, and the like, were bent to meet the new exigencies. Thus, private property and the acquisition of wealth were not deplorable per se, as early Christian doctrines would have it. Their moral status was dictated by the uses to which they were put. Aquinas legitimated private property on the basis of an implicit trust vested in its holders to use same for the benefit of the community. In addition, "human affairs are more efficiently organized if the proper care of each thing is an individual responsibility" (Aquinas, 1988, p. 72). In debunking old shibboleths, Aquinas took refuge in the sanctions of the natural law: "[In the case of private property, its status] is not against natural law but has been added to natural law by the inventiveness of human reason" (p. 72). (We may also take historical notice of Calvin's [1509-1564] contribution to the cause of secular political economy; see Weber, 1958.)

Under the banner of the Enlightenment, that display of reason would attach naturally to work: "Work becomes a medium for the realization of reason, one which will lift the human species out of a state of nature" (Lash & Urry, 1994, p. 62). It is here that we grasp the distinctions implied in Rousseau's often cited observation, to wit, that while the ancient political writers were fixated on virtue and morals, writers of his time substituted for these two principles money and commerce. In Kostas Axelos's (1976) partial sketch of the emerging "productive" man,

> The *ego* of the human subject is posed as *res cogitans* standing opposed to the (objective) world of *res extensa*. Representation and *ratio*, consciousness and science set the basis for the possibility of grasping the infinite world, and thought here enters on the course of development which will see consciousness, science, and technique unfurl the will to power. Mankind enthusiastically sets off to conquer the whole of reality in terms of objective works. (pp. 8-9)

Present here are the political economic implications of a Grotius, a Hobbes, and a Locke from whom it was but a short step to move from private property to the centrality of labor. Indeed, Locke (1952) has nicely sketched his *labor theory of value* in *The Second Treatise of Government*—a concept addressed in Chapter 6. By extension, the basic spirit of the concept was profoundly believed and relentlessly advocated by Voltaire, for whom work was the linchpin of great civilizations. Work, for Voltaire, keeps away the three great "evils" of need, vice, and boredom. In a retrospective look at the Greek and Roman civilizations, he relocated work at the center of the great achievements of these cultures. "Civilization is the product of work—*il faut cultiver*" (Weintraub, 1966, p. 54). Other Enlightenment figures such as Turgot, for example, did much "to make the cultivation of the soil more rewarding by wise legislation" (p. 55). Colbert, Louis XIV's crafty finance minister, sent spies abroad to steal new industrial secrets and even enticed skilled workers with attractive incentives (Manuel, 1982, p. 60).

We are now confronting "the work model of society" (Benhabib, 1986, p. 10). Labor now assumed center stage, ultimately allowing people, especially the populous classes, to situate themselves within the transforming currents of history. History is movement in which their praxes are deeply implicated.

The change is the paradigm shift mentioned above, one foreshadowed by the Enlightenment, which matured in the 19th century with industrialism. Labor's centrality in this new paradigm identifies with such thinkers as Francis Bacon, Adam Smith, and Karl Marx. For the first, scientific discovery and labor were the necessary combination for fulfilling God's purpose, "the relief of man's estate"; in Smith's hands, *homo oeconomicus* emerged from his entanglements with religious constraints so ably analyzed by Weber (1958) in *The Protestant Ethic and the Spirit of Capitalism* and by R. H. Tawney (1926) in *Religion and the Rise of Capitalism*. In both cases, one is struck by the manner in which private vices, such as usury and selfishness, became transformed into public virtues, from which new systems of ethics and morality resulted. Selfishness, for example, provided a cornerstone for Hobbes's morality based on "psychological egoism." In fact, selfishness acquired the power of "the most original" of the "Laws of Nature," which God, himself, "cannot alter"—Grotius's injunction (Chapter 6). For Marx, man became a productive subject. In combination, all alluded, with differing emphasis and directness, to a kind of labor-induced self-interest from which class conflict was inseparable and one in which culture would be pointedly expressed as the biased elements of cultural production of social classes and their concomitant political practices.

As a whole, the Enlightenment is regarded as the model for the self-development and self-fulfillment of humankind. Such an inference can be easily extracted from the earlier statements of Lash and Urry and Kostas Axelos. It is also to be drawn from my earlier analyses of Cartesian rationalism. But there are mishaps between word and deed. The Enlightenment betrays at least three major lines of analysis running through the definition and interpretation of culture. I will provide synopses of these inflections, the last of which culminates in Marxism as the variant that sets the stage for culture to be aligned systematically to praxis.

The first inflection is Cartesian. The tradition is anterior to the Enlightenment, but as the analyses in the previous chapters have shown, this body of thought was clearly the precursor to the Enlightenment. The aligning of ethical, political, and economic systems to the principles of the machine that we have encountered in the earlier chapters, especially in the thought of Helvetius, d'Alembert, and Voltaire, among others, is to be traced to this source. Indeed, we can dispatch Cartesian notions of culture with indecent haste. Recall that the mind-matter dualism on which Descartes's philosophy of consciousness is erected has no patience for the stuff from which culture is wrought (Chapter 5 and 6). Descartes called culture "custom and example" and isolated it as "*the* source of error" (Gellner, 1992, p. 38) from which the pursuit of certainty must be rescued. Even though the conceptualization and method differed, much the same suspicion was betrayed by Auguste Comte, whose positivistic formulations saw history (and, by extension, culture) finally gelling into science—the positive science of sociology.

The Cartesian spirit also pervades the approach taken by notable literary figures to culture. Take Croce, Ortega y Gasset, and T. S. Eliot. For them, culture enjoys substantial detachment from lived experience. For Croce, it is *poesia* as against *litteratura.* The first is a form of "pure intuition cleansed of all historical reference to reality." In turn, Ortega y Gasset speaks of culture as a phenomenon "without yesterday" ("la cultura salvaje, la cultura sin ayer, sin progresion, sin seguridad"). It is a culture freed of all notions of time and space. The final member of the trio, Eliot, is notorious for his defense of this detachment: "Eliot relinquishes not only the spontaneous link between literature and history . . . but he also surrenders the essential premises on which historical consciousness and literary sensibility could potentially be made to engage in some meaningful interaction" (Weimann, 1984, p. 81). As Terry Eagleton (1978) describes the Eliot-esque sense of tradition, "[It] is a labile, self-transformative organism extended in time and space, constantly reorganized by the present; but this radical historical relativism is then endowed with the status of absolute classical authority" (p. 147). The related conception of time "leaves out the combativeness with which individuals and institutions decide on what is tradition and what is not, what relevant and what not" (Said, 1993, p. 2). Mr. Eliot was not prepared to trust culture to be defined by the lowly orders of people; the present is directed by the past. And the purveyor of culture, say, poetry, is the individual separated from "the man who suffers and the mind which creates" (Venuti, 1989, p. 31).

Cartesian rationalism was extended to the Enlightenment tradition. As I indicated in Chapter 4, the tradition was like a reservoir into which different streams flowed. Implied here is a lack of ideational uniformity that clearly surfaces in this context. Not all of the *philosophes* abjured culture. To repeat what is indicated in Chapter 4, Montesquieu's (1906) *The Spirit of Laws* is, in part, unequivocal support for the histories and cultures of individual nations. Much the same sentiments break through in his observations on Grotius's application of natural law (Chapter 6). In his turn, Condillac would present identical support for culture in the counsels he provided for lawmakers of a nation: "[They] must study the character of the people, investigate their usages and customs. . . . Then [they] will preserve what is found to be good, and replace what is found to be bad, but only by means which conform most to the *moeurs* of the citizens" (cited in Bury, 1932, p. 209). Voltaire presents another example, despite his seemingly uncompromising stance against any culture except that of the elites. Berlin (1982, pp. 88-89) and Brumfitt (1970, pp. 124-125) find in his historical exercises a tendency to debunk but an equally powerful predisposition to forge the notions of "custom and opinion" into reliable history. As Brumfitt (1970) relays the paradox, "whilst Voltaire is becoming more deterministic, another concept is also becoming increasingly important in his historical writing: the concept of custom or opinion" (p. 124). It is partly for these reasons that Berlin offers him as an early exemplar of humanistic, as opposed to a positivistic, historiography.

This slight digression is not without its significance for the rise of the "work model of activity." For even though it is difficult to link Hegelian historicism directly with Montesquieu and Voltaire, the central place that history would gradually occupy did so obliquely. It came in the form of Hegel's attack on Kant's project of pure reason. Reason lost its apodicticity when Hegel integrated the contradictions that Kant dismissed as metaphysics—the stuff of *value*—into a synthesis defined by historical consciousness. In other words, Hegel's critique of Kant's pure reason comes with a substitution—"the necessity [to orient that critique] to a phenomenology of human spirit—the story of reason's historical and cultural becoming" (Benhabib, 1986, p. 344).

What can be detected from the extrusion of these culturohistorical asides of Cartesian determinism is the labor embeddedness lying dormant in the concepts of the Enlightenment. Parenthetically, Cassirer (1966) reminds us that historical thinking was always used by the philosophes "as one of the chief measures in the battle for its own ideals" (p. 217). In any event, Hegel's contribution to the pivotal role of labor in the new paradigm came by way of Marx's well known critique in which Hegel's *reflective* subject was eclipsed by Marx's *productive* subject.

Counterposed to the rationalist inflection to the Enlightenment tradition was a romantic trajectory, often referred to as "the counter-Enlightenment" (Berlin, 1982; Seidman, 1983). Within this trajectory are two main "moments," as I will refer to them: the one spearheaded by Johann Gottfried von Herder (1744-1803), the German poet and philosopher, while the other passes through Samuel Taylor Coleridge coming to its full flowering with the swift, critical counterstrokes of Matthew Arnold. These latter figures were English *belles lettres* who appeared at a critical time in British history when democracy as the dynamic extension of the work model of activity was threatening to define the total social fabric of British—and, by extension, capitalist society.

Herder and the Romanticists were fundamentally concerned with the disembodiment of the Subject occurring at the hands of the philosophes. Herder was showered with praise by Goethe for exposing the vibrant ties with the Subject and feeling, for showing the world as "a compost heap teeming with life" (cited in Cassirer, 1966, p. 219). Immediately, the significance of the Romanticists for culture, especially the ideas of Herder, emerged from the stress placed on "cultures" and not "culture." While the movement, as a whole sans Herder, betrayed strong affiliations with "the cause of the Christian Middle Ages [and] saw there the lost Paradise of humanity for which it longed and to which it wanted to return," (Cassirer, 1966, p. 222), it embraced a certain antimodernism that legitimated rhetorical forms, as I indicated in Chapter 4. This feature coupled with the stress on the existence and authenticity of cultures are the main contributions Romanticism brings to the notion of cultures as praxis. Herder is unsparing in his condemnation of cultural tyranny, even though he appears to detach culture from politics by inserting it within such idealistic forms as *nation,* and *volksgeist.* He thought it puzzling that the lives and cultures of other peoples were treated indifferently as though a mere footnote to European culture. Accordingly, "the very thought of a superior European culture is a blatant insult to the majesty of Nature" (cited in Williams, 1976, p. 19).

The romantic strain represented by Coleridge and Arnold reflected key notions of the broader movement. The courtship of spiritual perfection was paramount. In Arnold's words, "culture [has] its origin in the love of perfection. It moves by the force, not merely or primarily of the scientific passion for pure knowledge, but also of the moral and social passion for doing good" (Arnold, 1947, p. 36). By extension, he states that "culture indefatigably tries, not to make what each raw person may like, the rule by which he fashions himself; but to draw ever nearer to a sense of what is indeed beautiful, graceful, and becoming, and to get the raw person to like that" (p. 41). Here, as Robert Weimann (1984) informs us, Arnold is engaged in little more than a selection of his criteria from tradition. Tradition, in turn, derives, according to Robert Nisbet (1968, p. 76), from values rooted in the Middle Ages, hence that quality of pristine fixity and timelessness by which it is characterized from this perspective. There is hardly a historical dimension to this notion of culture, except to the extent that T. S. Eliot, one of its main advocates, locates that feature in the critic's imagination (Venuti, 1989; Weimann, 1984).

But Arnold's liberal affectations appeared to be feigned. He speaks of the attainment of "sweetness and light" for all and had certainly attacked the lethargy of the English ruling class, but his concept of culture was authoritarian. In 1866, when the English laboring classes agitated for the franchise, anarchy reigned. It was anarchy, as the people transgressed law and order, which, for him, was sacred. Moreover, freedom, for which thousands of workers agitated, carried a responsibility seemingly outside of their capacities to discharge: "It is not only a question of being free to speak but of a kind of national life in which people knew enough to have something to say" (Williams, 1980, p. 5). His was a detached, elitist, perspective. Surely, it inveighed, often justifiably, against the work model of activity, especially the encroaching domination of technology and poured scorn on "system makers and systems," such as Bentham, Comte, and by implication, Descartes; but he reserved a certain disdain for the way of life of the people. More out of a sense of omission, he displayed marked hauteur to any thought or action originating from this source that failed to reflect his notions of "sweetness and light." Peter Goodall (1995) catches these impulses rather well in the following summation: "The harmony which it is the job of culture to create is not the result of the consensus of the parts, worked through with compromise, but the surrender of the autonomy of the marginal elements to the authority of the center" (p. 19). Like the notions entertained by Herder, the Arnoldian (and, to an appreciable degree, the Coleridgean) perspective on culture was detached from political life. His notion of culture favored "an inward condition of mind and spirit, not . . . an outward set of circumstances" (Arnold, 1947, p. 39). "Culture was the outward flow of mind and feeling which met in a centre above politics or sectarianism" (Bradbury, 1971, p. 38). For Coleridge, whose contempt for political economy was hardly disguised, the worst form of aristocracy was preferable to the "oligarchy of glib economists" (Kirk, 1987, p. 114). In short, he was hostile to labor as a causal principle that allowed people to intervene in history and become active players.

But a materialist conception of culture is really a creature of a historicist rendering of human affairs, one which rubs shoulders with an idealist inflection. In short, the reference is to the historico-cultural perspectives of Hegel and Marx. Of course, it is Hegel who at once affirmed the idealist conception by linking reason to culture via the concept of civilization. Culture and the cultured were given a privileged, exalted status. It was their responsibility to bestow on lesser mortals and even to thrust it on them for their own good. Some, like Karl Popper (1971, p. 118), are not averse to the use of "some form of imperialism" to ensure this unquestionable good to humanity! Paradoxically, it was Hegel, the idealist and conservative, who supplied the basis for a Marxist materialist conception of history and—by extension—culture. Of course, I am referring to the well-known shadowboxing between Hegelian and Marxist dialectics alluded to in Chapter 2.

Under Marxist auspices, autonomy would shift from structure to agency via culture—those giving increasing validity to Karl Polanyi's countervailing position on the subject. But culture was still firmly yoked to economic definitions, expressed mainly in class terms. Listen to Gajo Petrovic (1967) in a widely quoted statement on the topic:

> Marx's conception of history is not "economic" if by this one means the view that the economic factor is the only determining factor in history, but it is "economic" if this term is used to designate the view that acknowledges the ultimately determining role of the economic factor. According to the view man is not *only* an "economic" animal . . . , but he is this and above all. (p. 94)

A materialist conception of culture, one situated in the established material organizations of life, is very much a creature of time. And when time is defined in terms of altered social arrangements, we are really speaking about the shift from a Platonic caste system, where the ingredients of culture take on a timeless, elitist, and ultimately transhistorical cast, to the revolt of the masses, to the "work model of society."

In their turn, the masses are situated in the central core of a world now defined principally by commodity production and distribution, with the lineaments of culture suffused with the dominant organizing principles of that order. Contestations are waged over rights, as uneven distribution of power holds center stage: "Wealth was no longer a characteristic of a people but rather a force for dividing a nation" (Jenks, 1993, p. 19).

In classical Marxism, culture forms part of the superstructure, of epiphenomena defined, if not controlled, by the economic instance. In its most vulgar usage—the kind in widespread fashion until a rash of neo-Marxist revisionism (Althusser, 1971; Poulantzas, 1975)—culture was viewed as a reflection of the economic workings of society. The neo-Marxist counterpoint is the "relative autonomist" position, one which, nonetheless, vests determining force in "structures" in the spirit of Lévi-Strauss, not in human agency, per culture, except in the omnibus context of social class. Culture was not seen as "a complex set of material-social practices"; rather, it was viewed as "a realm of representations—"consciousness" as opposed to "real activity," a symbolic domain, separated from, but controlled by, an economic domain" (Brenkman, 1987, p. ix). As long as economic structures remained relatively stable, such theories seemed to work; but the advent of globalism, including the dynamics of communications and aestheticization referred to above, would put them to the test. Indeed, the first major impetus in this direction would come from Marxism itself—the cultural Marxists of the Frankfurt School.

## ❖ Culture and Its Alignment to Praxis

The indications are clearly that culture en route to an autonomy underscored by human agency and not structural determinism had more to gain from cultural Marxism. It is evidently a rough passage across a river on whose far bank looms the imposing figure of Theodor Adorno, acting the part of Charon, Pluto's grim ferryman of the underworld.

The cultural Marxists, who were in the forefront of not only vesting some autonomy in culture, also did much to endow it with a political role. They were inclined, however, to blow hot and cold on the issues. In one breath, culture appears as an instrument of domination, especially in the writings of Horkheimer, Adorno, and Marcuse. It was an active force in creating a disenchanted modern society and aided directly in prefiguring domination through technology. The class struggle so central to Marxism was, according to Adorno, marginalized, and critique and praxis were to be situated in the aesthetic realm, if emancipation was ever to be effected.

Culture, then (at least modern culture, and the distinction appears to be vital, as we shall shortly see), could be said to be activist, to be praxiological. But these qualities were insinuated and, at their most assertive, propelled by desperation. Theodor Adorno represents the first inflection. Culture was negatively praxiological, in the sense that it served the interests of domination. In his famous book, coauthored with Max Horkheimer (1972), *Dialectic of Enlightenment*, he takes the position that reason, while activist, whether through culture or politics, was inherently oppressive. How could it serve the ends of freedom? Adorno, if not Marcuse, attempted to locate such a praxis in elitist cultural forms—classical music, for example. He could not get himself to locate the emancipatory moment in mass culture—the culture of the popular classes. On his view, mass culture lacks, among other things, the capacity to define and articulate what the popular (i.e., dominated) classes feel and express in their art. Capitalist domination made emancipation unavailing. Nor was critical theory, its exposure of processes of domination notwithstanding, an instrument of emancipation; as Jonathan Turner (1991) observed, negative dialectics could, at best, "allow humans to 'tread water' until historical circumstances were more favorable to emancipatory movements" (pp. 257-258). One of Adorno's most lasting insights on the question relates to the new form, the new use value assumed by commodities in a consumer-driven capitalism. It is that the exchange-value, per Marx's labor theory of value, has been superseded by a use-value driven and controlled by culture. We had to await the fullness of time to have this insight more clearly developed by such scholars and writers as Baudrillard, Featherstone, Lash and Urry, and Poster, who placed great stress on "symbolic" culture.

Finally, what about Gramsci? He deserves a far keener commentary than space will allow. His ideas do support culture as praxis, albeit in a somewhat indirect way. His concept of "hegemonic leadership" makes concession to the culture of the dominated classes as the means by which the dominant class exercises hegemony. In practice, these concessions get fed into politics and policy-making, thereby ensuring that the culture of the dominated forms part of the general culturo-political mix. Pluralist politics provide a good example.

## ❖ The Shifting Landscape: Nonmodern and "Backward" Cultures

What of the cultures in the non-Western and the formerly colonized societies of the world? This query has to be answered from two perspectives—that of the dominant and that of the dominated. But above everything else, the interplay of both sets of cultures under globalism suggests the arrival of a new shift. This shift is announced by a leveling of old dichotomies, due to such factors as hybridity, the persistence of traditional cultures, buttressed by their intrinsic validity and the suspect features of metropolitan culture (science and technology, for example).

From the perspective of the dominant. It is perhaps only a slight exaggeration to state that the really prominent ideas on the state of these cultures—those notions that have sedulously formed the basis for major development policy decisions—can be traced back to Collingwood's wry statement about history. To repeat: The central point of history is the sunrise of the modern scientific spirit.

In truth, an important disciplinary distinction must be made. Unfortunately, only a bare sketch is possible here. It seems evident from research on

Africa, for instance, that different disciplines have enjoyed uneven success and that much of this success (or lack thereof) bears a strong relationship to metropolitan policy issues related to socioeconomic development. The model of development required a science such as that which made a Germany or a France and, most gloriously, a United States flourish. While a long line of anthropologists (Evans-Pritchard, Griaule, Delafosse, and Horton, among others), historians (Anta Diop, James, and lately, Bernal, among others), literary figures (Rufus Lewis Perry, Cesaire, Fanon, and, lately, Ngugi wa' Thiong'o, among others) have, like John the Baptist, been crying in the wilderness in a voice that has now proved quite prophetic, that voice lacked the preferred cadences. Development required instead the wisdom of the social sciences—the voices of a Lerner, a Hoselitz, a Rostow, a Levy (non-Marxists) and a Baran, a Frank, or an Amin (Marxists).

The tack is a familiar enough one. Help is proffered, say, by providing assistance in drilling water wells or for any number of development projects. Then, almost inevitably, this lack in the "developing" country is extrapolated to its entire culture, with the "economic naturalization" thesis of a Mises or a Becker figuring prominently (see Chapter 2). Repeatedly, technological efficiency in this sense of modernization theory is used interchangeably with cultural backwardness. Even anthropology, a discipline that has done much to minimize misconceptions on so-called cultural backwardness, is not without sin. As Christopher L. Miller (1993, p. 219) reminds us

> Before the 1960s, Africa had almost been the province of anthropologists. African[s] were seen mostly as cultural objects than as producers of cultural interpretations; cultures were studied as systems, but African depictions of African cultures in literature were rarely given attention. (p. 219)

The myopia and conceptual difficulties were compounded largely by the imposition of European institutions (the nation-state, for example) and other definitions (tribe, for instance) on African cultural arrangements that were far more complex (Ranger, 1983). Once again, we are in the presence of *the A versus the not-A* scenario by which the relations of the two blocs are largely characterized.

At the time of this writing, these very development policies are still in vogue in those *structural adjustment* formulas implemented by the World Bank. Of course, the indigenous is marginalized. These policies are widely known to be aimed directly at economic as well as cultural dislocation; the process is pursued with a passion the equal of old-style colonialism. And yet there is increasingly less evidence suggesting a homogenization by metropolitan culture. We are situated in a global culture, where hybridity is often the rule (Buell, 1994; Robertson, 1992). Global cultural dynamics do not reflect the level of mimicry attributed to even heavily dependent cultures, as V. S. Naipaul contends in the cases of ex-British cultures in the Caribbean during the 1970s. Quite a diverse, yet related, range of causal factors cooperate in this very complex process: a corresponding coexistence of universalisms and particularisms (i.e., modernities and nonmodernities) in nonmodern *and* metropolitan societies (Keith, 1995a; Ngugi, 1990, p. 972; Robertson, 1992); the breakdown of cultural hegemony, resulting in part from the communications revolution (Appadurai, 1990); the natural hybridization long obscured by self-serving metropolitan ideologies now exposed by factors such as those indicated immediately above (Tomlinson, 1991). Cultural penetration suggests, increasingly, that cultural invention and not mimesis or replication has been occurring; that "Third World peoples were already post modern DURING the process of dependent modernisation."[4]

Relatedly, Anthony Appiah (1992) and Jonathan Friedman (1992) have indicated this nonmimetic quality in Third World appropriations of metropolitan cultural products. Friedman gives us some insights in the mind-set of the *sapeurs*—young, lower-class Congolese men who will do just about anything to be outfitted in the latest Parisian fashion. Are they apeing, afflicted by inferior complexes? No, their mind-set is rooted in the cosmological and symbolic universes and meanings of Congolese culture. Indeed, Appiah (1992) has keenly observed that "it might be said to be the mark of popular culture that its borrowings from international cultural forms are remarkably insensitive to, not so much dismissive of as blind to, the issue of neocolonialism or 'cultural imperialism' " (p. 149).[5] In the end, the anthropologist George Marcus, who now argues the case strongly for his discipline accepting a world of leveled dichotomies, speaks of a global culture defined less by struggle, than by negotiation. He speaks of the current global culture as being steeped in processes where identity formation results from "turbulence, fragments, intercultural reference and the localized intensification of global possibilities and associations" (Marcus, 1992, p. 315). All these developments tend to give greater credibility to Leslie Sklair's (1991) bold statement: "The global system at the end of the twentieth century is not synonymous with the global capitalist system, but the driving forces behind global capitalism are the dominant though not the only driving forces behind the global system" (p. 53). It is bold as there are many commentators who find the eclipse of the Soviet Union as the license for the metropolitan world to ride its coach and four through the Third World and other nonmodern cultures.[6]

What is there to be offered in the case of the Marxist tradition? It is true that it contributed appreciably in uncovering the dynamic processes of dependence. But in its definition of Socialist man, the tradition has certainly imposed stifling constraints of its own. These are directives by which the centrally defining endowments of the nonmodern cultures—often their indigenousness—are either expunged forthwith or treated as transitional to the march of those cultures to socialism. It is a commonplace that Marx (in the case of India) and Engels (in the case of Algeria) welcomed the utter destruction of these cultures preparatory to socialism. To take another example, at the Second International, held at Stuttgart in 1907, it was actually recorded that *natives* lacked the ability to mount and sustain emancipatory offensives. They were without the wherewithal to grasp the niceties of liberation praxis. We should likewise note the underlying implications of the cultural Marxists at the time of their most effective work, namely, their formulations during a period when the internationalization of capital and the rise of dependence were perhaps among the more compelling units for analyzing international capitalism and modernity. And yet their silence, except for peripheral asides from Marcuse, was deafening.[7] If Adorno were prepared to conceptualize a "negative dialectics" rather than envisaging the emancipatory moment in mass culture, his approach to the *Other(s)* as carriers was quite predictable. His analysis of jazz music, one of the cherished prizes of African American (indeed, all black) cultures, makes the point. For black people, as a whole, do not regard jazz only as their contribution to the modern world's limited number of new, genuine, art forms; jazz is viewed as the embodiment of what is "different," of what is culturally peculiar about them, which calls at once into play a politics of recognition and an ethic of difference. The example of Paul Gilroy (1993) is a case in point. He places much transformative force in black music. In his view, its expressive content and form provides the basis for the preferred "politics of transfiguration" over the modernist "politics of fulfillment." The politics of transfiguration betrays much of the rhetorical qualities opposed to modernity: It abhors the "modern, occidental separation of ethics and aesthetics, culture and politics" where, he continues, "the politics of fulfillment is . . . mostly content to play occidental rationality at its own game . . . the politics of transfiguration strives in pursuit of the sublime, struggling to repeat the unrepeatable, to present the unpresentable" (pp. 37-38).

The Adornian response is like a bucket of cold water in the face:

> The subject (the African American: added) which expresses itself expresses precisely this: I am nothing, I am filth, no matter what they do to me, it serves

> me right. Potentially this subject has already become one of those Russians, accused of a crime, and who, although innocent, collaborates with the prosecutor from the beginning and is incapable of finding a punishment severe enough. (Adorno, 1967, cited in Meszaros, 1989, p. 132)

The rather clear message is that there is a kind of collective ambivalence—Marxist and non-Marxist—about the legitimacy of these cultures. In my view, there is little to distinguish between Adorno, the *legislator* (to use Bauman's term), and Saul Bellow, who states, somewhat contemptuously, that Western civilization is prepared to read the Zulus when they would have produced a Tolstoy. (Even though in fairness to Adorno, many elements of emancipation surfeit his formulations—his ideas on identity, which attack the essentialist claims of the Enlightenment; see Sampson, 1993, pp. 84-89, for a crisp account.)

Successive revisionist efforts have done much to wean historical materialism of much of its economic and cultural determinism. Indeed, Zygmunt Bauman (1992, p. 221) can scarcely be faulted in insisting that Marxism remains a metanarrative, one even more restrictive than liberal democracy. To develop and supplement Bauman's position, one should note that liberal democracy is served by a critical dimension that is inseparable from its commitment to individual autonomy. In fulfilling its deepest aspirations, liberal democracy generates rights. Now, rights are standing knee-deep in difficulties, as the current literature on communitarianism testifies. But a dimension of this process is yet to be explored. For according as they legitimate the rights of universal citizenship and, by extension, universal dignity, liberal democratic traditions spawn a politics of recognition. More attention will be devoted to the issue in Chapter 10. Parenthetically, it is useful to make the point that a politics of difference has actually veered in from two directions—from the perspective of the Other(s), one often supported by what is intrinsic to the culture, broadly speaking, and from the wide angle and heterogeneous traditions of democracy, a spawning ground for principles and action metropolitan societies deem legitimate.

It is true that by the very nature of metropolitan domination much that represented the Other(s)' view of their culture was marginalized, or concertedly eradicated. But must they be nearly always seen as effects; can they ever function as major causal factors in shaping the socioeconomic environment in which they are located? In the later stages of neo-Marxist theorizing, such as I have mentioned earlier, revisionism around the notion of "relative autonomy" (of the state, of politics, of ideology, and so on) did much to release the vicelike grip of determinism to which historical materialism was prone. But structures, instead of human agency, were the phenomena receiving such relative autonomy. One type of determinism was merely replaced by another.

How is culture seen from the vantage point of the dominated? One can well begin a response to that question with a story involving the late jazz musician Miles Davis in connection with the birth of bebop. When Miles was informed that the white jazz afficionados had declared the arrival of a new type of music and that he (Davis) was one of the original forces, Davis is said to have quipped, "What! I've playing my horn like this for the past 15 years." In truth, what has been analyzed throughout as the *rhetorical* has been keeping pace, despite the continuing or diminishing corrosiveness of colonialism in all its guises and disguises. Although a single quotation is incapable of capturing what has clearly been persistent—with ignorance being the result of stilted and a largely one-dimensional reporting—one such quote from Kofi Anyidoho (1989), the noted Ghanaian poet, will be encumbered with that burden:

> Against the threat of total obliteration of the indigenous self, the New World slave fought back in quiet but firm rebellion. That quieting of the tongue was sometimes enforced by such rare devices as the iron muzzle. . . . Yet, as Kamau Brathwaite has clearly demonstrated . . . the imported African languages were never completely killed. They were compelled to submerge. But they gradually re-emerged, though constantly transforming themselves into new forms. (p. 23)

Anyidoho goes on, rightly, to designate language as "the strongbox in which the innermost soul of a people [is] hidden" (p. 23). This dimension provides, in part, the long, Third World, tradition of a praxiological culture. Several national leaders are proud poets and subscribers to the notion that culture is praxis: Fanon, Cabral, Neto, and Toure are unified on this issue. As Sekou Toure (1974) put it, "Culture is at a given time a social process, and infrastructure" (p. 69).

If the dynamics of the cultures of the dominated had consistently found expression in concrete political action, they were now conjoined to postmodern or post-Cartesian thinking for which culture was not the source of all errors. Far from being such an unspeakable hindrance, culture allows us to make sense of the world that we are constantly in the process of making and remaking. It is the source from which we derive the tools enabling us to get a grip of the complex, diverse world that we inhabit. Although I do find much of Burkean thought somewhat disagreeable, its comments on the proper relationship between "general prejudices" and constructive thought are certainly applicable to culture. We can explore more profitably what it reveals of our constitution and motivation; it will be our loss if it is treated as the repository for those human errors persistently dogging our path to that blissful illusion called *certainty*.

This chapter has brought within its purview the clear and distinguishing features of the phenomenon of culture as they relate to the major constructs of this book. Culture is freed to inform theory and practice. It has done so through a complex range of processes that became detached from abstractions and then attached to "the work model of society." But such a framework was, at first, hampered by the dominance of class relations that while foreshadowing certain emancipatory potentials of people, had to await yet another morphology within the social formation. The separation of consumption from production and distribution enabled the increasing autonomization of reflexivity and human agency. It is partly on these bases that culture assumed a praxiological posture, aided, of course, by a number of other epochal factors—the rise of risk society, the culturo-political syncretism supported by globalism, sophisticated communications systems, and so on. The part played by postmodernism in the process will be sketched in the next chapter.

## ❖ Notes

1. Alfred Ayer's positivist version is the most severe. Here there are only two classes of propositions grounding truth: (a) analytic propositions that depend for their truth on the meanings of the words by which they are expressed and (b) empirical propositions, whose truth (or falsity) derives from verifying propositions. Value judgments, many of which originate in culture, are meaningless. A difference-oriented attack on this position has gathered steam (see, for example, the tightly argued volume edited by Megill, 1994; also my earlier discussion in Chapter 7.

2. Structuralism, like Cartesianism, implies its own binarism. Determinate action resides in structures existing independently of human agency. Levi-Strauss states that the mind extracts knowledge in terms of pairs of opposites.

3. See Lash and Urry's (1994) elaboration. This form of reflexivity is "rhetorical," not "logic based."

4. I wish to thank Michael Allen of Bryn Mawr College, one of Sage's reviewers, for this observation.

5. Borrowing and the absence of mimicry exists in many areas. Faye Ginsburg (1994) speaks of the Australian Aboriginals' use of Western media technology to build their own "cultural future" (p. 365).

6. This erroneous view is held by MacCannell (1989): "The best indication of the final victory of modernity over other sociocultural arrangements is not the disappearance of the nonmodern world, but its artificial preservation and reconstruction in modern society" (p. 8). His myopia passeth all understanding! For a more accurate and realistic assessment, see Bamyeh (1993), Hannerz (1989), and Appadurai (1990). Also see John L. Comaroff's (1996) interesting comments on the effect of globalism: It underscores "an awareness of localism—and, in the process, reinforces it" (cited in Wilmsen & McAllister, 1996, p. 174).

7. Marcuse and Ernest Bloch are among cultural Marxists whose writings (later writings, in the case of the former) began to separate out art writ large as somewhat autonomous. Bloch, for example, locates in poetry, myths, and so on, histories and traditions inseparable from various social projects of the present. He speaks of elements of *concrete utopia* here. In turn, Marcuse (1987) yields to art another logic and sensibility that defies "the rationality and sensibility incorporated in the dominant social institutions" (p. 7). See Bloch (1971) and Marcuse (1978).

# *Chapter Nine*

# POSTMODERNISM AND THE REPOSITIONING OF CULTURE

*Hebraism and Hellenism—between these two points of influence moves our world.*
Matthew Arnold (1869, p. 69)

*Let us wage a war on totality: let us be witnesses to the unpresentable.*
Jean Francois Lyotard (1984, p. 81)

This chapter has as its focus the cultural dimensions of postmodernism. Why have I stressed the phenomenon, especially when other lines of the critique of modernity, such as communitarianism and a certain inflection to critical theory, have themselves endorsed culture as practice?[1]

Postmodernism is given priority because of its agreeable combination of analytic (and geographic) sweep and critical scope. In the area of social theory, postmodernism brings discourses to bear with transracial, transcultural, and transnational implications. Reality is *not* unitary, except perhaps for the blind and those who refuse to see. The above discourses are nothing if not the manifestations of a new reality defined by contiguity—a global one—and imperative interconnectedness in formulating definitions. Postmodern culture captures many of these heretofore related, but segregated, processes. This new omnibus feature results, as Kwame Anthony Appiah (1992) describes, from "a new way of understanding the multiplication of distinctions that flows from the need to clear oneself a space" (p. 145). The clearing of that space, I might add, has a symbolic rather than a narrow territorial definition, induced by changes such as sophisticated communications systems. Space clearing is also related to the consequences of agency and reflexivity, now global in nature.

Like communitarianism and critical theory, postmodernism also originated in narrow, metropolitan concerns. The first major work on postmodernism—Lyotard's (1984) *The Postmodern Condition: A Report on Knowledge*—was written on behalf of the Conseil des Universités of Quebec as a report on the state of knowledge in the most advanced modern societies. But its main focus—the poverty of logocentrism—fed neatly into much of the persistent epistemological contentions raised in the rhetorically suffused poetry of Aime Cesaire (its anti-Cartesianism, its humanistic communitarianism and *difference*), in feminism (due in part, to the contrasting epistemologies suggested by Carol Gilligan's [1982] *In a Different Voice*), and in the discourse on Nature (now that ecological science provides the earth with epistemological claims), among others. Loose and vague though its "theories" might be, postmodernism infuses such currently problematical concepts as power, narrativity, social movements, and so on, with the compulsions demanded by an expanded analytic framework. It also provides useful insights for new theoretical work, as I elaborate later.

On the other hand, communitarianism and critical theory are almost inseparably attached to the crisis situations in the metropolitan world. In one of the few attempts to take critical theory outside of this narrow orbit of discourse, Larry Ray (1993, *Rethinking Critical Theory*) has indicated that beyond pious suggestions for like initiatives from such scholars as Seyla Benhabib and Douglas Kellner, the myopia remains hale and well. Overall, the more enlightened analyses in both theoretical spheres are quite insightful. Seyla Benhabib's (1986) *Critique, Norm, and Utopia* has clearly taken major steps toward integrating the liberatory aspects of contextualism and postmodernism into a body of thought overly influenced by neo-Kantianism, conspicuously via Jurgen Habermas. And while she has avoided a measure of the neo-Kantianism by which a Habermasian analysis of globalism is blocked, she still has not built into her analysis the kind of expansiveness to accommodate our concept. I am quite aware that she is writing her own book, but one might say that an opportunity is missed and, perhaps, an obligation has not been met. Still, her commitment to a "politics of empowerment," which renders critical theory "more compatible with a radical, participatory, and pluralist conception of politics" (pp. 347-348), appears to be a step in the right direction.

Reconstructive theorizing, such that communitarianism and critical theory are admittedly undertaking, should assess their bearings with the Big Picture in mind. There is still an "internalist" tendency present. One looks in vain, for example, for any significant, direct theorization in Ben Agger's (1993) *Gender, Culture, and Power.* The project is clearly intended as one of cardinal import, namely, the birth of a new "feminist postmodern critical theory," but globalismic linkages have to be inferred. Feminist theory, broadly speaking, is inherently globalismic. There is not a single reference to "underdevelopment," the "Third World," or their equivalents in this book!

The fact is that myopia has not caught up with the new global reality. This inattention is due, in no small measure, to the persistence of what Zygmunt Bauman calls "ontological totalitarianism," of which the status quo is still in command. Qualitative changes at the global level are captured appropriately by the embracing orbit within which postmodernism operates: "It sees the world with some understanding of it as a historical whole" (Levin, 1988, p. 4). It has captured that sense of the world expressed by Heidegger as a total picture, representing the qualities of immediacy and a visual oneness associated with that metaphor. After all, this was the unabashed motive of capitalism!

An analytic note before I proceed. I have not completely accepted the total perspective of the postmodernists. Their wholesale condemnation of the Enlightenment, for example, is unacceptable. So, too, are the attempts to extricate their projects from any deliberate exercise in theory building. But much from their assault on logocentrism comports favorably with the neo-Enlightenment premises of this book. If the upcoming analysis appears at times to be debates within a debate, it is to be attributed to certain revisionist tasks I find unavoidable. Quite pointedly, I do not abandon completely the principle of foundationalism. In line with many prominent strands of feminist thought, the globalismic perspective grounds its epistemology on the foundation of difference.

## ❖ The Postmodern Interlude: The Triple Alliance

In the course of his analysis of culture, Raymond Williams observes that the concept is one of the two or three most complicated words in the English language. I support the candidacy of postmodernism for the fourth. As my charge in this chapter does not really require a definitional exercise that would clearly justify such a candidacy, I will, with pleasurable relief, extract from that corpus of ideas only that which is appropriate for our purposes.

Our starting point is a widespread admission from competing perspectives, postmodernism as well as other traditional positions often virulently opposed to it. Roughly, the two main positions that conflate are critiques of liberalism (communitarianism) and the attack on Marxism (postmodernism). The point of confluence exists in a common "Promethean conception" these principal positions share: "They view mankind as appropriating an essentially malleable nature, unfolding its talents and powers in the process of changing external reality" (Benhabib, 1992, p. 69). The common admission is that the universal organizing principles that modernity has used to control the world, whether as a civilizational responsibility or as naked domination, are losing their enabling power.

The crisis is a deepening of those conditions partly addressed by Lasch, Berger, and Lifton, among others (Chapter 2). But they should hardly be taken as narrow defects centered in the psychology of the metropolitan resident. They result from deeply embedded causal factors that ramify throughout the various levels of our common existential project—within the animate and the inanimate, within the social organizations that up to now have formed the theory and practice of everyday life. The plight is recorded in earlier chapters, so there is little need to rehash it here; perhaps, succumbing to whimsy, one should restate a Nietzschean admonition: "Ye have made your way from worm to man, and much within you is still worm" (Nietzsche, n.d., p. 6).

Critique also draws into the debate whether epistemological foundations on which modernity is erected are obsolete (the postmodernists) or are terribly disjointed but repairable (Agger, 1993; Benhabib, 1992; Giddens, 1990; Habermas, 1987). Accordingly, postmodernism is often counterposed to *high modernity, counter-Enlightenment, critical modernism, interactive rationality,* and the like. In any event, there is no mistaking the broad agreement shared on key issues, especially on those related to qualitative shifts in philosophical perspectives, from a gradually accepted obsolescence of a Philosophy of Consciousness to its replacement by a Philosophy of Language.[2]

The postmodernists, whose ideas have penetrated deeply into contemporary consciousness—as much a function of the probity and suggestiveness of their analyses—can be divided into three main strands. These are the postmodernists, narrowly defined (Lyotard, Baudrillard); the deconstructionists (Derrida, Paul de Man); and the poststructuralists (Foucault, Deleuze, and Guattari). The three strands are united, despite key differences, by their common sentence of death on the Enlightenment as a continuing viable principle for the present or any future social order. Their importance for situating interdependence within globalism rests on the emancipatory agendas often implicit in this rich, if controversial, body of formulations. *Implicit* is used because much that is germane to vitally needed theory building in our contemporary age of theoretical and praxiological flux exists as inferences, yet powerful ones, indeed! Postmodernists are notorious for their theoretical "vanishing act" (Thiele, 1986). Lyotard, in particular, appears to reject social theory *tout court.* But postmodernists, nonetheless, find theory building quite an abhorrent affair. And yet, if we should locate ourselves within the orbit of their discourses, such aversion becomes immediately understandable. I hardly think that there should be much controverting the suggestion that if deconstructionism has a message to convey, it is that the task of arriving at truth is difficult indeed. But a truly seminal body of ideas will stretch beyond the cognitive horizons of its originators, however prescient. Such is the case of Marx and historical materialism—there is Marx, the structuralist; Marx, the Freudian; Marx, the Leninist; Marx, the existentialist; Marx, the feminist; and so on. The evidence suggests increasingly that postmodernist thought, especially that of Derrida, carries implications way beyond his own evaluation of his contribution to the genre. Yes, there is evidence of a politics, an ethics, and a theory. In the end, Cornel West (1993) might just be a mite disingenuous in labeling Derrida's work as "rather monotonous, Johnny-one-note rhetorical readings" (p. 33) insensitive to the play of concrete military, economic, and social forces.

## ❖ Things Fall Apart?

Perhaps the most influential theoretical strand of postmodernism is that presented by Jean Francois Lyotard (1984).[3] The unifying cluster of forces that have kept modernity buoyant, he claims, is spent. According to Lyotard, modernity has been organized around what he calls "grandnarratives" (the individual, reason, the family, the nation, etc.). A simple way of putting it is that these strategic narratives—all with the individual neatly positioned at their centers—form a story line of his progress across time and space. Implicit here is a specific message: that he has a past and a future that can be defined by a discrete set of principles that give predictability to the nature and function of their contributing elements (the individual, the family, the nation, etc.). By extension—and Lyotard has spoken directly to this issue—this person (i.e., white, middle-class Western man) is no longer the model for all the other cultures of the world to emulate. Today, that universe of definition has collapsed and perhaps the clearest indicator of the drama is the loss of belief in the idea of Progress, itself primarily induced by the inherent limitations of a logic-driven characterization of the world. The tandem of Logic and Progress proved incapable of expunging those "myths and rigidities" at once germane to the Other(s) and nonresistant to the forces of modernist rationalism. If a central function of a philosophy is that it provides answers to the burning questions of its times, then modernity and its concomitant Philosophy of Consciousness is spent. For it has not been able to provide those answers that we are led to believe reside within the competence of the knowing Subject, Modern Man.

Progress and History—metanarratives originating in a logic-driven interpretation of reality—do, in Lyotard's view, suggest a level of social and existential unity now indefensible. Such foundational concepts applied to that end—unity, homogeneity, and totality—are snares. They are prison houses in which the Other(s) and the theory and practice of their diversity are historically held captive.

Descartes's spectator conception of the human Subject is now pushed aside and supplanted by the competing perspectives deriving from language games: "In the discursive justification and validation of truth claims no moment is privileged as a given, evidential structure which cannot be further questioned. It is the discourse of the community of inquirers" (Benhabib, 1992, p. 5). Calvin Schrag (1989b) can also be read to good effect on the consequences of this qualitative supplantation:

> To view language as a series of speech acts, issuing from the intentionality of serialized speaking subjects, somehow effecting a correlation of meaning and world, is still to accept a modernist epistemological paradigm that at once glosses the social sources of rationality, the role of the communicative telos of language, and the weight of tradition. Admittedly, it is the speaking subject that speaks and in his/her speech performance intends to say this and not that. Yet, these speech acts with their expressed intentions are always spoken *from* a language and *within* a tradition. The narratives of the speaking subject always remain embedded in the narratives of a wider sociohistorical tradition. An isolated speaking subject, searching for a correspondence of its intentions with states of affairs, is as much of an abstraction as is the lonely epistemological subject of modernity, severed from an objective, external world. (p. 95)

Totalitarian privileging is out. From the vantage point of the Other(s), this abolition of a single discourse now casts culture in the role of underpinning "an infinite range of realities" (Jenks, 1993, p. 141). In the transformation, culture will be released from the constraints of the fact-value framework in which it is rejected as a basis for a rational and scientific construction of reality. The new release clearly "opens the forum to the malcontents of an infinity of factional interests which 'must now be heard' " (pp. 145-146). Broad sketches of the possibilities of this "range" are presented in the next chapter.

This penchant for conflation, this abjuring of dichotomies, strikes at the Achilles's heel of modernity. For without a seemingly eternally situated Subject from which all cultures draw their definitions, the center cannot hold. Accordingly, from an optimistic point of view, modernity "is no longer exclusively the endpoint of the development of others, but rather the precarious point of departure for the further development of one's own . . . society" (Offe, 1987b, p. 2). Already we have it on the suggestion of Willard Quine (1975), that African languages do have many added perspectives from which Western social and philosophical thought can benefit (Chapter 7).

The postmodernists locate the main source of this collapse, one that leads to new forms of conceptualization, in the barrenness of the *logocentric* premises on which modernity is erected. It is bad enough, from this point of view, that logic is hopelessly constricted in its approach to defining reality; by way of extending the postmodernist position, I will analyze below this constriction in relation to rhetoric. It is worse that these all-embracing stories have taken on a timeless quality, less for their intrinsic validity than for the machinations of power (Foucault, 1973) or the oppression contained in the binary, metaphoric uses of language (Derrida, 1981). Terry Eagleton (1983) provides us with a crisp definition of the concept and hints at some of the inherent difficulties confronting it.

> [It is the commitment] to a belief in some ultimate "word," presence, essence, truth or reality which will act as the foundation of all thought, language and experience. It has yearned for the sign which will give meaning to all others—the "transcendental signifier"—and for the anchoring, unquestionable meaning to which all other signs can be seen to point (the "transcendental signified"). A great number of candidates for this role—God, the Idea, the World Spirit, the Self, substance, matter, and so on—have thrust themselves forward from time to time. Because each of these concepts hopes to *found* our whole system of thought and language, it must itself be beyond that system, untainted by its play of linguistic differences. It cannot be implicated in the very languages which it attempts to order and anchor. (p. 131)

The difficulty is hardly with logic per se; rather, it derives from a pervasive application of that logic such that it excludes other logics, rationalities, and epistemologies not adhering to its rules. (Postmodernism favors a subjective rationality, based on the "mytho-logic," which I will reintroduce in the next chapter.) To continue, it is in this sense that the Enlightenment tradition is labeled "totalizing." Not only does it betray that propensity in terms of its epistemological claims (its modern trajectory claiming to discover the permanent way of knowing), but it is exclusive in terms of the bearer of *the* message of truth. *He* is the white, middle-class male who has until now successfully withstood the Other(s). As Henry A. Giroux (1993) put it,

> Liberal and radical theorists have never been able to break away from Western models of authority that placed either the individual white male at the center of history and rationality or viewed history as the unproblematic unfolding of science, reason, and technology. (p. 115)

It is a significant attempt "to break away" that lies at the core of postmodernism.

These thinkers were certainly not the first to question the role of reason—there was, of course, Nietzsche—but this contingent had pushed its disclaimers the farthest. In a sense, immediate predecessors—Lasch and company—were prisoners of their contemporaneity, to borrow Agnes Heller's phrase. The existing recipes and remedies were remarkably nontranscendent, uniformly given over to an ethic of adjustment. For what seems apparent is a ritual of resignation to the command that whatever had to be done must occur within existing sociocultural parameters—a mind-set in the tradition of the accepted wisdom (one observes in Parsonianism, for instance) that capitalism is the best system of which human beings are capable. Take Peter Berger, for instance. His advice for the pathological condition of *homelessness* is that it be accepted as the price to be paid for the benefits of modernity. Robert Jay Lifton, for his part, stresses that protean man is without a model suited to his reconstruction but then takes refuge in a kind of historical recurrence: the capacity of humankind to rebound from even the most unseemly disaster (Lifton, 1971, p. 315). *Natura non facit saltus*!

On the other hand, the postmodern alliance sees no way out of the Faustian pact short of abandoning the logocentric. This cannot be accomplished by a return to ancient Greece, as in both cases the initiative will be to try propping up the Subject (Chapter 2). Nor will the instituting of a new constitutional religion a la Gellner do.[4] The alliance thinks perhaps even less of suggestions that logocentrism can be salvaged without the necessity of a major overhaul. Accordingly, postmodernists are dismissive of Anthony Giddens's forthright suggestion that the problems of modernity result from "design fault" and "operator failure" (Giddens, 1990, pp. 151-152). The problems are more fundamental than that. Such problems go well beyond suggested remedies that call for the modification of systems' designs or the substituting of more efficient operators. Especially in the works of Foucault (1973, 1982), the crux of the problem has to do with the overbearing and now obsolescent role of the individual as the sole measure of reality. Hence, Lyotard's uncompromising tone in the epigraph to this chapter. If nature has never taken leaps, it must do so now!

Indeed, Foucault has passed the death sentence on the individual qua the creature of the Enlightenment. That verdict issues from a deep tension between definition and performance—providing much fodder for the advocates of difference. The subject, the bearer of an "isolated mind and will," has not brought itself, let alone the world, under control through reason (White, 1991, pp. 2-3). The Subject, as Flax (1990) sees it, "is caught in a web of fictive meanings, in chains of signification, in which [it] is just another position in language" (p. 32).

In his turn, Habermas would make his concessions. His is perhaps the most powerful voice directed against postmodernism from within the Enlightenment tradition. His ideas form a part of the debates within the debate I mentioned at the beginning of this chapter. Briefly, the Habermasian perspective supports *difference* and *globalism* in its likewise abolition of the Subject, in the value it continues to place in rationality, and in the central role of language in the escape from domination. These are common positions of the postmodernists, but the similarities often end there. It is Habermas's avowed task to complete the project of the Enlightenment. The postmodernists have practically sworn to kill it! Take, for instance, the central place of language in both agendas. Habermas advocates a linguistic competence that is ambivalent on the point of the validity of Other-constructed claims. The postmodernists construct their language games in a fashion that gives a voice to difference, to those voices that "must now be heard."

Habermas's response was, like that of the liberals, pointedly coerced. Even though it would have surfaced with the general rough and tumble of debate, it was prompted by *ad hominem* challenges: Lyotard, for example, singled him out as the latter-day forger of consensus that "has become an outmoded and suspect value" (Lyotard, 1984, p. 66). Consensus is to be eschewed because attempts to coerce unity and homogeneity, where complexity is the rule, are really futile exercises. In turn, the recognition of complexity is the rejection of universalizability—the foundation principle of Habermas's communicative ethics. Universalizability does not take cognizance of the varying pace of different temporalities as experienced by different groups. I agree. Universalizability and its derivative, homogeneity, are myths that are constantly confounded by oppressive relations linked, for example, to race, gender, and class. It seems quite clear that the articulation and political operationalization of group identities and group specificities in terms of their difference is the antidote to the totalizing tendencies still lurking in concepts like universalizability. Many opponents detect a whiff of Kant here (Mestrovic, 1991; Walker, 1994).

Habermas and the postmodernists have carried on a running debate on a variety of issues related to the general topic (see his *The Philosophical Discourse of Modernity*, 1987, for example). For our purposes, however, I will confine the exchange to two main factors, both having important bearing on the validity of Enlightenment reason and, by extension, the interplay of culture and theory in fixing alternative perspectives of difference.

Habermas responds by claiming that the Enlightenment remains the dominant paradigm, although it has become impotent in certain key respects. He agrees that epistemologies derived from representation and the "paradigm of consciousness" are now supplanted by a "paradigm of communication." Conceptualizations that suggest the embrace of nature, history, and society do no longer make sense with the demonstrable collapse of the paradigm of consciousness. He, too, admits the problematic nature of the individual, of the subjective, which he addresses at some length in his copious writings (Habermas, 1975, 1986, 1987). Out of this has surfaced his theory of communicative ethics, which for the postmodernists possesses at least two features that are hotly contended. They do not accept the egalitarian presuppositions of communication ethics, as Habermas does not show how differentials of power will be eliminated—a good point on which I will comment later. Second, the species of emancipation contemplated rests, contradictorily, on the model of a universalizability that takes no cognizance of the naturally diverse state of reality. In short, Habermas is giving substance to ideologies that attempt to naturalize language and power relations. On globalism, especially as it relates to old First World-Third World relations, his theory is silent.

In sum, Habermas's project of rehabilitation is also rejected, leaving him to complain, with some justification nonetheless, that the postmodern alliance "suppresses the almost 200-year-old counterdiscourse inherent in modernity itself" (Habermas, 1987, p. 302). In his view, much that is criticized about modernity originates in the development of one form—a technical expression—of rationality; its distorting characteristics have taken precedence over "the jagged profile of rationality potentials that have been unevenly exploited" (Habermas, 1987, p. 348). Of course, his discourse on communicative rationality is one such area unevenly exploited. I will have a bit more to say on Habermas's criticism of postmodernism below.

The eclipse of the logocentric is the dissolution of a central force field holding relations of the individual vis-à-vis Nature, other individuals, and those relations on which Western domination is built. Postmodernists speak of a "de-centering," but their project is really one of disintegration. Let us take a look at the process of reconstruction, as it foreshadows much that could affect theories and practices of the Other(s).

## ❖ Difference Drives the Wedge

The tripartite alliance manages to expose areas of weakness in the Enlightenment tradition that form discrete points of departure for various expressions of Otherness. It might be weak in its direct theoretical inclinations, but there is no gainsaying the power of its critique, of its postmodern vision. Reliance on the Cartesian structure that I discussed in the previous chapters has diminished greatly, especially in the case of the Other(s). Mariam Thalos (1994, p. 532) aptly summarizes the main points of departure of feminists—perhaps the most active dissidents—and, by extension, the Other(s) (including Nature): (a) Others are the best placed to "produce true beliefs" about themselves; (b) logical foundations are inadequate and should be replaced by a more sociological and psychological approach to the determination and evaluation of beliefs; (c) the logical basis of knowledge is derived erroneously from classical philosophy's faulty reliance on cognitive objectivity.

From the rationalist dimension of classical philosophy, Otherness detaches itself from the technical, instrumentalist, aspects of reason. Empiricism, on the other hand, is rejected for its insistence that "synthetic generalizations of scientific validity" emerge directly via the physical senses. There is much unhappiness with the "scopic regime" of modernity, with the role of *vision* as the major defining sense of what is real. Much of this is covered in earlier chapters and should not delay us here. (I should indicate, however, that the rhetorical alternative to this scopic vision, one to which some postmodernists subscribe in the pivotal role they concede to language, has broadened the definitional perspective well beyond the physical senses.)

If the postmodernists avoided any active part in creating alternative theories, the other dissidents were not so dismissive. It has become more evident that the major disagreements of the dissidents were not centered on science and theorizing per se. Certain trajectories of feminist theory influenced by postmodernism could easily make their peace (correctly, in my view) with the broad principles of a general scientific agenda. Content and method of existing science are persuasively challenged, but the demand is not to abandon science and theorizing; it is mainly to modify them so as to meet the changes commanded by the Other(s) (Collins, 1991, chap. 10; Harding, 1986, 1987; Nelson, 1990, chap. 7). This compromise is not universally favored (Daly, 1978; Spender, 1980).

Let me sketch the process by which such a change is taking place. My purpose here is twofold. First, the sketch is offered as a counterpoint to the postmodernists' theoretical recalcitrance; second, it foreshadows an alternative theorizing to be undertaken in the next chapter.

The process begins with a shift in emphasis from a science and theorizing erected on logico-rational bases toward an alternative informed by the principles of rhetoric. Rhetoric, as I will explain, is far more than the art of colorful speech; it looms as the vital partner in the process of human knowledge and the interpretations of the complexities of reality that logic, its partner, abandoned. To continue, this process reveals much that is interesting about its fundamental attack on dichotomies and the network of dependence they institute. Two examples must suffice here. First, the Cartesian model is roundly challenged, as the "scopic vision" is pressured by the rhetorical perspective. Second, the mix of the discourses used by dissidents from the metropolitan world, where, presently, the offensive is most vigorous and intellectually sophisticated (the feminist and environmental movements, for example), makes substantial common cause with the erstwhile "primitives" and nonmoderns luxuriating in the backwaters of the globe. New social movements surface as the effective mirrors for these alliances, cross-fertilizations, and coordinated social and political strategies. It should be noted also that these movements "are carriers of alternative forms of modernity" (Ray, 1993, p. xviii)—I prefer the term *rationality*; they originate in the often suppressed dimensions of the Enlightenment of which Habermas speaks. These movements do not rest comfortably with instrumental rationality and its inherently dichotomizing propensities. Coextensively, they revolve less around production and distribution dynamics, due partly as a result of the diminishing significance of political economy as the key organizing principle of the current world order. Their rationale, one variously constructed—"postmaterialism," in Ronald Inglehart's (1990) view (see Chapter 2 of this volume)—is compounded by concerns with "the definition and valorization of personal and collective identities" (Plotke, 1995, p. 117); these compassion-driven expressions originate, on the broader canvas, from a vigorous contest between a philosophy of the heart (Schopenhauer) and Kant's philosophy of the mind (Mestrovic, 1991).

## ❖ The Suspect Nature of Postmodern Atheoreticity

Some of the more prominent postmodernists and their disciples have taken an intransigent position toward the question of theory building. Lyotard has often commented that such an exercise would result in grand narratives, encompassing systems of definition just as suffocating as those created by Enlightenment logic. (He makes no clear distinction between Enlightenment per se and its modernist aspect.) This injunction to avoid theory appears, on this view, to have linguistic and "anthropological" origins. In the discourse on deconstructionism, the implied totalization of Enlightenment logic is impossible "because our language is textual and subject to the laws of difference" (Zavarzadeh, 1994, p. 310). In other words, a single truth cannot exist because of the intrinsic limits of the Subject; Enlightenment rationality did (and could) not so outfit him, partly because of the inherent inadequacies of reason itself and, latterly, on account of the conceptual exclusion of all the vital stuff of lived experience. In the particular case of language, this totalization lays bare its pretense to be the instrument of truth revelation: There is no transcending one's social and historical context. Attempts to the contrary usually result in impositions "from above."

The anthropological trajectory gets explained by what is termed "weak thought" (*pensiero debole*). Weak thought is the result of the absence of those humanistic bases in which the critical capacity originates: In the words of Franco Crespi, this "absence of an absolute anthropological foundation" robs analysis "of references to ideals that call it to oppose itself to what exists" (cited in Pangle, 1992, p. 54). Before modernity succeeded in orchestrating the death of God, values and norms were derived from that source. The death of God "accelerated the spread of a latent culture of nihilism, cancer of the spirit, contagion of despair" (Levin, 1988, p. 4). Accordingly, defective humanism and the lack of substantive rationality are among the anthropological deficits that deny theory building.

In neither of these postures do we find a direct, explicit orientation to recast theory to meet the exigencies of an irredeemiably fallen Enlightenment. In fact, there are strong suggestions that some postmodernists, Gianni Vattimo, for example, disavow challenges mounted by "radical otherness," those forming the core of the Other(s) (Pangle, 1992, p. 54).[5] There is no overt and conscious effort at such exercises. Indeed, while the Lyotardian constructions of *game-ing* and "discourse theory" are applied occasionally, pointed, deliberate initiatives at fashioning emancipatory theories are conspicuously absent.

Postmodernists are uninhibitedly suspicious that such exercises will reintroduce new grand narratives. Michel Foucault (1982) appears, for instance, to define such activities as part of "the will to power," as the search for first principles, an overall frustrating and unfulfilling exercise. In the case of Richard Rorty (1989), the inclination is to abandon theory and embrace "contingency"—the notion that "anything goes." This has been described as a passion to "celebrate with a kind of resigned gaiety, the virtues of fragmentation, nonidentity, heterogeneity" (Jay, 1988, p. 121). Such unjustified withdrawal from theorizing does leave postmodernism often to the very serious, but unjustified, charge that it "demands faulty logic, mistakes, and accident as its methodological imperatives" (Jenks, 1993, p. 147).

But there are two ways of approaching this important issue. The first is dictated by what the postmodernists attribute to their formulations. The second approach, a far more reasonable and fruitful exercise, inheres in the theory and practice implications of those formulations. Here, determinations move outside the competence of the postmodernist; they assume characteristics of objectivity. They supersede the subjective test claimed by (and for) the postmodernist. Indeed, these two positions are hemmed in by a kind of anthropological imperative that immediately makes exercises in "resigned gaiety" and "contingency" unavailing. To theorize is really at the core of what we are as homo sapiens. The implicit capacity to be critical naturally sets up processes of action and thought in which results will be expected or adjudged in the context of continua or within existential milieux where the *is* and the *ought* are integral. This is an anthropological dimension that not only is nonextinguishable but seemingly supersedes the far inferior claims to theoretical avoidance allegedly represented by the absence of humanism and substantive rationality.

The anthropological imperative undergirding the exercise in theorizing is linguistically embedded and contingent in certain political situations. Thus, Karl Popper (1992, pp. 20-21) extracts the linguistic imperative from two of the four characteristics he finds inherent in language: the invention of descriptive statements that describe objective states of affairs and the argumentative function coextensive with it. On a more mundane, political, level, a similar embeddedness exists. There is a "veritistic" propensity to theorize commanded by a heterogeneous mix of human queries and experiences (Goldman, 1992). James Maffie (1995) makes a supporting argument: "Truth-centered reflection emerges on the contested terrain of clashing evidential judgments, norms, and practices" (p. 227). It should be noted as well that the necessity to theorize is immanent in other philosophical systems, like the Yoruba (Hallen & Sodipo, 1986) and examples drawn from India (Raju, 1971). Finally, Jung (1933) comments on the way theory is inveigled by anthropological uncertainties:

> [Man] protects himself with the shield of science and the armor of reason. His enlightenment is born of fear; in the daytime he believes in an ordered cosmos, and he tries to maintain this faith against the fear of chaos that besets him by night. (p. 162)

Indeed, what really remains to be debated, then, is whether *reason* provides the appropriate basis for the natural and expedient theorizing propensity. It is largely for these reasons that the advice to abandon theory, preparatory to the abolition of grand narratives, generates such a controversy. Ironically, grand narratives might not be the fixtures claimed on their behalf. The present global sociocultural climate might very well militate against their easy appearance, as I will suggest below.

Indeed, the "theory issue" has become a bone of contention between certain postmodernists and particular detachments of the Other(s). Jacques Derrida has drawn the bile of Henry Louis Gates Jr. (1992, p. 35) for suggesting that African Americans should abandon exercises in cultural theory directed at the dynamics of their identity. Jean Francois Lyotard fared no better for volunteering that women ought to do the same. Sabina Lovibond (1989) poses the dilemma: "How can anyone ask me to say goodbye to 'emancipatory narratives' when my own emancipation [as a woman] is still such a patchy, hit-and-miss affair?" (p. 12). In both cases, the quick of their respective objections is that such narratives form an important part of the politics of Identity that are vital for reclaiming and reconstituting Subjectivity. Lynn Hankinson Nelson (1990, p. 30) repeats similar sentiments from the perspective of a feminist science. She contends quite rightly that without incorporating the *differentia specifica* of women's activities and experiences, without grasping the reasons for their historical exclusion, the enterprise of science will remain incomplete.

The late Audre Lorde (1984) makes the same point from a black feminist perspective: "It is axiomatic that if we do not define ourselves for ourselves, we will be defined by others—for their use and to our detriment" (p. 45). In like vein is the position of the Latina, who, according to Ortega and Saporta-Sternbach (1989, "must dismantle the representation of stereotypes of herself" (p. 14). In his recent book, *Culture and Imperialism,* the indefatigable Edward Said (1993) alerts the victims of imperialism to the importance of "narrating" as a way of blocking other narratives from forming or emerging. Finally, Cornel West (1993, p. 31) adds another task to be done. His observation is that the Other(s) cannot be realistically explored without equal attention to the Self. The process not only will provide cues on how the Other was constructed but should also assist in a reconstruction without which the identity formation of the Other(s) is futile. The fortunes of Self and Other(s) are fundamentally inseparable (Chapter 2).

These objections are quite persuasive, given the nature of future theorizing, which itself must obey the vocabulary of difference. It seems to me that the novelist Toni Morrison suggests a worthwhile method regarding the African

American situation. How should theory in the American academy be structured to give African Americans their rightful place in American culture? One can hardly deny their contributions, which ooze copiously from all the interstices of American life. Her suggestion is that analytic exercises be undertaken, not to show why African Americans have been so excluded but, rather, to demonstrate how the dominant narratives were fashioned to exclude them. In Morrison's (1992) own words, the agenda is, "What intellectual feats had to be performed by the author or his critic to erase (Afro-Americans) from a society seething with their presence, and what effect has that performance had on the work?" (p. 11). Morrison is demanding nothing short of a deconstruction which, like that demanded by Isaac Julien and Kobena Mercer (1988), is not directed at compensating "the structured absences" (p. 3) of previous paradigms, but insists on the removal of forces disposed to creating binary oppositions in which such absences flourish.

The necessity for theory can hardly be contested. What is more crucial and immediate is the form it should assume. It is here that Ernesto Laclau's (1988) observation needs to be heeded: "Postmodernism cannot be a simple rejection of modernity; rather it involves a different modulation of its themes and categories" (p. 65). The difference in modulation must likewise acknowledge its own "social determination" within Enlightenment auspices—an acknowledgment that renders nugatory its claims to ahistoricity and to an atheoretical posture (Leys & Mandell, 1992, p. 6). Those who charge that postmodernism is, for these reasons, not different from the metanarratives it challenges, only that it is "greatly undertheorized," do appear to have a point (Thompson, 1993).

Reconstructive strategies of this kind apply to the entire array of Other(s). One cannot envision the possibility of constructing and redefining Subjectivity without initiatives of this sort. Such archaeological dredging is simply unavoidable and, in fact, should be encouraged, if the objective is to build unity without denying difference.

These exercises in identity definition strike at the heart of what is imperative about the global order taking shape around us. Pursue them we must, and when we do, the pursuit resides less in fabricated preferences or self-serving maneuvers for or against dominating power. Of course, such habits are endemic in the historically contentious relations of humankind. But such habits now fix on larger existential questions that make Claus Offe's earlier statement on theory linked to new paradigms quite persuasive. Of course, the compulsion springs from the growing persistence of the image of the world as a Big Picture. The dissidents are no longer rattling their sabres by the palace gates; they are now within!

One, particularly a member of a beleaguered Other, is understandably puzzled by the postmodernist's shunting between reprobation and approbation. How might the ploy be explained? It is possible that a well-known bias might be encroaching on an otherwise liberating body of thought. It is a brand of Eurocentrism to which I referred in the opening chapter. There still linger traces of the notion that there is a peculiar and far superior Eurocentric mind. As such, the basic existential principles mentioned above are of uncontestable paternity; it is one that exercises the power of life and death over the definitions and usages of these principles. One might be excused what is perhaps a momentary paranoia: Are we in the presence of a kind of legislating and interpreting, a form of elitism that even the well-intentioned find difficult to dislodge, due to a lingering imperialistic conditioning? Here are the etchings of the scenario at issue. Once there was a benevolent Europe that counseled, cajoled, or coerced the rest of the world to throw off their indigenous social and cultural accoutrement in exchange for enlightenment and prosperity. That agenda has failed. Today, there are benevolent and, often, penitential Europeans who, in their zeal to effect redress, proffer the dubious comfort of a Rorytan contingency! Some scholars, such as Ernest Gellner, view these concessions as *mea culpa* for colonialism, slavery, and the like. One hopes that such an explanation is frivolous.

The reviled and oppressed can never be satisfied with the news that the Big Dog is dead, particularly when the scars of painful wounds inflicted do remain whether in a foisted language or in debased cultures. Is a culture so afflicted not entitled to probe constructively questions such as, Is it true that our culture was so unserviceable? What made them survive and remain demonstrably congenial to countless generations before and even after the Big Dog made his inauspicious entrance? What allows "lesser" cultures to survive and command attention, even under the severest onslaught of modernity? Should women not be free to explore their socially and morally insupportable treatment? Many feminist scholars are familiar with William Edward Hartpole Lecky's (1890) chapter—"The Position of Women"—in his famous two-volume work on the history of European morals. The chapter is 97 pages long. In this work, published in 1890, the author clearly had to prepare himself for the unpleasantness of the task out of a sense of outrage. Even, then, the antiwoman sentiments could incur male displeasure. "Woman was represented as the door of hell, as the mother of all human ills" (Vol. 2, p. 338). Elisabeth Badinter's (1989) *The Unopposite Sex* and Nancy Tuana's (1993) *The Less Noble Sex*, one hopes, will send women scampering off in search of themselves!

If former dominating cultures are expected to adapt to diversity, how can this be achieved without engaging in projects of this sort? On the other hand, it is not enough to take the postmodernists at their word when they counsel the avoidance of theory. It makes little sense to state, as Linda Hutcheon (1989) does, that postmodernist counsels "have to be put on hold" (p. 15) until the Other(s)—feminists and postcolonialists, in this case—work out the issue of their subjectivity. bell hooks (1991) comments on the "often exclusionary" nature of postmodern literature, as it takes precious little stock of black *Otherness* and difference. Is it to be given on a silver platter? It seems to me that there might be a dereliction of duty here, although hooks rather engagingly suggests much from the black experience that could "enact a postmodernism of resistance" (p. 26). Building a theoretical framework to comport with the emerging global order requires no less than the injunction to cross borders of all kinds. And this can be done successfully only when the agenda is grounded in knowledge of one's identity.

To theorize is objectively and anthropologically situated. Consequently, the imperious order to abandon the trait is both impossible and ill-considered. Indeed, the truth might very well be as Newton Garver and Seung-Chong Lee (1994) and Simon Critchley (1992) suggest in the case of perhaps the most profound postmodernist—Jacques Derrida. It is the suggestion that the richness of this corpus of ideas does transcend the direct assessment of their author. The first two scholars point to Derrida's attack on metaphysics, with a remedial stress on rhetoric as the hub of meaning, and Critchley isolates an ethics greatly surfeited by impulses of Otherness. In the first case, the primacy of rhetoric is rooted in the notion that meaning is situated in experience and the epiphanies of life and that its import lies in language. In its turn, the emergent ethics is aligned to a politics of difference. Thus, in spite of himself and what appears to be a studied aversion to theory, Derrida is deeply implicated in the enterprise. Similar conclusions are applicable to Lyotard, whose contribution to "narrative" theory is already noted, and to Foucault, for his unintended, yet constructive, contribution to social movements (Plotke, 1995, p. 116). Other examples abound.

How plausible is the fear of grand narratives? It seems that a crucial point has been overlooked. A compelling argument can be made that the present state of global dynamics will make it very difficult for corrosive grand narratives to form as they did within a modernist totalitarianism. Initially, grand narrative building will be greatly impeded by the immediacy of sophisticated communications. History has shown rather clearly, in my view, that grand narratives tend to require for their growth and effectiveness a certain coexistence of time lapse and remoteness, expressed in geographical and systemic terms (in politics, philosophy, etc.). The new communications promote a new global openness and transparency that tend to inhibit the emergence of such a climate. Another detracting factor is the level of political awakening. Even as conservative a scholar as Zbigniew Brzezinski (1993) volunteers that the contemporary age is distinguished by "a population, [which] for the first time in history, is truly politically awakened" (p. 48). He suggests that political and ideological obfuscations of the past cannot be easily perpetrated. Writing in the realm of the politics of indigenous cultures, Franke Wilmer (1993, p. 20) couches identical sentiments in the context of the "moral suasion" that is now a significant part of global political discourse. In turn, James Rosenau (1990) considers this sharpening of the critical sensibilities of "today's person-on-the street" the major cause of contemporary international transformation; they are "the primary prerequisite for global turbulence" (pp. 13-15). It is perhaps for these reasons that Afrocentricity and the attempted grand narratives embodied in *The Bell Curve* (Hernnstein & Murray, 1994) are having such a rocky passage![6]

Let me, now, take the discourse back to Jurgen Habermas. The evidence is compelling that the Enlightenment tradition is not dead. Nor can the initially broad platform of reason on which it is erected be sustained. In the end, the postmodernist perspective draws more than it is willing to concede from that quarry. It is my contention that the rhetoric-driven epistemology that forms the subject of the next chapter owes much to the submerged, yet persistent, dimension mentioned in Chapter 4. Like a good many who have given him a sympathetic hearing, I, too, am yet to be convinced that the form of Enlightenment reason he selects to eclipse domination—namely, communicative reason—is satisfactorily grounded. How do matters of social class and power fit into this framework? His resistance to the "irrational" (in this book's context, "nonrational" seems more appropriate) is unconvincing. His privileging of cognition over all other forms of knowing "correspondingly devalues the faculty of perception, so that vision itself is so to speak colonized by cognition" (Lash & Friedman, 1992, p. 5).

Often, fresh perspectives or those marginalized and emerging from the dungeons of banishment owe much to the collective inadequacies and inconsistencies of theories. Habermasian notions of communication rationality, if unsatisfactory in its present form, do suggest attractive possibilities for the phenomenon of difference, despite his admission, in the case of the nonmodern world, that his is a "eurocentrically limited view" and is not intentionally directed at anything but advanced societies (see Habermas, 1986, p. 187).

Indeed, the same expansiveness yielded to postmodernist theorizing applies here. The fertility of Habermasian thought transcends the subjective yardstick of its author. Furthermore, his philosophical approach bodes well for a praxis in which difference can be successfully implicated. Unlike the mainstream of Enlightenment, he chooses to support what might be termed "a philosophy of deliverance" as against "a philosophy of truth"—the one, akin to the Marxist tradition, seeks to change social conditions impeding human emancipation; the other seems bent on the revelation of truth as an end in itself. On the issue of truth, Habermas has actually replaced the concept with a communicational model of argumentation. Here the crucial function of the dialogic, something of the thesis of negotiation increasingly advocated by the constructivists and the hermeneuticists (Bakhtin, Billig, and Gadamer, respectively), takes suggestive form. The tension here is that Habermas seems unprepared to place less emphasis on universality. Another shift congenial to difference is his aligning of norms to conditions in which rational consensus is determinant (Benhabib, 1986, p. 346). Of course, the "rational" in question should not be too heavily inflected by Descartes and Kant.

The very rich themes in Habermasian thought do capture the challenges faced in constructing what many consider to be sine qua non to a new global paradigm—namely, devising rationalities that sustain universality while preserving the particularities of difference. This is a huge challenge. In the next chapter, the larger rhetorical framework that could open up new possibilities for Habermasian thought is discussed.

## ❖ Notes

1. There were nonmodern challenges as well. Examples are Gandhi-ism, liberation theology, and Rastafarianism.

2. Less agreement exists on the shape of the end product. See the debates Habermas versus Gadamer (see Bernstein, 1986) and Habermas versus the postmodernists (see Bernstein, 1985; Habermas, 1987).

3. Lyotard's work does not reveal the depth of a Derrida. Its appeal rests in its easy and compelling identification with many of the deep riddles confronting the "marginalized"—a category that swells with each passing day (women, gays, and so on). His main concepts—logocentrism, for example—not only identify credible causal factors but strongly imply corrective strategies. His thoroughgoing support of difference has led to much emancipatory thinking and action among the Other(s). His fingerprints are all over feminism, for example.

4. Gellner (1992, pp. 91-96) patterns this alternative on a constitutional monarchy. The crux of his model flows directly from this statement: "It is a system that retains the ritual and symbolism of genuine monarchy, whilst transferring most of the real business of running society to a more technical, secular and unsacralized sphere" (p. 91). His ideas are only roughly sketched, but he appears to be lobbying for the legitimation of the gap that exists between utterance and perform-

ance—the putting of a permanent Band-Aid on an injury of an otherwise exemplary Enlightenment body!

5. Vattimo (1992, see especially chap. 1) shifts his position in *The Transparent Society*. Here, he gives much support to the Other(s).

6. In the present critical climate, they can maintain their essentialisms or exclusivisms only within their particular spheres of Otherness, which themselves are sites of healthy, critical contestations, as we see in the case of feminism.

# Chapter Ten

# CULTURE, RHETORIC, AND THE REFORMULATION OF THEORY

*Rationalism did not introduce order and wisdom where there was chaos and ignorance; it introduced a special kind of order.*
Paul Feyerabend (1994, p. 118)

*To understand reality, thought has to work methodically and logically without turning imagination and hopes into methods.*
P. T. Raju (1971, p. 16)

This chapter provides an account of the manner in which culture, as the beleaguered stepchild in the "fact-value" debate, is commanding a more direct role in theory building. The rhetoric-inflected endowments of the Other(s) now contest vigorously for an appropriate role in defining a globalismic social reality. To revert to an earlier characterization in Chapter 4, the shift is away from a preponderantly "rationalist" orientation to a more "historicist" one—a shift aided by a more social constructivist interpretation of the way human beings make sense of their world. The main armature is the logic-rhetoric dialectic.

First, what is this logic-rhetoric dialectic? Its meaning and implications are strewn throughout the preceding chapters, but a more precise account is required. In this chapter, I will set in place its basic structure. In the process, there are many major features to be noted, with other lesser features added to provide perspective. It must be noted that the tension between logic and rhetoric is common to most cultures, even though it receives its most thorough examination in the context of Western thought. The coexistence of logic and rhetoric resides in Indian thought (Radhakrishnan, 1969; Raju, 1971) no less than in the reflections of Ogotemmeli, the redoubtable Dogon sage of Marcel Griaule's philosophical adventures in Africa.[1]

Second, the tug-of-war has a distinct political ring to it, as the political tensions between the rationalists (Descartes and company) are clearly telescoped. Third, while the logic-rhetoric orbit *is* fundamentally linguistic, as conceded by Aristotle and Cicero, among others (Brown, 1987; McKeon, 1987, p. 66), the full implications of a linguistic construction of reality would be realized only in comparatively recent times. In short, the dominant message, though variously derived (from linguistics, sociology, psychology, for example), is that social reality is primarily mediated and defined by language. Language as is developed below, is not a dictionary of labels for preexisting phenomena created independently by the mind. Language, as Garth Hallet (1988, p. 42) stresses, is more than a synchronic definition, with syntax, grammar, semantics, and the like, accounting for reality. It is not a formal system of pure signs, closed on itself. It is more diachronic in nature captured nicely by Wittgenstein's (1967) famous phrase: "Only in the stream of life and thought do words have meaning" (p. 31).

This segment is followed by a brief analysis of a sample of derivative theories, especially fashioned by the Other(s). These initiatives carry important implications for a politics of recognition. The final segment sketches a grid of cultural affinities, markedly global in nature, from which the configuration of this politics can be discerned.

## ❖ Rhetoric Seizes the High Road[2]

The dialectic is one that is older than Western philosophy, even though it is here that it receives its most systematic and thoroughgoing treatment. From the classical Greeks through to the Romans, from Plato and Parmenides to Cicero, it was axiomatic that rhetoric was the key to knowledge and understanding. This was the "conjunctive" view of reality in which there is no clear distinction between "the world of thought and words and the world of things" (Lash, Szerszynski, & Wynne, 1996, p. 107). Indeed, rhetoric actually preceded logic, with the latter to emerge from the former. The process was preceded by a key question: Was it rhetoric, narrowly defined as primarily concerned with "imagination and hopes," or was it logic, a dynamic fragment of rhetoric and the ultimate creator of certainty and objectivity, that should form the basis of knowledge? Of course, much had to do with the tenor of the times, one where the stress in discovering "similarities based on commonplace association" gave way to the "emphasis on distinctions and dissimilarities" (Daniel, 1990, p. 138). Let me now provide a brief, skeletal account of this rivalry.

Mark Blackman, editor of Richard McKeon's (1987) essays on the subject (*Rhetoric: Essays in Invention and Discovery*), states that rhetoric has a variety of meanings. To the composition teacher, it is the "art" of writing; to the literary scholar, it is a "critical apparatus" the writer employs to establish rapport with the reader; to the philosopher of language, it is the "study" of misunderstandings and their remedies; to the "self-described" rhetorician, it is a "method." From the perspective of this book, there is a meaning for the epistemologist. True to form, logic is attempting to make of rhetoric an Other.

Rhetoric is not merely a verbal act. As Blackman put it, "it is a formative principle that both directs the systematic contemplation of any subject matter and contains the analytic tools necessary for the comprehension of diverse and often contradictory philosophical principles and systems" (p. viii). This "formative principle" is situated in the interpretive determinism of language from whose intrinsic structure we are able to grasp its scope. It inheres in *syntax* (which provides logical rigor), in *semantics* (which furnishes empirical content), and in *pragmatics* (which attaches to performance) (Brown, 1987, pp. 67-68). This integrated structure consists of two interrelated functions by which the parameters of knowledge and praxis are circumscribed: The first "tells the history of a particular piece of knowledge"; the second, which provides a context of justification, "explains [the content] of the first and the reasons for accepting it" (Feyerabend, 1987, pp. 110-111). In other words, rhetoric is the site of discourses, while logic provides the steps to ground them. Stephen Toulmin (1992, p. 27) notes that, for Renaissance scholars, rhetoric and logic were complementary; but this is only partly true. Logic originates in rhetoric.

These two contemporary philosophers of science have, by the nature of the respective functions of rhetoric and logic, placed rhetoric above logic in the process of apprehending reality. But there is a long, problem-ridden journey to this moment. It is a journey in which the secondary, impressive, but nonetheless, limited language of formal logic—especially that shard enshrined in mathematics and the calculative sciences—is subordinated to the formative and determinate principles of language. In the course of the journey, we are given evidence implicating rhetoric *qua* language as not merely existing as sites for discourses but providing their content as well.

The journey that rhetoric and logic have taken across time and space dramatizes the profound difficulty required in maintaining them in tolerable dialectical balance. One detects, beginning with the Ancients and the medieval thinkers, the paroxyms of thought the related issues engendered. These tensions were then mirrored in the ideas of the Renaissance figures, through to the Enlightenment, and finally to the present era, in which a historicist, or, more properly, a social constructivist, approach to knowledge assumes an increasingly compelling shape.

What seems clear from the history of the movements of these ideas is that rhetoric and logic would be caught by various shifts in the historical pendulum. In that broad sweep, we encounter competing theoretical positions on the roles of human cultures and their vital component—knowledge—in definitions of reality. In Parmenides (circa 450 B.C.) and Plato (427-347 B.C.) that definition, as we saw in Chapter 8, was the subordination of culture to a "*logos* [situated in] a realm of Being purged of inconstancy and uncertainty" (Habermas, 1971, p. 301). Today, rhetoric-driven approaches are retrieving the inconstant and uncertain that was relegated to "doxa [as] the realm of the mutable and the perishable" (p. 301). These shifts are accompanied by a conflict-inflected politics, expressions of which were deeply involved in the politics of Grotius, Descartes, and Hobbes, as they went about installing the modern project (Chapters 5 and 6). Now to the broad contours of this journey.

Reason for the Greeks and later the Romans was the basis of prudence (i.e., wisdom). Rhetoric and logic were seen to describe the ideal orbit. In Plato's view, rhetoric was powerful but inferior to logic; "mathematics was *the* paradigm of theoretical knowledge," although he was not dismissive of poetry. He saw the poet creating from natural talent guided by inspiration, "just like the seers and the oracles" (Feyerabend, 1987, p. 131). But Plato was fiercely antirhetoric, with a vehemence described as a "libel" (Toulmin, 1992, p. 31). Nonetheless, he was not as dismissive as Descartes, *vide* the frequent uses to which fables and allegories are made in his philosophy. In turn and prior to Plato, Parmenides also courted a turgid dualism: His mode of inquiry is "far from the footsteps of humans" leading to what is "appropriate and necessary"; the second limb is defined by "habit, born of experience" (Feyerabend, 1987, p. 120). He is partial to the first, typifying the beginnings of the shift from a "conjunctive" view of the world to the kind of exclusiveness (disjunctiveness) one associates with Cartesianism. There *is* a reality, but it has become cluttered and hidden by the dross of "habit born of experience," namely, myths, poetry, proverbs, and the like—the ingredients of "inconstancy and uncertainty." (It should be noted that there were thinkers—Epicurus [342-270 B.C.] and Lucretius [97-54 B.C.] who favored a rhetorically-derived rationality). Contrary to the concept that words are the signs for *ideas* detached from lived experience, the notion here, one shared substantially by the Romantics, is that "language develops from the general impulse of sensory-mimetic expression, which is innate in man, which is not a product of reflection but unconscious and unwilled" (Cassirer, 1955, Vol. 1, p. 148).

Cicero (106-43 B.C.) was no less sensitive to the significance of rhetoric. By his time, eloquence and wisdom were becoming separated. "Those who learned to analyze problems were unlearned in the arts of speech, while those who acquired eloquence were ignorant of what they talked about" (McKeon, 1987, p. 5). But Cicero conceived rhetoric to be more complex and used it to "establish the facts and resolve the "causes" by relating facts, words, values, and judgments" (McKeon, 1987, p. 6). For him, rhetoric straddled the now commonplace separation between logic and rhetoric, whereby the latter is mainly about the excessive embellishing of speech to render it "unreasonably persuasive" (Shotter, 1993, p. 2). Cicero captures an all-embracing rhetoric in a framework encompassing five dimensions—invention, disposition, elocution, memory, and pronunciation. These do encompass logic and the more narrowly conceived notion of rhetoric as persuasive speech. Rhetoric writ large was "an art of making in all phases of human activity" (McKeon, 1987, p. 2). In other words, language was at once the instrument to formulate distinct concepts and to provide the stuff of their meaning. It described a "conjunctive" reality (Reiss, 1982a).

We have a clear and recurring sense of the place of logic that results directly from the need for action to be anchored to some notion of certainty. After all, there is a struggle, a contest, with Nature. In Cicero's schema, this function, in which logic is implicated, falls under the heading of *invention,* referred to as *ratio iudicandi* or those processes and procedures we associate with induction, deduction, proof, and so on. In Cicero's view, this function was secondary to *ratio inveniendi,* the processes and procedures of discovery in which rhetoric inheres. Clearly in the Middle Ages, rhetoric formed the core of "civil philosophy," embodying three kinds of *oratory:* deliberative, judicial, and demonstrative (McKeon, 1987, p. 125).

As Richard McKeon (1987) shows in his most illuminating essays, "Rhetoric in the Middles Ages" and "Poetry and Philosophy in the Twelfth Century: The Renaissance of Rhetoric," Rhetoric (a capital R is used to signify its omnibus position embracing reality through language) began to fragment. Here, logic as *ratio iudicandi* appeared to have gathered strength with the rise of mathematical calculations then showing their distinctiveness. But Rhetoric, that element of it that was now counterposed to logic—rhetoric (with a small r)—now came to be associated mainly with poetic and dialectic.

Campanella, for example, divides his philosophy into grammar, dialectic, rhetoric, and poetic. Rhetoric "deriv[es] its arguments from dialectic and its matter from morals; it does not treat of all questions but is limited to persuasion and dissuasion of good and evil" (McKeon, 1987, p. 163). In the hands of Robertelli, "the end of poetic . . . is the 'imitating word,' as the end of rhetoric is that 'persuading word' " (pp. 163-164).

Cicero hardly realized that invidious distinctions between rhetoric and logic would eventuate as a basis for colonialism and imperialism in the 19th and 20th centuries. But he provided insights as to why the ultimate dichotomy creating the Big Ditch—a separation based on superior and inferior epistemologies—should be regarded as suspect. A good example appears in the epistemological uses of the faculty of memory—the much-maligned, "value-laden" phenomenon. Cicero uses the insights of Simonides, the Greek poet (556-468 B.C.) to provide the illumination:

> Simonides has been commissioned to present a poem in honor of his host at a banquet. In the course of his poem he also praised Castor and Pollux, and his patron, when the poem had been read, argued that the praise had been divided and proposed to pay only half of the fee that had been set for the panegyric. At that point Simonides was notified that two young men wished to see him outside. In his absence the roof of the banqueting hall collapsed, crushing the diners so badly that it was difficult to identify the corpses. Simonides used his memory of the places at which the guests had been seated to identify the persons, and he argued that the faculty of memory may be trained by selecting places, forming mental images of the things to be remembered, and placing them in the places distinguished, so that the order of the places would preserve the things, likening the places to a wax tablet and the images to the letters written on it. (McKeon, 1987, p. 26)[3]

Simonides gives expression to a mode of acquiring knowledge to which rhetoric in the vulgarized sense, as *value,* is central. It points to the long traditions of oral history in the so-called backward and nonmodern societies of today. Culture-specific renditions of Simonides's method form the bases of much of the oral and narrative traditions of today. We know of the prominent place these traditions occupy in nonmodern cultures such as those of Africa. In the case of India, orality was consciously adopted, even though its cultures had access to writing. It was felt that the oral tradition took one closer to the truth (Oliver, 1971, pp. 22-30). Today, their significance does not escape the attention of moral philosophers and ethicists, who argue that moral reasoning is inseparable from narrative (Hauerwas, 1981; MacIntyre, 1984): As G. B. Madison (1990) offers in support, "We understand ourselves by narrating ourselves" (p. 184); this process of narrating, storytelling, derives from the use of the imagination not as organizing sensations that are, according to a Cartesian definition of reality, of little definitional significance—man, on the view, being a cognitively intuited entity.

Rhetoric held the prominent position up to the Renaissance. It was to provide "the source of doctrines which have since become the property of other sciences" (McKeon, 1987, p. xv). Such a development was merely a fulfillment of its intrinsic, multidimensional nature (per Cicero). Indeed, at the time of the Renaissance, logic as a separate sphere, one associated with action as against words and eloquence, seized center stage. We observe the shift and classificatory consolidation in the writings of the scholars of the day. Thus, John Buridan, the 14th-century scholastic, identified rhetoric as an *instrumental science*; its counterpart was a *principal science* that dealt with "the proper things of the science" whose tools are logic and dialectic. On the other hand, the instrumental science involved "not only the doubtful and the true but also the need to stir the desire as it bears on understanding, and a special moral logic or dialectic is required that is divided into two parts, rhetoric and poetic" (McKeon, 1987, p. 162). Philosophy was, at the same time, divided by John of Jandun in a fashion that made rhetoric a subdivision of logic. Up to the time of Campanella and Robertelli, the mid- and the early 16th century, respectively, the space occupied by rhetoric resulted from logic's particular designation as against the "universal" correlate.

The next stage begins with the Renaissance, when a sharp distinction between "essence" (consistent with logic and science) and "appearance" (consistent with rhetoric and those things now categorized as nonscientific, as *values*) began to harden. One witnesses the reappearance of the distinction between eloquence and wisdom as one between art and nature, value and fact, the humanities and the sciences (McKeon, 1987, p. 9). It was a veritable paradigm shift from the tandem of rhetoric and reason, linked to a prudential reality, toward an instrumental variant of reason. The one was fixed on "the good life and an interpretation of possible actions in light of this ideal" (Brown, 1987, p. 72); the other appeared as instrumental rationality influenced by Paramenides. Instrumentalism was responding to complaints, which surfaced frequently in the late 17th century, that rhetoric distorts the human capacity to think (Brown, 1987, p. 82).

The Cartesian revolution was next. But many held a fairly grounded, though not undebated, view toward language. Generally, reality was taken to occur *within* language, with traces of a few demurrers. Most notable, perhaps, though prior in time, was that of William of Ockham, the 14th-century theologian. He posited a distinction between man and nature, accordingly introducing dualisms and distinctions between cognition and sensation, between logic and faith, with preponderant influence placed on culturally and historically detached, decontextualized "interminably logical subtleties" (Wallace, 1972, Vol. 2, p. 54). In the process, language would serve a largely nominalist function enshrined in the so-called Ockham's razor, which enjoins that concepts should not be introduced where they are not necessary. It was a rule that later led to the principle of logical economy, of positivism, of Russell's mathematical language.[4] In a sense, logic was the horse that drew the cart of knowledge, not the historically and culturally inflected elements of language, which had to be excised of these saturations to which language is prone.

The Cartesian revolution repeated a strategy that, in line with the impulses of first principles and geometry, it applied to the law of God vis-à-vis the law of Nature. I will repeat Paul Hazard's (1963) quote that presents the strategy quite well: The novelty of this strategy, which is an artificial act of disaggregation, "lay in the patent separation of the two terms; in the no less evident tendency to stretch their opposition; and then in an attempt to reconcile the two, which of itself implied that the rift was a real one" (p. 271). Cartesian logic and rationality are inherent in language. In quite the same way that Grotius and the Naturalists attempted to use the law of Nature to fix the weaknesses of the law of God—namely, violence, disorder, war, and so on—Cartesian logic strove to prune language of parallel defects. If the defects of the law of God situate God, the All-Knowing, at the center of an embarrassing contradiction, so did the defects of language vis-à-vis the reason He counsels must be at the heart of human affairs. The logical and the rhetorical are both expressible in language, but it is the logical that will expunge what language countenances in rhetoric as limitations of knowledge and truth—myths, legends, history, intuitions. These are parallel to the irrationalities of which God is guilty in the application of his now suspect law of God. For Descartes, there was a universal language. Cassirer (1955) captures the essence of that position quite well:

> Since only the One identical, fundamental form of knowledge, the form of human reason, recurs in all branches of knowledge really deserving of the name, all speech must be based upon the one, universal, rational form of language, which, though cloaked by the abundance and diversity of verbal forms, cannot be hidden entirely. (Vol. 1, p. 128)

We detect here distinct associations with Ockham's thought. For that legacy arrived as a hugely compressed, or decontextualized language urged in the service of a limited number of concepts.

The truth is that logic is itself a language but one that does not embrace the totality of human experience. As Wittgenstein demonstrates, mathematical principles and logic state nothing of sensuous reality but, rather, have their explosions of meaning within linguistic rules internal to these principles and logic. Logic possesses insight into its constructs only according to its own plan.

It is true that this language provides a species of certainty that is quite impressive when the sum and substance of human experience are reduced to the logic of a machine, as I have discussed in Chapter 5. In this scheme of things, the more general conception of language is not completely absorbed into mathematics; what is left of it serves the purpose of providing labels for the stuff of Cartesian reality. This reality does not inhere in language as the *primum mobile* of reality, such as can be gleaned from Cicero, certain Renaissance thinkers, and Romantic philosophers like Johan Georg Hamann and Herder who offer that reason inheres inextricably in language. It was the "bone" on which Hamann "gnawed" and was prepared to do until death (Cassirer, 1955, Vol. 1, p. 150). Apropos of Herder and the Romantic philosophers, "man comes to know himself by expressing and hence clarifying what he is and recognizing himself in his expression. The specific property of human life is to culminate in self-awareness through expression" (Taylor, 1975, p. 17). In other words, because these expressions exist as myths, proverbs, allegories, stories, and the like, they are centrally implicated in self-awareness and, by extension, theoretical explorations of reality. Indeed, suggested here is a linguistic ontology, with its methodological principles based, as we shall see below, on intersubjective communication.

Indeed, the marginalization of rhetoric appears to have been achieved by a somewhat indirect process. The abhorring of rhetoric came primarily with its derivation from Matter. Recall, in Chapter 5, that Descartes could not find it congenial to incorporate human bodily expressions, namely, the stuff of rhetoric, into his epistemology. Rhetoric succeeds by *persuasion;* truth inheres in certainty that requires that which *commands,* such as logic does. As for the oral historical tradition typified by Simonides, Descartes countered with disdain; for history is like foreign travel that broadens the mind but does not deepen it. Progressively, attempts to situate rhetorically constructed explanations fell prey to gathering forces of positivism and its rash of nomothetic laws—social scientific concepts possessing the specificity and generalizability of natural laws.

The rise to prominence of the quality of generalizability restricts the role of language. It appears to receive its list of duties from reason. And the dimension so privileged to issue those orders is logic. Descartes and Locke based the primacy of the logic embedded in language on logical correlations between its signs and the ideas formulated by reason: "The ideas represented by our linguistic signs already exist in logical relations to one another before we have signs for them" (Garver & Lee, 1994, p. 64). The Hobbesian absolutist state and the Grotian law of nations—both of which we have encountered in other contexts—preexisted. Their revelation lay in the use of appropriate linguistic signs to give expression to their antecedent existence. This is expected,

> [because] signs represent ideas and that an idea is something that can stand in semantic contrast or contradiction to another idea—and can be seen to stand in such contrast or contradiction without reference to contexts of communication, to "voices resounding in the corridors," or to how they figure in the stream of life. (p. 67)

In other words, signs as representative of language were nuggets of reason detached from the dross of historical manifestations of concrete life. In Bacon's view, these signs, defined by logic, were at the heart of any right method, and method is the basis of "legitimate" knowledge of reality (Reiss, 1982b, p. 221). Language was to be univocal, not ambiguous. A similar position was taken by Hobbes and Locke: "Names are signs for concepts and not signs for objects themselves" (Cassirer, 1955, Vol. 1, p. 134).

But neither Leibniz's *ars combinatoria* (the possible combinations of signs would correspond to the scientifically possible combinations of things) nor the notion of language as the product of Cartesian reason, nor the rendition of language systems embedded in empiricism (Bacon, Hobbes, Locke) proved satisfactory. Indeed, even though arithmetic and calculus (in Leibniz's case) and Euclidean geometry (in Hobbes's case) were unable to dissolve the natural ambiguity of language, thinkers such as Locke, Hume, and Bentham attempted to cripple its rhetorical aspect. Locke went as far to suggest "that if a child had poetic leanings the parents should labor to stifle them" (Levine, 1988, p. 3). In fact, even poets and belles lettres, august figures like Alexander Pope and Samuel Johnson, succumbed to the tyranny of logic, so much so that the former fashioned a poetic code to comport with the principles of mathematics, and the latter, in turn, prepared a dictionary "with the aim of fixing univocal meanings in perpetuity, much like the univocal meanings of standard arithmetic terms" (pp. 3-4). The writing of history was not exempt. Henry Thomas Buckle (1821-1862) attempted to use a scientific, Cartesian, approach in his unfinished *History of Civilisation in England.* But even the formalization of the social sciences under the sway of Weberian "value neutrality" could not dislodge the inherent ambiguity of language, in spite of rigorous attempts at univocality. The voluminous literature on the issue is well-known and need not be cited.

Univocality was impossible because the cart was being placed before the horse. In truth, reason, itself conditioned and defined by language, could get at the meaning and specificity of the ideas only through language. Reason, as Susan Langer (1953, p. ix) put it, is not a "primitive endowment" coexistent with the prehistory of language and myth—reason is man's *achievement* springing from the intrinsically linguistic context in which it inheres. Reason is posterior to the dynamics of language, as, operationally, we, as the harnessing agents of reason, cannot do so outside the determinacy of language that is prior and formative. This insight is clearly embedded in Vico's comment that "man is properly only mind, body, and speech, and speech stands as it were midway between mind and body" (Vico, 1744/1984, p. 393).[5] In his turn, Nietzsche (1911) provides more explanatory specificity:

> Language is "a movable host of metaphors, metonymies, and anthropomorphisms: in short, a sum of human relations that have been poetically and rhetorically intensified, transferred, and embellished, and that, after a long usage, seem to people to be fixed, canonical, and binding. (cited in Garver & Lee, 1994, pp. 54-55)

This brilliant insight, coupled with Vico's systematic account of the process, is transforming current conceptions. Language provides an ontological base to social life, one that operates within a communicative or interlocutive methodology. On the first count, there is no subjectivity to be established outside of the fundamental practice of utterance. Our subjectivity is impossible without telling someone what we mean, and this can be achieved only by language. As Francis Jacques (1991) put it, "the speaking subject is ultimately not the subject of saying [Descartes's detached, sovereign subject] nor the self-sufficient subject of utterance, but that which is finally constructed in the course of the interlocution" (p. 318).

The ontological dimension involved in this truism is fashioned from the reformulation of the mind-matter dualism. The interposing of speech suggested by Vico puts its stamp of language as constitutive and symbolic. Mind and matter are apprehended through lived experience, which, in turn, makes sense through language. Thereupon, reality takes on a " hermeneutical-existential" meaning (Madison, 1990, p. 165). Language fashions and communicates lived experience! (see Benveniste, 1971; Jacques, 1991; Madison, 1990). The result is the absence of the nonlinguistic subjectivity a la Descartes, a correspondence thesis distinguishing between our clear and distinct ideas and things that exist in themselves.

Reality is analogical as well as symbolic—fundamentally linguistically derived qualities that are captured aptly in the working of metaphors. First, growing research on metaphors establishes this linguistic device as a transference of conceptual meaning from diverse but interrelated linguistic, lived experience, domains. A metaphor "is fundamentally a borrowing between and intercourse of thoughts, a transaction between contexts" (Richards, 1936, p. 94). In amplification, "The metaphor invok[es] and filt[ers] different but associated conceptual systems. The interaction generates a novel semantic context, and goes beyond the literal meaning of the terms of the metaphor itself" (Hodgson, 1993, p. 19). In other words, metaphors are deeply and irretrievably implicated in reality. Language as a device incorporating the integrative mechanisms that link conceptual domains as well as one that is "poetically and rhetorically intensified," carries many crucial implications for the process of arriving at meaning.

Language does not respect the antagonistic division made between logic and rhetoric. Indeed, we begin to appreciate rhetoric. As Donald McCloskey (1995) has shown, the metaphor can serve this function within the narrow bounds of a logicdriven science (economics, in his example); it can also cross-fertilize the logic-driven and the rhetoric-driven, as in the case of the allegorical uses made of metaphor and the story format. "Mainstream economics combines a metaphor of free exchange with a story of the bourgeois journey" (p. 216). In fact, the metaphor may combine with the purely rhetorical in ways that legitimately create knowledge and appropriate methods for its expression. These are displayed, for instance, in myths, allegories, stories, proverbs, and the like—all of which abound in the nonmodern and the so-called backward worlds. Often these linguistic forms and modes of ascertaining the meaning and complexities of life are the most reliable media for representing the experiences of the cultures. Heidegger (1962, cited in Brown, 1987) captures the relationship aptly with the use of an architectural metaphor: "Language is the house of Being" (p. 205) and as such it contains the world, not the other way around. Accordingly, the stuff of the world to be delineated by science or other means is already caught within the infrastructure of language. The infrastructure consists of myths, metaphors, allegories, fables, and so on. Ernst Cassirer (1953) strengthens the argument via a point of departure from Descartes:

> Descartes said that theoretical science remains the same in its essence no matter what object it deals with—just as the sun's light is the same no matter

> what wealth and variety of things it may illuminate. The same may be said of any symbolic form, of language, art, or myth, in that each of these is a particular way of seeing, and carries within itself its particular and proper source of light. (p. 11)

Allegories, stories, myths, and metaphors are the symbolic forms used by human beings in pursuit of meaning. "A conception is fixed and held only when it has been embodied in a symbol" (Langer, 1953, p. ix). In turn, a conception does not have an independent existence, as Descartes suggests. Although, generally, they may be either discursive or imaginative (i.e., logical or rhetorical) to use the terms adopted in this chapter, concepts "are mere formulations of thought which, instead of giving the true forms of objects, show us rather the forms of thought itself" (Cassirer, 1953, p. 7). What is of crucial significance is the *perspective* from which the logical and the rhetorical emerge. That perspective originates in language, with its two main forms—logic and rhetoric—obedient to the sensuous, which (per Herder) already has within it a basic element of "reflection" (Cassirer, 1950, p. 319, Vol. 1). What this implies is that there is no extralinguistic reality to which rational concepts or rhetorical forms relate in terms of the provision of meaning. Indeed, the organizational and interpretive dimensions of the perspective provided by language (i.e., metaphorical thinking) are common to the mythopoetic thinker as well as the rationalist. "The nature and meaning of metaphor is what we must start with if we want to find, on the one hand, the unity of the verbal and the mythical worlds and, on the other, their difference" (Cassirer, 1953, p. 84).

This situation has really led to a conclusion giving much legitimacy to *difference*. While a detached reason and the attempt to use language as mere description are now suspect, and although the notion that reality is unitary becomes increasingly problematical, there is still some accommodation for logic as determination via quantities and mathematical correlations. Now, instead of being the hub of the wheel of knowledge, it is one of many determinants. Consequently, this broadened and more inclusive interpretation of language compels a legitimate, independent view, which Donald Levine (1988, p. 29) expresses in the case of the Amhara culture of Ethiopia: Rhetorical knowledge "finds its natural medium in some sort of ambiguity, whether the form be spiritual parable, philosophic parable, lofty allegory, subtle symbolism." But "ambiguity" is a function of the limitations of a logic-driven approach to language; it is a positive quality in language induced by the complexities of its rhetorical forms. (Max Muller reinforced this point in reference to the obfuscatory role of ideology. He states that "there is mythology now as there was in the time of Homer, only we do not perceive it, because we ourselves live in the very shadow of it, and because we all shrink from the full meridian light of truth"; cited in Cassirer, 1953, p. 5.)

As we now view the present terrain, we see the substantial figure of Vico's ghost eliciting the definition of reality from a diverse mix of cultural forms, lived experiences, and habits of mind (intuition, imagination, and the like). *Other-driven* theory (a term used interchangeably with *rhetoric-driven*) is now acquiring its ammunition from a variety of sources, some of which are recorded below. For the realm of rhetoric abounds in cultural forms that do no longer march to the command of the fact-value rhythms orchestrated by Kant or Weber or Sir Alfred Ayer.

The raid is properly directed against the Greeks. Recall the charge made against Plato's mysticism and irrationalism; in his turn, Spinoza had his swipe at Descartes's "occultism" (Chapter 7). In the special case of emotions—expressions that the rationalists treated with disdain—some Greeks, Plato, for instance, appear not to have legislated a complete divorce between emotions and reason. Reason was accorded the role of jockey to exert the necessary constraint (Jaggar, 1989, p. 145). In like fashion, Huston Smith (1992) sketches the primacy of intuition, imagery, and insight:

> Logic can show us that if we were to approach the world with an eye to embracing rather than controlling it, or asking how it might school us rather than serve us, it would reveal a different guise. But what that guise would be, it cannot say. For this latter report, insight is required. (p. 214)

Formal logic is secondary to these rhetors and is never the source of new knowledge. Morton Kaplan (1971) deserves to be quoted in full on the question:

> Intuitions provide knowledge—sometimes better and more useful knowledge provided by scientific method. We do not, for instance, know how to build a computer capable of complex recognition patterns that the human mind is capable of. The experienced craftsman who observes a metal alloy under conditions of flame can often specify [the] components of the alloy to a precision not yet obtainable by scientific method except through the most expensive and time consuming methods, and sometimes not even then. Tea and wine tasters perform their work with subtlety that mechanical contrivances cannot yet achieve. The rules for acquiring such knowledge often cannot be transmitted, although identifications can be made and, in some cases, confirmed. (p. 10)

It should be noted that Cartesianism eschews psychology—a discipline on which a good many claims of difference rest. That spectator model of knowledge abhors "the voices resounding in the corridors." Philosophy, for Descartes, requires a process of inquiry and investigation that seeks out general principles by which particulars can be connected. The clear Cartesian injunction is that we listen to the voice, "the ego, that . . . well-concealed citadel in the brain—*arcem in cerebro tenens*—to repeat Pierre Gassendi's acerbic swipe at Descartes's unencumbered mind" (Horkheimer, 1947, p. 107).

A rhetoric-driven approach to knowledge, then, seeks meaning and "knowing" from within the social, psychological, and historical spheres of life. It might be remarked that the study that perhaps is responsible more than any for the entrenchment of feminism in the sphere of Otherness is psychological. Carol Gilligan's (1982) *In a Different Voice* helps to found feminine difference (and the authenticity of a different, but legitimate, voice) in the quality of expressivity or an ethic of responsibility or care. The ethic of care and the ethic of rights are different moral points of reference cardinally important in the socialization of women and men respectively. Accordingly, women's experiences should no longer be devalued but ought rather to be construed as a legitimate and different point of view. At once, this scientific claim is grounding "women's need [for] equality with men [and claiming] protection for their differences from men" (Fox-Genovese, 1991, p. 55).

Richard Rorty has, as part of his well-documented recoiling from philosophy, given the stamp of approval to literature. Here, he does so not as the firm adherent of theory building. We have Rorty stating that imagination, rather than reason, allows us to grasp the basic connectedness that has been eroded by the Enlightenment: Imagination "extends our sense of 'we' to people whom we have previously thought of as 'they' " (Rorty, 1989, p. 192). Of course, we should recall in Chapter 7 the rehabilitation of myths by Hans Blumenberg. Not only are they found to be integral to the development of science, but they appear pivotal as complements to a fuller understanding of reality. Recall Blumenberg's forceful argument that the reason-science alliance is technically, psychologically, and psychically inadequate for the tasks mapped out for it.

If logic and rhetoric are originally seen as operating in dialectical harmony and if the latter has operated preemptively, postmodernism now places greater interpretive stress on rhetoric. Of course, this is old hat for many Third World and nonmodern cultures whose civilizations and worldviews have been erected on rhetoric-based foundations. In truth, the principal value of the breakdown is the authenticity of the rhetorical.

Postmodernism dismisses modernity's pretensions that truth is whole. Truth is partial. One of the complementary positions in the new scientific ethos it spawns, despite its reluctance, is that we experience more than we know and we know more than we express: "Hence the unreflected, signified world is always larger than whatever version of it becomes canonized into formal knowledge. The land is always larger than the maps, and in mapping it in one official way we narrow awareness of alternative ways of experiencing the terrain" (Brown, 1990, p. 191). It does not "leave out" what cannot fit snugly into a predetermined space. The process of exclusion is less possible because of the way knowledge is now conceptualized. Severely damaged is the notion of the Subject's Archimedeanism, namely, his standing imperiously outside of lived experience to plot a predetermined course—a path that has sedulously attempted to avoid social and historical contexts and instead courts the neat symmetries and certainties of mathematical abstractions. As Donald McCloskey (1988) puts it wryly, "We have no way to get outside our own human conversations and get in the mind of God in order to tell whether such and such an argument is True" (p. 27). Science and knowledge must recourse to language (Black, 1962; Hodgson, 1993; Lakoff & Turner, 1989)—a statement that sits rather well with the Wittgensteinian axiom that words really acquire their meanings only in the stream of life.

In the end, a rhetoric-driven orientation toward theory incorporates two processes. The first is really to make the *appearances* embodied in lived experience take on a direct, specific involvement in the definition of a complex world. This is the result of the ontological character of language to which the notion of a cultural imperialism of social reality and meaning is uncongenial. Leibniz, for all his best intentions, was concocting a mischief when expressing a delight "in variety, particularly if it is reduced to unity" (cited in De Rougemount, 1966, p. 127). The nature of that mischief, as Iris Young (1990) states it, is that "by claiming to provide a standpoint which all subjects can adopt, [a logic-driven framework] denies the difference between subjects" (p. 10).

The second process, one also situated in language, is more procedural in nature. It is to be found working more closely with new sociological approaches in social reality construction with hermeneutics and social constructionism. From the former, which makes a very strong case for the authenticity of nonrepeatable social experiences (i.e., idiographic "laws") to the latter, where reality is taken as being socially constructed, we arrive at the principle of social negotiation. Reality, whether national or global, is not legislated; it is negotiated. Negotiation requires dialogue as against the "self-celebratory monologues" of Cartesianism (Sampson, 1993, chap. 1). In context, as Ernest Gellner (1992) defines the associated "cognitive elitism," "it did indeed hold all men and minds, but *not* all cultures and systems of meaning, to be equal" (p. 37). Coextensively, dialogue calls forth the "argumentative" necessity as a basic communicative function. The necessity, John Shotter (1993, p. 2) argues, is methodological. The more appropriate picture of social reality now being signaled by hermeneutics and social constructionism, one—I might add, that reinforces the legitimacy of difference—demands it. Basically, the necessity and ability "to [answer] back, with equal and opposite claims" in the marketplace of ideas, from which realities must now be negotiated (Benhabib, 1992, p. 5), is a sine qua non. Conversation is the only context in which knowledge is to be understood, as we have no place to stand outside of our beliefs and, more envelopingly, our language. Stated somewhat cavalierly but substantially true, there are no facts, only interpretations, as Nietzsche declared. These interpretations form a "deliberative rhetoric" that "broadens the space of rhetoric to include the common good . . . the interests of the rhetors and the hearers alike, and the rationality of practical wisdom as a guide for deliberation and action" (Schrag, 1989a, p. 183). Involved here, too, is a dramatic shift in the constituents of understanding, for rhetoric has become epistemic in the sense that what constitutes truth—now a multiple phenomenon—in which narrative (giving rise to a "narrative paradigm") (Fisher, 1984) and imagination (a Vichian characterization (Verene, 1981) and its postmodern model (Madison, 1990) provide the foundations.

The foregoing account sketches the broad outlines of a metamorphosis. Logic and rhetoric are being integrated to eliminate the often crude and indefensible dichotomies on which global relations have been erected. Let us now see how practice is—or is not—supporting theory.

## ❖ Some Forays Into Theory Building

What follows are examples of theoretical exercises influenced, in part, by the rise of the new rhetorical twist discussed above. I make no determined effort to present a critical account of them.

*Standpoint Theory.* This theory—in fact, it seems proper to refer to "theories" and, better still, "standpoint epistemologies"—remains the subject of much problematizing, though one should be thoroughly impressed with the strides being made toward substantive theories. Their main difficulties appear to be twofold. The first relates to the thorny issues associated with new theory building. For example, when one speaks of "women" as an Other with substantial claims to difference, we discover that this constituency is heterogeneous and quite fractious to boot. There are splinter standpoint epistemologies. One such example is the *Afrocentric feminist epistemology,* the main contradictions of which Patricia Hill Collins (1991) captures below. Her main point is that at certain junctures in this perspective, an Afrocentrist feminist thought is multinucleated: "On certain dimensions [of this theorizing], Black women may more closely resemble Black men; on others, white women; still on others Black women may stand apart from both groups" (p. 207). Here, Afrocentric feminist epistemology claims subsidiary differences within two parent differences (feminism and Afrocentricity), while clinging somehow to the political antipathies of these two to the status quo. This exemplifies some of the divisiveness in which difference is mired, despite a shared antipathy to the status quo (see hooks, 1981; Lorde, 1984; Mohanty, Russo, & Torres, 1991).

Second, standpoint theory comes face to face with an anticipated opposition—white male-oriented epistemology. Among the new themes repudiated by the status quo are (a) politics as a central variable, (b) the issue of scientific objectivity (after all, variables that are improperly from the realm of "value" are incorporated into this regime), and (c) the sacrilege committed by suggesting that there is more than one way to discover how to discover—the Cartesian-Kantian way. In one of her many well-directed arrows at establishment science, Sandra Harding (1987) courts history as her ally: "At any moment . . . there are many 'subjugated knowledges' that conflict with, and are never reflected in, the dominant stories a culture tells about social life" (p. 188).

The first comprehensive explication of standpoint theory is Nancy Hartsock's (1983) pioneering essay, "The Feminist Standpoint: Developing the Ground for a Specifically Feminist Historical Materialism." As the title suggests, this version of standpoint epistemology takes Marxism as its point of departure. The pivotal Marxist notion here relates to the dynamics of class conflict and the claim that a true understanding of a class society can be gathered only from the vantage point of the oppressed classes engaged in political struggle. Its derivation is from Marx and Engels' *The German Ideology* (1972).

The specific focus on the Other(s) originates in a revamped scientific—a more diversity-oriented—approach that at once abandons the so-called impartiality of status quo science. This discourse is located in the knowledge and interest of the Other, that is to say, from the standpoint of a reality viewed from a necessarily partial, but privileged, position. In this way, the suffocating aspects of the scientific impartiality insisted on by the status quo are avoided. Now the privileged standpoint extends "to women, [to] people of color, [to] nature as a historical agent, [to] the truth value" (Aronowitz, 1992, p. 258). As for the interest-based, rhetorical nature of knowledge, Gianni Vattimo (1991) captures the mood, via a Nietzschean insight:

> Yet the chemical analysis of the process of knowledge reveals that it . . . is impossible because it is nothing more than a series of metaphorizations. This

> series goes from the thing to the mental image, from the image to the word which expresses the individual's state of mind, from this to the word which social conventions determine to be the "right" one, and then once again from this canonical word to the thing, which we now see only in terms of the traits which may most easily be metaphorized in the vocabulary that we inherited. (p. 167)

*Afrocentric Theory.* Afrocentric theory, as we know it today, has quite a distinguished lineage. The persistent claim that people of African descent and their heritage command exclusiveness is the recurrent theme of many scholars and writers who have made the African condition his or her bailiwick: from the mere, but distinct, flicker of a vision in Maria W. Stewart, who in 1831 exhorted African American women to desert pots and kettles for a more edifying pursuit of the mind; from the pages of *The Souls of Black Folk,* where DuBois thunders "the blacker the mantle, the mightier the man"; from the Senghorian version of Negritude, with its cousin status eternally sedimented in his signature statement, *L'émotion est nègre comme la raison hellène (emotion is black as much as reason is Greek)*; from Aimé Césaire, whose celebrated poem "Cahier d'un retour au pays natal (A Return to my Nativeland)" is partly a diatribe directed against modernity in the name of difference; from Cheikh Anta Diop and his powerful and convincing tropes on African civilization; to the task of distillation now in the hands, chiefly, of Molefi Kete Asante. These clusters correctly imply shades of meanings and interpretations. And although Afrocentricity is clearly a distillation, it shifts depending on whether one deals with its politico-ideological value or its theoretical efficacy.

On the first count, it enjoys increasing appeal, as it gives shape and pronounced expression to the varieties of summonses for freedom by the peoples of the African diaspora. As old definitions become increasingly suspect, as the perception of an age-old racial tension sharpens in the present, the Afrocentric star has a wider sphere in which to shine. Mind you, it has competition, especially from Islam, and its ascendancy owes much to the theoretical uncertainties exposed by postmodernism regarding the Big Picture. But its tentacles are spreading, as one observes its increasing educationally reconstructive work within many urban school systems (Camden, New Jersey, and Washington, D.C., for example). Its basic message that redemption begins with an intimate knowledge of blackness, one that eradicates the angst of inferiority, is quite powerful. Indeed, it has managed to weather the onslaught of criticism—from whites as well as blacks—precisely because of the strength of this appeal.

But some confusion reigns in the realm of theory. Is it an essentialist theory? Is the basis of the theory that "blackness and Afrocentricity reflect longstanding belief systems among African peoples" (Collins, 1991, p. 27)? Does this mean that all peoples of African descent are indissolubly tied to such systems that have identical definitional effects on their worldviews wherever they may be?

This essentialism has led to fierce criticism, not directed so much at the underlying claim to difference as it is to the all-inclusive definition of what is African. Scholars like Paul Gilroy (1993) and Kwame Anthony Appiah (1992) attack the cavalier sweep of its inclusiveness and its alleged essentialism. Appiah, in the first instance, reserves the identical critique he extends to African philosophy; Africa is an "invention," as the continent is really an agglomeration of hundreds of languages and dialects and their cognate cultures—all with significantly nuanced forms as to frustrate any attempt of this kind of totalizing. Gilroy is troubled by the apparent lack of contamination and hybridity with which Afrocentric essentialism seems to be invested by its advocates.

After persistent and quite persuasive critiques of this kind, the main branch of the Afrocentric school, led by Molefi Asante, has made some distinct modifications. A newly fashioned posture posits Afrocentricism as meaning that any meaningful and authentic study of peoples of African descent must begin and proceed with Africa as the center, not periphery. And Jerome Schiele (1994, p. 152) adds the qualification that there are distinct cultural differences between African and European peoples, but these initiatives are widely regarded as insincere, as the burden of the critique has not been squarely addressed. Nonetheless, the theory has many elective affinities with the other dissident theories, which I will address later.

At present, the appeal of Afrocentricity lies less in its theoretical efficacy—though at some early point political responses on the subject should be abandoned. Its appeal is mainly ideological. Opponents might scoff at Molefi Asante's (1987) scholarship, particularly with reference to what is interpreted as a thinly disguised and insupportable essentialism, and the claims he makes relative to Egypt (Kemet)—claims that, by the way, have been largely substantiated by Martin Bernal (1987). But these critiques—many of which are not without merit—are somewhat counterbalanced by a huge restitutive potential; it is the reconstructive process that the related archaeological work of the Afrocentrists animates. Ideologically and politically, the agenda has much in common with the founding of the state of Israel. This initiative, as is well known, was the consolidation of peoples of the Jewish diaspora into a nation. Resuscitation required—or certainly received—nothing less than the use of the past, where reality and fiction operated side by side to forge a national consciousness.

*Resistance Theory.* Briefly, resistance theory may be explained as a reaction to domination. In short, these theories address the complex and varied ways in which people exposed to domination negotiate spaces in which to function and even forge frontal attacks on hegemony. Especially in the context of Marxist and other radical forms of critique, there is a tendency to see domination as total and overemphasize the determinant role of structures and institutions. In cases in which revolutionary and other forms of transformative offensives are not in evidence or are deemed rudimentary or absent, the assumption is capitulation by these subject populations. But as Aronowitz and Giroux (1993) put it, "[There is] an underemphasis on how human agency accommodates, mediates, and resists the logic of capital and its dominating social practices" (p. 96) that is mistaken. Culture strongly mediates the ultimate shape a regime, capitalist or socialist, will take. And its largely autonomous character renders its processes less prone to vulgar determinism, structural or otherwise.

A fair measure of research has shed much light on the kinds of activity taking place within the shadows of domination. Within metropolitan societies, resistance theory focuses on the ways in which inner-city minority students, for example, resist oppression. Many of these strategies are often found to represent counterhegemonic undertones (Sutcliffe & Wong, 1986; Willis, 1977).

Similar activity has now moved to center stage in the Third World. We may recall Paulo Freire's (1970) well-known and rather effective *Pedagogy of the Oppressed.* Of course, that agenda consists of the empowerment of illiterate peasants through the use of their indigenous culture to forge liberating knowledge and praxis (Freire, 1970; Freire & Macedo, 1987). It is now common to speak of the "weapons of the weak" (Scott, 1976, 1985), of "reverse discourses" directed at "unfreezing some of the structures of domination" (Slater, 1994, p. 29), of "performance texts" in which culture is employed to subvert the established order and infuse the disadvantaged with new empowering ideologies (see Chinweizu & Madubuike, 1980; Ngugi, 1986)—all these are political expressions and forms directly influenced by culture.

*Postcoloniality.* Postcoloniality has not, up to now, been defined with much satisfaction. Kwame Anthony Appiah (1992) defines it, somewhat unenthusiastically, as "the condition of what we might ungenerously call a comprador intelligentsia: of a relatively small, Western-style, Western-trained, group of writers and thinkers who mediate the trade in cultural commodities of world capitalism and the periphery" (p. 149). Appiah provides an imprecise and unsatisfactory "definition" of postcoloniality because of his fundamental disagreement with the agenda. But there is a postcolonial theory that Henry Giroux (1992) defines rather well:

> it represents a space in which to retheorize, locate, and address the possibilities for a new politics based on the construction of new identities, zones of cultural difference, and forms of ethical address that allow cultural workers and educators alike to transform the languages, social practices, and histories that are part of the colonial experience. (p. 28)

But a postcolonial theory, even if its specific definitions are currently quite elusive, is vitally necessary in the Age of Difference. The more prescient of colonial administrators, Warren Hastings, in the case of India, for example, points to the increasing liberating role and the complementary rehabilitation of authenticity indigenous languages and literature would play "when the services which [they] once yielded of wealth and power are lost remembrances." Today, we witness the stress for cultural and ethnic authenticity in, for example, the postures of African writers and scholars such as Ngugi wa thiong'o (Kenya), Chinweizu (Ghana), and Narogin (Native Australia).

Writing in Gikuyu, Ngugi's work has taken on a truly revolutionary potential for the Kenyan people. His *The Misfortunes of Mitigari* is a case in point. Kole Omotoso shows the fear it drove into the hearts of the Kenyan ruling class from the excerpt below:

> Security officers came to the offices of the publishers and requested all copies of *Mitigari.* As they took *Mitigari* away, the security people warned that the publisher should not reprint. "In Kikuyu or in English?" the publishers wanted to know. . . . "In Kikuyu," replied the security people. (cited in Anyidoho, 1989, p. 21)

But any number of thorny issues plague the formation of this theory, despite the crucial nature of the exercise for any number of frequently repeated social, psychological, and political rehabilitations (of Self and Other[s]). In the first instance, there is the cardinal issue of the carrier: Who shall be the authentic voice? The people or intellectuals? Against what has been viewed as an elitist and, perhaps, co-opted (or co-optable) position is the view that the voice that must be heard via postcoloniality is that of the people. On the first count, Gyatri Chakravorty Spivak's (1988) stance is to the effect that the voice of the people has been silenced by the machinations of imperial processes, and as such, it is the voice of the postcolonial intellectual like herself that should be representative. Against this view is that of Aijaz Ahmad (1992), one that bristles with the misgivings and vitriol of Marxism.

Second, to what extent should white colonial ex-settlers (Australia, New Zealand, and so on) be included in the genre? Is a single genre possible, given the diverse range of colonial experiences (Africa, with its immense variety, the Caribbean, the white settler colonies?). Will this not lead to a rash of "bogus universals," to use Anne McClintock's (1994, p. 299) term? Is there not enough cultural "contamination" to frustrate the objectives of such agendas (Appiah, 1992; Parry, 1994)? Is grounding postcoloniality in transcendental categories of psychoanalysis, such as Homi Bhabha (1994) does, borrowing from Jacques Lacan, really a suitable replacement for historical analysis: Is historical analysis really replaceable (Dirlik, 1994; Young, J., 1990)? Can postcoloniality be successfully grounded in linguistic categories (Dirlik, 1994)?

In the end, the broad agenda almost compels a theory that acknowledges difference as part of a well-articulated expression of oppositional postcoloniality. But there appears to be a far way to go; even so, it is a project that must not be frustrated into inactivity because of its complex nature.

Finally, let me comment briefly on a central conceptual and methodological issue that remains largely unresolved in many of these cases. Is every difference-oriented theory free to formulate its theory and practice arbitrarily? Is every social grouping free to view these processes as rational, merely by following certain socially accepted (group accepted) rules? No. These remain "suggestions, which have to be proven not only in regard to the material already available, but also in regard to the future historical practice(s) of human beings" (Wellmer, 1971, p. 33). (I have pluralized *practice* in the quote to give legitimacy to the diverse nature of reality, to avoid any Marxian universality to which Wellmer's quote might be prone. This does not, however, support the passion for relativism one finds expressed in these theories from time to time.)

## ❖ The Politics of Recognition: Unity in Diversity

Normally, when people from the metropolitan world cooperate in the political affairs of the rest of the world, it is usually against the backdrop of the anarcho-realist principles (Chapter 2). And yet if the powerful ideologies spun from the cross-fertilization of power, wealth, and influence acted mainly as blinders, the scales should now be falling away from our collective eyes. On the socioeconomic plane, the pressures of survivalism arrive laden with psychic and anthropological imperatives, as illustrated throughout the text. We must cooperate or we die! On the political plane, there is a politics of recognition ramifying into subsets of which a politics of affinity is perhaps the most promising. In short, the identical arguments that have legitimized the politico-legal status of the individual, complete with his or her rights, contain within them, as Charles Taylor (1994, pp. 25-73) and, less so, Michael Ignatieff (1986) have demonstrated, a powerful set of counterarguments for a politics of recognition. Recognition is commanded by the requirements of identity. Lately, Will Kymlicka (1995) grounds a persuasive case for certain "collective rights" for minority cultures. Denial of identity—a violation of many of the principles of autonomy, self-determination—generates psychic, social, and self-definitional distortions of which the Other(s) complain. Is not one of democracy's forte the support of a politics of equal recognition? (Kymlicka, 1995; Taylor, 1994, p. 27). Yes. Invoking Plato and Hegel, Francis Fukuyama (1992) remarks that "the propensity to feel self-esteem arises out of the part our soul called *thymos*. It is like an innate human sense of justice" (p. xvii). The propensity feeds into the historical process from which its relevance to political life springs. So with this fact comes the notion that an Other-oriented politics resides within Western liberal political traditions, even if such a claim cannot be successfully extracted from the notion of difference drawn preponderantly from nonmodern and traditional milieux.

But problems of implementation abound. Prominent among them is the liberal principle of neutrality. In theory, no particular claim or conception is given superiority, as that would yield preference to a particular definition of the good. Charles Larmore (1987) suggests that particular definitions of the good reside (should reside?) in the private sphere, as in the public realm he or she appears (should appear?) as a self without any insistent vision of the good, thereby betraying the requisite neutrality. In practice though, the experience is that particular norms prevail largely as a function of power relations, with the priorities of sectional interests flushed in the guise of universalities. Indeed, as Sheldon Wolin (1992) observes, "Some of the more powerful groups are organized for the express purpose of using political and legal means to deprive other citizens of their rights or to restrict the exercise or scope of them" (p. 245).

In its turn, a politics of affinity owes much of its substance to feminist theorizing (Flax, 1991; see Donna Haraway, 1988, for example). It surfaces as a nascent political form with the possibilities of eliminating or reducing obstacles to an alternative political agenda anchored to difference. For whereas the pluralism implicit in what Wolin expresses above favors, at least in principle, some notion of equality, it does not subscribe much to the exercise of justice. Pluralism often is merely satisfied with ensuring that each constituency gets its moment in the political sun, with the issue of its capacity to secure justice of less importance. Indeed, form cannot gel with substance—as inherent in a rights-based perspective, as it is currently inveigled by liberalism—is an abdication of personal responsibility to the conscience-freeing characteristics of the market.

In its main outline, this politics, which extends in its implications to the entire array of the Other(s), works at forging practical solutions to the concepts of identity and recognition—concepts so riddled with tensions and contradictions. We are assaulted by these problems in the copious literature on feminism and environmentalism, so the citation of examples is superfluous. This politics is really pointing to the difficulties in forging pure or even substantial theories and formulations of identity; much of the difficulty, on this view, stems from hybridity and a congenital form of essentialism claimed by some Other(s). No culture can claim, convincingly, the absence of contamination by other cultures, *ergo* the essentialism of Afrocentricity is spurious, as its critics intone. A woman-centered essentialism, such as that represented by Solanas (1969), Spender (1980), and Daly (1978), in which man and woman are as different as east is from west, just will not do. As a voice in rebuttal put it, "Women no less than men, though undoubtedly in a different fashion, are products of a culture and cannot coherently claim for themselves an *a priori* purity or absence of contamination by its values, its language or its myths" (Gatens, 1991, p. 87).

What, then, is the nature of the approach? First, this politics is about the search for connections to enable the Other(s) to cooperate in a common process of emancipation. These connections must somehow recognize the elements that separate Other from Other (Afrocentrists are, in principle, antigay) as well as the strains existing *within* an individual Other (white women and black women) and stress and operationalize the elements that unite. In the end, what is being sought is an effective mechanism to join "partial views and halting voices" into a collective thrust against the forces of domination (Haraway, 1988, pp. 586-590). In this general context of "multiple subject positions," Chantal Mouffe (1988a, p. 90) speaks of subjectivity now characterized by many such positions defying the concept of unity; it is "the locus of multiple possible constructions, according to the different discourses that can construct that position" (p. 90). The call demands a politics "that can recognize and legitimate group difference while resisting fragmentation into discrete and local entities, and the kind of solidarity that becomes possible if we give up the presumption of an undifferentiated humanity" (Phillips, 1993, p. 2). We can detect the broad possibilities of this politics of affinity in the current politics of the new social movements within and across the metropolitan world and across the nonmodern world. In both geographical spheres, repeated references are made to a "postmodern" politics, or a "quotidian" politics where notions of the unitary self are beset by key notions of fragmentation. Crisscrossing political action is rife, exemplified by a multinucleated self displaying the capacity to make claims on behalf of a wide range of dimensions (race, class, gender, ethnicity, for example) in which politics now consists, not as islets of independent existence but sites of multiple existential forms (gay, black, man, and so on) that in the rough and tumble of a more open political age, give rise to conflicts and contradictions. Immediately, these politics betray a number of unusual features extending the political terrain.

First, culture is overly present, as economic considerations decline in relative importance. Second, there is a very high level of tolerance for democracy in the sense that groups and interests that were hitherto impeded by some variant of pluralism or hierarchization now appear to be provided a "representational space" to maneuver (Robertson, 1992, p. 47). These are movements that attempt "to [find] practical ways of organizing that did not reproduce hierarchical, patriarchial patterns (Falk, 1992, p. 20). The third feature of these movements has been referred to as "solidarity across groups" (Rosenau, 1992, pp. 145-146). Solidarity is expressed as the protection of the interests of neighbors (Walker, 1988), giving succor to the marginal (Luke, 1989), and forming coalition—issue-oriented politics—to combat common crises (ecological problems, for example). In this mix of involvement, two distinct currents can be discerned. The first is linked to new statuses, like the postmaterialism analyzed by Inglehart (1990) in which politics shift from narrow economic issues to those related to empowerment, esteem, and self-actualization. The second is distinctly influenced by the issues raised and discussed as Dependence II—by issues linked to *risk*, for example (Chapter 2). A "risk" society moves distinctly away from one in which there is a distribution of "goods" accompanied by competing interests. It becomes situated in new, threatening conditions defined by a sharing of the "bads." These bads do not discriminate and consequently unify the competing groups against a common enemy (pollution, ecological decay, etc.) (Lash et al., 1996, p. 2). Implicated here, of course, are the roles being played by agency and reflexivity, whose impact on individual emancipation has also been remarked on in the broader context of Dependence II.

But caveat emptor. It cannot be overemphasized that there are deeply embedded difficulties implicit in the agenda that a politics of affinity has set for itself. One should have no illusions that the project will be anything but a problem-plagued one. Now, let me proceed to the presentation of certain clusters of elective affinities by which such a politics, and the broader political agenda, is, at least, partially defined.

## ❖ A Politics of Recognition: A Fretwork of Affinities

There is a fretwork of affinities shared by many of the Other(s) that suggests the arrival of new political forms. We detect an unprecedented critical massing of dynamic social transformative fragments giving a new global politics a realistic potential. Among the major fragments are (a) dynamic anti-status quo sentiments, once accompanied by predictable vulnerabilities (histrionics) but now marked by a strong sense of solidarity; (b) realistically shared goals, based on identical strategies created by a basically common source of domination; and (c) a globalismic impetus, extracted from commonalities that are progressively dismantling the separating walls erected on the Big Ditch principle.

Let me attempt to address these components in the interlocking manner in which they do often appear. It should be noted that the list is far from being exhaustive. The dynamic anti-status quo expressions of difference, to which I infer, have been mentioned partly in my earlier account of standpoint theory and Afrocentricity. Here, I am using standpoint theory to embrace other activist forms of difference, the claims of indigenous peoples, for example. To be integrated as well are key concepts drawn from cultural criticism and theory, such as hybridity—a concept aligned to postcoloniality. Below are major examples of confluences, *elective affinities,* between the varieties of the Other(s) striving to fashion politically viable accommodations:

1. There is a general antipathy to an all-embracing domination—one that moves beyond the histrionics that characterized early forms of antipathies directed against domination. The antipathy is greatly strengthened by the clearly visible chinks in the armor of modernity. Perhaps the chink that exposes metropolitan domination to its greatest challenges appears as deep crises in its fundamental systems of thought. The counteroffensive of the Other(s) draws much of its ammunition from these vulnerabilities.

2. The basic notion that difference owes its origins and its emancipation to self-conscious political struggle. Less reliance is placed on the role of the state, the public sphere. This element is raised in the case of feminism (Eisenstein, 1983); in Afrocentric feminist epistemology (Collins, 1991, p. 27); in Afrocentricity (Bekerie, 1994, p. 143); in indigenousness (Mies & Shiva, 1993, pp. 84-86); in the Green movement (Spretnak & Capra, 1986; and in resistance theory, where a clear distinction is drawn between a consciousness linked to the possibilities of political action and mere "oppositional" tactics (Aronowitz & Giroux, 1985).

3. A shared belief that their domination has been instituted in part by forms of cultural seduction and cultricide. The common approach is a form of mass abandonment of the politics of Gramscian hegemony propagated by the state. Accordingly, women grasp at their capacity to nurture; African peoples retrieve their essentialism; native Americans rehabilitate their earthbound philosophy. In the ensuing search many of these commonalities get aligned. Take orality and narrativity. It might be remarked that often these characteristics are central to anti-status quo political initiatives within and outside of the metropolitan world. An example of the first is finding increasing application in education via "resistance theories." Good examples are to be found in the pedagogy in certain African American schools in the United States and among the peasantry in Latin America. Likewise, certain branches of the feminist movement, those advocates influenced by Lacan (Julia Kristeva and Helene Cixous, for example), find primary explanatory force in narrativity, allowing them the possibility of making common cause with Other(s) of like cultural ancestry.[6]

4. The correspondence between the ethic of care with much of the cosmological and axiological aspects of Afrocentricity, with the earth philosophy of indigenous peoples, ecofeminism (the intuition of biocentric equality). The peculiar claims of the Other(s) and the inanimate—Nature, for example—form part of this potential coalition. Ecofeminism and deep ecology are good examples.

5. The special case of power. This is a phenomenon that is receiving a recasting under the new aeges. Much of this work surfaces in feminist theorizing but finds favorable points of contact with certain Third World philosophies and those of indigenous peoples. Specifically, the distinction turns on whether, according to Hannah Arendt (1969), Fritjof Capra (1996, p. 10), and Jean Baker Miller (1992), *power to be* and *power as influence of others* should now replace the hierarchical *power over.* Capra maintains that power must now be properly exercised within "networks" typical of ecological dynamics. C. B. MacPherson (1973) does likewise abjure the limited attention devoted to this form of power. In his view, this neglected aspect of the phenomenon is "power as ability to use and develop essentially human capacities" (p. 49). That this form of neglected power is the preserve of women is the thesis of Nancy Hartsock (1983, p. 12). Men, by virtue of the domination they exercise over women and, by extension, the Other(s), as a whole, use "power-over" as the natural outgrowth of their "instrumentally" defined status. Women, on the other hand, are anthropologically aligned to the other kind of power, namely, "power to," a species that relates to "energy, capacity, and potential" (p. 210). The implication here is that this latter rendition of power is more democratic in its application and more integra-

tive, as people are empowered "to do." "Power to" is taken as being fundamentally different; it is one having links to similar characterizations expressed by Others; one that breaks down the binary oppositions consistent with the "power for" model; and one that has as its stage all the world, inasmuch as the breakup of binary oppositions merely signals the potential interconnectedness of corresponding elements of difference across barriers of all kinds.

So, in the overall, global politics is still linked in some fashion to the noblesse oblige germane to the realist model of international relations. To the contemporary realist who finds in Hobbes a mentor, such displays may surely qualify as acts of prudence, not expressions of playing to the exigencies of morality. But the patterns discussed above clearly beckon to a politics grounded in shared interests. Of course, these are interests, it should be noted, that ignore national barriers. Furthermore, they are rooted in the Self-Other interplay and, as such, should take their cue from a reading of W. E. B. Dubois's interpretation of his place in America as a black and an American provided by Elizabeth Fox-Genovese (1991): "Fidelity to that twoness requires holding fiercely to both its elements" (p. 139).

But important cautionary notes must be sounded. One such is that claims of difference can disguise discrepant constituencies themselves defined by the logic of difference. We have already encountered an example in the case of Afrocentric feminist epistemology above. Another example is the "unthinkable" alliance between blacks in certain London neighborhoods and the National Front, where the former are known to join the latter in a campaign against gays (Mercer, 1990, p. 49). The National Front is a fascist organization, whose hatred of blacks and Jews amounts to a mania.

The contents of this chapter have really touched tangentially on many crucial issues serving to reorient the project of theory building and thereby call into account a new global politics. To be discerned in the flow of the analysis are certain qualitative shifts allowing three interrelated developments. First, the bases of social definition and interpretation—here "social" is used in its broadest terms—are expanded from a narrow dependence on facts in the rationalistic sense. Second, that process of expansion allows language, which has been long marginalized, to play a primary role as against the traditionally supportive role it has been assigned to logic, especially in modern societies. Now cultural forms are visibly providing fundamental bases for grounding theory and action. Third, the combination of the prior two developments has added legitimacy to the concept of difference. It is largely by insisting on its related claims that the Other(s) are making their demands to play a central role in the definition of the emerging global order.

## ❖ Notes

1. Modernity-biased writers (e.g., Drucker, 1993, pp. 25-27) leave the impression that rhetoric and logic (*techne*) exist on a continuum. Cultures still immersed in rhetoric are backward, incomplete. Research shows, however, that some cultures, even though having access to logic and writing, chose elements of rhetoric as being more revealing of truth and knowledge; see Olivier (1971) in the cases of Ancient India and China. Some African societies (the Akan of Ghana, for example; Ackah [1988]) locate rhetoric at the heart of the search for truth. The Asante word *nokware* means truth, truthfulness, honesty, probity; it derives from *ano*, which means the mouth and *kor*, which means one or single (see Ackah, 1988, pp. 25-26).

2. The "linguistics" in this chapter draws heavily on Brown (1987), McKeon (1987), Hallett (1988), Heidegger (1982), Gadamer (1975), Daniel (1990), Oliver (1971), Prelli (1989), and Verene (1981).

3. Much is currently made of memory as the basis of an epistemology of "recollective imagination," one in which the main elements of memory (memory itself, imagination, and invention) form the foundation of the primary faculties of the mind. Recollective imagination, sharing much of Vichian thought, is said to provide answers for the dichotomous and dualistic formulations inherent in the traditional pattern of the philosophy of *Geist* (spirit) and the philosopy of *Leben* (life) (see Verene, 1981, intro. and chap. 4).

4. Russell's perfect language was based on the symbolic calculus of his *Principia Mathematica*. Its mathematical basis was undermined by Carnap, among others, who found several different calculi, effectively suggesting the possibility of several languages! (see Urmson, 1960, chap. 9).

5. This has been Vico's much tested and much adopted thesis: linguistic forms, mainly myths and metaphors, permit knowledge. These forms provide us with a referent derived from the mythic and figural that exists as the product of a community. Meaning, then, proceeds as metaphoric signification in which language provides the expressed associations and their content: "Discourse is made meaningful within the determinate though anonymous context of the communal dictum of mythic expression" (Daniel, 1990, p. 133); see also Kolakowski (1989, chap. 7), who firmly locates myth in the process of thought, in the fact that thinking rests inescapably on the interplay of opposites: "In saying that something is such and such, we know what we are saying only when we know that some other thing is what this thing is not" (p. 61). Kolakowski cogently argues that "what this thing is not" is inescapably anchored to mythical thinking. For insightful accounts of Vico's locating rationality within "the communal dictum of mythic expression," see Daniel (1990, chap. 5; Verene, 1981).

6. These feminists demonstrate the complex nature of creating women as Other. Both recoil from active politics—an activity sine qua non to most strains of feminist theories.

# Part IV

# Chapter Eleven

# CONCLUSION

## Interdependence Without Illusions

*All the king's horses and all the king's men . . .*

*[at] night . . . all cows are black*
Hegel

In the opening chapter, the reader was warned that this book would, at best, be the broad outlines of a new framework. The task has been accomplished mainly by revealing the outmodedness of many key concepts and formulations of the Enlightenment. Cartesian rationalism and its Kantian extensions are caught in the web of a radical paradigm shift toward globalism—a concept that connotes, in part, the unfulfilled promises of modernity, which set the tone for global interdependence.

These promises are of two types. The first comes with the pathologies that seemingly increase in direct proportion to society's capacity to cater to escalating material fetishes of dubious social and psychological validity. These pathologies surface as the failure of liberalism to reconcile individual freedom with the cannibalistic "freedom" inherent in the market, where our ethics, morals, and codes of behavior and performance take their cues from the principles of supply and demand. Unfulfilled promises of the second kind reside in rationalities, though legitimate even by Enlightenment principles, have become marginalized and even eradicated by the exclusivist nature of modern, apodictic reason. It is a species of reason against which Adorno warned as having at its core a propensity to dominate. For their part, these latter rationalities form the centerpieces to the theoretical and praxiological alternatives now counterposed by the marginalized cultures (Third World and nonmodern cultures) to the modern, First World cultures.

Together the marginalized rationalities inhere in the concept of *difference*, on which the book's definition of interdependence is based. In the course of the analysis, it is determined that the taint of backwardness that usually attaches to difference is not necessarily deleterious. The truth-claims by which the concept is underpinned are to be found prominently and seemingly immovable in metropolitan settings. Difference, which also incorporates the inanimate (Nature, for example), is found to implicate deeply the social, psychic, and psychological definitions of constituencies firmly situated within First World milieux—women and racial and ethnic minorities, for example. Accordingly, the old dichotomy between First World and Third World, between modern and traditional or backward, is now an embarrassing anachronism.

But the interdependence conceptualized here is a special rendition of the phenomenon. It is quite unlike the existing versions served up by liberalism (Vernon), or the conservatives (Waltz and Morgenthau), or radicalism (Frank, Amin). None of these approaches is prepared to yield to difference the capacity for fundamental change on the scale this work implies and begins to demonstrate. In addition, the advocates of these approaches are not as sanguine as I am about the eclipse of the modernist Enlightenment model, even though I am not prepared, like the postmodernists, to have it jettisoned completely.

This book has worked its way along the labyrinthine paths leading to the citadel of modernity. Conversely, it has walked, partly backward, from this citadel, tripping over several piles of rubble properly attributed to modern theories of society. Nature and the environment as well as our own sense of social identity are in severe crisis and modernity has played a large role in it. Conversely, the phenomenon of difference, on which this definition of interdependence rests, suggests much that is reconstructive of a new global order. For, among its distinctive features, this concept leads the offensive against the practice of dichotomization, one in which Western culture is valorized at the expense of the Other(s). If difference supplies its own arguments for inclusion within a new theorizing of globalism, aided by the principles of status quo liberalism (see Chapter 9), the concept does likewise reinforce the crucial part that must now be played by dialogue and negotiation. These two features that inhere in the hermeneutic/social constructivist turn, have increasingly put in question the nomothetic, ex cathedra, single-path-to-glory approach of Cartesian and Kantian provenance. Dialogue and negotiation reinforce a democracy of views, complete with the theoretical wherewithal, albeit existing nodally but encouragingly, to demand that he/she who alleges must prove. Despite a superficial identification with relativism, anything does *not* go!

An epidemic of rejoicing appears to be in order. For seemingly at last the opportunity to be released from many of the mixed blessings of modernity is truly on us. Instrumentalism has finally been shown to be the proverbial emperor without clothes. But that is not to be—at least not yet. At the best of times, it is never a simple matter to move from vigorous critique, in which time-hallowed concepts or worldviews are shattered, to broad conceptual agreement, let alone implementation. We must haggle; such is the inviolable legacy of the Enlightenment. Presently, the obstacles are initially of an ideological nature, even though fierce intramural theoretical exchanges exist among those who find the idea of a new paradigm generally congenial.

The ideological impediments exist on either side of the Big Ditch—the one the metropolitan sphere, the other, the nonmodern and sometimes non-Western societies (members of the Other[s], as I have defined the concept). Almost out of habit, one ingrained by a culture of hegemonic superiority, the metropolitan world finds it difficult to reorient its thinking, even in the face of compelling evidence. As we saw in the case of "ecological modernization," the science of ecology has undermined much of the dichotomous thinking on which the man-versus-Nature dichotomy is erected. The summons is for economic arrangements more in keeping with sustainability and a respect for the delicate ecosystems defining Nature. Yet the prevailing economic principle of *technology for growth* is so deeply entrenched as to command accommodation, as a matter of course, rather than the massive theoretical reconceptualization required. The holes are predrilled; the task is to insert the pegs, which must all be, or made, round; if not, leave them out! While the law of enthropy, the revolt of Nature, and the depletion of strategic resources command a qualitative change of approach, theories, practices, and related policies remain intransigently aligned to modernity. In truth, the aphorism of Mark Twain is frighteningly apposite: The tool we have been using all along is a hammer, which explains why our problems appear unerringly as nails!

Metropolitan ideological stubbornness is also displayed in the area of power politics. For the hegemonic powers, realist and neorealist politics have served the ends of metropolitan domination rather well. Zbigniew Brzezinski (1993), the author of *Out of Control,* introduced many of the riddles associated with this general posture. To his credit, this former Secretary of State in the Carter Administration concedes the emergence of "a single and increasingly interdependent global political process" (p. xiii) and the corrosive nature of modern culture ("permissive cornucopia"). Even though there is general agreement on the existence of crippling social pathologies, the correctives he suggests are disappointingly exclusionary. Recognition of the position and contribution of the Other(s) are conspicuously absent. Indeed, his position is different from that of the late Raymond Aron (1967, p. 74) largely with respect to the locus of world leadership. For Aron, the West is dying as "a separate culture," but would become the center of a "universal" society. Brzezinski, for his part, pointedly excludes Europe and cites America's role in executing "effective global control." His main preoccupation is hardly with the locus of leadership; that is self-evident. It is rather with the difficulties inherent in certain conditions from which "permissive cornucopia" derives. The degraded and nonprogressive value systems in which American society is immersed present a profound threat to its ordained leadership.

At the same time, hegemonic rivalry—the natural legacy of Westphalia—could hardly be avoided. Indeed, Brzezinski volunteered that neither Brussels (the proposed capital of a United Europe) nor Tokyo would be proper for the task. In Europe's case, it will remain "headless and soulless" until "[it] acquires a political identity and imbues the vision of its unity with a more ambitious and globally appealing content" (Brzezinski, 1994, p. 145). Not being prepared to be scoffed at, the East ventured its own agenda in *The Voice of Asia* (1996), coauthored by Mahathir Mohammad, the Prime Minister of Malaysia, and Shintaro Ishihara, a prominent Japanese businessman. The message is curt: In the coming century, Asia will replace the West as the center of the world.

Where is the rest of the world? Generally, the region remains, especially for those embracing the realist posture, the proverbial tail to be wagged by a dog of admittedly different constitution. It is quite different, but its favorite bone remains the one on which is inscribed "power is power only if it is exercised over others." Thus, Thomas Pangle (1992), a disciple of Socrates and Montesquieu, for whom morality must take the Kant (1981) of *Grounding for the Metaphysics of Morals* as its *vade-mecum*, is blunt to the point of being dismissive. The current fits and starts reflected in postmodernity are merely summonses for a return to unfulfilled features of a glorious past, with Europe at the helm. That the rest of the world is an afterthought shines brightly through the following quotation:

> The highest task of good Europeans would then be not only to define the foundations of human nature, but to try to make out something of its peaks and heights; not only to guarantee the dignity that is common to every human being, but to seek to clarify and honor those qualities that distinguish and make truly

> admirable the few who can and should be beacons for the rest; not only to secure human rights, but, on the basis of those rights, to explore competing human values. No doubt high among those virtues will be the thoughtful compassion and generosity that ought to be exhibited in Europe's concern for the suffering mass of mankind dwelling outside Europe and North America, the vast majority of our fellows who lack the security and opportunity implicit demanded by the most basic human rights. In this regard, Europeans will have to avoid the pitfalls of both sentimental pity and obtrusive paternalism. (pp. 86-87)

There is an unspoken notion that this bloc will merely reappropriate its adjunct role, even though there is much to suggest unspeakable human retrogression should such a course be sustained. We pursue old dichotomous behavior at our collective peril, for if there is a single message current events proclaim it is that nonmodernities are B's and *not* not-A's. One-way transfers of knowledge and technology for which metropolitan economies are known must give way to codetermination. The patent failures of the one-way flow are not merely "side effects" susceptible to tinkering within a paradigm that is fundamentally sound. The quick of the problem lies in the framework itself that now has no choice but to engage in two-way transfers (Marglin & Marglin, 1996). Narrow conceit shrouded by pseudoscientific twaddle must be replaced by justified inclusiveness such as that presented by the dynamics of difference.

If we view hegemonic politics dispassionately, we ought not to escape the conclusion that these are powerful obstacles lying across the path this book has sketched for interdependence. Of course, that a formidable opposition in this context is a probability is likewise a given. Can we anticipate anything but immensely complex processes, whether we confront the old practices of the world, as a whole, or those of the projected United Europe? In the latter case, old rivalries and the suspicions they continue to engender; cultural and political differences; the fear of being dominated by a powerful unit within the Union; the fear that freedom of movement will enure to the disadvantage of the more prosperous units; the volatility of a common currency—all these (and any one singly) have the potential to keep negotiations protracted and reinforcing the view that we are caught in the throes of the Grand Illusion.

And yet the rest of the world cannot afford the luxury of indifference to the events occurring here. Globalismic interdependence is unthinkable without significant metropolitan participation. The explanation lies in the Self-Other dynamics discussed throughout the book. In more practical terms, the world is truly a village; no longer does it make sense to think in the zero-sum terms reminiscent of realist theory. It might just be the primary role of the Other(s) to keep on shouting even though their voices threaten to become hoarse! Emmanuel Levinas might truly be correct in his insight that the Other(s) are the conscience of the Self, and, consequently, the armature around which a new reality must be erected (see Bauman, 1993; Critchley, 1992; George, 1995, on the immense suggestiveness of this body of thought).

Before reintroducing the fierce intramural theoretical exchanges that impede global interdependence, I should comment briefly on the ideological obstacles on the other side. One should not leave the impression that the nonmodern world, especially the Third World, stands ready for an agreeable ritual of codetermination. Examples are strewn in earlier chapters of a saturnalia of wantonness in such areas as agriculture, population, the environment, and resources (flora and fauna). Nonmodern societies have not been models to be emulated, not necessarily well-prepared partners. On the face of it, one could question the wisdom of cooperating as partners with cultures that, despite an abundance of water, find it difficult, or are unwilling or unable, to link many of their huge nutritional and public health problems to the avoidable scourge of filth and squalor that proper, cheap water technology would easily alleviate. Ghanaians of the Cape Coast region might have every good reason for dissuading Western tourism from appropriating their sparkling white sand beaches. One does not think that using these precious gifts of Nature as lavatories is either effective or self-serving. Indeed, it is downright backward! In such cases, these realities cannot be reasonably blamed on colonialism and imperialism. Multiple regression can be taken only so far.

In context, one could be excused taking seriously Thierry Verhelst's earlier statement (Chapter 2) that the First World must look to the Third World for solutions to its follies and ineptitudes. Like similar apparent paradoxes presented by many Other(s)—feminist politics and ethics, for example—there is much to precipitate an often unfounded, yet institutionalized, ridicule from status quo sources. And yet proper distinctions must be made, and in fairness to Verhelst, he was quick to insert the important qualification that we avoid the "myth of paradise lost"—the notion that the metropolitan world is horribly corrupted while the Third World luxuriates in pristine innocence (Verhelst, 1990, p. 26).

The truth is that we need to develop quickly the will and the capacity to keep constantly in focus the new Big Picture. Indeed, the command is directed to all parties, those still clinging to modernity as well as the Other(s), whose suspicion of modernity, though largely justified, must now cooperate in establishing a new sense of mutual trust. It becomes more difficult, with each passing day, to take refuge in such tired aphorisms as the now contextually inapt old Eastern philosophical standby mentioned in the Preface. Yes! This, too, will pass into realms of greater complexity, confusion, and redefinitions bearing testimony to the new global realities of survivalist interdependence that is our present inheritance.

We should also be circumspect in our evaluation of programs of change. Countless attempts are in progress, for instance, in the key area of sustainability in Africa and Asia, yet positive results appear to be scarce. In a series of studies on environmentalism in Southeast Asia, for example, the preface to that collected work indicates that the authors and discussants were unable to identify "much that is 'sustainable' in the present and prospective pattern of resource use" in those societies (Brookfield & Byron, 1993, p. vii). It is a constant refrain, even though conclusions such as these must be judged in the context of process. The process of implementation is so huge that significant change appears as the proverbial pin in the haystack. Impressive and encouraging gains are being made. That should be the filip, less so the formidable distance yet to be covered, daunting as it might be. Conversely, the African or the Asian must exercise a corresponding patience with their metropolitan neighbors. While the status quo media will hardly report it, the metropolitan world is gradually coming to grips with the modernist equivalents of feces on the Ghanaian beach! (One thinks immediately of the growth of indigenous medicine: Data in 1996 show that Americans spent some $14 billion outside of their traditional medical insurance coverage on alternative medicine.)

The analysis provided in this book has certainly supported Richard Falk's contention that there is a globalization-from-below in the offing. Other-inflected values, norms, practices, and habits of mind are making their way into new global definitions. The suspect premises of the Enlightenment have been exposed in part by postmodern theory, new social movements theory, liberation theory, Gandhi-ism, Rastafarianism. But it is hardly as though the process is (or even substantially) a one-way street. What needs to be stressed with monotonous regularity is the appropriateness for Self and Other(s) to point accusing fingers at each other. One culture's Cape Coast beach is another culture's destruction of Nature or insensitivity to humanism. The next step after acknowledging each culture's "right" to reciprocal finger-pointing—once this process was a one-way street—is formulating mutually reinforcing theory and practice created against the relief of the new Big Picture.

But problems exist here as well, which leads to a brief comment on theoretical infighting, some examples of which are indicated throughout the latter portion of the book. Whether we focus on the disputes within the ecological movement (social ecology versus deep ecology; social and deep ecology versus ecofeminism—see Fox, 1989, and Ferkiss, 1993, for excellent accounts of the disputes) or those discrepant fragments within feminism (white woman versus black woman; straight woman versus lesbian; feminism as inevitably an activist political agenda versus the antipolitical postures of Lacan-inspired feminists—Kristeva and Cixous, for example), we should take proper stock of a perceptive Hegelian insight. Here Hegel speaks of the deceptions inherent in the existence of "the night in which all cows are black."

The demand for epistemological diversity is unassailable, but we must distinguish knowledge from opinion, ideology from scientific theories, twaddle from engaging discourse. We have treated (and should) with suspicion claims to difference made by those who would use the available, congenial space opportunistically. One thinks immediately of the effort of certain sections of the gay community to lay claims to a "queer brain" or the seemingly irreconcilable feminism of Mary Daly and Dale Spender, which places woman and man at poles as far apart as east and west, with ne'er the twain to meet! (Chapter 10). To repeat an earlier analysis in Chapter 9, it is difficult to fault the initiatives of the liberated and inspired Other(s) in engaging in the kind of archaeological work centered on a search for Identity. But the search that should be directed at how domination was instituted and how Identity should be restored, must then function as the *terminus a quo* and not the *terminus ad quem*. We search and will find; then we rehabilitate as a joint, interpenetrating process between Self and Other(s). Narrow identity politics possess a short-term ideological value attached to a psychology of recognition (Taylor, 1992), but in the end, they should not be pressed beyond their constructive limits. Political opportunism bred by narrow identity politics is a necessary evil that should never be allowed to escape the proper cage in which it must be held captive.

Theorizing in the general areas encompassing difference has been sufficiently developed so as to reassure us that Stygian though the darkness might be, we can make crucial distinctions between the black, the brown, and the white cow. The task is getting the cows to recognize themselves without relying on the flawed "ocular-centric" perspective (Jay, 1992), "the empire of everyday seeing" (Levin, 1988) by which our ways of perceiving and conceptualizing are deeply influenced. To pursue this bovine metaphor further, all the cows should be able to identify themselves, even in the dark, through the aid of sounds, smells, gait, and so on. But just as crucial is the imperative not to lose the sense that they are all cows nonetheless! Such is the timely injunction against essentialisms that needs to be communicated with engaging regularity. An essentialism such as that underlying nationalism makes difference a weapon of utter destruction. In my view, there is nothing fundamental about such a claim that makes its destructive potential inevitable and internally supportable. What needs to be recognized are the compulsions and their consequences that should render these threats increasingly insupportable and unavailing, perhaps, moreso, as our growing enlightened views of what we are and what we are capable of accomplishing as human beings make these largely pathological expressions shameful contradictions. Refresher courses are splendid for the constructive energy they invariably impart. It seems that one such course, which appears in Hegel as something in the nature of an anthropological constant, could stand our search for answers in good stead. It appears in the context of love in the family setting:

> Love means in general terms the consciousness of my unity with another so that I am not in selfish isolation but win my self-consciousness only as the renunciation of independence and through knowing myself as the unity of myself with another and of the other with me. (cited in Frost, 1996, p. 143)

"Standpoints" will flourish and it is in the nature of difference that they do so. But an immediate task awaits our unified attention and initiative. Theory and practice must continue to find ways of grounding standpoints without the kind of exclusivity that leads far too often to carnages initiated by primordial rectitude, whether a Bosnia or a Rwanda. It seems to me that one of the truly liberatory aspects of epistemological diversity is the provision of the broad sketches of such a framework. Already, much useful work on the politics of difference (Phillips, 1993), of affinity (Haraway, 1988), of border crossings (Giroux, 1993), and so on have set the stage. What is needed is the continuing operationalization of these efforts within the nook and cranny of our global culture. It will not be a short-term initiative. But that is one of the strengths of humankind, namely, that there is a future whose justifiable compulsions put in the relative shade our instincts for immediacy.

I would like to end this chapter on a note of exhortation. Surely, there are enough instances of the "doomsday" syndrome to place the burden of proof even more squarely on the shoulders of those who allege. Nonetheless, the truth is that our first responsibility is hardly to look at precedent, less so if it draws its authority from the usual scientific stock of knowledge. The foundation of precedent, especially touching areas covered by this book, if not flawed, is quite suspect. Precedent is usually expressed in deference to modern, instrumental science that has demonstrably shown itself as anything but the definitive answer to old wives' tales, proverbs, and all those expressions labeled "values" against which modern science wages an uncompromising battle. Now we are beginning to appreciate that this species of science is truly the Sorceror's Apprentice.

If proof had not been veering in from diverse disciplines and perspectives—from the natural sciences, philosophy, the social sciences—one would almost be tempted to speak of a bandwagon effect set in motion by an irresistible fad. But that is not the case. Evidence that we are on the cusp of a new axial age is compelling. The simultaneity of this discovery by all branches of knowledge simulates the proverbial moths drawn to a common flame. In unison, we must all view carefully the composition of the flame that has universally struck us with the peculiarity and the civilizational strangeness of its structure.

As rhetoric forms a central plinth of this work, it seems only appropriate that it should be invoked in conclusion. I will do so with a few chosen lines from one of my favorite poets, W. H. Auden. The lines are from his much celebrated "September 1st 1939."

> All I have is a voice
> To undo the folded lie;
> The romantic lie in the brain
> Of the sensual man-in-the-street
> And the lie of Authority
> Whose buildings grope the sky:
> There is no such thing as the State
> And no one exists alone;
> Hunger allows no choice
> To the citizen or the police;
> We must love one another or die.[1]

There is a community-oriented message here that I will translate in political theoretic language. It is that we handle with care and indeed use decreasingly the notion that we are solely the bearers of rights. Instead, we must fashion the elements carrying the powerful incentives and definitions of rights into epochally appropriate notions of a global good(s)—of global community. The derived morality appears to best realize itself, given the nature of our present world, within the framework of structures that at once acknowledge and celebrate some sense of individuality and the attachment of that individuality to embracing definitions of community. We must now speak not of "national" citizens but "world" citizens. We must get away from the Kantian notion of an individuality that is the sole legitimator of morality (i.e., the individual as the only moral agent in which what is right, what is moral, is to be determined).

## ❖ NOTE

1. From W. H. Auden's *Poems, Essays and Dramatic Writings 1927-1939,* edited by Edward Mendelson; used by permission of Faber and Faber Ltd.

# REFERENCES


Abu-Lughod, J. (1989). *Before European hegemony: The world system A.D. 1250-1350.* New York: Oxford University Press.

Ackah, C. A. (1988). *Akan ethics.* Accra, Ghana: Ghana Universities Press.

Adams, M. (1989). African visual arts from an art historical perspective. *African Studies Review, 32*(2), 55-108.

Adorno, T., & Horkheimer, M. (1972). *Dialectic of enlightenment* (J. Cumming, Trans.). New York: Herder & Herder.

Agger, B. (1993). *Gender, culture, and power.* Westport, CT: Praeger.

Agonito, R. (1977). *History of ideas on woman: A source book.* New York: Perigee.

Ahmad, A. (1992). *In theory: Classes, nations, literatures.* London: Verso.

Aiken, H. D. (1984). *The age of ideology.* New York: Meridian.

Albrow, M., & King, E. (Eds.). (1990). *Globalization, knowledge and society.* London: Sage.

Alger, C. F. (1990). Grass-roots perspectives on policies for development. *Journal of Peace Research, 27*(2), 155-168.

Allsopp, B. (1972). *The garden Earth: The case for ecological morality.* New York: William Morrow.

Althusser, L. (1971). *Lenin and philosophy.* New York: Monthly Review Press.

Alvares, C. (1991). *Decolonizing history.* New York: Apex.

Amin, S. (1974). *Accumulation on a world scale* (2 Vols.). New York: Monthly Review Press.

Amin, S. (1976). *Unequal development.* New York: Monthly Review Press.

Amsden, A. H. (1979). Taiwan's economic history: Case of *Etatisme* and a challenge to dependency theory. *Modern China, 5*(3), 341-380.

Anderson, W. T. (1992). *Reality isn't what it used to be.* New York: HarperCollins.

Anyidoho, K. (1989). *The pan African ideal in literatures of the black world.* Accra: Ghana Universities Press.

Apel, K. O. (1980). *Towards a transformation of philosophy.* Boston: Routledge & Kegan Paul.

Appadurai, A. (1990). Disjuncture and difference in the global cultural economy. *Public Culture, 3*(2), 1-24.

Appiah, K. A. (1992). *In my father's house: Africa in the philosophy of culture.* New York: Oxford University Press.

Aquinas, St. Thomas. (1988). *St. Thomas Aquinas on politics and ethics* (P. E. Sigmund, Ed., Trans.). New York: Norton.

Arendt, H. (1969). *On violence.* New York: Harcourt, Brace Jovanovich.

Aristotle. (1984). *Politics* (C. Lord, Trans.). Chicago: University of Chicago Press.

Arnold, M. (1869). *Culture and anarchy.* London: Smith Elder.

Arnold, M. (1947). *Four essays on life and letters.* (E. K. Brown, Ed.). New York: Appleton-Century.

Aron, R. (1966). *Peace and war: A theory of international relations.* Garden City, NY: Doubleday.

Aron, R. (1967). *18 lectures on industrial society.* London: Wiedenfeld & Nicholson.

Aronowitz, S. (1992). *The politics of identity.* New York: Routledge.

Aronowitz, S., & Giroux, H. A. (1985). *Education under siege.* South Hadley, MA: Bergin & Garvey.

Asante, M. K. (1987). *The Afrocentric idea.* Philadelphia, PA: Temple University Press.

Asinoff, R. (1985, December 1984/January 1985). India accident raises questions of corporate responsibility. *In These Times,* 9, 3, 10.

Attfield, R. (1994). *Environmental philosophy: Principles and prospects.* Aldershot, UK: Avebury.

Avineri, S. (1971). *The social and political thought of Karl Marx.* London: Cambridge University Press.

Axelos, K. (1976). *Alienation, praxis, and techne in the thought of Karl Marx* (R. Bruzina, Trans.). Austin: University of Texas Press.

Axinn, J., & Stern, M. J. (1988). *Dependency and poverty: Old problems in a new world.* Lexington, MA: Lexington Books.

Bacon, F. (1974). *The advancement of learning and the new Atlantis* (A. Johnston, Ed.). Oxford, UK: Oxford University Press.

Bacon, F. (1994). *Novum organum* (P. Urbach & J. Gibson, Ed., Trans.). LaSalle, IL: Open Court.

Badinter, E. (1989). *The unopposite sex.* New York: Harper & Row.

Bahro, R. (1984). *From red to green: Interviews with new left review.* London: Verso.

Bahro, R. (1986). *Building the green movement* (M. Tyler, Trans.). Philadelphia, PA: New Society Publishers.

Bamyeh, M. A. (1993). Culture. *Current Sociology, 41*(3), 40-65.

Banton, T. (1996). *The greening of Marxism.* New York: Guilford.

Baran, P. (1957). *The political economy of growth.* New York: Monthly Review Press.

Barrett, W. (1959). *Irrational man.* New York: Doubleday.

Barry, B. (1989, October). The light that failed? *Ethics,* 160-168.

Barry, B., & Goodin, R. E. (Eds.). (1992). *Free movement.* University Park: Pennsylvania State University Press.

Barry, J. (1986, March 13). Preventing chemical disasters. *Daily World,* pp. 9-12.

Bartley, W. W. (1988). Theories of rationality. In G. Radnitzky & W. W. Bartley, III (Eds.). *Evolutionary epistemology, rationality, and the sociology of knowledge.* Lasalle, IL: Open Court.

Bates, R. H., Mudimbe, V. Y., & O'Barr, J. (Eds.). (1993). *Africa and the disciplines.* Chicago: University of Chicago Press.

Bauman, Z. (1989). *Modernity and the Holocaust.* Cambridge, UK: Polity Press.

Bauman, Z. (1992). *Intimations of postmodernity.* New York: Routledge.

Bauman, Z. (1993). *Postmodern ethics.* Oxford, UK: Blackwell.

Bauman, Z. (1995). *Life in fragments: Essays in postmodern morality.* Oxford, UK: Blackwell.

Beck, U. (1992). *Risk society: Toward a new modernity.* Newbury Park, CA: Sage.

Beck-Gernsheim, E. (1996). Life as a planning project. In S. Lash, B. Szerszynski, & B. Wynne (Eds.), *Risk, environment and modernity* (pp. 139-153). London: Sage.

Becker, G. (1976). *The economic approach to human behavior.* Chicago: University of Chicago Press.

Bekerie, A. (1994). The four corners of a circle: Afrocentricity as a model of synthesis. *Journal of Black Studies, 25*(2), 131-149.

Bellah, R. N., Madsen, R., Sullivan, W. M., Swidler, A., & Tipton, W. H. (1992). *The good society.* New York: Vintage.

Ben-Amos, P. G. (1989). African visual arts from a social perspective. *African Studies Review, 32*(2), 1-54.

Benhabib, S. (1986). *Critique, norm, and utopia.* New York: Columbia University Press.

Benhabib, S. (1992). *Situating the self.* New York: Routledge.

Benhabib, S., & Cornell, D. (Eds.). (1987). *Feminism as critique.* Minneapolis: University of Minnesota Press.

Benveniste, E. (1971). *Problems in general linguistics.* Coral Gables, FL: University of Miami Press.

Berger, P. L. (1986). *The capitalist revolution.* New York: Basic Books.

Berger, P., Berger, B., & Kellner, H. (1974). *The homeless mind: Modernization and consciousness.* New York: Random House.

Berlin, I. (1982). *Against the current: Essays in the history of ideas* (H. Hardy, Ed.). Hammondsworth, UK: Penguin.

Bernal, M. (1987). *Black Athena* (Vol. 1). New Brunswick, NJ: Rutgers University Press.

Bernstein, R. J. (1983). *Beyond objectivism and relativism.* Oxford, UK: Basil Blackwell.

Bernstein, R. J. (1985). *Habermas and modernity.* Cambridge: MIT Press.

Bernstein, R. J. (1986). What is the difference that makes a difference? Gadamer, Habermas, and Rorty. In B. Wachterhauser (Ed.), *Hermeneutics and modern philosophy.* Albany: State University of New York Press.

Bhabha, H. (1994). *The location of culture.* London: Routledge.

Biebuyck, D. P. (1983). African art studies since 1957: Achievements and directions. *African Studies Review, 26*(3, 4), 99-118.

Billig, M. (1987). *Arguing and thinking: a rhetorical approach to social psychology.* Cambridge, UK: Cambridge University Press.

Birnie, P. (1992). International environmental law: Its adequacy for present and future needs. In A. Hurrell & B. Kingsbury (Eds.), *The international politics of the environment* (pp. 53-88). Oxford, UK: Oxford University Press.

Black, M. (1962). *Methods and metaphors: Studies in language and philosophy.* Ithaca, NY: Cornell University Press.

Blanshard, B. (1991). *Reason and analysis.* LaSalle, IL: Open Court.

Blaut, J. M. (1993). *The colonizer's model of the world.* New York: Guilford.

Blier, S. P. (1993). Truth and seeing: Magic, custom, and fetish in art history. In R. H. Bates, V. Y. Mudimbe, & J. O'Barr (Eds.), *Africa and the disciplines* (pp. 139-166). Chicago: University of Chicago Press.

Bloch, E. (1971). *On Karl Marx.* New York: Herder & Herder.

Block, F. (1990). *Postindustrial possibilities: A critique of economic discourse.* Berkeley: University of California Press.

Bloom, A. (1987). *The closing of the American mind.* New York: Simon & Shuster.

Bluestone, B., & Harrison, B. (1982). *The deindustrialization of America.* New York: Basic Books.

Blumenberg, H. (1990). *Work on myth.* Cambridge: MIT Press.

Boggs, C. (1986). *Social movements and political power.* Philadelphia, PA: Temple University Press.

Booth, A. L., & Jacobs, H. M. (1990). Ties that bind: Native American beliefs as a foundation for environmental consciousness. *Environmental Ethics, 12*(1), 27-43.

Botwinick, A. (1993). *Postmodernism and democratic theory.* Philadelphia, PA: Temple University Press.

Bradbury, M. (1971). *The social context of modern English literature.* New York: Schocken.

Brenkman, J. (1987). *Culture and domination.* Ithaca, NY: Cornell University Press.

Bricker, P., & Hughes, R. I. G. (Eds.). (1990). *Philosophical perspectives on Newtonian science.* Cambridge: MIT Press.

Brodbeck, M. (1972). Descartes and the notion of a criterion of external reality. In the Royal Institute of Philosophy (Ed.), *Reason and reality* (p. 5). London: Macmillan.

Brookfield, H., & Byron, Y. (Eds.). (1993). *South-East Asia's environmental future.* New York: United Nations University Press.

Brown, L. R., Flavin, C., & Wolf, E. C. (1988, July/August). Earth's vital signs. *The Futurist,* pp. 5-15.

Brown, L. R., & Jacobson, J. L. (1986, December). Our demographically divided world. In *Worldwatch Paper* (No. 74). Washington, DC: Worldwatch Institute.

Brown, R. H. (1987). *Society as text.* Chicago: University of Chicago Press.

Brown, R. H. (1990). Rhetoric, textuality, and the postmodern turn in sociological theory. *Sociological Theory, 38*(2), 188-197.

Brumfitt, J. H. (1970). *Voltaire: Historian.* London: Oxford University Press.

Brzezinski, Z. (1993). *Out of control.* New York: Collier.

Buchdahl, G. (1981). *The Image of Newton and Locke in the Age of Reason.* London: Sheed & Ward.

Buell, F. (1994). *National culture and the new global system.* Baltimore, MD: Johns Hopkins University Press.

Bull, H. (1981). Hobbes and the international anarchy. *Social Resarch, 48,* 717-738.

Burdett, H., Fornos, W., Kinkade, S., & Meyer, D. (1988). A continent in crisis: Building a future for Africa in the 21st century. In *Toward the 21st century* (pp. 47-73). Washington, DC: The Population Institute.

Bury, J. B. (1932). *The idea of progress.* New York: Macmillan.

Cammack, P., Pool, D., & Tordoff, W. (1993). *Third World politics.* Baltimore, MD: Johns Hopkins University Press.

Capecchi, V. (1989). The informal economy and the development of flexible specialization in Emilia-Romagna. In A. Portes, M. Castells, & L. A. Benton (Eds.), *The informal economy* (pp. 189-215). Baltimore, MD: Johns Hopkins University Press.

Capra, F. (1996). *The web of life.* New York: Doubleday.

Capra, F., & Pauli, G. (Eds.). (1995). *Steering business toward sustainability.* Toyko: United Nations Press.

Cardoso, F. E., & Falleto, E. (1979). *Dependency and development in Latin America.* Berkeley: University of California Press.

Carmody, D. L. (1992). *Mythological woman.* New York: Crossword.

Carmody, J. (1983). *Ecology and religion: Toward a new Christian theology of nature.* New York: Paulist.

Carpenter, B. (1990, April 23). Living with our legacy. *U.S. News & World Report,* pp. 60-65.

Carroll, J. (1977). *Puritan, paranoid, remissive: A sociology of modern culture.* London: Routledge & Kegan Paul.

Carson, R. (1962). *Silent spring.* New York: Knopf.

Cassirer, E. (1946). *The myth of the state.* New Haven, CT: Yale University Press.

Cassirer, E. (1953). *Language and myth.* New York: Dover Publications.

Cassirer, E. (1955). *The philosophy of symbolic forms.* (3 Vols.). New Haven, CT: Yale University Press.

Cassirer, E. (1966). *The problem of knowledge.* New Haven, CT: Yale University Press.

Caton, H. (1988). *The politics of progress: The origins and development of the commercial republic, 1600-1835.* Gainesville: University of Florida Press.

Chernoff, J. M. (1979). *African rhythm and African sensibility: Aesthetics and social action in African musical idioms.* Chicago: University of Chicago Press.

Chinweizu, O., & Madubuike, I. (1980). *Toward the decolonization of African literature.* Enugu, Nigeria: Fourth Dimension.
Chiras, D. D. (1992). *Lessons from nature: Learning to live sustainably on Earth.* Washington, DC: Island Press.
Cioran, E. M. (1993). *The trouble with being born.* London: Quartet Books.
Cixous, H., & Clement, C. (1986). *The newly born woman.* Minneapolis: University of Minnesota Press.
Clastres, P. (1974). *La Societe contre l'etat.* Paris: Editions de Minuit.
Cliffe, L. (1985). Rural political economy of Africa. In P. C. W. Gutkind & I. Wallerstein (Eds.), *Political economy of contemporary Africa* (pp. 117-143). Newbury Park, CA: Sage.
Cockcroft, J., Frank, A. G., & Johnson, D. (Eds.). (1972). *Dependence and underdevelopment.* New York: Doubleday.
Collingwood, R. G. (1969). *The idea of history.* London: Oxford University Press.
Collins, P. H. (1991). *Black feminist thought.* New York: Routledge.
Comaroff, J. L. (1996). Ethnicity, nationalism, and the politics of difference in an age of revolution. In E. N. Wilmsen and P. McAllister (Eds.), *The politics of difference.* (pp. 162-183). Chicago: The University of Chicago Press.
Commoner, B. (1972). *The closing circle.* New York: Knopf.
Commoner, B. (1990). *Making peace with the Earth.* New York: Pantheon.
Conn, S. A. (1990, April). Protest and thrive: The relationship between global responsibility and personal empowerment. *New England Journal of Public Policy* [Special issue] (163-177).
Constanza, R. (Ed.). (1991). *Ecological economics.* New York: Columbia University Press.
Contrucci, J. (1988). *Rape of the wild.* London: Women's Press.
Cox, H. (1984). *Religion in the secular city.* New York: Simon & Schuster.
Critchley, S. (1992). *The ethics of deconstruction: Derrida and Levinas.* Oxford, UK: Blackwell.
Daly, M. (1978). *Gyn-ecology: The metaethics of radical feminism.* Boston: Beacon.
Daniel, S. H. (1990). *Myth and modern philosophy.* Philadelphia, PA: Temple University Press.
Daston, L. (1994). Baconian facts, academic civility, and the prehistory of objectivity. In A. Megill (Ed.), *Rethinking objectivity* (pp. 37-63). Durham, NC: Duke University Press.
Davidson, B. (1992). *The black man's burden.* New York: Random House.
Delafosse, M. (1927). *Les Negres.* Paris: Rieder.
De Rougement, D. (1966). *The idea of Europe.* New York: Macmillan.
De Santis, F. (1959). *The history of Italian literature* (2 Vols.). New York: Basic.
Denton, J. (1985). The underground economy and social stratification. *Sociological Spectrum,* 5(1, 2), 31-42.
Derrida, J. (1981). *Positions* (A. Bass, Trans.). London: Athlone.
Descartes, R. (1984). *Discourse on method* (G. Heffernan, Ed., Trans.). Notre Dame: University of Notre Dame Press.
Diop, C. A. (1974). *The African origin of civilization: Myth or reality.* Westport, CT: Lawrence Hill.
Dirlik, A. (1994). The post-colonial aura: Third World criticism in the era of global imperialism. *Critical Inquiry, 20,* 329-356.
Donovan, J. (1985). *Feminist theory.* New York: Ungar.
Dos Santos, T. (1970). The structure of dependence. *American Economic Review, 15*(2), 231-236.
Douglas, M. (1986). *How institutions think.* Syracuse, NY: Syracuse University Press.
Draper, J. W. (1904). *The intellectual development of Europe* (2 Vols.). New York: Harper & Brothers.
Drucker, P. F. (1993). *Post-capitalist society.* New York: HarperCollins.
Dublin, M. (1992). *Futurehype—The tyranny of prophecy.* New York: Plume.

DuBois, W. E. B. (1940). *Dusk to dawn: an essay toward and autobiography of a race concept.* New York: Harcourt, Brace and Company.

DuBois, W. E. B. (1970). *W. E. B. DuBois speaks: Speeches and addresses, 1890-1919* S. Foner (Ed.). New York: Pathfinders Press.

Duerr, Hans-Peter. (1985). *Dreamtime: Concerning the boundary between wilderness and civilization.* Oxford, UK: Basil Blackwell.

Dunlap, R. E., Gallup, G. H., Jr., & Gallup, A. M. (1992). *The health of the planet.* Princeton, NJ: George H. Gallup International Institute.

Durning, A. B. (1988). Action at the grassroots: Fighting poverty and environmental decline. *Worldwatch Paper* 88. Washington, DC: Worldwatch Institute.

Dworkin, R. (1977). *Taking rights seriously.* Cambridge, MA: Harvard University Press.

Dwyer, A. (1990). *Into the Amazon.* San Francisco: Sierra Club Books.

Eagleton, T. (1978). *Criticism & ideology.* London: Verso.

Eagleton, T. (1983). *Literary theory.* Minneapolis: University of Minnesota Press.

Easterbrook, G. (1989, January 26). The revolution in medicine. *Newsweek,* pp. 40-74.

Eder, K. (1993). *The new politics of class.* London: Sage.

Edgerton, S. (1976). *The Renaissance rediscovery of linear perspective.* New York: Harper & Row.

Edwards, M., & Hulme, D. (Eds.). (1992). *Making a difference: NGOs and development in a changing world.* London: Earthscan.

Ehrlich, P. (1968). *The population bomb.* New York: Ballantine.

Eisenstein, Z. (1981). *The radical future of liberal feminism.* New York: Longman.

Esteva, G. (1992). Development. In W. Sachs (Ed.), *The development dictionary* (pp. 8-25). London: Zed.

Evans-Pritchard, E. E. (1946). *Nuer Religion.* Oxford, UK: Oxford University Press.

Evans-Pritchard, E. E. (1976). *Witchcraft, oracles and magic among the Azande* (E. Gilles, Ed.). London: Oxford University Press.

Faber, D. (1992). The ecological crisis of Latin America: A theoretical introduction. *Latin American Perspectives,* 19(1), 3-16.

Falk, R. (1992). *Explorations.* Philadelphia, PA: Temple University Press.

Fals-Borda, O. (1990). The application of participatory-action research in Latin America. In M. Albrow & E. King (Eds.), *Globalization, knowledge and society* (pp. 79-97). London: Sage.

Fanon, F. (1967). *Black skins, white masks* (C. L. Markam, Trans.). New York: Grove.

Farah, D. (1993). The lost decade: Central America is staggering under its '80s legacy. In P. Goodwin, Jr. (Ed.), *Latin America* (pp. 180-183). Guilford, CT: The Dushkin Publishing Group.

Farber, M. A., & Nelson, J. A. (Eds.). (1993). *Beyond economic man: Feminist theory and economics.* Chicago: University of Chicago Press.

Farber, S. (1991). Local and global incentives for sustainability: Failures in economic systems. In R. Constanza (Ed.), *Ecological economics* (pp. 344-354). New York: Columbia University Press.

Farrington, J., & Bebbington, A. (1993a). *Reluctant partners? Non-governmental organizations, the state and sustainable agricultural development.* London: Routledge.

Farrington, J., & Bebbington, A. (1993b). Governments, NGO's and agricultural development: Perspectives on changing inter-organizational relationships. *Journal of Development Studies,* 29(2), 199-219.

Featherstone, M. (1992). Postmodernism and the aestheticization of everyday life. In S. Lash & J. Friedman (Eds.), *Modernity and identity* (pp. 265-290). Oxford, UK: Blackwell.

Feibleman, J. (1968). *The theory of human culture.* New York: Humanities Press.

Felski, R. (1995). *The gender of modernity.* Cambridge, MA: Harvard University Press.

Ferkiss, V. (1993). *Nature, technology, and society.* New York: New York University Press.

Ferry, L. (1995). *The new ecological order.* Chicago: University of Chicago Press.

Ferry, L., & Renault, A. (1992). *From rights of man to the republican idea.* Chicago: University of Chicago Press.

Feshbach, M., & Friendly, A., Jr. (1992). *Ecocide in the U.S.S.R.* New York: Basic Books.

Feyerabend, P. (1979). *Against method.* London: Verso.

Feyerabend, P. (1994). *Farewell to reason.* London: Verso.

Finsterbusch, K., & McKenna, G. (Eds.). (1990). *Taking sides* (6th ed.). Guilford, CT: Dushkin.

Fisher, J. (1993). *The road to Rio: Sustainable development and the nongovernmental movement in the Third World.* Westview, CT: Praeger.

Fisher, W. R. (1984). Narration as a human communication paradigm: The case of public moral argument. *Communication Monographs, 51.*

Flax, J. (1990).*Psychoanalysis, feminism and post-modernism in the contemporary West.* Berkeley: University of California Press.

Flax, J. (1991). *Thinking fragments: Psychoanalysis, feminism, and postmodernism in the contemporary west.* Berkeley: University of California.

Forsberg, R. P. (1990). *Thomas Hobbes' theory of obligation.* Wakefield, NH: Longwood Academic.

Foster-Carter, A. (1978, January-February). The modes of production controversy. *New Left Review,* pp. 47-77.

Foucault, M. (1973). *The order of things: An archaeology of the human sciences.* New York: Vintage.

Foucault, M. (1978). *The history of sexuality.* New York: Pantheon.

Foucault, M. (1983). The subject of power. In H. Dreyfus & P. Rabinow (Eds.), *Michel Foucault: Beyond structuralism and hermeneutics* (pp. 208-226). Brighton, UK: Harvester.

Foucault, M. (1988). The ethic of care for the self as a practice of freedom. In J. Bernauer & D. Rasmussen (Eds.), *The Final Foucault* (pp. 1-20). Cambridge, MA: MIT Press.

Fox, W. (1989). The deep ecology: Ecofeminism debate and its parallels. *Environmental Ethics, 11,* 5-25.

Fox-Genovese, E. (1991). *Feminism without illusions.* Chapel Hill: University of North Carolina Press.

Fox Keller, E. (1985). *Reflections on gender and science.* New Haven, CT: Yale University Press.

Frank, A. G. (1969). *Capitalism and underdevelopment in Latin America: Historical studies.* New York: Monthly Review Press.

Frankel, C. (1956). *The case for modern man.* New York: Harper & Brothers.

Fraser, S. (Ed.). (1995). *The bell curve wars.* New York: Basic Books.

Frazer, E., & Lacey, N. (1993). *The politics of community.* Toronto: University of Toronto Press.

Freire, P. (1970). *Pedagogy of the oppressed.* New York: Continuum.

Freire, P., & Macedo, D. (1987). *Literacy: Reading the word and the world.* South Hadley, MA: Bergin & Garvey.

French, H. F. (1994, January). Can the environment movement survive industrial demands? *USA Today Magazine, 122* (2584), 66.

Freud, S. (1962). *Civilization and its discontents* (J. Strachey, Ed., Trans.). New York: Norton.

Friedman, J. (1992). Narcissism, roots and postmodernity: The constitution of selfhood in the global crisis. In S. Lash and J. Friedman (Eds.), *Modernity & identity* (pp. 331-366). Oxford, UK: Blackwell.

Friedman, M. (1962). *Capitalism and freedom.* Chicago: University of Chicago Press.

Froebel, F., Heinrichs, J., & Kreye, O. (1980). *The new international division of labor.* Cambridge, UK: Cambridge University Press.

Froebenius, L. (1936). *Histoire de la Civilisation Africaine.* Paris: Gallimard.

Frost, M. (1996). *Ethics in international relations: A constitutive theory.* New York: Cambridge University Press.

Fukuyama, F. (1992). *The end of history and the last man.* New York: Basic Books.
Fuller, S. (1991). *Social epistemology.* Indianapolis: Indiana University Press.
Gadamer, Hans-Georg. (1975). *Truth and method.* New York: Seabury.
Garner, R. (1994). *Beyond morality.* Philadelphia, PA: Temple University Press.
Garver, N., & Lee, S-C. (1994). *Derrida & Wittgenstein.* Philadelphia, PA: Temple University Press.
Gatens, M. (1991). *Feminism and philosophy.* Bloomington: Indiana University Press.
Gates, H. L., Jr. (1992). *Loose canons: Notes on the culture wars.* New York: Oxford University Press.
Gay, P. (1966). *The Enlightenment: An interpretation.* New York: Vintage.
Gellner, E. (1992). *Postmodernism, reason and religion.* New York: Routledge.
Genovese, E. D. (1965). *The political economy of slavery.* New York: Vintage.
George, J. (1995). Realist "ethics," international relations, and postmodernism: Thinking beyond the egoism-anarchy thematic. *Millennium: Journal of International Studies, 24*(2), 195-223.
Georgescu-Roegen, N. (1971). *The entropy law and the economic process.* Cambridge, MA: Harvard University Press.
Gergen, K. J. (1991). *The saturated self.* New York: Basic Books.
Giddens, A. (1990). *The consequences of modernity.* Stanford: Stanford University Press.
Gies, F., & Gies, J. (1994). *Cathedral, gorge, and waterwheel.* New York: HarperCollins.
Gill, S., & Law, D. (1988). *The global political economy.* Baltimore, MD: Johns Hopkins University Press.
Gilligan, C. (1982). *In a different voice.* Cambridge, MA: Harvard University Press.
Gilroy, P. (1993). *The black Atlantic: Modernity and double consciousness.* Cambridge, MA: Harvard University Press.
Ginsburg, F. (1994). Embedded aesthetics: Creating a discursive space for indigenous media. *Cultural Anthropology,* 9(3), 365-382.
Giri, A. K. (1995). The dialectic between globalization and localization: Economic restructuring, women and strategies of cultural reproduction. *Dialectical Anthropology, 20*(2), 193-216.
Giroux, H. A. (1993). *Border crossings.* New York: Routledge.
Goldberg, D. T. (1994). *Racist culture.* Oxford, UK: Blackwell.
Goldman, A. (1992). *Liaisons: Philosophy meets the cognitive and social sciences.* Cambridge: MIT Press.
Goodall, P. (1995). *High culture, popular culture: The long debate.* Sydney, Australia: Allen & Unwin.
Goozner, M. (1987, July 19). Age old tradition bankrolls Koreans. *Chicago Tribune,* section 7, pp. 1-2.
Graham, A. C. (1992). *Unreason within reason.* LaSalle, IL: Open Court.
Greenfield, H. (1995). *Invisible, outlawed, and untaxed: America's underground economy.* Westport, CT: Praeger.
Griaule, M. (1965). *Conversations with Ogotemelli.* London: Oxford University Press.
Grieco, J. (1990). *Cooperation among nations: Europe, America, and non-tariff barriers to trade.* Ithaca, NY: Cornell University Press.
Grier, P. T. (1990). Modern ethical theory and Newtonian science: Comments on Errol Harris. In P. Bricker & R. I. G. Hughes (Eds.), *Philosophical perspectives on Newtonian science* (pp. 227-239). Cambridge: MIT Press.
Griffin, S. (1980). *Woman and nature.* New York: Harper Colophon.
Grimaldi, A. A. (1958). *The universal humanity of Giambattista Vico.* New York: S. F. Vanni.
Griswold, W. (1994). *Cultures and societies in a changing world.* Thousand Oaks, CA: Pine Forge.
Grotius, H. (1903). *Rights of war and peace* (Introduced by D. Hill). New York: A. Walter Dunne. (Original work published in 1625).

Grove-White, R. (1996). Environmental knowledge and public policy needs: On humanising the research again. In S. Lash, B. Szerszynski, & B. Wynne (Eds.), *Risk, environment and modernity* (pp. 269-286). London: Sage.

Grunebaum, J. O. (1987). *Private ownership*. London: Routledge & Kegan Paul.

Gurtov, M. (1988). *Global politics in human interest*. Boulder, CO: Lynne Rienner.

Gyekye, K. (1987). *An essay on African philosophical thought: The Akan conceptual scheme*. New York: Cambridge University Press.

Habermas, J. (1972). *Knowledge and human interests*. Boston: Beacon.

Habermas, J. (1975). *Legitimation crisis* Boston: Beacon.

Habermas, J. (1986). *Autonomy and solidarity* (P. Dews, Ed., Trans.). London: Verso.

Habermas, J. (1987). *The philosophical discourse of modernity*. Cambridge: MIT Press.

Habermas, J. (1989). *The Theory of Communicative Action*. 2 Vols. (Thomas McCarthy, Trans.). Boston: Beacon.

Hagen, E. E. (1975). *The economics of development*. Homewood, IL: Irwin.

Hajer, M. A. (1996). Ecological modernisation as cultural politics. In S. Lash, B. Szerszynski, & B. Wynne (Eds.), *Risk, environment and modernity* (pp. 246-268). London: Sage.

Hale, J. R. (1971). *Renaissance Europe, 1480-1520*. New York: Harper & Row.

Hall, J. A. (1985). *Powers and liberties: The causes and the consequences of the rise of the West*. Oxford, UK: Blackwell.

Hall, S. (1991). Old and new identities, old and new ethnicities. In A. D. King (Ed.), *Culture, globalization and the world-system*. Binghamton: State University of New York at Binghamton.

Hallen, B. (1995). Some observations about philosophy, postmodernism, and art in contemporary African studies. *African Studies Review, 38*(1), 69-80.

Hallen, B., & Sodipo, J. O. (1986). *Knowledge, belief and witchcraft: Analytic experiments in African philosophy*. London: Ethnographica.

Hallet, G. L. (1988). *Language and truth*. New Haven, CT: Yale University Press.

Halliday, F. (1988). Three concepts of internationalism. *International Affairs, 64*(2), 187-198.

Hannam, M. (1990). The dream of democracy. *Arena, 90*, 109-116.

Hannerz, U. (1989). Notes on the global ecumene. *Public Culture, 1*(2), 66-75.

Hanson, D. (1984). Thomas Hobbes's "highway to peace." *International Organization, 38*(2), 329-354

Haraway, D. J. (1988). Situated knowledges: The science question in feminism as a site of discourse on the privilege of partial perspective. *Feminist Studies, 14*(3), 574-599.

Hardin, G. (1974). Lifeboat ethics: The case against helping the poor. *Psychology Today, 8*, 38-43.

Harding, S. (1986). *The science question in feminism*. Ithaca, NY: Cornell University Press.

Harding, S. (Ed.). (1987). *Feminism & Methodology*. Bloomington: University of Indiana Press and Milton Keynes: Open University.

Hargrove, E. C. (Ed.). (1986). *Religion and environmental crisis*. Athens: University of Georgia Press.

Harries, K. (1996). *The ethical function of architecture*. Cambridge: MIT Press.

Harris, E. E. (1954). *Nature, mind and modern science*. London: Allen & Unwin.

Harris, E. (1990). Ethical Implications of Newtonian Science. In P. Bricker & R. I. G. Hughes (Eds.), *Philosophical Perspectives on Newtonian Science* (pp. 211-225). Cambridge, MA: MIT Press.

Harris, N. (1986). *The end of the Third World*. New York: Meredith.

Hartsock, N. M. (1983). The feminist standpoint: Developing the ground for a specifically historical materialism. In S. Harding & M. B. Hintikka (Eds.), *Discovering reality* (pp. 283-310). Boston: Reidel.

Hassard, J., & Parker, M. (Eds.). (1993). *Postmodernism and Organizations*. London: Sage.

Hauerwas, S. (1981). *A community of character*. Notre Dame: University of Notre Dame Press.

Hazard, P. (1963). *The European mind.* New York: Meridian.
Heap, S. H. (1989). *Rationality and economics.* Oxford, UK: Basil Blackwell.
Hebdige, D. (1979). *Subculture: The meaning of style.* New York: Methuen.
Hegel, G. W. F. (1969). *Hegel's science of logic* (A. V. Miller, Trans.). New York: Oxford University Press.
Hegel, G. W. F. (1989). *Lectures on the philosophy of world history.* Cambridge, UK: Cambridge University Press.
Heidegger, M. (1982). *On the way to language.* New York: Harper & Row.
Held, D. (Ed.). (1991). *Political theory today.* Stanford, CA: Stanford University Press.
Hernnstein, R., & Murray, C. (1994). *The bell curve: Intelligence and class structure in American life.* New York: Free Press.
Hettne, B. (1978). Current issues in development theory. *SAREC REPORT,* R.5, c/o SIDA, 105 25 Stockholm, Sweden.
Hettne, B. (1990). *Development theory and the three worlds.* London: Longman.
Himmelweit, S., & Mohun, S. (1977). Domestic labour and capital. *Cambridge Journal of Economics, 1,* (1), 15-31.
Hirschman, A. (1977). *The passions and the interests: Political arguments for capitalism before its triumph.* Princeton, NJ: Princeton University Press.
Hirshleifer, J. (1977). Economics from a biological viewpoint. *Journal of Law and Economics, 20*(1), 1-52.
Hirshleifer, J. (1982). Evolutionary models in economics and law: Cooperation versus conflict strategies. In R. O. Zerbe, Jr., & P. H. Rubin (Eds.), *Research in Law and Economics.* (4), 1-60.
Hobbes, T. (1962). *Leviathan* (M. Oakessott, Ed.). New York: Collier.
Hobsbawm, E. (1975). *The age of capital, 1848-1875.* New York: Scribner.
Hobsbawm, E., & Ranger, T. (Eds.). (1983). *The invention of tradition in Africa.* New York: Cambridge University Press.
Hodgson, G. M. (1993). *Economics and evolution—Bringing life back into economics.* Ann Arbor: University of Michigan Press.
hooks, b. (1981). *Ain't I a woman: Black women and feminism.* Boston: South End.
hooks, b. (1991). *Yearning: Race, gender, and cultural politics.* Boston: South End.
Hooykaas, R. (1972). *Religion and the rise of modern science.* London: Scottish Academic Press.
Horkheimer, M. (1947). *Eclipse of reason.* New York: Oxford University Press.
Horton, R. (1967). African traditional religion and Western science. *Africa, 37*(1 & 2), 50-71, 155-187.
Horton, R., & Finnegan, H. (Eds.). (1973). *Modes of thought.* London: Faber & Faber.
Hoselitz, B. (1960). *Sociological aspects of economic growth.* Glencoe, IL: Free Press.
Hountondji, P. (1983). *African philosophy: Myth or reality.* Bloomington: Indiana University Press.
Hurrell, A. (1993, March). Green conditionality. *Overseas development council policy paper.* London: Overseas Development Council.
Hutcheon, L. (1986-87, Winter). The politics of postmodernism: Parody and history. *Cultural Critique,* pp. 179-208.
Hutcheon, L. (1989). Circling the downspout of empire: Postcolonialism and postmodernism. *Ariel, 20*(4), 149-175.
Hutchins, R. M., Murray, J. C., Buchanan, S., Reznick, P., Wheeler, H., & Gordis, R. (1966). *Natural law and modern society.* New York: Meridian.
Idowu, E. B. (1973). *African traditional religion: A definition.* London: SCM Press.
Ignatieff, M. (1986). *The needs of strangers.* New York: Penguin.
Inglehart, R. (1990). *Cultural shift in advanced industrial society.* Princeton, NJ: Princeton University Press.
Irigaray, L. (1977). *This sex which is not one.* Ithaca, NY: Cornell University Press.
Irigaray, L. (1985). *Speculum of the other woman.* Ithaca, NY: Cornell University Press.

Jackson, J. G. (1990). *Introduction to African civilizations.* New York: Citadel Press.

Jacob, M. C. (1976). *The Newtonians and the English revolution 1689-1720.* Brighton, UK: Harvester.

Jacoby, R., & Glaugerman, N. (Eds.). (1995). *The bell curve debate.* New York: Times Books.

Jacques, F. (1991). *Difference and subjectivity.* New Haven, CT: Yale University Press.

Jaggar, A. (1983). *Feminist politics and human nature.* Totowa, NJ: Roman and Allenheld.

Jaggar, A. (1989). Love and knowledge: Emotion in feminist epistemology. In A. M. Jaggar & S. R. Bordo (Eds.), *Gender/body/knowledge* (pp. 145-171). New Brunswick, NJ: Rutgers University Press.

James, G. M. (1954). *The stolen legacy.* New York: Philosophical Library.

Jameson, F. (1984). Postmodernism, or the cultural lag of modern capitalism. *New Left Review, 146,* 83-93.

Jay, M. (1988). *Fin de siecle socialism.* London: Routledge.

Jay, M. (1992). Scopic regimes of modernity. In S. Lash & J. Friedman (Eds.), *Modernity and identity* (pp. 178-195). Oxford, UK: Blackwell.

Jenks, C. (1993). *Culture.* London: Routledge.

Jones, E. L. (1981). *The European miracle.* Cambridge, UK: Cambridge University Press.

Jones, R. A. (1994). Ambivalent Cartesians: Durkheim, Montesquieu and method. *American Journal of Sociology, 100*(1), 1-39.

Jordan, W. D. (1974). *The white man's burden.* New York: Oxford University Press.

Julien, I., & Mercer, K. (1988, Autumn). Introduction: de margin and de centre. *Screen,* pp. 2-10.

Jung, C. G. (1933). *Modern man in search of a soul.* (W. S. Dell & C. F. Baynes, Trans.). New York: Harcourt Brace Jovanovich.

Kahn, H., Brown, W. & Martell, L. (1976). *The next 2000 years.* New York: William Morrow.

Kant, I. (1981). *Grounding for the metaphysics of morals* (J. W. Ellington, Trans.). Indianapolis, IN: Hackett.

Kaplan, M. A. (1971). *On historical and political knowing.* Chicago: University of Chicago Press.

Katz, R. (1973). *A giant in the earth.* New York: Stein & Day.

Kavka, G. S. (1986). *Hobbesian moral and political theory.* Princeton, NJ: Princeton University Press.

Kay, C. (1989). *Democracy and development in Latin American economies.* New York: Routledge.

Keith, N. W. (1995a). East is East and West is West: Informalization in the age of interdependence. *Peace and Conflict Studies, 2*(2), 3-31.

Keith, N. W. (1995b). Indigenousness as a new global norm: Barter and the related ethic of self-reliance. *Peace and Conflict Studies, 2*(1), 18-28.

Keller, E. F. (1985). *Reflections on gender and science.* New Haven, CT: Yale University Press.

Kennan, G. F. (1996). *At a century's end: Reflections, 1982-1995.* New York: Norton.

Kimball, R. (1990). *Tenured radicals.* New York: Harper & Row.

King, P. (1974). *The ideology of order.* New York: Barnes & Noble.

Kirk, G. S., & Raven, J. E. (1957). *The pre-Socratic philosophers.* Cambridge, UK: Cambridge University Press.

Kirk, R. (1987). *The conservative mind.* Chicago: Regnery.

Kline, M. (1980). *Mathematics: The loss of certainty.* New York: Oxford University Press.

Klingender, F. D. (1970). *Art and the Industrial Revolution* (A. Elton, Ed.). New York: Schocken.

Knaplund, P. (1927). *Gladstone and Britain's imperial policy.* London: Allen & Unwin.

Knappert, J. (1995). *African mythology.* London: Diamond Books.

Kolakowski, L. (1989). *The presence of myth.* Chicago: University of Chicago Press.

Kolakowski, L. (1993). The demise of historical man. *Partisan Review, 58*(3), 461-470.

Korman, S. (1996). *The right of conquest.* New York: Oxford University Press.

Koselleck, R. (1988). *Critique and crisis.* Cambridge: MIT Press.

Krieger, M. H. (1973). What's wrong with plastic trees? *Science, 179,* 23-28.

Kuhn, T. (1970). *The structure of scientific revolutions.* Chicago: University of Chicago Press.

Kymlicka, W. (1995). *Multicultural citizenship.* New York: Oxford University Press.

Laclau, E. (1988). Politics and the limits of modernity. In A. Ross (Ed.), *Universal abandon?* (pp. 63-82). Minneapolis: University of Minnesota Press.

Laclau, E. (1991, December). God only knows. *Marxism Today,* pp. 56-59.

Lacoue-Labarthe, P. (1989). On the sublime. In L. Appignansi (Ed.), *Postmodernism: ICH documents* (pp. 19-26). London: Free Associations Books.

Lakoff, G., & Turner, M. (1989). *More than cool reason—A field guide to poetic metaphor.* Chicago: University of Chicago Press.

Langer, S. (1953). Translator's preface to Ernst Cassirer. In *Language and myth.* New York: Dover.

Larmore, C. (1987). *Patterns of moral complexity.* Cambridge, UK: Cambridge University Press.

Larrain, J. (1989). *Theories of development: Capitalism, colonialism, and dependency.* London: Polity.

Lasch, C. (1979). *The culture of narcissism.* New York: Norton.

Lasch, C. (1995). *The revolt of the elites and the betrayal of democracy.* New York: Norton.

Lash, S., Szerszynski, B., & Wynne, B. (Eds.). (1996). *Risk, environment and modernity.* London: Sage.

Lash, S., & Urry, J. (1994). *Economics of signs and space.* London: Sage.

Lawson, H. (1985). *Reflexivity: The post-modern predicament.* La Salle, IL: Open Court.

Lecky, W. E. H. (1890). *History of European morals* (2 Vols.). New York: Appleton.

Lee, R. (1994). Globalization and cultural change. *Current Sociology, 42*(1), 26-37.

LeFebvre, G. (1973). *The coming of the French Revolution.* Princeton, NJ: Princeton University Press.

Leiss, W. (1990). *Under technology's thumb.* Toronto: McGill-Queens University Press.

Lerner, G. (1993). *The creation of feminist consciousness.* New York: Oxford University Press.

Levin, D. M. (1988). *The opening of vision: Nihilism and the postmodern situation.* New York: Routledge.

Levine, D. N. (1988). *The flight from ambiguity: Essays in social and cultural theory.* Chicago: University of Chicago Press.

Levinson, C. (1971). *Capital, inflation, and the multinationals.* New York: Macmillan.

Levy-Bruhl, L. (1949). *Les Carnets de Lucien Levy-Bruhl.* (Preface by Maurice Leenhardt). Paris: Presses Universitaires de France.

Leys, C., & Mandell, M. (Eds.). (1992). *Culture and social change.* Montreal, Canada: Black Rose Books.

Lifton, R. J. (1971). Transformations. In L. Rubinoff (Ed.), *Tradition and revolution* (pp. 97-125). Toronto: Macmillan.

Lipovetsky, G. (1992). *Le Crepuscule du devoir* [The twilight of duty]. Paris: Gallimard.

Lloyd, G. E. R. (1992). Democracy, philosophy, and science in ancient Greece. In J. Dunn (Ed.), *Democracy: The unfinished journey, 508 B.C. to A.D. 1993.* Oxford, UK: Oxford University Press.

Locke, J. (1952). *The second treatise of government* (Edited with introduction by T. P. Peardon). Indianapolis: Bobbs-Merrill.

Long, M. (1993). Pollution is growing threat in Argentina. In P. Goodwin, Jr. (Ed.), (1994). *Latin America* (6th ed.; pp. 199-200). Guilford, CT: Dushkin.

Lorde, A. (1984). *Sister outsider.* Trumansberg, NY: Crossing Press.

Lovibond, S. (1989, November-December). Feminism and postmodernism. *New Left Review, 178,* 5-28.

Luard, E. (1987). *War in international society.* New Haven, CT: Yale University Press.

Luke, T. (1989, Fall/Winter). Class contradictions and social cleavages in informationalizing post-industrial societies: On the rise of new social movements. *New Political Science,* 125-154.

Lyons, J. D., & Nichols, S. G., Jr. (Eds.). (1982). *Mimesis—From mirror to method, Augustine to Descartes.* Hanover, NH: University Press of New England.

Lyotard, J. (1984). *The postmodern condition: A report on knowledge.* Manchester, UK: Manchester University Press.

MacCannell, D. (1989). *The tourist: The new theory of the leisure class.* New York: Schocken.

Machiavelli, N. (1935). *The prince.* London: Oxford University Press.

MacIntyre, A. (1984). *After virtue: A study in moral theory.* Notre Dame, IN: University of Notre Dame Press.

MacIntyre, A. (1988). *Whose justice? Which rationality.* Notre Dame, IN: University of Notre Dame Press.

MacPherson, C. B. (1962). *The political theory of possessive individualism.* London: Oxford University Press.

MacPherson, C. B. (1973). *Democratic theory: Essays in retrieval.* Oxford, UK: Oxford University Press.

Macy, J. (1991). *World as lover, world as self.* Berkeley: Parallax.

Madison, G. B. (1990). *The hermeneutics of postmodernity.* Indianapolis: Indiana University Press.

Maffie, J. (1995). Towards an anthropology of epistemology. *The Philosophical Forum, 26*(3), 218-241.

Mansbridge, J. J. (Ed.). (1990). *Beyond self-interest.* Chicago: University of Chicago Press.

Manuel, F. E. (1982). *The age of reason.* Westport, CT: Greenwood.

Manzo, K. (1991). Modernist discourse and the crisis of development theory. *Studies in Comparative International Development, 26*(2), 3-36.

Marcus, G. (1992). Past, present and emergent identities: Requirements for ethnographies of late twentieth-century modernity worldwide. In S. Lash & J. Friedman (Eds.), *Modernity and identity.* Oxford, UK: Blackwell.

Marcuse, H. (1964). *One-dimensional man.* Boston: Beacon.

Marcuse, H. (1968). *Negations.* Boston: Beacon.

Marcuse, H. (1978). *The aesthetic dimension: Toward a critique of Marxist aesthetics.* Boston: Beacon.

Marglin, F. (1990). Losing touch: The cultural conditions of worker accommodation and resistance. In F. Marglin & S. Marglin (Eds.), *Dominating knowledge: Development, culture and resistance.* Oxford, UK: Clarendon.

Marglin, F. A., & Marglin, S. A. (Eds.). (1996). *Decolonizing knowledge.* New York: Oxford University Press.

Marnell, W. H. (1968). *Man-made morals: Four philosophies that shaped America.* Garden City, NY: Doubleday.

Martell, L. (1992). New ideas of Socialism. *Economy and Society, 21*(2), 152-172.

Martinez-Alier, J. (1991). Ecological perception, environmental policy and distributional conflict: Some lessons from history. In R. Constanza (Ed.), *Ecological economics* (pp. 118-136). New York: Columbia University Press.

Martinez-Alier, J. (1995). Distributional issues in ecological economics. *Review of Social Economy, 13*(4), 511-528.

Marx, K. (1975). *Capital* (3 vols., F. Engels, Ed.). New York: International Publishers.

Marx, K., & Engels, F. (1972). *The German ideology* (C. J. Arthur, Ed.). New York: International Publishers.

Masolo, D. A. (1994). *African philosophy in search of identity.* Bloomington: Indiana University Press.

Mastanduno, M. (1993). Framing the Japan problem: The Bush administration and the structural impediments initiative. In J. G. Stein & L. W. Pauly (Eds.), *Choosing to co-operate* (pp. 35-64). Baltimore, MD: Johns Hopkins University Press.

Mathews, F. (1990). *The ecological self.* London: Routledge.

Maybury-Lewis, D. (1992). *Millennium: Tribal wisdom and the modern world.* New York: Viking.

Mazrui, A. A. (1990). *Cultural forces in world politics.* London: James Currey, Heinemann.

McClelland, D. (1961). *The achieving society.* New York: Van Nostrand.

McClintock, A. (1994). The angel of progress: Pitfalls of the term "post-colonialism." In P. Williams & L. Chrisman (Eds.), *Colonial discourse and post-colonial theory: A reader* (pp. 291-304). New York: Columbia University Press.

McCloskey, D. N. (1988). The consequences of economic rhetoric. In A. Klamer, D. McCloskey, & R. Solow (Eds.), *The consequences of economic rhetoric.* Cambridge, UK: Cambridge University Press.

McCloskey, D. N. (1993). Some of the consequences of conjective economics. In M. A. Farber & J. A. Nelson (Eds.), *Beyond economic man: Feminist theory and economics.* Chicago: University of Chicago Press.

McCloskey, D. N. (1995). Metaphors economists live by. *Social Research, 62*(2), 215-237.

McClure, K. (1992). On the subject of rights: Pluralism, plurality and political identity. In C. Mouffe (Ed.), *Dimensions of Radical Democracy* (pp. 108-127). London: Verso.

McDaniel, J. (1989). *Earth, sky, gods and mortals: Developing an ecological spirituality.* Mystic, CT: Twenty-Third Publications.

McKean, M. A. (1981). *Environmental protest and citizen politics in Japan.* Berkeley: University of California Press.

McKeon, R. (1987). *Rhetoric: Essays in invention & discovery* (M. Blackman, Ed.). Woodbridge, CT: Ox Bow Press.

McLaren, P. L. (1991). Schooling the postmodern body: Critical pedagogy and the politics of enfleshment. In H. A. Giroux (Ed.), *Postmodernism, feminism, and cultural politics.* Albany: State University of New York Press.

McMullin, E. (1978). *Newton on matter and activity.* Notre Dame, IN: University of Notre Dame Press.

McNamara, R. (1982). Demographic transition theory. *International Encyclopedia of Population* (Vol. 1.). New York: Macmillan.

McNeill, W. H. (1967). *World history.* New York: Oxford University Press.

Meadows, D. H., Meadows, D. L., Randers, R., & Behrens, W. H., III (1972). *The limits of growth.* New York: Universe Books.

Meadows, D. L., Meadows, D. H. (1974). *Dynamics of growth in a finite world.* Cambridge, MA: Write-Allen Press.

Meeks, W. A. (1993). *The origins of Christian morality.* New Haven, CT: Yale University Press.

Megill, A. (Ed.). (1994). *Rethinking objectivity.* Durham, NC: Duke University Press.

Mercer, K. (1990). Welcome to the jungle: Identity and diversity in postmodern politics. In J. Rutherford (Ed.), *Identity: Community, culture, difference* (pp. 43-71). London: Lawrence & Wishart.

Merchant, C. (1980). *The death of nature: Women, ecology and the scientific revolution.* San Francisco: Harper & Row.

Mestrovic, S. (1991). *The coming fin de siecle.* New York: Routledge.

Meszaros, I. (1989). *The power of ideology.* New York: New York University Press.

Metz, C. (1982). *The imaginary signifier: Psychoanalysis and cinema.* Bloomington: Indiana University Press.

Meyer, C. A. (1995). Opportunism and NGO's: Entrepreneurship and green North-South transfers. *World Development, 23*(8), 1277-1289.

Meynell, H. (1991). Habermas: An unstable compromise. *American Catholic Philosophical Quarterly, 45*(2), 189-201.

Midgley, J. (1994). The challenge of social development: Their Third World and ours: 1993 Daniel S. Sanders Peace and Social Justice Lecture. *Social Development Issues, 16*(2), 1-12.

Mies, M., & Shiva, V. (Eds.). (1993). *Ecofeminism.* London: Zed.

Miller, A. S. (1991). *Gaia connections.* New York: Rowman and Littlefield Publishers.

Miller, C. L. (1985). *Blank darkness: Africanist discourse in French.* Chicago: University of Chicago Press.

Miller, C. L. (1993). Literary studies and African literature: The challenge of intercultural literature. In R. H. Bates, V. Y. Mudimbe, & J. O'Barr (Eds.), *Africa and the disciplines* (pp. 213-232). Chicago: University of Chicago Press.

Miller, J. B. (1992). Women and power. In T. E. Wartenberg (Ed.), *Rethinking power* (pp. 240-248). Albany, NY: SUNY Press.

Mingione, E. (1992). Informalization, restructuring and the survival strategies of the working class. *International Journal of Urban and Regional Research, 7*(3), 311-339.

Mingione, E. (1994). Life strategies and social economies in the postfordist age. *International Journal of Urban and Regional Research, 118*(1), 24-45.

Mitchell, R. J. (Ed.). (1980). *Experiences in appropriate technology.* Ottawa, Canada: Hunger Foundation.

Mitsch, W. J. (1991). Ecological engineering: Approaches to sustainability and biodiversity in the U.S. and China. In R. Constanza (Ed.), *Ecological economics* (pp. 428-448). New York: Columbia University Press.

Mitsch, W. J., & Jorgensen, S. E. (Eds.). (1989). *Ecological engineering: An introduction to ecotechnology.* New York: Wiley.

Mohamad, M., & Ishihara, S. (1996). *The voice of Asia: Two leaders discuss the coming century.* Tokyo: Kodasha International.

Mohanty, C. T., Russo, A., & Torres, L. (Eds.). (1991). *Third World women and the politics of feminism.* Indianapolis: Indiana University Press.

Molyneux, M. (1979, July-August). Beyond the domestic labour debate. *New Left Review, 116,* 3-27.

Montesquieu, Baron de. (1906). *The spirit of laws* (2 Vols.) (T. Nugent, Trans.). London: George Bell & Sons.

Morgan, F. (Ed.). (1989). *A misogynist's source book.* London: Jonathan Cape.

Morgenthau, H.J. (1968). *Politics among nations.* New York: Knopf.

Morrison, T. (1992). *Playing in the dark: Whiteness and the literary imagination.* Cambridge, MA: Harvard University Press.

Mouffe, C. (1988a). Hegemony and new political subjects: Toward a new conception of democracy. In C. Nelson & L. Grossberg (Eds.), *Marxism and the reinterpretation of culture* (pp. 89-101). Champaign-Urbana: University of Illinois.

Mouffe, C. (1988b). Radical democracy: Modern or postmodern? In A. Ross (Ed.), *Universal abandon? The politics of postmodernism* (pp. 31-45). Minneapolis: University of Minnesota Press.

Mudimbe, V. Y. (1988). *The invention of Africa: Gnosis, philosophy and the order of knowledge.* Bloomington: Indiana University Press.

Mudimbe, V. Y. (1994). *The idea of Africa.* Bloomington: Indiana University Press.

Mudimbe, V. Y., & Appiah, K. A. (1993). The impact of African studies on philosophy. In R. H. Bates (Ed.), *Africa and the disciplines* (pp. 113-138). Chicago: University of Chicago Press.

Mulhall, S., & Swift, A. (1992). *Liberals & communitarians.* Cambridge, MA: Basil Blackwell.

Munroe, T. (1990). *Jamaican politics: A Marxist perspective in transition.* Kingston, Jamaica: Heinemann.

Murray, A. (1995). *Who's who in mythology.* London: Bracken.

Naess, A. (1973). The shallow and the deep, long-range ecology movement. *Inquiry, 65,* 95-100.

Naess, A. (1988). Sustainable development and the deep, long-range ecology movement. *The Trumpeter, 5*(4), 138-142.

National Center for Health Statistics. (1990). Advance report of final mortality statistics. *Monthly Vital Statistics, 41*(7).

Needham, J., & collaborators. (1954-1984). *Science and civilization in China* (6 Vols.). Cambridge, UK: Cambridge University Press.

Neimark, P. (1990, July-August). My kingdom for a horse. *Business Marketing*, p. 50.

Nelson, L. H. (1990). *Who knows*. Philadelphia, PA: Temple University Press.

Ngugi wa Thiong'o. (1967). *A grain of wheat*. London: Heinemann.

Ngugi wa Thiong'o. (1986). *Decolonising the mind: The politics of language*. Portsmouth, NH: Heinemann.

Ngugi wa Thiong'o. (1990, September 14-20). Return of the native tongue. *Times Literary Supplement*, pp. 972, 981.

Nicholson, L. (1990). *Feminism/postmodernism*. London: Routledge.

Nietzsche, F. W. (1911). On truth and falsity in their ultramortal sense. In *The complete works of Friedrich Nietzsche* (Vol. 2) (O. Levy, Ed.). London: Macmillan.

Nisbet, R. (1968). *Social change and history*. New York: Oxford University Press.

Noddings, N. (1984). *Caring: A feminine approach to ethics and moral education*. Berkeley: University of California Press.

Nooter, M. H. (Ed.). (1993). *Secrecy: African art that conceals and reveals*. New York: Museum for African Art.

Norgaard, R. (1995). Beyond materialism: A coevolutionary reinterpretation of the environmental crisis. *Review of Social Economy, 13*(4), 475-492.

Notestein, F. W., Kirk, D., & Segal, S. (1963). The problem of population control. In P. M. Hauser (Ed.), *The population dilemma*. Englewood Cliffs, NJ: Prentice Hall.

Nozick, R. (1974). *Anarchy, state, and utopia*. New York: Basic Books.

Nozick, R. (1993). *The nature of rationality*. Princeton, NJ: Princeton University Press.

O'Briant, W. H. (1974). Man, nature and the history of philosophy. In W. T. Blackstone (Ed.), *Philosophy and environmental crisis* (pp. 79-890). Athens: University of Georgia Press.

Offe, C. (1987a). Challenging the boundaries of institutional politics: Social movements since the 1960s. In Charles Maier (Ed.), *Changing boundaries of the political*. New York: Cambridge University Press.

Offe, C. (1987b, April). Modernity and modernization as narrative political principles. *Praxis International*, 1-15.

O'Hara, S. U. (1995). Sustainability: Social and ecological dimensions. *Review of Social Economy, 8*(4), 529-551.

Okin, S. M. (1979). *Women in Western political thought*. Princeton, NJ: Princeton University Press.

Oliver, R. T. (1971). *Communication and culture in ancient India and China*. Syracuse, NY: Syracuse University Press.

O'Neill, O. (1991). Transnational justice. In D. Held (Ed.), *Political theory today (pp. 276-304). Stanford, CA: Stanford University Press.*

Ortega, E., & Saporta-Sternbach, N. (1989). At the threshold of the unnamed: Latina literary discourse in the eighties. In A. Horno-Delgado (Ed.), *Breaking boundaries: Latina writings and critical readings* (pp. 3-23). Amherst: University of Massachusetts Press.

Oruka, H. O. (1985). *Punishment and terrorism in Africa*. Nairobi, Kenya: East African Literature Bureau.

Outlaw, L. (1991). Lifeworlds, modernity, and philosophical praxis. In E. Deutsch (Ed.), *Culture and modernity* (pp. 24-49). Honolulu: University of Hawaii Press.

Pacey, A. (1990). *Technology in world history*. Cambridge: MIT Press.

Paddock, W., & Paddock, P. (1967). *Famine 1975! Who will survive?* Boston: Little, Brown.

Padron, M. (1987). Non-governmental development organizations: From development aid to development cooperation. *World Development, 15*(Suppl.), 69-77.

Pangle, T. (1973). *Montesquieu's philosophy of liberalism: A commentary on the spirit of the laws*. Chicago: University of Chicago Press.

Pangle, T. (1992). *The ennobling of democracy*. Baltimore, MD: Johns Hopkins University Press.

Parker, M. (1993). Life after Jean-Francois. In J. Hassard & M. Parker (Eds.), *Postmodernism and organizations* (pp. 204-212). London: Sage.

Parry, B. (1994). Resistance theory/theorizing resistance and two cheers for nativism. In P. Hulme (Ed.), *Post-colonial theory and colonial discourse*. Manchester, UK: Manchester University Press.

Passmore; J. (1974). *Man's responsibility for nature*. London: Duckworth.

Pateman, C. (1988). *The sexual contract*. Cambridge, UK: Polity Press.

Patterson, O. (1991). *Freedom: Freedom in the making of Western culture*. New York: Basic Books.

Paul, S., & Israel, A. (1991). *Nongovernmental organizations and the World Bank: Cooperation for development*. Washington, DC: World Bank.

Percival, R. (1989, August). Malthus and his ghost. *National Review, 41*, 30-33.

Petrovic, G. (1967). *Marx in the mid-twentieth century*. New York: Anchor.

Peukert, H. (1984). *Science, action, and fundamental Theology*. Cambridge: MIT Press.

Phillips, A. (1993). *Democracy and difference*. University Park: Pennsylvania State University Press.

Piore, M., & Sabel, C. (1984). *The second industrial divide: Possibilities for prosperity*. New York: Basic Books.

Plamenatz, J. (1960). *Alien rule and self-government*. London: Longman.

Plato. (1969). Phaedo. In L. R. Loomis (Ed.), *Plato: Five great dialogues* (pp. 83-153). New York: Gramercy.

Plotke, D. (1995). What's so new about new social movements? In S. M. Lyman (Ed.), *Social movements: Critiques, concepts, case studies* (pp. 113-136). New York: New York University Press.

Plumwood, V. (1993). *Feminism and the mastery of nature*. London: Routledge.

Popper, K. R. (1966). *The open society and its enemies* (2 Vols.). Princeton, NJ: Princeton University Press.

Popper, K. R. (1968). *Logic of scientific discovery*. New York: Harper & Row.

Popper, K. R. (1971). *The open society and its enemies*. (2 Vols.). Princeton, NJ: Princeton University Press.

Popper, K. R. (1992). *In search of a better world: Lectures and essays from thirty years*. London: Routledge.

Portes, A., Castells, M., & Benton, L. A. (Eds.). (1989). *The informal economy*. Baltimore, MD: Johns Hopkins University Press.

Poster, M. (1990). *The mode of information*. Chicago: University of Chicago Press.

Poulantzas, N. (1975). *Classes in contemporary capitalism*. Atlantic Highlands, NJ: Humanities Press.

Prelli, L. J. (1989). *A rhetoric of science*. Columbia: University of South Carolina Press.

Putnam, H. (1994). *Reason, truth and history*. Cambridge, UK: Cambridge University Press.

Quijano, A. (1971). *Nationalism and capitalism in Peru*. New York: Monthly Review Press.

Quine, W. V. O. (1975). The nature of natural knowledge. In S. Gutterspan (Ed.), *Mind and language* (pp. 58-75). Oxford, UK: Oxford University Press.

Rabinow, P. (Ed.). (1984). *Foucault reader*. New York: Pantheon.

Radhakrishnan, S. S. (1969). *Eastern religions and Western thought*. London: Oxford University Press.

Radnitzky, G., & Bartley, W. W., III. (Eds.). (1987). *Evolutionary epistemology, rationality, and the sociology of knowledge*. Lasalle, IL: Open Court.

Rahnema, M. (1992). Poverty. In W. Sachs (Ed.), *The dictionary of development* (pp. 158-176). London: Zed.

Raju, P. T. (1971). *The philosophical traditions of India*. Pittsburgh, PA: University of Pittsburgh Press.

Ranger, T. (1983). The invention of tradition in Africa. In E. Hobsbawm & T. Ranger (Eds.), *The invention of tradition in Africa* (pp. 211-262). New York: Cambridge University Press.

Rappaport, R. (1979). *Ecology, meaning and religion.* Richmond, CA: North Atlantic Books.
Rawls, J. (1971). *A theory of justice.* Cambridge, MA: Harvard University Press.
Ray, L. J. (1993). *Rethinking critical theory.* Newbury Park, CA: Sage.
Redclift, M. (1987). *Sustainable development: Exploring the contradictions.* London: Routledge.
Reed, G. (1986). A Native American ethic: A homily on Black Elk. In E. C. Hargrove (Ed.), *Religion and Environmental Crisis* (pp. 25-37). Athens, GA: University of Georgia Press.
Reed, J., & Wake, C. (Eds.). (1976). *Leopold Sedar Senghor: Prose and poetry.* London: Heinemann.
Reeve, A. (Ed.). (1987). *Modern theories of exploitation.* London: Sage.
Reeve, A. (1991). The theory of property. In D. Held (Ed.), *Political theory today.* Stanford, CA: Stanford University Press.
Regan, T. (1986). *Matters of life and death: New introductory essays in moral philosophy.* New York: Random House.
Regan, T. (1991). *The thee generation.* Philadelphia, PA: Temple University Press.
Reich, R. B. (1988). *Tales of a new America.* New York: Vintage.
Reiss, T. (1982a). *The discourse of modernism.* Ithaca, NY: Cornell University Press.
Reiss, T. J. (1982b). Power, poetry, and the resemblance of nature. In J. D. Lyons & S. G. Nichols, Jr. (Eds.), *Mimesis: From mirror to method, Augustine to Descartes* (pp. 215-247). Hanover, NH: University Press of New England.
Renner, M. (1991). Jobs in a sustainable economy. In *Worldwatch Paper* (No. 104). Washington, DC: Worldwatch Institute.
Richards, I. A. (1936). *The philosophy of rhetoric.* Oxford, UK: Oxford University Press.
Roberts, B. (1994). Informal economy and family strategies. *International Journal of Urban and Regional Strategies, 18*(1), 6-23.
Robertson, R. (1992). *Globalization.* Newbury Park, CA: Sage.
Rodney, W. (1972). *How Europe underdeveloped Africa.* London: Bogle-L'Ouverture.
Rolston, H., III. (1986). *Philosophy gone wild.* Buffalo, NY: Prometheus.
Rolston, H., III. (1988). *Environmental ethics: Duties to and values in the natural world.* Philadelphia, PA: Temple University Press.
Rorty, R. (1979). *Philosophy and the mirror of nature.* Princeton, NJ: Princeton University Press.
Rorty, R. (1989). *Contingency, irony, and solidarity.* Cambridge, UK: Cambridge University Press.
Rosenau, J. N. (1990). *Turbulence in world politics.* Princeton, NJ: Princeton University Press.
Rosenau, P. M. (1992). *Post-modernism and the social sciences.* Princeton, NJ: Princeton University Press.
Rosenberg, J. (1994). The international imagination: IR and "classic social analysis." *Millennium, 23*(1), 85-108.
Rostow, W. W. (1962). *The stages of economic growth: A non-Communist manifesto.* Cambridge, UK: Cambridge University Press.
Ruggie, J. G. (1993). Territoriality and beyond: Problematizing modernity in international relations. *International Organization, 47*(1), 139-174.
Russell, B. (1956). *Our knowledge of the external world.* New York: Menton.
Sachs, W. (Ed.). (1992). *The development dictionary.* London: Zed.
Sahlins, M. (1976). *Culture and practical reason.* Chicago: University of Chicago Press.
Said, E. (1978). *Orientalism.* New York: Vantage.
Said, E. (1990). Third World intellectuals and metropolitan culture. *Raritan,* 9(3), 27-50.
Said, E. (1993). *Culture and imperialism.* New York: Knopf.
Sampson, E. E. (1993). *Celebrating the other.* Boulder, CO: Westview.
Sandel, M. (Ed.). (1984a). *Liberalism and its critics.* New York: New York University Press.
Sandel, M. (1984b). *Liberalism and the limits of justice.* Cambridge, UK: Cambridge University Press.
Sanderson, S. E. (Ed.). (1985). *The Americas in the new international division of labor.* New York: Holmes & Meier.
Schapiro, J. S. (1963). *Condorcet and the rise of liberalism.* New York: Octogon.

Schiele, J. H. (1994). Afrocentricity: Implications for higher education. *Journal of Black Studies, 25*(2), 150-169.

Schlatter, R. (1951). *Private property.* New Brunswick, NJ: Rutgers University Press.

Schneider, B. (1988). *Barefoot revolution: A report to the Club of Rome.* London: Intermediate Technology Publications.

Schrag, C. O. (1989a). *Communicative praxis and the space of subjectivity.* Bloomington & Indianapolis: Indiana University Press.

Schrag, C. O. (1989b). Rationality between modernity and postmodernity. In S. K. White (Ed.), *Life-world and politics—Between modernity and postmodernity: Essays in honor of Fred Dallmayr* (pp. 81-106). Notre Dame, IN: University of Notre Dame Press.

Schumacher, E. F. (1977). *A guide for the perplexed.* New York: Harper & Row.

Schumpeter, J. (1943). *Capitalism, socialism, and democracy.* London: Allen & Unwin.

Schwarzenberger, G. (1964). *Power politics.* London: Stevens & Sons.

Sclove, R. E. (1995). *Democracy and technology.* New York: Guilford Press.

Scott, J. C. (1976). *The moral economy of the peasant: Subsistence and rebellion in Southeast Asia.* New Haven, CT: Yale University Press.

Scott, J. C. (1985). *Weapons of the weak.* New Haven, CT: Yale University Press.

Seabrook, J. (1991, January). The David Lynch of architecture. *Vanity Fair,* pp. 74-79, 125-129.

Seidman, S. (1983). *Liberalism and the origins of European social theory.* Berkeley: University of California Press.

Sen, A. K. (1977). Rational fools: A critique of the behavioral foundations of economic theory. *Philosophy and Public Affairs,* 6(4), 317-344.

Serres, M. (1995). *The natural contract.* Ann Arbor: University of Michigan Press.

Sethuraman, S. V. (1981). *The urban informal sector in developing countries.* Geneva: International Labor Organization.

Sethuraman, S. V. (1985). The informal sector in Indonesia: Policies and prospects. *International Labor Review, 124*(6), 719-735.

Shapin, S. (1996). *The scientific revolution.* Chicago: University of Chicago Press.

Shapin, S., & Schaffer, S. (1989). *Leviathan and the air pump: Hobbes, Boyle and the experimental life.* Princeton, NJ: Princeton University Press.

Shakespeare, W. (1980) *The complete works of William Shakespeare* (Preface by Philip Brockbank). London: Octopus Press.

Sheehan, W. M. (1978). *Stop global drift.* Santa Anita, CA: Center for the Future.

Sherman, H. J. (1987). *Foundations of radical political economy.* Armonk, NY: M. E. Sharpe.

Shiva, V. (1989). *Staying alive: Women, ecology and development.* London: Zed.

Shotter, J. (1993). *Cultural politics in everyday life.* Toronto: University of Toronto Press.

Sica, A. (1988). *Weber, irrationality, and the social order.* Berkeley: University of California Press.

Simon, J. L. (1983, August). Life on earth is getting better, not worse. *The Futurist,*7, 4, 7-14.

Skinner, Q. (1966). The ideological content of Hobbes's political thought. *Historical Journal,* 9, 286-367.

Sklair, L. (1991). *Sociology of the global system.* Baltimore, MD: Johns Hopkins University Press.

Slater, D. (1994). Power and social movements in the other Occident: Latin America in an international context. *Latin American Perspective, 21*(2), 11-37.

Smith, A. (1937). *An inquiry into the nature and causes of the wealth of nations* (E. Canaan, Ed.). New York: Modern Library. (Original work published in 1776)

Smith, F. L., & Kushner, K. H. (1990, April 1). Good fences make good neighbors *National Review, 42*(6), 31-33, 59.

Smith, G. (1994). Towards an ethnography of idiosyncratic forms of livelihood. *International Journal of Urban and Regional Research, 18*(1), 71-87.

Smith, H. (1992). *Beyond the post-modern mind.* Wheaton, IL: Quest Books.

Snow, D. M. (1992). *Distant thunder: Third World conflict in the new international order.* New York: St. Martin's.

Snowden, F. (1970). *Blacks in antiquity.* Cambridge, MA: Harvard University Press.
Solanas, V. (1969). The S.C.U.M. manifesto. In B. Roszack & T. Roszack (Eds.), *Masculine/feminine.* New York: Harper & Row.
Snyder, L. L. (Ed.). (1962). *The imperialism reader: Documents and readings in modern expansionism.* Princeton, NJ: Van Nostrand.
Spender, D. (1980). *Man made language.* London: Routledge & Kegan Paul.
Spinoza, B. (1982). *The ethics and selected letters* (J. B. Schneewind, Ed.). Indianapolis, IN: Hackett Publishing.
Spivak, G. (1988). Can the subaltern speak? In C. Nelson & L. Grossberg (Eds.), *Marxism and the interpretation of culture.* Urbana: University of Ilinois Press.
Spivak, G. (1990). *The Post-colonial critic: Interviews, strategies, dialogues* (S. Harasym, Ed.). New York: Routledge.
Spretnak, C. (1981). *Lost goddesses of early Greece.* Boston: Beacon.
Spretnak, C., & Capra, F. (1986). *Green politics.* Santa Fe, NM: Bear & Co.
Stannard, D. E. (1992). *American holocaust.* New York: Oxford University Press.
Stone, R. D. (1992). *The nature of development.* New York: Knopf.
Stromberg, R. N. (1966). *The intellectual history of modern Europe.* New York: Appleton-Century-Crofts.
Stuart Mill, J. (1875). A few words on non-intervention. In *Disquisitions and Discussions* (Vol. 3, pp. 167-168). London: Longman, Green, Reader & Dyer.
Sutcliffe, D., & Wong, A. (Eds.). (1986). *The language of the black experience.* Oxford, UK: Basil Blackwell.
Szerszynski, B. (1996). On knowing what to do: Environmentalism and the modern problematic. In S. Lash, B. Szerszynski and B. Wynne (Eds.), *Risk, environment, and modernity* (pp. 104-137). London: Sage.
Taussig, M. (1987). *Shamanism, colonialism, and the wild man.* Chicago: University of Chicago Press.
Tawney, R. H. (1926). *Religion and the rise of capitalism.* New York: Harcourt, Brace.
Taylor, C. (1975). *Hegel.* New York: Cambridge University Press.
Taylor, C. (1989). *Sources of the self: The making of the modern identity.* Cambridge, MA: Harvard University Press.
Taylor, C. (1991). *The ethics of authenticity.* Cambridge, MA: Harvard University Press.
Taylor, C. (1994). *Multiculturalism and the politics of recognition* (A. Gutmann, Ed.). Princeton, NJ: Princeton University Press.
Taylor, P. W. (1986). *Respect for nature.* Princeton, NJ: Princeton University Press.
Tewari, D. D. (1995). The Chipko: The dialectics of economics and environment. *Dialectical Anthropology, 20*(2), 133-168.
Thalos, M. (1994). The common need for classical epistemological foundations: Against a feminist alternative. *The Monist, 77*(44), 531-553.
Thiele, B. (1986). Vanishing acts in social and political thought. In C. Pateman & E. Gross (Eds.), *Feminist challenges* (pp. 30-43). Boston: Northeastern University Press.
Thompson, P. (1993). Postmodernism: Fatal distraction. In J. Hassard & M. Parker (Eds.), *Postmodernism and organizations* (p. 97). Newbury Park, CA: Sage.
Thurow, L. C. (1984). *Dangerous currents: The state of economics.* New York: Vintage.
Todd, J. M. (1971). *Reformation.* Garden City, NY: Doubleday.
Tomlinson, J. (1991). *Cultural imperialism.* Baltimore, MD: Johns Hopkins University Press.
Toulmin, S. (1983). *The return of cosmology: Postmodern science and the theology of nature.* Berkeley: University of California Press.
Toulmin, S. (1992). *Cosmopolis.* Chicago: University of Chicago Press.
Touraine, A. (1969). *The post-industrial society.* London: Wildwood.
Touraine, A. (1977). *The self-production of society.* Chicago: University of Chicago Press.
Toure, S. (1974). A dialectical approach to culture. In R. Christian & Nathan Hare (Eds.), *Pan-Africanism.* Indianapolis, IN: Bobbs-Merrill.

Toynbee, A. (1976). *Mankind and mother earth*. New York: Oxford University Press.
Trainer, F. E. (1989). *Developed to death: Rethinking world development*. London: Green Print.
Trevor-Roper, H. (1969). The religious origins of the Enlightenment. In *The European witch-craze of the sixteenth and seventeenth centuries and other essays*. New York: Harper Torch Books.
Tribe, L. H. (1974). Ways not to think about plastic trees. *Yale Law Journal, 83*, 1315-1348.
Tuana, N. (1993). *The less noble sex*. Indianapolis: Indiana University Press.
Tucker, R. W. (1977). *The inequality of nations*. New York: Basic Books.
Tunkin, G. I. (1974). *Theory of international law*. Cambridge, MA: Harvard University Press.
Turner, J. (1991). *The structure of sociological theory*. Belmont, CA: Wadsworth.
Urmson, J. O. (1960). *Philosophical analysis*. Oxford, UK: Clarendon.
Valery, P. (1958). *Reflections on the world today* (F. Scarfe, Trans.). New York: Oxford University Press.
van Tongeren, P. (1984). Development co-operation awareness in European cities. *IFDA Dossier, 40*, 27-38.
Vattimo, G. (1991). *The end of modernity*. Baltimore, MD: Johns Hopkins University Press.
Vattimo, G. (1992). *The transparent society*. Baltimore, MD: Johns Hopkins University Press.
Vaughan, C. E. (1960). *Studies in the history of political philosophy* (Vols. 1 & 2). New York: Russell & Russell.
Venuti, L. (1989). *Our halcyon dayes—English prerevolutionary texts and postmodern culture*. Madison: University of Wisconsin Press.
Verene, D. P. (1981). *Vico's science of imagination*. Ithaca, NY: Cornell University Press.
Verhelst, T. (1990). *No life without roots*. London: Zed.
Vernon, R. (1971). *Sovereignty at bay*. New York: Basic Books.
Vico, G. (1984). *The new science of Giambattista Vico* (T. G. Bergin & M. H. Fisch, Trans.). Ithaca, NY: Cornell University Press. (Original work published in 1744)
Viswanathan, G. (1989). *Masks of conquest*. New York: Columbia University Press.
Voltaire (Francois-Marie Arouet). (1962). *The philosophical dictionary*. (Peter H. Gay, Ed. and Trans.). New York: Basic Books.
Von Mises, L. (1960). *Epistemological problems of economics*. Princeton, NJ: Van Nostrand.
Von Mises, R. (1951). *Positivism*. Cambridge, MA: Harvard University Press.
Wai-Andah, G. (1981). West Africa before the seventh century. In G. Mockhtar (Ed.), *UNESCO general history of Africa: Vol. 2. Ancient civilizations of Africa*. Paris: UNESCO.
Walker, R. B. J. (1988). *One world, many worlds: Struggles for a just world order*. Boulder, CO: Rienner.
Walker, R. B. J. (1994). Norms in a teacup: Surveying the new normative approaches. *Mershon International Studies Review, 38*(2), 265-270.
Wallace, W. A. (1972). *Causality and scientific explanation* (2 Vols.). Ann Arbor: University of Michigan Press.
Wallimann, I. (1994, March). Can the world industrialization project be sustained? *Monthly Review*, pp. 41-51.
Waltz, K. (1979). *Theory of international politics*. Reading, MA: Addison-Wesley.
Ward, K. (Ed.). (1990). *Women workers and global restructuring*. Ithaca, NY: Cornell University Press.
Weber, M. (1958). *The Protestant ethic and the spirit of capitalism* (T. Parsons, Trans.). New York: Scribner.
Weber, M. (1968). *Economy and society* (3 Vols., G. Roth & C. Wittich, Eds.). New York: Bedminster.
Weeks, J. (1995). *Invented moralities*. New York: Columbia University Press.
Weimann, R. (1984). *Structure and society in literary history*. Baltimore, MD: Johns Hopkins University Press.
Weintraub, K. J. (1966). *Visions of culture*. Chicago: University of Chicago Press.
Weir, D. (1988). *The Bhopal syndrome*. San Francisco: Sierra Club Books.

Weisman, L. K. (1994). *Discrimination by design: A feminist critique of the man-made environment.* Chicago: University of Illinois Press.

Wellmer, A. (1971). *Critical theory of society.* New York: Herder & Herder.

West, C. (1990). The new cultural politics of difference. In Russell Ferguson et al (Eds.), *Out There: Marginalization and Contemporary Culture.* Cambridge, MA: MIT Press.

West, C. (1993). The new cultural politics of difference. B. W. Thompson & S. Tyagi (Eds.), *Beyond a dream deferred* (pp. 18-40). Minneapolis: University of Minnesota Press.

Westrum, R. (1991). *Technologies & society.* Belmont, CA: Wadsworth.

White, L. (1962). *Medieval technology and social change.* London: Oxford University Press.

White, L., Jr. (1968). *Machina ex Deo: Essays in the dynamism of Western culture.* Cambridge: MIT Press.

White, S. K. (1991). *Political theory and postmodernism.* Cambridge, UK: Cambridge University Press.

Wiegand, B. (1992). *Off the books: A theory and critique of the underground economy.* Dix Hills, NY: General Hall.

Wight, M. (1973). The balance of power and international order. In A. James (Ed.), *The bases of international order.* London: Oxford University Press.

Williams, E. (1966). *Capitalism and slavery.* New York: Capricorn.

Williams, R. (1973). *The country and the city.* Oxford, UK: Oxford University Press.

Williams, R. (1976). *Keywords.* New York: Oxford University Press.

Williams, R. (1977). *Marxism and literature.* Oxford, UK: Oxford University Press.

Williams, R. (1980). *Problems in materialism and culture.* London: Verso.

Williams, R. (1981). *Culture.* New York: Fontana.

Williams, R. (1986). Towards many socialisms. *Socialist Review 85, 16*(1), 45-65.

Willis, P. (1977). *Learning to labour: Why working class kids get working class jobs.* Westmead, UK: Saxon House, Teakfield.

Wilmer, F. (1993). *The indigenous voice in world politics.* Newbury Park, CA: Sage.

Wilson, W. J. (1991). Studying inner-city dislocations: The challenge of public agenda research. *American Sociological Review, 56*(1), 1-14.

Winner, L. (1980). Do artifacts have politics? *Daedalus, 109,* 125-136.

Wiredu, K. (1995). *Conceptual decolonization in African philosophy: Four essays.* Ibadan, Nigeria: Hope Publications.

Wittgenstein, L. (1967). *Zettel* (G. E. M. Anscombe & G. H. von Wright, Eds.). Oxford, UK: Blackwell.

Wolfe, A. (1989). *Whose keeper? Social science and moral obligation.* Berkeley and Los Angeles: University of California Press.

Wolin, S. (1992). What revolutionary action means today. In C. Mouffe (Ed.), *Dimensions of radical democracy* (pp. 240-253). London: Verso.

Wooton, D. (1992). The levellers. In J. Dunn (Ed.), *Democracy—The unfinished journey 508 BC to 1993 AD* (pp. 71-89). Oxford, UK: Oxford University Press.

World Commission on Environment and Development. (1987). *Our common future.* Oxford: Oxford University Press.

Wright, L. B. (1935). *Middle-class culture in Elizabethan England.* Ithaca, NY: Cornell University Press.

Yankah, K. (1995). Displaced academies and the quest for a new world academic order. *Africa Today, 42*(3), 7-25.

Young, I. M. (1990). *Justice and the philosophy of difference.* Princeton, NJ: Princeton University Press.

Young, J. (1990). *Sustaining the earth.* Cambridge, MA: Harvard University Press.

Zavarzadeh, M. (1994). Ideology, poststructuralism, and class in politics: Rethinking ideology critique for transformative feminist politics. In A. Kibbey, K. Short, & A. Farmanfarmian (Eds.), *Genders 19: Artifice.* New York: New York University Press.

# INDEX

# About the Author

**Nelson W. Keith** is Professor of Sociology as well as the founder-director of the Institute for International Development at West Chester University in West Chester, Pennsylvania. A former diplomat, Dr. Keith is a barrister-at-law, a member of the Honourable Society of the Inner Temple in London. Later, he secured a Ph.D. in sociology, with an emphasis on political economy, from Rutgers University.

Before joining the faculty at West Chester, Dr. Keith taught at Rutgers University, New Brunswick, in the School of Urban and Regional Policy, as well as at Temple University. Wedged between his professional exploits is a period of consulting, mainly in the sphere of international development. He has traveled extensively and through his institute has worked closely with many foreign universities in the general areas of development and in faculty and student exchanges.

He has published widely, resulting in three books and numerous other publications. His book, *The Social Origins of Democratic Socialism in Jamaica* (1992), co-authored with Novella Keith, is well received and is thought by a number of reviewers and others to have the makings of a classic. He has also received commendation for the research he is currently undertaking in the area of indigenousness. His next book, a sequel to *Reframing International Development: Globalism, Postmodernity, and Difference,* is devoted to that topic.